Cultivate Your  and Wisdom

"Hear counsel and receive instruction, that thou mayest be wise in thy latter end." This verse from Proverbs 19:20 is probably about the best literal description of Qabalah in print. Qabalah means "getting wise" in the broadest possible sense.

There are two principal ways to bestow Wisdom. One is to spoon feed it in ready-made form to the uninstructed and unprepared, and expect them to adapt themselves to it by whatever means are available. The other way is not to reveal Wisdom directly, but to offer a practicable means for individuals to find it by their own efforts in their own time. This is the Qabalistic way.

Any genuine exponent of the subject simply says to enquirers in effect: "There is your material. Here are the tools with which to work. These are the ways in which others have worked according to their special skills. Now start for yourself, and we will provide what help and encouragement we can. The rest lies between thou and That."

And this is exactly what William Gray gives to his readers in *Growing the Tree Within* (formerly titled *The Talking Tree*). Here you will discover a different and more logical way of looking at the Qabalah; learn the origin of the Tree design, its nature, purpose and plan; and explore detailed delineations of each of the 22 paths with tarot card meanings. Here you receive everything you need to begin or continue your exploration of the Tree of Life, your own inner source of wisdom.

The Tree will talk about anything you are interested in. Initiate yourself into its ways and talk with Divinity inside yourself. Talk *with*, not *to*, and receive your answers. That is Qabalah.

About the Author

William G. Gray was born in Harrow, Middlesex, United Kingdom. His mother was an astrologer and psychic consultant—young Bill's first introduction to the occult and to the Golden Dawn.

His writing career commenced when he completed two projects left unfinished at the death of Dion Fortune, founder of the Society of the Inner Light. One manuscript became *The Talking Tree*, and the other, *The Magical Mass* (which later became *The Sangreal Sacrament*). However, it was Israel Regardie's enthusiastic response to the manuscript published as *The Ladder of Lights* that provided the impetus for Gray's works to reach the public.

Since that time, Gray has written several books on Western esoteric ceremonialism, devoting particular attention to what he calls the Sangreal concept.

To Write to the Author

We cannot guarantee that every letter written to the author can be answered, but all will be forwarded. Both the author and the publisher appreciate hearing from readers, learning of your enjoyment and benefit from this book. Llewellyn also publishes a bi-monthly news magazine with news and reviews of practical esoteric studies and articles helpful to the student, and some readers' questions and comments to the author may be answered through this magazine's columns, if permission to do so is included in the original letter. The author sometimes participates in seminars and workshops, and dates and places are announced in *The Llewellyn New Times*. To write to the author, or to ask a question, write to:

William G. Gray
c/o THE LLEWELLYN NEW TIMES
P.O. Box 64383-268, St. Paul, MN 55164-0383, U.S.A.

please enclose a self-addressed, stamped envelope for reply, or $1.00 to cover costs.

Llewellyn's New World Magic Series

Growing the Tree Within

Patterns of the Unconscious Revealed by the Qabbalah

William G. Gray

A New Edition of *The Talking Tree*

1991
Llewellyn Publications
St. Paul, Minnesota, 55164-0383, U.S.A.

FIRST LLEWELLYN EDITION
FIRST PRINTING

First publication *The Talking Tree* by Samuel Weiser, Inc. Copyright 1977.

Cover illustration by Robin Wood

Library of Congress Cataloging-in-Publication Data:
  Gray, William G.
    [Talking tree]
    Growing the tree within : patterns of the unconscious revealed by the
  Qabbalah / William G. Gray.
        p.   cm. — (Llewellyn's new world magic series)
    Reprint. Originally published: The talking tree. New York : S. Weiser,
  1977.
    ISBN 0-87542-268-3
    1. Occultism. 2. Cabala. 3. Tarot. 4. Tree of life—Miscellanea
  I. Title. II. Series.
  BF1999.G715 1991
  135'.4—dc20   99-10202
                                                                      CIP

Llewellyn Publications
A Division of Llewellyn Worldwide, Ltd.
P.O. Box 64383, St. Paul, MN 55164-0383

Llewellyn's New World Magic Series

The European re-discovery of the "New World" was much more than a geographic confirmation of the "Lands to the West."

For the members of various esoteric groups, America was to be the "New Atlantis," a utopia free of ignorance, superstition, fear and prejudice—incarnating a Great Plan for the spiritual evolution of this planet. Central to the political foundations of this *New Order for the Ages* is the intellectual freedom to pursue knowledge and wisdom unrestrained by the dictates of Church and State, and to publish and speak openly that all the people may grow in wisdom and attainment.

At the very core of this vision is the recognition that each person is responsible for his or her own destiny, and to freely pursue this "Happiness" requires that one throw off domination by "personal devils" of psychic nature, just as the American Colonies rebelled against the despotism of the British King.

We must be free of that which hinders our Vision and obstructs the flowering of the Life Force. For each of us that which obstructs is our *inner* personal Evil, and it is the Great Work of the magician to accept responsibility for that Evil and to transmute its powers into personal Good. Therein lies the secret of spiritual growth.

And with personal transformation comes our enhanced Vision and Power to work with magical responsibility in the outer world and to transmute those Evils resultant from human ignorance and fear, superstition and prejudice. We move forward as we perceive such Evils as originating from within ourselves and as we challenge them in their true nature.

We live in perilous times, but a "New Age" is at hand as the techniques of personal magic are used by more and more people to accept responsibility for Evil, and to redeem it for the Good—for individual growth and success, and for the Good of the planetary life within which we have our being.

New World Magic is visionary, recognizing the role of the individual practitioner in the world in which we live, and accepting the promise of a "New Order for the Ages." It is magic that is psychologically sound and spiritually committed. It is magic that builds upon older traditions in the knowledge that within them are our roots, and it is magic that looks to new understanding to ever expand the potential into which we grow.

New World Magic is for all who want to make a *New World*!

To

DION FORTUNE

The substance of a promise
made in shadow
for the sake of
LIGHT.

And a pledge so far unbroken
that the Western Word be spoken.

"L"

Contents

The Nutshell

An intelligent commentator read through the whole material of this "Pathbook," and said: "Do you think it would be possible to put everything in a nutshell so to speak, in order to give people a positive understanding of how the Paths came to be where they are in the first place? Readers simply get the Tree design thrown at them whole as it were, rather than developed from absolute origin. So many get the idea that the Paths were placed where they are because of some whim on the part of early authorities rather than by definite laws. Could you clarify things for them right down to rock bottom. Nobody seems to have done this anywhere." Very fair comments and suggestions indeed. Here is the outcome.

First a quick recapitulation of the Spheres.
1. *The Crown or Summit.* Life closest to God above all else.
2. *Wisdom.* The ability of learning everything in Life.
3. *Understanding.* The ability of appreciating all in Life.
4. *Mercy.* Compassion of all lesser lives.
5. *Severity.* Control of powers by discipline and duty.
6. *Beauty.* Universal health, harmony, and happiness in Life.
7. *Victory.* Achievement of what is right in Life.
8. *Glory.* The honour of being alive for the sake of Spirit.
9. *Foundation.* Faith in Life and its fertility.
10. *The Kingdom.* Our world of natural Life as we live it.

It should never be forgotten that all this comes out of Nothing. Zero. Nor again forgotten that the Law says: "Ten Holy Spheres. Ten. Not nine or eleven, but Ten. Think this out carefully, and make sure you understand it."

To connect ten equal circles together on paper, all we need is a pair of drawing compasses. First make a circle of any convenient size, then put the point of the compasses anywhere on its edge and draw another similar circle so that the outside of this goes through the exact center of the first circle. Do this again from the other side. When ten circles are linked this way, outer to inner edges, we shall have Figure 1.

Looking at the center points of these circles, we should see they are very nearly the Tree of Life pattern. In fact they seem to go rather one better, since they are all so closely and beautifully related as a whole. If we connect them together by the simplest system of straight lines, we shall have Figure 2. Count up these lines or paths, and there should be twenty-two. The same number as letters in the Hebrew alphabet. So we could use one letter per Path to identify them. If we are Hebrews. If not, plain numbers will do, or we can use the English alphabet adapted.

It could be said that Figures 1 and 2 represent the Tree of Life as it ought to be if everything were perfectly balanced and all life-factors related to each other the best possible way. Experience tells us otherwise, and legend relates our "Fall" from heavenly grace. The most modern ideas postulate humans making an earthfall" on this planet from higher and more advanced conditions of Cosmos. Moreover, it seems fairly plain that if we ever want to "regain Heaven," or achieve our original spiritual status in this universe or any other, we shall have to become very much better people than we are now. The Paths of Life on the Tree are in fact supposed to show us how to climb steadily and slowly back to such a level. So we shall have to show our "Fall" somehow on the Tree design.

That is why the last Sphere of the Kingdom on the Tree was called the "Fallen Sphere"; it is the Kingdom of Nature on Earth inhabited by humans "fallen from Heaven." Since we cannot put an extra Sphere on a Tree that has to be "Ten but never Eleven," we shall have to move one out of place toward the Earth end of the Tree. That will leave a blank space near the top and push a Sphere out of the bottom. Which Sphere do we alter? Obviously the second one down has to move. If we imagine this dropping a space and pushing the two beneath it at the same time, we shall obtain the familiar figure of the Tree and its Paths as it Figure

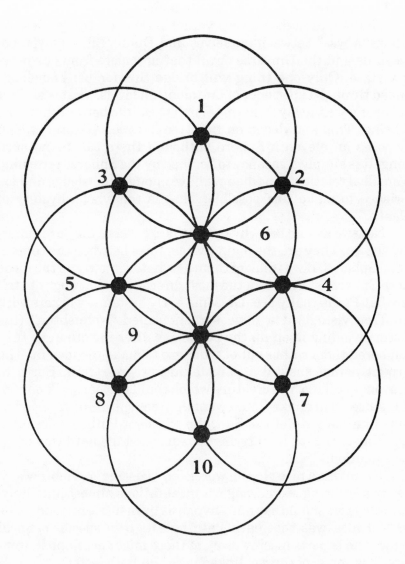

Figure 1
THE TEN PERFECT SPHERES

3. There are still twenty-two Paths, but now there is a space on the Tree where the center of a Sphere used to be.

That space makes a very valuable Symbol. It signifies the gap or "Abyss" between ourselves and Divine Life—maybe between us and the Universe or all that is remote from our here-now state. Only one thing will bridge this for us; knowledge gained through experience of Life along all levels. That is all that will ever get us away from this Earth back into better conditions of being. This knowledge on the Tree is called "Daath," which supposes an eleventh Sphere, although there can be no such thing. It is simply a vacancy to be filled by the Spheres returning to an ideal relationship when we have enough knowledge and experience to make this possible. That is the whole mystery of "Daath."

Now we should see why the Paths are where they are generally shown. They are the main contact lines between the centers of the Spheres. If we think of them as whatever joins up the ideas those Spheres stand for in the most direct way, that ought to tell us what Paths really are. On some early systems, workers with the Tree visualized a huge serpent called "Nehushtan" (the Hisser) winding itself up the Paths one after the other, so they numbered them rather out of sequence to make the idea fit. The serpent notion showed a painstaking progress from Earth to Heaven up a Tree by a creature which could neither walk nor fly. Also since great snakes often went up trees spiralling from left to right like the path of the Sun, the "Serpent-Path" represented the "Way of Light"; Man trying to reach God the hard way of cyclic evolution.

There was a nice play on words too. "Hissing" in Hebrew also meant muttering secret magical incantations almost inaudibly. Nowadays we should say auto-hypnosis by mantric methods. The general idea was that each Path had its own special magical sound, and experts hissing away at these might accomplish wonders. The sonic, of course, linked with the Path letter.

Since the Tree of Life is composed of counterbalancing concepts, what would be the opposite to a Serpent? Oldtimers seeing that as a slow and winding way of getting to Heaven had to think of something fast and straight coming from Heaven to Earth. In those days that was a lightning-flash. Indeed, perhaps there might be some far-back human memory of reaching this planet

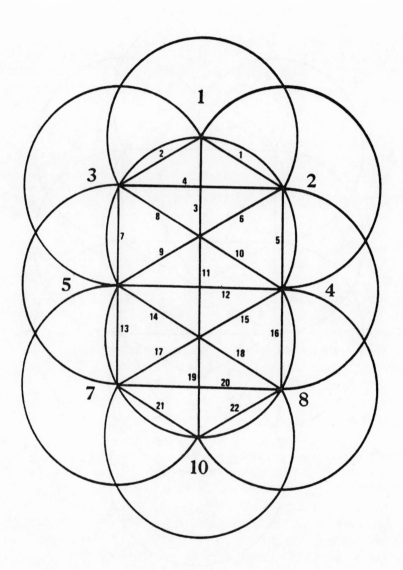

Figure 2
THE TWENTY-TWO PERFECT PATHS

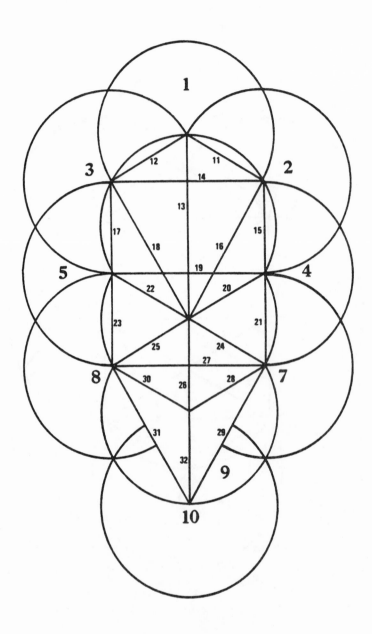

Figure 3
SPHERES AND PATHS AFTER "FALL"

by "fast as lightning" means powered by some kind of "super-electricity." In all events, we can see this counter-symbolism in Figures 4 and 5, if we use this most logical Path enumeration.

Like other ancient races, Hebrews used letters of the alphabet for numbers, so it was natural for them to number the Paths this way. Most of mankind's early alphabets were evolved for commercial, military and other mundane reasons and consisted largely of consonants, vowel sounds being especially holy and used in God-names. There was another good reason for a consonant alphabet. It made a good workable commercial and other shorthand only readable by those who knew how to fill in the gaps. Take a modern example in English. "Buy six cows, four sheep, and twelve goats." Now which makes the most sense here, consonants or vowels?

"B-y s-x c-ws f-r sh-p -nd tw-lv- g-ts."
"-u- -i- -o- -ou- -ee- a- -e-e -oa-."

There is scarcely much doubt which is readable to any literate person. Even a computer could scarcely make sense of the vowels alone. That is why the English alphabet fits on the Tree minus its vowels.

Apart from anything else, there is one very good reason for using numerals and letters to identify the Spheres and Paths on the Tree of Life. It is because those are the elements of our normal awareness in this world and the links we use trying to make contact with others. We are so used to thinking in figures and words that our lives here are involved with them all the time. Sadly enough, few of our words have much spiritual meaning, and we use numbers mainly for money, time, or mathematical calculations. Yet both of those can help us climb our Trees closer to Cosmic consciousness if we learn to associate them with metaphysical values. That is the real reason for attaching them to the Tree Paths.

For instance, what does anyone think of when plain numbers 2 and 3 are mentioned? Seldom more than just quantities of anything. On the Tree these are Wisdom and Understand. So suppose whenever those figures are encountered in ordinary living, ideas or injunctions towards the principles of Wisdom and Understanding arise automatically? In such case a sense of real

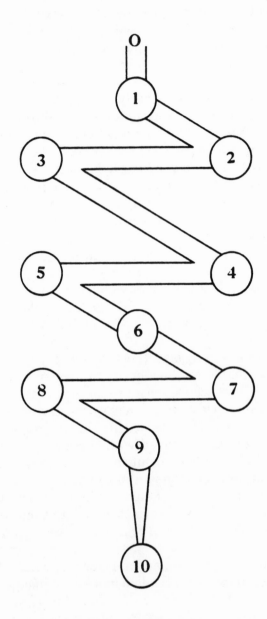

Figure 4
THE LIGHTNING FLASH

Life-values would keep coming ever closer to normal human awareness. We might even develop into people with a sense of perpetually present Spirit. Who knows?

If numbers help us realise spiritual realities, letters can help us find the different relationships between them. Sometimes this alphabetically arranged code even in English can be surprising. Take for example attribution, which symbolizes the nature of God. It works out as:

G	*Wise Mercy*
O	*(or a U*
	Truth
O	*sound)*
D	*Absolute Beauty*

How much better can our ideas of Good and God be than that? Now try the opposite: EVIL, or Devil.

D	*High Beauty*
E	*The Power of Air*
V	*Glory and Conquest*
I	*The Power of Fire*
L	*Severity or Mercy*

A rather accurate description really. Mythically our Devil was described before his "Fall" as the most beautiful of all the Archangels. He is called the "Prince of the Powers of the Air." His downfall was supposedly due to Glory and Conquest because of pride, and he is usually associated with Fire. Lastly, unless Divine Mercy spared us the worst of Life, the Devil would make things very severe for us. "God" and the "Devil" are words personifying principles of Good and Evil as the best or worst that Life might hold for us as humans.

Apart from numbers and letters, all sorts of symbols may be attached to the Tree Paths, and most people have their own pet theories. Probably the most popular are the Tarot cards. In this case, the numbered suits from one to ten obviously belong to the Spheres of the Tree, and the twenty-two pictures known as trumps must go with the Paths. The Kings, Queens, Knights and

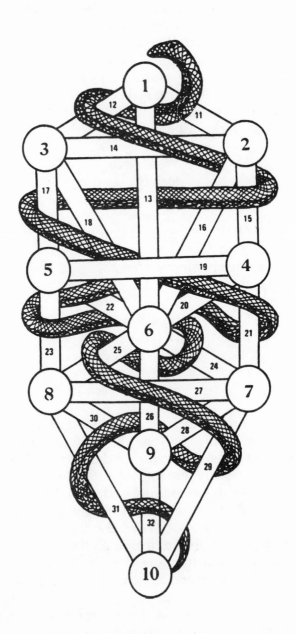

Figure 5
THE SERPENT AND PATHS

Pages have to signify the "Four Worlds" or stages of Cosmos between God and Man. That is to say they correspond to the fourfold Life-process by which we arrive in this world physically, i.e.,

Impregnation	Male Seed implanted	**King**
Conception	Female egg fertilized	**Queen**
Gestation	Development in womb	**Knight**
Parturition	Separate being born	**Page**

Other interpretations are possible of course.

As might be expected among humans, bitter and fruitless arguments go on about which Tarot trump to put with each Path. The system given here is based on ideological principles, and seems quite sane and sensible. We have to think of them as being what best links the concepts of the Spheres themselves together in the most direct way. If we take the fundamental ideas behind the trumps *per se* we shall see they classify into ten main groups like this.

1. *Cosmic Ideas.* **Moon, Sun,** and **Stars**, or reaching from Earth to Outer Space in that order.

2. *Fatal Ideas.* **Wheel of Fortune, Justice**, and **Judgment**, or how Life deals with us on three levels from bottom to top.

3. *Exo-and Esoteric Ideas.* **The Hierophant** and the **Hermit**. Outer and Inner Life. A Hermit lives inside himself to make relations with God, and a Hierophant lives out of himself to make relations with God for others.

4. *Alteration Ideas.* Death and the Devil. Death alters our Life-condition, and we alter ourselves to avoid or adapt with the "devil" or adversity in Life.

5. *Compensation Ideas.* The Hanging (or dependent) Man, and Temperance. The first hovers between Earth and Heaven, touching neither, and the second always determines a middle course in Life.

6. *Ruling Ideas.* The Emperor and Empress. Men and women governing their own powers of Life properly.

7. *Energy Ideas.* Strength, and the Blasted Tower. The first

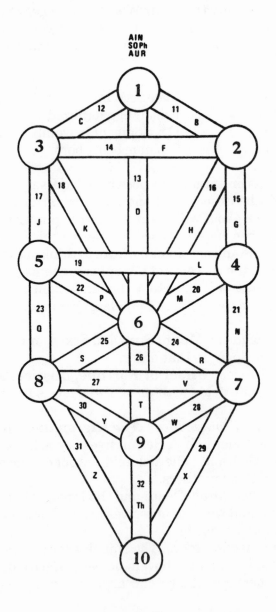

Figure 6
THE LETTERS AND PATHS

is power applied carefully with control, and the second is power let loose drastically.

8. *Moving Ideas.* The Chariot and the Lovers. A Chariot or vehicle takes us all through Life, and the Lovers keep Life moving from one generation to another.

9. *Inspirational Ideas.* **The Magician** and the Priestess. Men and women trying to solve the secrets of the Universe and Life by devotion to science and religion or the arts in general.

10. *Who and What Ideas.* **The Fool** (or Innocence abroad) and the **World**. People and Places. The Fool is all of us with everything to learn about Life, and the World is where, when, and how we actually live.

Ten sets of ideas. Two sets of three, and eight sets of two. They will fit the paths very well indeed, but only on one way. This may be analysed by a sort of table that will explain why. To make it clear, we will classify the Tree design into these categories.

Three Pillars	Right, Center, and Left
Three Levels	Top, Middle and Bottom of Pillars
Top Complex	Paths combining at top of Tree
Center Complex	Paths combining at middle
Lower Complex	Paths combining at bottom of Tree

First, we make up the Middle Pillar like this:

Middle Pillar

Card	from Sphere	to Sphere	Because
Star	Crown	Beauty	It represents life from other systems linking with ours.
Sun	Beauty	Foundation	It is the central beauty of our system and basis of life energy.
Moon	Foundation	Kingdom	It is closest to our Earth and it links with tides of fertility.

Next we build up the three levels from side to side of The Tree.

Three Levels

Card	from Sphere	to Sphere	Because
Judgment	Wisdom	Under-standing	True Judgment should depend on both Principles
Justice	Mercy	Severity	Justice makes us deserve either or both Principles.
Wheel	Victory	Glory	Hopes of these make us take chances in Life.

Now we set up the side Pillars.

Left Pillar

Death	Under-standing	Severity	We need to understand the strict need for Life-change across the Abyss separating us from God.
Devil	Severity	Glory	We gain best glory in Life by dealing with its severe stresses and temptations.

Right Pillar

Emperor	Wisdom	Mercy	All right living people should rule themselves by these principles.
Empress	Mercy	Victory	It is a good rule of Life to achieve victories by Mercy.

Now the internal Path complexes.

Top Complex

Hermit	Crown	Under-standing	Inner Life must seek itself contemplatively.
Hierophant	Crown	Wisdom	Outer Life must find itself actively.
Hanging Man	Under-standing	Beauty	We must understand how to balance Life beautifully by our dependence on Divinity.

| Temperance | Wisdom | Beauty | We need real Wisdom to lead temperate and beautiful lives. |

Center Complex

Card	from Sphere	to Sphere	
Tower	Severity	Beauty	There is severe beauty in awe some effects of power relesed like lightning or the blasting rays of the sun.
Strength	Mercury	Beauty	The merciful use of strength is truly beautiful like the genial warmth of the sun.
Chariot	Beauty	Glory	It is glorious to go everywhere in Life seeking true Beauty.
Lovers	Beauty	Victory	The victories of genuine Love in Life are so Beautiful.

Lower Complex

Magician is	Glory	Foundation	The glory of Magical science working with Nature's secret and fundamental Life-forces.
Priestess	Victory	Foundations	Devotions to the very deepest foundations of Life are needed for gaining spiritual victories.
Fool	Glory	Kingdom	The glories of this world are often foolish, and we have to become as "little children" (innocents) in the Kingdom of Glory.
World	Victory	Kingdom	We are in the natural Kingdom of this world to make a spiritual success of four human living.

Anyone is of course entitled to place Tarot Cards anywhere on the Tree of Life he likes—providing there are as good or better reasons than these for doing so.

So there in a nutshell is the basis of this book. The rest is necessary enlargements and extensions, going for brief excursions along each Path in turn. Actually, we do not live Paths one after the other so much as all at once with different parts of ourselves. On the whole, the higher up the Tree we climb, the finer and better levels of our natures are used for Pathworking. Most of us are likely to be quite active on the lower Paths, maybe familiar with middle ones, but perhaps not so advanced along the top ones. We can at least study their lay-out as a whole while looking for Light along our individual Paths to Perfection. Which is really what they are all about anyway.

The Talking Tree: Its Nature

Surely every serious student of what might be called Western Occultism has heard about the famous Qabalistic Tree of Life? Some study it in detail, others cannot find any cause in it to make them devote more than a passing effort of thought in its direction. The Tree either compels attention or rejects it. There are seldom any half-measures about it, and one rarely encounters triflers, wool-gatherers, or any of the "do it for kicks" brigade bothering themselves very greatly with the Tree. Why should they? They see no value in it for themselves, and because of what they are as those selves, this is perfectly true. Firstly it does not strike such people that if they altered their own approach-angles they might well discover a whole World of Inner wealth, and secondly that the Tree might provide them with the keys making this very alteration possible.

What really puts people off the Tree of Life and its possibilities is their instinctive realization of its magnitude as a work problem, and inability or unwillingness to tackle it on their own initiative. They may be prepared to buy other people's ready-made thoughts and findings about the Tree in the forms of books and study courses, but they are most unprepared to carve up the raw wood for themselves, so to speak. That is precisely what the Tree demands or expects of those who show interest in it—a will to work with it, and a skill to act with it, rather than indolent opulence waiting to purchase the finished products obtained by the efforts of true craftsmen. Nothing but painstaking care and devoted effort will develop real skill in a soul on any level of expression, and this especially applies to the spiritual abilities necessary for the practice of Qabalah as an Inner activity. Being very well aware of this, any genuine exponent of the subject simply

1

says to enquirers in effect: "There is your material. Here are the tools to work it with. These are the ways in which others have worked according to their special skills. Now start for yourself, and we will provide what help and encouragement we can. The rest lies between thou and That."

What actually is the Qabalah anyway? Why should it apply particularly to the Western Tradition of Occult teaching? Many people are under an impression that Qabalah is purely a Jewish affair of obscure pseudo-origins and doubtful meanings, hardly worth the intelligent attention of an educated modern mind. Though this is very far from the truth, there are indeed various reasons why it should still be current in certain circles. Firstly, the word itself. It derives directly from the Hebrew QBL, which means to receive or obtain. It also signifies to admit or allow a law, and to embrace instruction. The word is used in that sense in Proverbs 19:20, "Hear counsel and receive instruction, that thou mayest be wise in thy latter end," probably about the best literal description of Qabalah in print. Qabalah means "getting wise" in the broadest possible sense, and surely every human being on Earth is here for that very reason? Why then, the connection between Qabalah and any kind of specialized Occult or "Secret Wisdom"?

This implication comes purely from the suffix "h" on the word, turning it into an unfinished query. There is no definite article like our "he", but an "h" is placed at the beginning of the word to which it is attached. Thus, Qabalah can be read as "receive the instruction of the —————" or, with an enquiring inflection of tone, "receive instruction of the —————??" This is much in the same sense as someone might say to another, "Are you going to —————?", leaving the definite specification of the query unspoken because each knows what is in the other's mind and, being an extremely private matter, it is not intended for overhearing. All this implies caution, secrecy, discretion, information known among select circles but unspoken of elsewhere, and linkage between uttered words and inner meanings comprehensible to those "in the know." Qabalah.

Gaining Wisdom that it is un-Wise to expose before those who have not found it for themselves. That is Qabalah. There are two principal ways of reaching Wisdom. One is presenting it in ready-made form to the uninstructed and unprepared, then expecting them to adapt themselves to it by whatever means are available. This works, but not without considerable trouble and difficulty. The other way is not to reveal Wisdom directly, but to offer a practicable means for individuals to find it by their own efforts in their own time. Such is really the difference between Outer and Inner Schools of thought. With Exoteric systems, prepared information is pushed at the pupils in a definite pattern rather like programming a computer. Their education consists of their individual and collective reactions to those stimuli. With Esoteric Systems, no empiric teaching is thrust upon the students at all, but their natural abilities for intuitive learning and experience are fostered by every possible means, and they are provided with self-instructional devices for arriving at the required ultimates by exercising their own Wills in those directions. This is the Qabalistic Way. It obviously applies only to those souls willing to proceed along its Paths of their own accord. Others automatically rule themselves out.

Qabalah is the Inner Wisdom we have to reach as spiritually evolving entities in our own right, and as human souls seeking their Divine objectives. Although this applies to everyone, there are naturally various methods to suit particular needs of humans in different categories of consciousness, stages of evolution, ethnical groupings, and other classifications right down to personal peculiarities. Fundamentally, of course, Inner Wisdom derives from a single Source of Consciousness which we may term Divine if we please, or by any other name we accept as an adaptive word between ourselves and It—That—call It what we Will. Since the fact of our humanity diversifies us into specialised types of soul-entity, so therefore should we expect to find our most suitable spiritual means of progression along whatever lines approximate closest to our deepest and truest state of soul as this stands at its present point of Inner Evolution. The actual recognition of this Inner Reality by a seeking human soul is indeed a major Initiation of a unique kind. When Inner Awareness and Outer Experience meet in a closed "Magic Circle" of Consciousness, Life is liveable on both levels of Being, and we realize our immortal identity. That is what humans are instinctively looking for throughout their whole existence, and who knows how many incarnations it may take before souls even suspect this while working through human bodies? We differ so widely in our main approaches to the same Eternal Problems.

One of the broadest divisions among Mankind on this Earth is what we might call the Eastern and the Western mind. There is no need to analyse this difference here, but only to note its necessity in the arrangement of our common spiritual structure as evolving entities of this Earth. There is no question of "rightness and wrongness" involved whatever—or ever was. It is simply a matter of categorical types of consciousness being called for to fulfill especial functions through specific fields of spiritual energies. Both Eastern and Western Inner conditions of consciousness have vital purposes in the spiritual economy of Mankind as a whole. Neither will gain by useless opposition to the other, nor should members of either category abandon their heritage and try to change their courses into the other direction. Both East and West, for what they are and will become, are as necessary to the body of Mankind as an arm and a leg are vital to an individual being. Either we learn how to coordinate with each other in this world or we paralyze our progress entirely by pointless and idiotic conflicts on most levels of living.

The Inner Traditions of East and West, though built up from the same basis, are essentially different in character like the Pillars or Columns of the Tree-Pattern. Though each should respect and recognize the other's validity and purpose in the Master Plan, individual initiates ought to concern themselves primarily with their own particular Tradition, so that this becomes as true to its Archetype as possible. All may be assured that a sort of "Middle Pillar" exists, which is composed of advanced souls who have grown into independence on their own accord, and so are capable of operating along a median accord, and so are capable of operating along a median Light-Line common to both extremities of Awareness and extensible beyond the limits of either.

During our early Earth-history, divergence between what we now call the Eastern and Western Traditions was not so outwardly evident as it appears today, because of geographical population distribution. The Western hemisphere of the world remained comparatively unpopulated and uncultured. As this position changed down the centuries, the tendency was for people with a "Western" outlook to migrate permanently and develop their cultures in their own way, while those of an "Oriental" nature consolidated themselves in the Eastern half of the globe.

Thus, the great difference between East and West is fundamentally an Inner one on very deep soul-levels, and those souls who naturally belong to one group or the other become incarnated in their appropriate racial and ethnical categories which now have mainly a geographical and political meaning rather than their ancient religious variations.

There have always been "Middle Pillar" types of soul who operate principally "behind the scenes" independently of any racial, political, or denominational category. Their function is not unlike that of the spinal cord in a human body—keeping both right and left portions of the anatomy in some kind of coordination so that the occupying soul may use them properly. Also, like the spinal cord, such souls are hidden away in the framework of the corpus, doing their work quietly and unobtrusively, directing the energies of consciousness where these are needed to produce effects. These specialised souls may even be compared with Paths upon the Tree of Life, or the nervous system of a body. Without them, humanity as a whole could not be adequately directed by the "ruling Consciousness" originating from the Great Entity we loosely term "God," the "Supreme Spirit," or whatever expression is preferred.

These "central Souls" may or may not be objectively aware of their own natures and functions. This depends on their degree of development as spiritual beings. Broadly speaking, the more evolved a soul, the more conscious of their Inner structures and purposes they are, unless for some special reason their objective consciousness is screened from direct contact with their deeper percipience, which may well be most necessary for a number of reasons. Those who know what their work is and also the best ways of doing it, might be called Initiates of a most esoteric kind. They are unlikely to be recognized by other humans outside their category, and it is most improbable that they would show any trace of their Inner identity in any public way without very exceptional cause. Yet they are far from faultless or infallible, and none are better than they have become by their own efforts in evolution. They mediate Inner energies according to their conditions of spiritual advancement, and that is all even the Ultimate Itself could demand of anyone.

As the East-West divergence of humanity increased, so also arose an increasingly greater need for spiritual balance to be maintained between the two by Initiated centralisers. The human Initiate-agents employed in this work found their task an almost impossible one owing to the violence of conflict repeatedly breaking out along the widening East-West axis. This was ostensibly on the grounds of religious opinions, though based, of course, on much more primitive motivations of greed and hate. Additionally, three great religious Faiths grew up in the world which were openly opposed to all the older Traditions as such, and avowedly dedicated to the suppression of every belief save their own authorized versions. Each had a "Party line" for adherents to follow, and their own penalties for noncompliance. The mildest of these three were the Buddhists, whose sphere of influence lay mainly in the far East. In sharp contrast was the Christian Faith dominating Western Europe with an almost unequalled history of persecution and blood-shed. Then arose the Islamic Faith of the Middle East, opposed to all who sought guidance beyond the limits of the Koran. There remained only one course open to Initiates of the Inner Mysteries—secrecy of awareness and action which allowed their freedom of function, yet would remain inviolable by any kind of Earth-bound antagonism. How they achieved this and maintain it in modern conditions must remain their own private affair even today.

Naturally, such Initiates operated on far higher levels than those of specific sects or creeds, even though they might apparently be quite orthodox members of these Faiths, and outwardly conform with whatever political or other ruling opinions prevailed among the section of humanity those Initiates were associated with. Since the bulk of their real work lay in Inner Spheres, they had virtually no physical network to be discovered, seldom made contact with each other on material levels, and remarkably little on paper pointed in their direction except to those who spoke the same Inner language. Only in such a way could they carry out their assignments and do the necessary duties imposed on them by their spiritual status. Over the centuries a surprisingly efficient and valuable sort of "Secret Spiritual Service" became very solidly established and staffed by Initiate-agents capable of directing energies between Inner and Outer Dimensions of Existence.

Despite all this secret structure and elaboration of caution, evidence of its existence could not be absolutely concealed.

Changes of method and procedure became inevitable. In early times it was possible to entrust great portions of Inner Wisdom to those who committed it entirely to memory, and might be relied on to hand it down intact among their successors. Disguised as fairy stories, myths, poems, songs, and what we now call "folklore," ancient teachings and Traditions could continue quietly enough while favorable conditions for their reception lasted. With the spread of learning and the printed word, systems of Inner Intelligence had to alter. In fact, those responsible for these developments were themselves working from Inner compulsion. Besides this, fringes of the Inner Organisation began to show up in various forms of what we would now call "underground movements." In Europe came the appearances of semi- and pseudo-secret bodies like the Troubadours, the Rosicrucians, and other vehicles for use by far more recondite controlling sources of consciousness. Among these Westernizing trends of Inner influence was an obscure and apparently Jewish system of occult activity called Qabalah.

In quite a number of minds, the term "Qabalah" evokes images of elderly and perhaps senescent Jewish scholars whom much learning has made at least peculiar, playing around with intellectual puzzles involving figures and letters like some crazy crossword that they hope will explain the whole Universe if they ever manage to solve it. A harmless occupation for retired Rabbis maybe, or a pastime for theological students. Something of that nature, anyway, and not to be taken seriously by those with more robust or entertaining psychic proclivities. Such is often a kindly, if contemptuous, viewpoint held by many who see Qabalah from a distance through the wrong end of their astral telescopes. On the other hand, a more sinister side to Qabalism may be pictured, in which evil-looking Hebrews in black gowns covered with squiggles are trying to raise all sorts of nasty demons by means of diagrams and chanting, combined with suffocating fumes of cannabis or other confusion-causing stenches. The choice of either totally inaccurate imagining depends rather upon whether one is pro- or anti-Semite.

Why, in fact, did an association arise between the Western Tradition and anything peculiar to Hebrew erudition? It might be tempting to assume that Jewish commercial instincts were seeking fresh fields for development in new territory, but such was not the case at all, since commercially inclined Semites had no interest whatever in Qabalah and, in fact, so far as Orthodox opinion decreed, Qabalah was heretical, unauthorised, and generally frowned upon as being foreign to customary beliefs, with far too many pagan implications for the comfort of most congregations. Whatever connection Jewish scholars had with Qabalah, therefore, was always in a private capacity. How was it then, their writings have given us the impression today that Qabalah is purely or exclusively Jewish?

This was, of course, because the only available writings and manuscripts for translation which dealt with Qabalah as such were in Hebrew, and set down in Hebrew terms and idioms. Why should this be so? To understand the reasons, we must remember the conditions prevailing throughout the Western world at the period these works were written. Religious intolerance and persecution were general. Political intrigues and sectional interests caused as much trouble in all directions as they do today, though, of course, in the manner of their age. In short, the Western world was, and still is, in no state for any dissemination of Inner Wisdom to other than a very select minority whose consciousness has reached a point where it is able to function on levels transcending the average to a considerable degree. Suppose individual Initiates of such spiritual status decided to convene as earthly entities and exchange energies between themselves which might be recordable in related human language and symbology. How would they manage this practically during the Middle Ages?

Leaving transport difficulties aside, the religio-political position presented the most formidable problems. For top-grade Initiates of a Secret Tradition with ostensible positions in Christian, Muslim, Jewish, or other Faith in addition to their national or racial distinctions, any form of publicizable convention or suspected collusion would have been disastrous. Suppose today, some equivalent individuals with American, Russian, Chinese, European, African, and other associations met for a similar purpose without the approval or authority of their respective governments? They might meet more subtle kinds of trouble than their medieval brethren, but the same opposition would positively be levelled against their work. Nevertheless, there must always be souls on Earth able to operate far above compulsions from political, national, commercial, religious, or other sectional forms of domination. Those alive in medieval times had their particular problems to deal with, and so they adopted methods which seemed appropriate to their circumstances.

We must remember that Latin was commonly used among Europeans of University educational standards. Greek was a good second. This ruled these out for any form of Occult recording in written characters. Ordinary national languages were too uncertain and quite unsuitable at that period. Arabic might have been useful except for fanatical Muslim opposition to such matters. Oriental languages already had their quota of Qabalah suitable to their ethnical and other requirements, and besides did not adapt properly for the purpose in mind. Codes and cyphers could have been, and were actually used, but these were very clumsy contrivances then, slow to manipulate, and with much to go wrong. What was left? The possibility of Hebrew suggested itself as a natural alternative for a number of reasons.

Firstly, because it was associated with sacred scriptures of antiquity shared by Christian, Muslim, and Jew alike. Secondly, it was an ancient written language still in use among a very limited class of thinking humans. Even ordinary Jews found their scriptural forms of Hebrew almost beyond interpretation, and spoke a very different version of it among themselves. Though not unknown to non-Jewish Universities, Hebrew was only studied by a relatively small section of theologicals and classicals. Commercial and political circles certainly had no use for Hebrew or the slightest interest in it. Perhaps above all, Hebrew has always been a unique language in which to hide meanings behind meanings behind meanings to very great depths. Being without proper vowels, and depending on accentation and "pointing" to reach any conclusive meaning at all, it proved amazingly adaptable to the implantation of Inner ideas among apparently ambiguous or irrelevant outer arrangements. It was not only good as a code or cypher, but was in itself that very thing in a most practical form.

In addition to all this, although Orthodox Jewry might strongly disapprove of heterodox material, they were in no position to persecute their members for heresy as Christians did, or banish them to galleys, mines, and other sorts of slavery like Muslims might. If the worst came to the worst, and writings in Hebrew reached the wrong hands, Israel as an everlasting scapegoat would have to bear whatever blame might be apportioned. Actual risk of this was slight, since who was likely to care much about the mystical meanderings of what seemed at that time an unimportant minority of Jewish sectarians, apparently unsupported by the bulk of their own people?

Then, too, since the Dispersion, Jews no longer had a country of their own. They were scattered throughout the whole of Europe and travelled extensively throughout the Western world. Wherever they went, they made contacts through every possible circle, yet maintained a curious system of communication among themselves from one end of their hierarchy to the other. As a people, they were generally intelligent, hard-working, extremely cautious, lovers of art, literature, and most civilized forms of culture, and possessed of an inherent curiosity beyond ordinary bounds which led them along original lines of investigation. Faults they had in plenty, but especially during that difficult medieval period of Western development, the right type of Jews proved invaluable agents of the Inner Initiates seeking to direct Humanity as a whole toward its Divine purpose. Since they automatically sought for loyalties that lay above their countries of sojourn, they were open to interests and impulses coming from much wider spheres of influence. Their traditional language again was a product of what we now call the Middle East, which was once to the West of human civilization. It was neither of the Far East, nor of the European West, having roots in both directions, and so was useful as a kind of *lingua occulta* for Initiates seeking contact with the human mind by all ways or Paths via what we now call the "Middle Pillar" method.

In common with other Faiths, Jews had their linkages with the Ancient Traditions going well back into pre-history. Granted that many primitive customs such as blood-sacrifice, etc., had served their purpose, and should be superseded by more evolved formularies of Inner approach; nevertheless, it was and is of considerable importance to maintain contact with the original impulse that started Man-kind climbing toward Divinity. The Christian church was doing its utmost to suppress all traces and survivals of its pagan predecessors, regardless of value or detriment to humanity. Islam took the same attitude, though scarcely the same procedures, even forbidding artists to depict anything alive as much as a blade of grass, for fear of breaking the Commandment against making the likeness of anything in the Heavens, the Earth or the Oceans.

Although Jewry officially forbade idolatry in various forms, there remained a fairly intact Mythos stemming from olden times, with existent nomenclature of Inner energies personified as Angels and so forth, plus different Divine Names which roughly equated with those of other Pantheons and Systems. Moreover, a fairly strict code of morals and ethics had become rooted in the "common consciousness" of the Jewish people as a whole. In many ways this was stern, unbending, and, in modern times might be considered hopelessly unpermissive or restrictive, but it did have the property of developing a type of spiritual strength and discipline which carries communities through almost unbelievable odds, and overcomes opposition sometimes by sheer survival alone. If Inner Traditions, especially those of the West, are to continue, that particular type of integrity and faith is as necessary now as in medieval days, and neither Jews nor any particular group of people have any special right to monopolize it. They never did, but in the period we are considering, the Jewish soul clung with almost desperate obstinacy to its Inner beliefs, simply because those were all that preserved the individuality of that soul in a world threatening its extinction.

Perhaps one of the best reasons in the end why Hebrew was so suitable for dissemination of the Western Tradition during the Middle Ages, was because the Jews had no civil power in their own right, and their spheres of influence extended through Inner fields of force only. As physicians, scholars, and in other positions where they were able to affect the destiny of humanity from Inside, they could be of great service by bringing subtle but incredibly potent spiritual energies to bear exactly where and when these were needed. On the other hand, Jews were completely powerless to institute programs of persecution and destruction on those who disagreed with their opinions or attempted to work beyond the limits of belief fixed by Church and State alike. They were in no position to prevent individuals among their own peoples from acting as agents of Inner and older Traditions. However greatly Orthodox Jews disliked the idea, they were most unlikely to betray those yet attached officially to their Faith by bonds of birth and observance of custom. Christians, on the other hand, were cheerfully burning their "deviationists" literally in heaps.

For all these reasons alone, Hebrew became the most obvious language and System to be adopted in the Middle Ages by those Inner Initiates responsible for the maintenance and furtherance of the Secret Tradition of Europe and the West. It was mainly a question of availability and practicality. An enormous amount of the Western Tradition lay scattered around in Britain, but was in no condition to be reconstituted at that period. If it could be kept alive at all in legend and local customs, this would serve until its moment came for reawakening. The tale of Arthur and his knights asleep in an underground cave awaiting their call to action again, at the time of their people's greatest need, is of very deep and real significance. All people need the Inner strength deriving from their own ethnical roots when stresses against them increase beyond normal bearing. Who should understand this better than the Jews of the Middle Ages whose only homeland was an ancestral memory and a pious hope? They had to draw upon their Inner resources the whole time.

Notwithstanding all this, the Qabalah, properly understood, is no purely Jewish invention or system. It entirely transcends specific racial or religious origins, although it harmonizes most closely with what we might call the Westernizing and modernizing tendencies of the human mind and soul. The medieval formularies of Qabalah were arrived at by a number of souls from various ethnic groupings whose entire concern with the Hebrew languages, customs, or people, was that these were suitable for service to a far wider section of Humanity whose spiritual needs called for much closer contact with Inner Intelligence than were available through other Earth-reaching channels of communication. There have always been souls in incarnation capable of operating on scales of consciousness a good deal advanced from those in common usage. We may think of them euphemistically as Leaders toward light if we please. They still need formation-patterns into which their consciousness may be cast, and which may be used also for the training and development of evolving souls to take their place in due course of Cosmos. This was a major aim of those who loosely termed themselves "Qabalists." Receivers. Receivers of what? from whence? Of whom? How? All interesting matters for investigation even at this distance of time, especially since our world today faces just the same issues presented in a different manner.

Exactly what were the Qabalists seeking? Their main objective was the same as other Mystery Schools, namely the discovery and knowledge of the Elements of Existence in terms of Fundamental Energies, and the codification of Consciousness as the Pattern (or Paths) of Cosmic Relativity. They were looking for the most basic construction of Creation itself, and the best means of using such knowledge for the advancement of humanity toward Divinity. They realized perfectly well that Life begins and terminates from Within, and that ability to control Inner conditions will determine Outer effects. So, of course, did other Systems, but the Qabalists' aim was to find a sort of Master-Formula for the Plan and Process of our Inner Identity which would afford maximum assistance to those souls already in the vanguard of humanity and on whom devolved the responsibility for leading Mankind toward Ultimate Light. Since most of these souls were incarnating in a steadily increasing Western Stream, the Formula had to be suitable for these new necessities of adapting the most Ancient Energies into constantly modernizing forms of expression.

The type of Enlightenment received by souls of such categories which is classed as "Qabalah," or "of Inner Origin," is not generally obtained in a condition suitable for indiscriminate distribution to the public at large. Firstly, it cannot be contained in literary forms they would properly grasp or appreciate, and secondly, they are not at a point of spiritual evolution to benefit from it in its advanced and concentrated state. The real essence of Qabalah is that all living souls must find it for themselves through their own Inner contacts with its spiritual source of supply. When they all start coming to the same conclusions as a result of their individual efforts, they will realize they are on the right track or Path of Inner progress. As a kind of utility Key to the "Kingdom of Heaven" which lies inside human soul-entities, the unique Glyph of the "Tree of life" was devised and used by Initiates of the inner Mysteries of Light as a practical means of achieving their spiritual identities at first hand. That was, and still is, the principal purpose of the Tree-Symbol—To act as an "Open-It-Yourself" Master to every inner Door a seeking human soul is likely to encounter in the Quest of Light.

Those who can make use of such Keys should do so. Others

must take whatever becomes available to them through the efforts of these Initiates on behalf of their less enterprising fellow beings. There is no question of "inferior information" involved in any way whatever here. It is simply a matter of individual spiritual evolution and nothing else. We all have to pass the same Points of Progress sooner or later as we go along our Lines of Light. Everything depends on our ability to absorb this incredible Inner Energy, and then reflect its radiance in ways that may benefit others less able to endure its intensity as Source-strength is approached. Perhaps this is why so little is written directly about "Qabalah" itself. We do not write much of Alphabets, but we do write everything imaginable with them. Nor do we use figures for their own sake in mathematics, but for what can be done with them. The Tree of Life Formula is for working with in Inner Dimensions of Life in spiritual terms that equate more or less with the basic concepts of figures and letters in our ordinary world of consciousness as human beings. We may think of it as an Inner Alphabet and an Inner Numerical System. With those, the whole Inner World lies open to intelligent investigators.

If we consider even a moment, it will be obvious that our civilization and development as a human species on Earth is linked in the closest ways with our capabilities of "writing and reckoning," for which Figures and Letters are the basics. We might well call them the true Elements of Education, whereby our latent and inherent qualities are led out of us so to speak, that we may stand in our own True Lights. Why then, should we not be able to civilize and develop ourselves as spiritual subjects of an Inner and Eternal Kingdom by similar means? In fact, we can, and the Tree of life provides this very valuable facility. It does more. By its intrinsically ideal nature, it not only allows us to approach Inner Existence as we may find it, but more importantly, to construct Inner Cosmos in accordance with the Divine, or True Will, acting through us.

The working plan of the Tree may seem very complicated to non-Qabalists, but is really simplicity itself. It is to be used Inwardly just as we use numbers and letters Outwardly, but the values of the Symbols are based on a totally different currency so to speak. Instead of a numerical decade, we have a decimal System of primal Concepts relative to spiritual Absolutes. In place of an Alphabet, there are resultant Concepts derived from dual combinations of the Prime set. These constitute our basic terms of Inner education. Once these important elements of Inner Intelligence are grasped, the rest will follow as a matter of experience and arrangement. We say of Earthly matters that something is "as simple as A.B.C.", and this applies in wider Worlds of Inner Awareness also. In learning the Tree of Life characteristics, we are "becoming as little children" and entering an Inner Kingdom where, in order to grow up properly, we first have to "Learn our letters." In other words, we shall be learning to think, speak, act, and eventually become "like unto Gods—immortal." That is what Qabalah is for.

It is, after all, a question of coordinating and relating the energies of Consciousness according to a Master-System based on technically irreducible Elements of active Awareness. Just as our entire physical state of Existence is composed of chemical Elements arranged in patterns which combine to make up the whole of differentiated Creation, so is our Spiritual state of Existence composed along the same lines of light. What our physical knowledge of chemistry is accomplishing for humanity is of secondary importance when compared with what our knowledge of spiritual "al-chemy" might do for us as souls. Qabalah is the art and work of gaining such knowledge for ourselves with the aid of those Inner Entities willing to assist our efforts. This is true Alchemy, which from its literal roots means "Divine heating." For "God," read whatever in ourselves impels us to an ever-extending Ultimate, and for "heating" read the energy generated in us by that Impulse making us act as we do in search of Its nature and Itself. That is what Alchemy means, and where should we derive this needed "Divine heat" from, if not from the Light shining Within us, or the Sun of Truth we dare not look upon and live?

With the Tree of life Formula, we commence with a related Pattern shared by Ten Concepts, a Universal Nil or all-emanating Zero, and an "X Outcome" or calculable result. The Nil or Zero is the Ain Soph Aur, the Concepts are the Sephiroth, and the Outcome is "Daath," or Knowledge and Experience. All these have been dealt with very exhaustively by many writers, and they will only be passingly referred to in this work. What we shall concern ourselves with mainly are the "Paths," or "Letters" of the Qabalistic Inner Alphabet which have their basis as resultants of reaction between two Principle Concepts or Sephiroth. In former times, such a System was linked to the Hebrew Alpha, but is now forthcoming at last in plain English characters. The principles remain unchanged, only the equivalents in Earth language are altered to suit modern needs.

Nevertheless, it is impossible to grasp the significance of the "Inner Letters," or use them to make "Words" with, until living experience has been gained of and with the major Concepts or Sephiroth. Just as no child can learn an Alphabet of any kind before it realizes that the things and affairs of this world connect with each other in some kind of order and Pattern, so must we first appreciate the salient points of the Inner life Pattern and Order as represented by the Sephiroth. There is only one way to do this, which is by Internalizing our consciousness concerning them by means of Meditation, and Externalizing this Awareness by "Magic," or Meditation through Intentional Expression. First we look at the Concepts, and next we turn them round and work *with* them, just like making up Words and whole strings of meanings out of basic Figures and Letters. In the case of the Tree, we make the Letters themselves out of Figure combinations, so these have to be handled first.

The Ten Basic Concepts presented by the Qabalistic Tree of Life are, of course, the familiar Sphere-System of:

0. **Zero**. Nil, the Unmanifest. All that Will be.
1. **The Crown** or Summit of Perfection. Divine Rulership.
2. **Wisdom**. Projective Awareness. Inspiration, etc.
3. **Understanding.** Perceptive Awareness, Intuition, etc.
4. **Mercy**. Right, Compassion, Encouragement, etc.
5. **Severity**. Might, Discipline, Restraint, etc.
6. **Beauty**. Harmony, Balance Poise, etc.
7. **Victory**. Incentive, Hope, Devotion, etc.
8. **Glory**. Initiative, Honor, Determination, etc.
9. **Foundation**. Faith, Purpose, Dedication, etc.
10. **Kingdom**. The Human status and its possibilities.

Plus: Experience and knowledge as an issue of living with this Scheme. This is Qabalistically termed "Daath."

There it is. A practical outline (or Tree) of Life composed of vital Principles needed for the progression of a human soul from its Earthly condition of incarnation to whatever Ultimate it may achieve in unison with Divinity. Possibly one of the first things an outside observer might notice about it is an absence of anything suggesting evil. Critics might say this presents merely a sort of dream-world, born of wishful thinking as an escape from their "real" human world, which all admit is still burdened with evils and imperfections. Critics, however, are seldom of the slightest help to others. Certainly the Tree Scheme excludes evil, since Qabalists do not believe that any evil whatever formed part of the Original Intention responsible for Creation, nor should it exist in a Scheme intended to achieve and arrange life in accordance with that same Intention or True Will behind Being. There is no question of denying evils or wrongs prevalent among humanity on Earth, but there is every question of denying the admission of such undesirable issues into the construction of Inner Cosmos under Creation by the consciousness of Divinity acting through Mankind awakening to life in Spiritual Space. The Tree Scheme outlines a Plan of Perfection, and how can even the slightest trace of evils be admissible therein?

Humanity has to work out its salvation by imagining Heavens and either attempting to reach them entirely on Inner levels or else trying to make them come true in Earthly terms. We have probably suffered more on Earth from human ideas of Heaven, than our worst fears of Hell threatened. With their own Heavenly notions, sections of humanity have gladly inflicted Hell on everybody else. By and large, the Eastern approach is to visualize Perfection as a purely Inner state, for the sake of which Initiates should utterly abandon this "wicked world" in order to obtain Liberation. Conversely, the Western approach, while admitting a theoretically perfect Inner Existence, considers this impractical until its equivalent achievement is possible right here on Earth. The East seeks spiritualization of Matter, and the West, materialization of Spirit. The Qabalah postulates a mid-Line of Enlightenment.

This is done by accepting the framework of ten Points or Principles as a fundamental basis for becoming what is best for the human soul to ultimately be. Into that framework every single soul may put WHAT THEY WILL in the way of individual effort to achieve their own emancipation as an entity in ENTITY. All will become what each attains. In order to commence this achievement in the Way of Qabalah, it is essential to "Learn the Tree," as an actually experienced relationship of those Principles within oneself. When we have put the Tree-Principles in ourselves into the Pattern outlines by the notation shown through the Tree-Glyph, we shall be ready to learn the "Inner Language" of its "Letters." This is why so many Qabalists make use of Rite and Ritual means of rearranging themselves on very deep Life-levels so as to correspond with the Tree Plan. Such is, after all, the most valuable purpose of Ritual as an activity. To formulate Patterns and Paths for the fundamental Forces of our Inner Existence, according to the Will Within us. Most Qabalists have their own ways of constructing Rituals out of natural components, using the Ten Principles of the Tree as a building Plan. In any case, whether with Ritual or other means, the sense and realization of the Sephiroth as Spiritual types of Inner Energies must be definitely experienced to a marked degree before the Initiate is properly prepared for the Paths of the Tree.

We can identify with the Tree-Scheme by any practical method presenting itself for the purpose. First, it must obviously be read and thought about in order to obtain material for studies and practices. The diagram of the Glyph should be drawn and dissected in a variety of ways and colors, and the entire Pattern must eventually be so familiar that it becomes part and parcel of living as it were. When the appearances and circumstances of everyday life begin to suggest the Sephirotic Principles, of their own accord almost, this will show that the Tree Scheme has indeed "taken root" in fertile Inner Fields. If a blue sky makes one think of Mercy and Compassion, and yellow or gold flowers put one in mind of Harmony and Beauty, for example, then the Tree is growing nicely. It is flourishing even better when the colors and associations alone actually encourage one into a real state of Compassion, Harmony, or other condition of being expressed as a Tree-Concept. That will come about in time, if sufficient care and effort is expended on the enterprise. When every single encounter with Life points along some Path leading to Light, it may be known that the Tree is well established and branching out as it should.

There are all kinds of Invocations, associative Symbolism and technical devices of Ritual calculated to condition the consciousness of an operator with specific Tree-Concepts. While these are definitely helpful to those with abilities and facilities for working them, undoubtedly the finest method of realizing the Concepts is simply to live them in ordinary and extraordinary practice, and then build them into relative relationship with each other as in the Tree-Plan itself. Even if the humblest start is made by the old and tried system of living through the Concepts at the rate of one per day, this will do far more than enthusiastic leaps that lead to nowhere except disappointment and loss of interest. After all, the Concepts are Qualities or Attributes which are common (or should be) to Divinity and Humanity alike. As Human souls, we ought to have at the very least some vestige of each somewhere in our make-up. The rest is a matter of developing and arranging them as the Tree indicates.

Supposing we follow the broadest outline of the Tree from its structure at our Human end to its connection with the Highest Concept of Divinity we can reach—and beyond. At Point 10, the Kingdom, we take our status on Earth as whatever we are, and begin to climb from that. At Point 9, we need a Foundation of Faith and basic beliefs. At Points 8 and 7, Glory and Victory, we need Initiative and Incentive, Intelligence and Devotion, to bring us to our vital Point G, Harmony, Balance, Poise, and one might say Central Spiritual Integrity. Once this is reached, we shall appreciate how to use Points 5 and 4, Discipline and Compassion, in order to Bring the Gulf (Abyss) between ourselves and Divinity and acquire Points 3 and 2, Understanding and Wisdom through Experience and Knowledge (Daath). Then and then alone, we shall be fitted to rule ourselves by directions of the Divine Will in us at Point I, the Crown or King. If we reach any such analogous condition, then we shall be free to BE WHAT WE WILL through the mysterious Nil-State of Zero which the Eastern Tradition terms Nirvana, and the Western Tradition has no terms for at all beyond saying, "The rest is—SILENCE." Such is the significance of the conventional greeting, "Pax Profundis."

What if anyone should say, "But I lack most of those qualities cannot handle even what I have properly. How can I ever use the Tree?" The answer is quite simply that the Tree does not call for specific amounts of its indicated qualities in or from anybody, but for the deliberate patterning and lay-out or perhaps "circuitry" in modern terms, of whatever traces of those particular qualities exist in any human being. Granted that most of us are sadly deficient of them in one way or another, and probably have far too much of some and not nearly enough of others. Who is unreasonable enough to expect perfection in human beings?

Whatever our condition may be, the thing to do with the Tree is apply its Pattern to ourselves and sort out its qualities in us into the Plan it presents, whether such qualities are little, over-much, or scarcely at all obvious in our natures. Once this arrangement is made, and the Plan followed out, all the qualities will interact with each other through the connections or "Paths" between them, and sooner or later they will relate with themselves in such a way as to evolve our entire beings into far better specimens of humanity, and even samples of Divinity, than we might otherwise have remained. Everything depends upon putting ourselves into the Tree-Order according to its indicated instructions. In a sense, this is not unlike a Do-It-Yourself electronic kit. There we have a number of components, a book of instructions, and most importantly, a circuit diagram. If we put the pieces together according to the instructions in the plan shown by the diagram, we shall have a finished apparatus which will work perfectly when electrical energy is applied. The Tree of life is a straightforward circuit diagram of Do-It-Yourself Divinity, and if its pieces are set up as shown, the Inner Energy of Divinity acting through us will operate the finished construction. That is the true purpose of the Tree.

Surely the overall layout of the Tree is easy enough to follow mentally if not immediately otherwise? As humans, we have to find enough faith and belief to make a foundation from which to commence climbing the Tree. (A launching pad is the first essential of a Space rocket) This should result in the dual energies of Incentive and Initiative lifting us from mere materialism toward our spiritual objectives. Then we ought to achieve Poise, or Space-stability in Inner Dimensions which allows us to live and function properly as souls. When this state is gained, it enables us to use the controls of Might and Mercy so as to steer us toward the Star we aim for. The Experience and Knowledge acquired by this time gives us the ability to project ourselves across the Abyss of the Lost, and arrive at an awakened condition of consciousness equal to Wisdom and Understanding in a different state of being from our previous one. At last we shall reach our objective, and be able to rule our own Universe from its Ultimate Point AS WE WILL. Not even here do we end, but what lies before us then is beyond any Tree to include, so the Glyph indicates the Great Unmanifest as outside the scope of its structure, linked only to the

Plan at the Point of Highest Light. Not at all unlike a journey through Inner instead of Outer Space.

That is naturally only the barest and widest coverage of the Tree. So how shall we learn all its finer and more intimate details that will connect us personally and individually with its spiritual structure? From the Tree itself, of course. Where else? If all its "branches" are Paths, and every Path has its own significance which might be summed up as a symbol equivalent in Inner terms to an alphabetical Letter in Outer usage, then the Tree ought to speak its own messages in ways of "Words" and whole sentences intelligible to our awakening spiritual consciousness. Moreover, it should be capable of putting such messages through in phraseology which even our ordinary consciousness might comprehend. Theoretically, The Path-System of the Tree should act like a translating machine, interpreting purely Inner energies of Intelligence into relative terminology phrased in Earthly forms of speech and comprehension. This, it will and does do for those willing to learn the "Language" and "Grammar" of this strange mid-speech between entirely different Dimensions of Life. That is the purpose of the Paths or Branches on the Tree of Life Symbol. How we may arrive at the realization of, and begin to use, such "Letters" is the object of our present study.

In the Middle Ages of course, the Tree of Life with its Principles and Paths was geared to the Hebrew Alphabet exclusively, which mainly confined its use to students of and in that tongue, whether they were of Jewish origin or not, which by no means all Qabalists were or ever will be. The needs for such secretive and selective courses of action no longer apply for ostensibly religious reasons, even though necessity for discretion always remains. There is no reason now why the Tree of Life should not speak to anyone in their own way with their own language. Plain English is a very good language to receive Qabalah with. What better nowadays? After the universal language of mathematics, which expresses the fundamental Principles of the Tree, English is now the leading literary and cultural tongue of the Western Tradition and the consolidating Middle Way. When the natures and realities of the Principles or Spheres of the Tree have become clear to us as Concepts connected with a Scheme of mathematical notation and values, we should discover the amazing possibilities of relationships between these becoming a familiar Alphabet of our

Mother-Tongues which will talk to us in our own ways about the Inner actualities Mankind has sought since his inception in the Mind of his Maker. More. The Tree will talk about anything we are interested in. What instructed child does not know the story of the Talking Tree whose leaves told everything to those who listened carefully? That is the Tree of Life in reality. A means whereby anyone initiated into its ways may talk with Divinity inside themselves as it is reputed Adam and our noteworthy forefathers did. Talk *with*, be it noted, not talk *to*. Anyone can talk to anyone else, Divinity included, but who receives answers? That is Qabalah. Receiving answers to what we ask via the language of the Tree. For us in particular, the Earthly form of this happens to be English, and therefore we may as well adjust our Tree-talk to suit ourselves. Let us hear how it sounds in practice.

The Purpose & Plan of the Paths

Most people find the relatively straightforward principles of the Sephiroth simple enough to deal with, but when it comes to all the multiplicities and complications of the Paths on the Tree, things either seem too confusing to bother with, or too fanciful to make any sense from. What with all the decoration of Hebrew letters, Tarot cards, colors, astrological signs, etc., the whole heap of arcana seems muddled beyond all meaning. For some souls, it is this very tangle which exerts a fascination of its own, as rather grubby and disorderly junkshops have an almost hypnotic effect on matching human personalities.

How did these associations become attached to the Tree-Paths in the first place? The alphabetical linkage is reasonable enough for identification purposes. All sorts of Path systems have been developed from time to time, and the present one in use does not seem to have arisen before the Middle Ages, or to have become at all complicated by accretions until the era of the Golden Dawn. The numerations of the Paths have always been somewhat arbitrary after the first obvious four. Between trying to make the muddle mean something, and fasten preconceived ideas into precarious Tree-positions, it is small wonder so many explorers of its Labyrinthine twistings found such small returns for all their efforts.

Confusion of any description was never the initial intention behind the Path-design. Such was simply a side effect experienced by those failing to follow its real purpose. A useful side-effect in some ways perhaps, since it certainly discouraged inquisitive meddlers while providing them with enough material to keep them happily playing with harmless puzzles. Actually the Paths had and have far more to offer than those pleasantries.

Their true purpose and Inner Intention is to offer means for clarifying consciousness in such a way that its energies may be directed through all levels of Life extending greatly beyond those defining our limits as mere mortals. If we like to make them a modern analogy, and think of the Paths as the circuit-construction of a walkie-talkie set putting its owner in touch with Inner Intelligence unreachable with an ordinary vocal range, this will be a fair comparison. Again, we might think of them as being the basic terms of a language spoken between Divinity on one hand and Mankind on the other—the so-called "Tongue" of the Angels, or "Enochian," by which a human being might establish intelligent contacts of consciousness with far more developed life-types than his own. If we accept that consciousness is actually the energy of existence as entity, then it seems obvious there must be some medium of exchange which is acceptable on all levels, and this is what the tree-paths purport to be.

The working principles of this System are simple enough. Take a relationship between any two Spheres or Concepts, treat this as a unit of Awareness in its own right, then adjust Consciousness to operate on that new level of expression. It is then a question of exchanging one type of Awareness for another, a normal process for any intelligent human. After all, babies do not think in terms of any particular language, and only when they become able to collect their consciousness into circles of energy called "Words," can they deal properly with affairs of this world in relationship with other humans. Learning the "Inner Speech of Spirit" is much the same sort of process. We have to collect our consciousness of spiritual values in terms of prime figures into secondary circles which will become the "letters" of our new "Inner Alphabet," arrange these again into "Words," and then into sentences making sense to those Entities employing this type of conscious communion among their own circles of association. The Tree of Life provides us with the Prime Concepts out of which a whole Cosmos of Inner Consciousness may be constructed with what we might call "The Language of Light." By linking this associatively with our ordinary forms of human speech and thought, we can establish channels of communication, or Paths, between our normal selves and the deepest levels of our Innermost Identity. This objective is shared commonly by every Magical, Mystical, Religious, or other System of spiritual operation. The

Qabalah alone propounds a Scheme of Enlightenment based on living and learning according to the "letters" of the Laws that link every single soul directly with its own Inmost Origin.

To obtain these "Letters," we "mate up" the Spheres of the Tree by pairs and obtain their product. This must be realized and symbolized into some form of convenience for our human consciousness to handle. Formerly, this was done with a character of the Hebrew Alphabet, which, of course, had a dual value as a number and some physical item, in addition to its phonetic use as a unit of speech or writing. Later on, the Tarot card System appeared as numerical ideographs which fitted the Tree in various ways that never seem to have met with universal acceptance. Eventually came a craze for "Attributing" everything and anything to the paths of the Tree, almost as if it were a Christmas Tree with everybody trying to hang up their intellectual presents intended for each other. This rather untidy decoration somewhat spoiled the Tree's appearance for those who sought its admirable simplicity. The original notion of taking a number, linking it with an idea, then juggling with the figures in a purely mathematical field and obtaining resultants that translated it to totally new ideas, became observed especially to a Westernizing culture that did not link its Alphabet with numerical values, and thus dealt with its deep ideology in separate fields of consciousness. We think in either words or figures. To a learned Hebrew scholar, these would be interchangeable, but we see them in quite distinct categories because of our traditional training in constructing circles of consciousness. There is no question of one way being right and the other wrong. It is simply a difference of method. To make the fullest and best use of the Qabalistic Tree, all should follow their most natural means of approach and ascent. In our case, this happens to be along literate lines of the English language, and therefore it is the one we shall employ.

Since the whole system of Anglicized Tree-linkage had been set out in *Magical Ritual Methods* (Helios 1969), it will only be necessary to epitomize this here, and then embark on a deeper investigation of the individual Paths and methods of employing them. In the first place, the Tree-Form we shall deal with is the traditional one of the Qabalah, but its basis of consciousness derives from pure Concepts rather than a network of numbers. In the older Hebraic system, the mathematics of the Tree eventually became more important to its users than the meanings of such figures in terms of living experience and relationship with Inner Reality. This was largely because of the universality of mathematical values as a means of exchanging conscious energies between individuals of widely differing species. Those who could not speak a word of each other's language bargained well enough together by means of upheld fingers or numerical knocks. Ancient Semitic and other traders were well accustomed to this instinctive decimal system. It seemed only reasonable to suppose that if one could communicate with otherwise unintelligible fellow-mortals in such a way, why might one not invent something of the sort for communicating with the "Gods" themselves? So intelligent humans began making decimal codes of consciousness aimed at dealing directly with Inner Intelligence far beyond their normal range of reach. Poor little mortals sending secret signals to their Divinity! Man, holding up his fingers for God to count. Why should it be surprising to discover that responses were indeed duly received from Heavenly Quarters?

In the case of the Qabalistic Tree, there are but twenty-two Paths which are letter-numbered neatly enough by means of the Hebrew Alphabet. To replace this with our English Alphabet, it is tempting at first to add two extra Paths, until one remembers that vowels were "extras" in Hebrew, and fitted in with consonant-formed words in order to give those words their real meaning according to the spirit in which they were intended. The vowels were originally very special sonics indeed, being mostly used for "God-names" and other sacred purposes. Consonants gave words their bodies, but vowels alone put soul into them. If we follow this valuable idea with the English Alphabet, we shall extract the vowels and equate them with the *Magical Elements of the Cosmic Cross,* so:

A	to	EARTH at	North
E	to	AIR at	East
I	to	FIRE at	South
O	to	WATER at	West
U (OO) to		AETHER	around and about. (The

"element" of Universal Truth.)

This, of course, leaves only twenty-one letters, and there are twenty-two Paths. The simplest solution is to use the old and very practical letter Th, or "thomb," which need never have been dropped from our Alphabet since we write it so frequently otherwise.

The allotment of the consonants to the Paths is a natural enough process if we connect the Sephiroth in their normal order of 1-2, 1-3, 1-6, (since there is no Path between Sephirah 1, and 4 or 5), then carry on accordingly with the other Sephiroth. This produces a full Table of:

Path	Sephiroth	Letter
11	1 Crown—Wisdom 2	B
12	1 Crown—Understanding 3	C
13	1 Crown—Beauty 6	D
14	2 Wisdom—Understanding 3	F
15	2 Wisdom—Mercy 4	G
16	2 Wisdom—Beauty 6	H
17	3 Understanding—Severity 5	J
18	3 Understanding—Beauty 6	K
19	4 Mercy—Severity 5	L
20	4 Mercy—Beauty 6	M
21	4 Mercy—Victory 7	N
22	5 Severity—Beauty 6	P
23	5 Severity—Glory B	Q
24	6 Beauty—Victory 7	R
25	6 Beauty—Glory 8	S
26	6 Beauty—Foundation 9	T
27	7 Victory—Glory 8	V
28	7 Victory—Foundation 9	W
29	7 Victory—Kingdom 10	X
30	8 Glory—Foundation 9	Y
31	8 Glory—Kingdom 10	Z
32	9 Foundation—Kingdom 10	Th

We now have a System of Elementary Energy-Ideas linked with vowels, and dualized Concepts attached to consonants of our ordinary everyday Alphabet. It will be easiest to understand if overall relative Symbols are found to epitomize each Path. The usual method of doing this is by means of the Tarot Trumps or "Major Arcana." Many ways of arranging these have been tried, mostly by juggling with their conventional enumeration, which has resulted in very odd positioning indeed. The way we propose to adopt, in this instance, is to take the fundamental ideas of each

Tarot Trump, and align these with whatever seems their most appropriate position of the Tree itself. The card-concepts have a distinct pattern of their own, and may be outlined by two triplicities which will give the central upright Pillar, and the cross-bars of the Tree, followed by eight pairs to complete the rest of the Path-Pattern.

The *triplicities* are:

Moon, Sun, Star: marking the cosmic levels by stages away from our world toward lnfiinity.

Wheel of Fortune, Justice, Judgment: signifying the decisive types of Inner Intent which lead us from Humanity to Divinity.

The *pairs* are:

Fool and World: Us and our Earthly environments if taken at lowest level, and our final freedom from Evolution if seen as an ultimate aim.

Magician and Priestess: Science and Sentiment, or the two main streams of Inner seeking which lift us off purely material ground for living.

Chariot and Lovers: Ambition and Affection, Hope and Happiness, or the best motives in ourselves for becoming better beings than mere mortals.

These three pairs or six Concepts are connected with what might be called the most human of our characteristics which tend to make us plod the Paths leading from mortality as Man to Immortality as Ultimate Entity. The next three pairs are connected with our somewhat more arcane extensions of Existence. They are:

Blasted Tower and Strength: The complementary uses of Energy for integrating and disintegrating our Cosmic constructions AS WE WILL in the courses of perfecting their arrangements and natures.

The Devil and Death: Tribulation and liberation, or the "needs must when the Devil drives," and our continual changing condition of life through excarnation and rebirth which allows us to improve over a succession of incarnations. These two make up the Left Hand Pillar of the Tree.

The Empress and Emperor: Rulership of our Empathy and Id-Entity, or the forces by which we both FEEL and KNOW our relationship with Divinity. These are the Right Hand Pillar of the Tree.

The last two pairs form a sort of quarternal group which links our highest faculties with our point of Ultimate Aim. As usual with the Tarot, they are really Principles represented by Personifications, which are:

The Hanged Man and Temperance: Duty and Discretion, or the realizations of what we ought to do because such courses are the correct ones for us according to the True (or Divine) Will behind our being.

The Hermit and Hierophant: Ourselves as individually related with Divinity, and as related through that Divinity with all other individual beings. The I Am and WE ARE of every and all Existence.

If the Tarot Trumps are laid out in this way in the design of the Tree-Pattern, they will show the whole of our progression from where we are as humans to where we might be if we sought a better state of being. They will also show us how to arrange ourselves so as to achieve at least some degree of such an objective. What is more, if we equate them with our Alphabet, they might even tell us something in English we would grasp with our ordinary working minds. Therefore, if we incorporate each duality of Sephirotic Concepts forming the Paths of the Tree into the single Hieroglyph of a Tarot trump, and then think of this as conveniently linked with a consonant Letter of our Alphabet, we shall have a very practical means of connecting our normal human conditions of consciousness with the most arcane Awareness of which we might be capable if we Willed to Work that Way. So we make out another kind of symbolic "shopping list" which runs:

Letter	Tarot Trump	Tree-Concepts	Path
B	Hierophant	Crown-Wisdom	11
H	Temperance	Wisdom-Beauty	16
J	Death	Understanding-Severity	17
K	Hanged Man	Understanding-Beauty	18
L	Justice	Mercy-Severity	19
M	Strength	Mercy-Beauty	20
N	Empress	Mercy-Victory	21
P	Blasted Tower	Severity–Beauty	22
Q	Devil	Severity-Glory	23
R	Lovers	Beauty-Victory	24

S	Chariot	Beauty-Glory	25
T	Sun	Beauty-Foundation	26
V	Wheel of Fortune	Victory-Glory	27
W	Priestess	Victory-Foundation	28
X	World	Victory-Kingdom	29
Y	Magician	Glory-Foundation	30
Z	Fool	Glory-Kingdom	31
Th	Moon	Foundation-Kingdom	32

To appreciate just why this arrangement is made in its particular way, the entire layout of the Tree and these Ideas should be studied as shown by the frontispiece Figure. It shows how the Concepts combine with each other to form the design they do, and where the pieces of individualized consciousness fit in with each other to make up more meanings and open other ways of Will-working.

We have now constructed a somewhat unique piece of mental machinery. It amounts to a circuitry of consciousness which is powered by actualities of subjective experience, and productive of resultants from these in units of our normal Alphabetically based awareness as homo sapiens. This is rather like feeding electrical impulses of varying strengths and frequencies into a television receiver, and obtaining results in terms of sound and vision our ordinary ears and eyes can appreciate. The main difference in this comparison is, that with a T.V. set we only need money to obtain it and pay for its running, while in the case of the "Talking Tree," we need what no money will ever buy—constant and consistent efforts of intelligent application. In fact, the Paths were even called "The Paths of Intelligence," because that is exactly what they are, specific channels of consciousness which inform and enable souls who speak their language to gain the spiritual status their efforts entitle them to achieve.

After all, this is how intelligence of any kind reaches us, and how we send it out of ourselves to accomplish any particular purpose. All that is capable of affecting our awareness, or that we can reach by means of our Will-directed consciousness, has its own particular Pathway or channel corresponding with its nature. It is through these Paths alone that consciousness operates, and if we learn how to control the force-flows along them, then we may do WHAT WE WILL with those incredible energies. That, surely, is the whole point of working with Paths on the Tree of Life? The

Magical method of developing and applying this necessary control is via the Key-Symbols appropriate in each case. The Hebrews used Number-Letter Keys and we shall use Ideograph-Letter ones. Otherwise the principles are the same.

The Sephiroth, or Primal Decade of the Tree have each to be considered from four main standpoints or "Worlds" that connect Non-Existence with Existence as we know it. First of all, things Originate, and since this lies with Divinity alone, a specific and suitable God-Name or Attribute denotes the Origination of each Sephirah. Next, Creation comes, and so an "Archangelic" or functional Name applies. After that, everything Formates, or becomes its particular self as a formulation of Creative Consciousness. This is designated by an "Angelic Order." Lastly is Expression, or Manifestation in terms appreciable to human awareness. With the Sephiroth, this is equated with Cosmic phenomena such as the Planets, Zodiac, Nebulae, Space, Time, etc. After that come more mundane associations such as colors, perfumes, instruments, and so forth. These four Angles of Awareness naturally link up with the Elements, Tarot suits, and other Quarternities. In a sense, they are the principal points of the circles of consciousness we have to trace around everything in a Magical Way, in order to experience existence from all Cosmic angles. This process of course, must be applied to the Paths of the Tree as well as the Sephiroth, through we are no longer in necessity of finding elaborate Hebrew titles to describe what we find, providing the underlying principles are followed faithfully.

The whole idea is, first, to grasp the nature of each Sephirah properly, then consider them as pairs producing a concept between them, and then analyze this product in the same four ways as the Sephiroth themselves, so that they link on all these levels. There is no reason why we should not term those stages of Existence: Divine, Archangelic, Angelic, and Mundane, if we wish to. They are really qualities or properties constituting the network or circuitry that connects our Humanity with an ultimate spiritual condition behind our being. Knowledge and use of such a System will undoubtedly advance our evolution in accordance with the Will responsible for our existence in the first place.

There are four main ways of familiarizing ourselves with the Sephiroth and their Paths, or for that matter with any other topics whatever. The first is by pure Meditation or direct Inner approach. The second is by study and conscious consideration of the subject. The third by Ritual or other means of representational experience. Lastly comes actually living the Sephiroth and Paths as a normal *modus vivendi* on all their Life-levels. These relationships between individual souls and their spiritual aims correspond with the Qabalistic "World" quarternity. We Originate in ourselves by contemplative meditation, Create by constructive consciousness, Formate by ceremonial and Symbol, and then Express by objective living. The whole process may be continued around its cycle in reverse order, of course, and by "folding back" our lives into ritual Symbology, this into conscious considerations, and that again into contemplative meditation, we can directly relate our lives with the Infinite Being. What is important is the order in which all this is carried out. It must be done sequentially by its proper stages.

Relatively few souls who seek Inner or "Occult" ways of progression, realize exactly how essential such Order is. Their Outer lives may be models of ordered and well-arranged affairs, while their Inner Existence remains no more than a junk-heap of discarded ideas and futile fancies. They will keep their bodies in excellent condition, their homes splendidly, and their material concerns even magnificently, while living in a state of spiritual squalor they would be utterly horrified to observe if this were projected into physical terms. This indeed does happen when the "Dweller on the Threshold" is encountered. Yet if we would make any sort of spiritual progression at all, we must work as Divinity Itself does—Cosmically—and Cosmos simply means Order, implying that all becomes arranged accortling to the Will directing such a process. Once this Will is known, realized, and put into effect, Cosmos follows. That is the meaning of DO WHAT THOU WILT. The Tree of Life, with its Sephiroth and Paths sets out an Order (or Cosmos) which all may use in accordance with their True (or Divine) Wills working consciously from one end of their Existence to the other in perfectly arranged patterns of Living light. The Sephiroth show the 1,2,3,4's of this Cosmic procedure, and the Paths show the A,B,C,D's of it. Grasp those, and all else become possible. That is their real Qabalistic value.

Before we progress through the Paths Letter by Letter from their four main viewpoints, it is best to bring those points themselves to life in the character of the Elemental Vowels. This will not only explain and demonstrate the working principles of the whole process, but will provide a most useful exercise in its practice.

In the first place, it should scarcely be necessary, though it might be opportune, to remind ourselves that the Four Magical Elements of Life—Earth, Air, Fire, and Water—are NOT, nor ever were intended to be, identified with the purely physical phenomena described by those names. These material manifestations are simply valid Symbols, appreciable by our ordinary consciousness, to represent the four principal aspects of the Universal Energy behind Life itself, and consequently our own entities therein. If we accept that Life emanates from One Source which we are approaching from four distinct angles plus a collective factor common to all, we are quite entitled to call those Primals A.E.I.O. and U. as sonic summative Symbols. Very briefly indeed, these headings indicate:

A. Earth Matter, the body, its flesh and bones, solidity, Expression, etc. The Shield.
E. Air The Breath of Life, mind, animation, gaseity, Formation, etc. The Sword.
I. Fire Illumination, spirit, consciousness, natural heat, radiance, Origination,etc. The Rod.
O. Water Feeling the soul, emotions, blood, liquidity Creation, etc. The Cup.
U. Aether Universality, contact between all varieties
    (Truth) of being, Continuity, etc. The Cord.

Taken together in combination, the Vowels will "spell" the Name of the Living One: I.A.O.; IEOA; HU; YAH; etc. Whichever way they are connected, they signify Divinity enlivening Existence, and hence were sacred in all ancient Magical practices. Consonants do not make sense however we string them together, and thus are considered "dead" or lifeless letters, but as soon as vowels are related with them properly intelligent meanings appear everywhere. Thus the vowels are to language just what Life and Consciousness are to Existence. They make sense and sentience out of everything. This alone should be enough to set them apart as something very special in the way of Symbols. Now we will try putting them through the four processes or relationships with ourselves and the Living Entity Itself.

Contemplative meditation with Vowels should not be very difficult. A state of Inner sonic resonance to any Vowel can easily be set up and maintained as a background against and out of which, evocative imagery of that particular character may be constructed. In the case of "I," for instance, the sound should be felt Inwardly at a comfortable level while imaginative awareness builds up impressions of Light, warmth, intelligence, and other associative links between the Divine and human ends of entity and Id-entity. There may even be a sense of "I"-ness as an ego and individual. A very great deal may enter and emerge from this Originative way of working. Creatively, the "I" can be maneuvered about almost incredibly. It may become a line of progress, a line of information and enlightenment, a Symbol of Uprightness, the Pillar of Light between heaven and Earth, the guide-rod of the Supreme Shepherd, a pointer to Paradise, absolutely anything associated with Living Light in a Creative way. Enthusiasm, warm feelings, the "I" of Illumination, the Rod of Rulership, all these ideas and many others will come along by themselves to be considered by a consciousness tuned to an "I" Concept.

Formatively, by means of ritual practice, an operative magician can really do things with an "I." Every match becomes an "I," to light up. Candles and tapers are all illuminated "I"s. The Rod of Power is an "I." Every shaft of light writes the Letter. The eye sees it everywhere. The "I" of Invocation is in constant ritual use, and so is the "I" of Inclinaton, Intellect, and an Infinity of other Items concerned with the Magical Element of Fire in a formalised Symbolic manner. Expressed into material living, "I-Fire" is appreciable and applicable in all kinds of commonplace ways. We can switch on electrical lamps and heaters which are powered by current coming along the conducting "I"s of copper cable. Heat-driven engines propel railway carriages along "I" rails. The "I" control-rods are the safeguards of an atomic pile. Light is the longest "I" we can imagine. All direct lines are "I"s in principle. The Symbol of the Rod and "I" go together. "I" means also upright and worthy behavior among other humans, a standard or rule to observe, and is the general sign of enlightened people. We need not look very far to find all sorts and conditions of "I"s, all relatable with ourselves and the Inner Life-Element of Fire which is synonymous with Light in its spiritual sense.

Then, of course, we have the "U" vowel, symbolized by the

Cord. This binds things together securely, connects any two or more points with each other, and otherwise acts as a medium of contact around, across, through, or any other direction discoverable in Cosmos. Elementally, it aligns with "Universal Truth," or whatever links any particular unit of Life or Existence with others. It signifies our contact and connection with the rest of Creation from one end to another right around the Circle of Consciousness. Magically, it joins anything to anything, and when we link Vowels or Letters together in order to make sense with them, the "U" Symbol is needed. We might even think of it as being like the little loop-links joining the letters of our alphabet together in cursive writing, or the split-second sonic alterations and spaces that make our speech intelligible. "U" is most Useful in an Undeniable way. We might even realise that the notches on the carriage escapement-bar of a typewriter which enable words to be typed are U-shaped in principle.

So, when we combine our "I" with other Letters or Vowels, we must not forget the Ubiquitous "U" making this possible. It can be contemplated as Union, considered Symbolically as a quadrant of a Circle, or Pillars set up on Earth and open to Heaven, formated ritually with a Cord, and expressed in whatever ways we join in with living as humans. Properly understood and applied, the "U" Symbol is of the highest importance, for without it we could never make any kind of continuum. It is well shown and expressed by the up-raised arms in the ritual gesture of supplicating the Universal Spirit in terms of "You, Who, etc." Man's ancient Names for the Divinity were indeed: IU and HU. What, in fact, makes up a Universe for anyone? Themselves and all else. I and U. The Symbology of our Four Vowel-Elements and their common Truth-Union together, gives us a complete picture and practice of Cosmos in the most workable way.

For the practical ritualist using Qabalistic formulae, this EIUOA ("You Are") Cosmic Symbol is the whole basis of all ritual practice. Get it right and get it going, and everything else will follow along quite naturally in the course of Cosmos. Most operatives devise or use even a collection of Rites for this purpose, but ritual, like everything else, can easily become over-encumbered and uneconomical. All that is really necessary is a "Temple sized" Rite for working the Temple or Lodge conditions, and a "Pocket" edition of the Rite for practice at any convenient occasion. This latter is usually a species of the "Sign of the Cross," or "occult orientation" of oneself in relation to the Inner Points of Power. It takes the form of a head to foot, side to side, around and hold-in-center gesture, normally done with the right hand, and the mental attribution of some particular Inner quality or Concept to each angle and section of this Solar Cross pattern of Cosmos. A conventional formula is; "In the Name of the Wisdom (above head), the Love (heart), the Justice (right shoulder), and the Infinite Mercy (left shoulder), of the One Eternal Spirit (circling), AMEN." (Hands together at breast). It is quite permissible to visualize oneself in the center of a Magic Circle at the same time, and acknowledge the Elemental Points at East, South, West, North, and around by evoking images of the Archangels concerned, or simply the Vowel-headings of E, I, O, A, and U. Neat, concise, and most effective Rites can be adequately devised from these basics, which are very much part of a Magical operative's training. In fact, it is tempting to consider that particular opus as an essential "trade-test." There are quite a number of such Rites in print here and there, but none are equal to the one that each Initiate of Magic must make for himself. Unless a practitioner develops the ability to make a Rod from a hedge-cutting, a Sword from a sharp flint, a Cup from a hollowed hand, and a Shield from whatever cover Nature provides, he or she will never be able to make Magical Instruments from even the most wonderful pieces of artwork money can buy.

The major aim and end-product of the Vowel Rituals is to effect a fully cosmated consciousness relatively geared to the Inner and Outer actualities of Existence, and "Keyed" by the "Master-Code" of the "Word" A.E.I.O.U. The utility of this should need no explanation. Whatever dodge or device of thinking or ritual can be worked out for this purpose should be given a chance. Sometimes the very simplest things prove the most effective. Suppose, for instance, we try associating the Vowels as ordinary exclamations to be used whenever we turn our attention to any one Element in particular. As for example:

"AH"	(A)	in connection with Earth.
"AI or HI"	(I)	in connection with Fire.
"OH"	(O)	in connection with Water.
"EE"	(E)	in connection with Air, and
"OO	(U)	in connection with any conjunction of

Elements, or virtually anything at all that signifies a true relationship.

One rather delightful method of doing this is while bathing. Concentrating on the Air, with its scents, breeze, etc., "EEE" is sonated. "AIIIII" denotes the pleasant warmth and the brightness of the Sun. "OHHHHH" signifies the sea if it is there, but otherwise the moisture in the atmosphere, or maybe Water as plain sweat or body-fluids. With "AAHH" the good Earth should be felt and appreciated. lastly the happy comfort of the whole situation should be summed up in "OOOOOOOOO" or "HUUUUUU". If this type of exercise is practised properly and persistently, the outcome should be that the final "Key" of "UOOOOOOOOOOOOU" or of "HOUUUUUUUUUU" alone, should be sufficient to induce the state of spiritual Cosmos required for true Inner living.

This is how the "HOOOOOOOU" of the Sufi works, or the "AUM" of the Hindus and Buddhists. In the case of the "AUM," it is again reducible to a final "MMMMMMMMMMMM" sonic, right down to a minimal physical sound which yet has a maximum effect in Inner Dimensions. Neither "HOUUU" nor "AUM", or any other Master Key will accomplish anything by themselves for those who do not know and have not practised all the prerequisites needed to make them what they are—major controls of living consciousness. Without such "conditioning" (which may take considerable time and trouble), the "Magic Words" or HU, AUM, or other Keys are no more than "noises off."

There is no real point in proceeding with Qabalistic Pathworking until at least some practical experience is gained in these vital Elemental exercises. Trivial perhaps as they may seem to those expecting much more spectacular marvels of Magic, the Elementary associative meditations, considerations, rituals, and expressions do indeed construct the essential nucleus of Cosmative Consciousness out of which all else will emerge. The Path-Letters will only make messages and convey intelligence to those who already have set up the Vowels in positions to explain everything.

Perhaps the most practical program for anyone to follow who intends to live and work in what might be called the Qabalistic Way, is to begin with the Circle-Cross cosmation of the Life-Elements, then grasp the Sephirotic Scheme of the Tree, and after that proceed along all the Paths, Letter by Letter at first, and then whole "Inner Words" at a time. In this method, everything should explain itself as progress is made, and clearly point out the next step to be taken. Thus, the Tree of Life will really become a Magic "Talking Tree" and tell those who have learned its language all the Inner information they need to know for the sake of their spiritual enlightenment. It should, of course, be theoretically possible to run these three activities as parallel procedures after some initial successes have been scored with each. They also correspond with the Qabalistic "Worlds." The Circle-Cross procedure is Originative, the Sephirotic Scheme is Creative, the Path-Pattern Formative, and the outcome in terms of individual, collective, or other effects is Expressive. It is always best to follow the natural in-built lines of any arrangement, and those are the ones which link up the Points of Light that make up the Qabalistic Cosmos just as every star and planet of our spatio-temporal Universe links our lives with Ultimate Life Itself.

Again and again, as we proceed along the Paths of the Tree, we must keep reminding ourselves of their essential nature and function. They are NOT a collection of Tarot cards, Alphabetical Letters, or anything of the sort. The Paths, Channels, Links, Rays, Media, Connections, or whatever the communicative System of the Tree of Life is called, are direct lines of relationship between the Primary Points of Life as indicated by the specific decade of Spheres, and that is that. What happens if we combine, say, Wisdom and Harmony? Or Severity and Understanding? Severity and Mercy? Achievement and Glory? Something, or a lot of things, must eventuate from, or be relative to, those particular combinations of conscious energies. Whatever those somethings may be, and there must be untold variations of them, they ARE the Paths of the Tree. We may term them what we please, or work out any feasible nomenclature to describe or identify them, but basically they are interactive energies between the Living Principles upheld by the Tree of Life, and consequently are actualities of consciousness in the fields of its Universal Energy. Just as force-fields arise between the poles of a magnet, the electrodes of a battery, or a Star and its planets, so do relative states, stresses, surges, and similar phenomena occur between the Spheres of the Tree, and those ARE its "Paths." Such, and neither more nor less.

Purely for the purpose of relating ourselves via those Paths with the Life-Principle Itself in all Its Aspects, we shall use a Symbolic Code which is indicative of, but NOT identified with, the Tree-Paths. As a combinative system, we are using the Tarot Hieroglyphs because of their suitability. As a link with literacy, since we are "word-thinkers," we shall use a system of Letter equations based on our mother-tongue. These are not "attributions," but designations. The end-aim is that these summative Symbols will combine with each other like Alphabetical Letters on very deep levels of Awareness, and by making "Words" intelligible to a consciousness functioning through those Inner Dimensions of Life, will extend our existence as sentient souls into increasingly higher states of being than our present condition.

To plod (or plot) the Paths, we must do just what we did with the Elements, which will make quite a lot of work. There is no "instant initiation" to be had in mastering this mystery! The quickest and best way in the end is to fulfill the Will or Intention behind all the Paths, and experience each one properly before we can expect to put them together and make sound spiritual sense from our newly learned language of the Talking Tree. Sometimes the word "Path" itself confuses those who would otherwise seek to study them. Part of the Magic in the Qabalah is that it automatically repels quite gently the attentions of many who would be unsuitable souls for its System. Sensing a closed spiritual door, such people usually cease wasting their time unprofitably and go elsewhere for fulfillment. To those who are ready for the Tree-Paths, however, they soon begin to explain themselves in terms of a mutually established Inner Language.

A Path in anyone's language can scarcely be other than a means of personal procedure from one point to another, and that is just what the Tree-Paths are. The ways by which all categories of Consciousness, and consequently of souls who exist by this Energy, proceed from one State (or Sphere) of Life to another. The Paths of the tree are the condition of Consciousness in Kinesis or active Existence. While we are using our energies of consciousness as thinking, for instance, we think from one point to another. How do we do it? What carries our awareness from here to there so to speak? A Path. Neither more nor less, whatever its condition or limits. Paths vary enormously. Some are easy and some almost impossible. Everybody uses the commonplace ways of a city, but how many traverse the perilous paths across mountain faces? One might almost believe that the higher they go the harder they get. It is certain that the more difficult a path, the more highly specialized and trained or experienced a soul must be who hopes to use it.

The Paths of the Tree are no different from others in this respect. They start with relative ease, and become progressively more difficult as souls ascend the Tree. For that reason some other Systems used a Holy Mountain allegory which commenced with broad highways in the Cities of the Plain at its base, then became ever narrower and trickier as the Mountain was climbed until they finally petered out altogether and each climber had to make his way across virgin ground with nothing but the Apex of the Mount to indicate his way ahead. In the case of the Tree-allegory used in Qabalah, the broad trunk is easy at the base, and most of the branches bear weight for much of their length, but as we get higher the branches become thinner and riskier, until it is evident that if we insist on making further progress, we shall either have to become less substantial ourselves, or wait indefinitely until the branches grow strong enough to support us.

A Qabalist meeting such an inevitable point where personal progress appears impractical, seeks a Way beyond it along a parallel Path on a higher (or sometimes a lower) level. When physical progress comes to an end, mental Paths are followed, and when they give out, spiritual levels are used. Beyond these, the only hope of progress is to link up with living Entities in other states of Existence altogether and ask for transport. Even so, we may never be mere passengers along the Ways of Life all of us must take for ourselves. Up to a point we may be given lifts, but sooner or later we shall be set down to walk the rest of the way, and there is nothing to compare with the exercise. This is what happens with the Tree-Paths. We can easily obtain "lifts" by means of other people's thoughts and go along with them, but these only go so far, and eventually every traveler must either be prepared to push on by his own power or else postpone his progress. When we deal with the Paths of the Qabalistic Tree as specified and laid out in the standard design of the Tree-Glyph, it is perhaps as well to bear in mind that remarkably few travelers among them have recorded or published their findings in any readily comprehensible or practical way. If all available information concerning the Tree-Paths under that particular heading had to be gathered together in print, there would be little enough to choose from. Such scarcity of supply alone makes the subject a fascinating one. Why, with a subject leading in every direction through all conditions of Consciousness, should there be so little light thrown on the formula itself? Possibly because of its tenuous nature and difficulty of placing any great weight of heavy opinion on these higher branches, and probably also on account of the extreme effort needed to find terminology and means of expressing Inner experiences in Other ways. What cannot be adequately written can scarcely be read rewardingly.

It was largely for that reason much of the older work on Qabalah seems so obscure and meaningless to modern minds. It was not that writers in those days had no knowledge or experience of their topic, but they were indeed restricted as to recording or coding such consciousness into communicative formulae with other souls. That was mainly why they had to invent all kinds of novel Symbols which had no significance except for those who accepted them as having recognisable Inner values. Even today we speak of mysterious or incomprehensible symbols as being "cabalistic." Yet there was no original intention of deception or mystification, but the beginnings of a language foreign to Earth which was only intelligible to souls who understood sophisticated spiritual speech. Once this could be successfully linked with ordinary Alphabets, our human minds might approach it the more easily. So it happened.

The principles by which Tree-Paths are linked with Letters are very straightforward. First identify the Path in question by its actual nature as a relationship between Sephiroth, giving it a numerical value for reference, and a Letter value as a unit of literate consciousness. Then sum up all this with a Master-Symbol having the deepest possible connections with fundamental awareness. The Tarot Hieroglyphs will do this nicely. We now have four joined-up factors consisting of:

1. An Energy-exchange between fundamental Life-Principles.

2. A reference figure for this.

3. A Letter-value for its incorporation into verbally categorised consciousness.

4. A Key-Symbol with implications and linkages reaching as far as it will extend our awareness in this particular direction, or

Path.

Four extremely useful items indeed when we combine them crosswise to explain themselves, as the Master-Word of Creation is said to do with I.H.V.H. Qabalism is normally based on four-fold procedures for establishing the existence of anything, its decimal scale being derived from the Four Worlds of Life, the Three Rings of Time-Space-Events, the Two Pivots or Pillars of Power, and the One Principle of Poise in the Center of this Cosmos. To get further meanings out of our Paths, we shall have to relate them with the Worlds and other Qabalistic denominations of Existence in its various categories.

The "Four Worlds," after all, are only arbitrary stages between the Infinity of Nil and the definite Existence and Expression of any "Something" at all. Since only Divinity can Originate anything, this faculty is reckoned as "God-Aspect" or "property," and so described. Then comes Creation, or building the Archetypal Idea into a definite identity, which the old Qabalists called an Archangelic process of consciousness. After that follows Formation, or bringing the Original Idea right down to a sharply focused and fully finished product except for actual manifestation as an Earth-expression. This was said to be the work of an Angelic type of intelligence. Finally, of course, is the Expression itself of the Idea into something which manifests in ways we can recognize in our mundane world. The type of consciousness engaged with this was loosely classified as "spirits." Sometimes these have a human body around them, and sometimes they do not.

As humans ourselves, we have some degrees of this Consciousness in each of us with varying proportions. To Originate some Idea, or "bring it out of nothing" so far as any soul is concerned, is a Divine act for himself, no matter how often other souls have invited it into them from their "Great Nil". Few humans do this very often in their lives to any remarkable degree. How far do most people rise above the lowest average of taking other ready-made ideas and pushing these around in tangible or other evident ways?

Initiates of Qabalah and other Systems seek to raise themselves, or increase their degrees of conscious Energy toward tlie Divine, or Originative condition of Being. The more we Originate, the more Divine we shall become, the more we Create, the nearer to Archangels we grow. Our degrees of ability at Formation increase our Angelic properties, and the better we Express matters (including ourselves), the more improved we shall be as humans. Throughout this whole process the factor of Quality is paramount. It is little use simply hurling stuff into Existence for the sheer sake of it like the early volcanic activities of our planet in its productive history. All must be modified by a spiritual sense of "Rightness" which most Initiates believe in as "Love" under one description or another. With Will through Love must ALL BE, if we are to become WHAT WE OUGHT TO BE.

As ordinary human beings, of course, we cannot actually Originate anything in the sense of making it BE independently of ourselves. If we could, then we could think lumps of anything around us which would immediately materialize. That, fortunately, is beyond our ability. Our relative originative faculties are individually internal to us, and have to go through the rest of the Creative and Formative processes before they can be Expressed, if indeed they ever get so far. Still, even though we are yet far from being Divine, if we behave in remotely relative Divine ways for a sufficiency of Existence, we may quite reasonably expect to achieve some degrees of spiritual status inour own right. Even our comparatively short experience on this Earth alone has shown such possibilities for us already. Therefore, we should deal with our Life-Worlds as if we had the necessary qualities of Divinities, Archangels, Angels, and Spirits in ourselves, and we shall develop these very potentials as we go along.

All this was a principal reason why it has always been a maxim of magical practice that a sincere operator must make as many as possible of the magical "props," such as Instruments, vestments, and physical Symbols, for himself. The process of Inventing, Designing, Forming and Finishing all this equipment was itself a most valuable and inimitable exercise in living right through the Four Worlds from Divine to Human ends. To Invent anything, the magicians had to use a God-like faculty in themselves—to Design it, Archangelic properties were called for, in the actual shaping and forming up of the production, angelic gifts were needed, and when ultimately the magicians held whatever it was in their hands and used it, they had to do so according to the spirit of the purpose producing it. Thus, when these magi attempted communion with Beings of distinct Inner categories or

Orders of Consciousness, they had already mastered the rudiments of the Inner spiritual "speech" used by those Entities of higher than human Life. It is true that we can develop these needed qualities in ourselves by other ways than making up magical paraphernalia, but the process and order of procedure is the same in principle, no matter how it is worked out in actual production. To make the Tree-Paths practical propositions, therefore, we shall have to live them through the Four Worlds like everything else. Since the best place to begin anything is obviously at its nearest point to Nil, this is where we shall start living our Paths on this journey from their earliest emergence out of Nil toward our manifestation as Mankind made of Matter. Because the Decade of the Sephiroth constitutes the primary figures of the Tree-Plan, the internal Paths will commence their Alphabetical sequence at eleven, and begin with B in this case, as A represents the Element of Earth as a Vowel-sonic.

The Formulae that now follows is only one typical series of relevance, and is not intended as other than an example of working. It need in no way be taken as ultimate, conclusive, or unimprovable. The set-up as it stands is simply to show the Four-way method of dealing with each Path, and arrive at a practical outcome which will assist our further progress along ever-exalting levels of the same Paths leading us steadily and surely toward whatever our Ultimate state of Spirit may be. Let us see how far we can go at present, if we follow these Paths one by one.

The Eleventh Path

SPHERE—LETTER CODE:	Crown 1 B 2	Wisdom
DIVINE ORIGINATION:	AHIH—IHVH	The ALL
ARCHANGELIC CREATION:	Metatron—Ratziel	Intention
ANGELIC FORMATION:	Chioth ha Qodesh— Auphanim	Extension
APPARENT EXPRESSION:	Nebulae—Zodiac	Conduction
TAROT SYMBOL:	HIEROPHANT	

We may sum this up by thinking of a Supreme Hierophant or Pontiff-Principle acting for all of us with the Will or Intention of everyone to extend themselves in Existence by the conduction of Consciousness throughout Cosmos.

There has to be some kind of relationship between us all as souls, and the Supreme Life-Spirit as our sole Source and Sum of Being. Traditionally this relationship was personified here on Earth by a Hierophant, Pontiff, or Priest-King, who offered himself in the Holy Mysteries as a Mediator. These are the principles of Kingship and Wisdom, rulership of, by, and for the sake of, pure Rightness alone. We should remember the Qabalistic text: "He is all Right, and in Him there is no Left hand Path." This is symbolized by depicting the Ancient One as a dignified and bearded Face showing its Right profile. What higher faculty could we possibly ask of Divinity than the ability to rule ourselves rightly? If we could only do this, no wrongs or ills would ever occur in our existence. This is the main message which the Hierophant-principle in each of us is trying to impart. At one time it was called "Conscience." Knowing together.

It should be noticed that the Path-links with the Four Worlds are simply presentations of the same fundamental Idea taken four ways. Other representative headings might have been used, but the intention behind this particular system is to deal mainly with the principles rather than particulars which will fit themselves in anyway, once the principles are grasped. To take one Idea and push it four (or more) ways, is the underlying principle of Cosmos, and the working of the I.H.V.H. or any other Tetragrammatic Formula. After all, every single Idea that ever was or will be, and in fact everything altogether in the whole of Existence emerges from ONE IDEA, and That is That. Call it "God," Divinity, or any Name at all, IT IS WHAT IT IS. So, when Qabalism trains its Initiates to get in the habit of taking any particular portion of this ONE IDEA, and developing it in at least four directions, it is helping those souls to behave in a "God-like" way, as one might consider small children to be gently guided by older members of their families into adult ways. If we are to be the Children of Light, then we really ought to try and learn what our Elders are attempting to impart for our benefit.

On every Path then, we must take our topic and see it from the four viewpoints of its cosmos. From the Spirit originating it, the Soul creating it, the Mind formating it, and the Body that expresses it. So one thing leads out of another and into another again until there will literally be no part of Cosmos we cannot enter with our consciousness. Given the basics of the Sephiroth and the paths, the complete Consciousness of Cosmos, or the Entity of Existence as "God," or whatever Personification may be approached, will be available to those who "speak the Language." Wherever we Will go in all Creation, something or somebody has to lead into it from somewhere that connects with each and all of us, however remotely. To get there ultimately, we simply have to "follow our noses" along the Paths between us and whatever it is, however long this may take even from lifetime to lifetime. The Tree-Plan is intended to be the meeting place of *all* Life-Paths, so if we start from there every time we want to go somewhere in Consciousness, we may not go very far wrong, and if we should stray, it is not too difficult to return to our Hierophants. We can conduct our own tour of Cosmos wherever we Will or intend to extend ourselves.

Hierophant is a term deriving from "hieros," meaning holy, consecrated, pertaining to Divinity, etc., and signifies an initiating priest-mediator. The Latin equivalent of Pontiff is literally a Bridge-builder, or one who bridges the difference between Divin-

ity and Humanity. A Sovereign-Pontiff, or King-Priest like Melchizadek is one who offers himself on behalf of all his people so
that they and THAT will unite. That is why such a Symbol occupies this particular Path between the Principles of Wisdom and
the Sovereign Spirit of Life. A bridge has to begin somewhere,
and this is where it starts from Ultimate Spirit to reach intimate
union with each individual soul, and it is the Pontiff-principle in
all of us that begins building it.

The Tarot Symbol of the Hierophant we shall study for this
Path is that of the Waite pack, as are the rest of the Trump Symbols in this work. This is because there is such an absolute wealth
of concealed meanings in them not found elsewhere. Of late years
this remarkable pack has suffered from some neglect, probably
owing to the over-abundance of its symbology, which calls for
quite prolonged and deep investigation before the hidden details
come to light. Few people seem prepared to penetrate such
depths, and so the Waite cards have often been passed over in favor of the starker and cruder Marseilles designs. It seems a pity
to lose such wonderful study opportunities in connection with the
Life-Tree, and so we shall take one Trump apart at every Path
and see what extra information may be gained thereby.

We note first that the Pontiff Figure is throned between two
Pillars which look alike at a casual glance until we observe a difference in the carving at their heads. This may only be slight, but
there is enough to tell a practised eye that the right Pillar is male
and the left female, as with the Tree. The Pillars are of grey stone
(the tone of Chockmah, or Wisdom, where the Symbol connects)
indicating that the common material from which both human
sexes are constructed. The background of the card is grey, too,
and so is the throne on which the Hierophant sits. Grey is the
mediating shade between the Black of "Nay" and the White of
"Yea," therefore it is an appropriate ground for the crowned mediator working toward Wisdom along this Path. Somewhere between Yea and Nay we shall find all the answers we seek in Life
and achieve Wisdom thereby. The little dots shown as descending and ascending the Pillars indicate sent-forth individual egos
entering into the Limits of Living in search of identity through
incarnation and ultimately a triumphant return with every secret of Life solved.

On one side of the throne head is incorporated a single ornamental boss, and on the other are two. These indicate the Male-Female nature of the Pontiff's polarity, and can also show the Path connection between Sephiroth 1 and 2. In the case of the Waite pack, it is necessary to look very closely indeed for the least oddity of design or unlikely discrepancy. There is more than probably some quite significant meaning to discover which might otherwise have been missed.

A careful study of the Pontiff's face reveals its androgynous cast of feature, common to most of the Waite figures. The Hierophant might be Male or Female or both. Let us assume both. The golden triple tiara signifies the sovereignty of Mind, Soul, and Spirit over Body, though this tiara looks ostensibly Christian, with a sacrificial Cross at mid-point. At the very summit may just be seen part of the letter "SHIN," the Hebrew Mother-letter with Aleph and Mem. SHIN is the letter linked with Fire in old Qabalistic lore, and here we may see it as the triple illumination of Spirit above all. The descending gold lappets of the tiara signify the division of Light to Right and Left of Creation so that illumination may be experienced to the full extent of our Existence.

The Hierophant Figure is clothed in a blue underrobe with a crimson "seamless garment" over it, while the inner sleeves are white. Red and blue by themselves signify Might and Mercy respectively, and the white sleeves mean purity of intent in action. The right hand is raised in priestly blessing while the left hand is also raised to grasp the Standard of the Golden Rule. This is the triple Tau which forms the backbone of the Tree-Pattern, and is the Measure of Man as he should be, neither above nor below the "golden mean." The proportions and arrangement of the levels on this Standard are of great significance, and will repay meditation. The left thumb of the Figure upholding the Standard is hidden behind its stem, showing that the Divine Will which intends us to keep the Golden Rule of loving God wholeheartedly, then one's fellow man and oneself in equal shares, is seldom revealed directly to us. Revelations of Divine Will are usually met through mediatorship as in the case of the Hierophant.

Joining right and left shoulders together is the pallium which centers in a descending strip with three crosses and a terminal square on it. Here we have the Tree-symbology again, where we find the principle of connecting extremities by a Path, and then keeping a mid-line state of balance. The three crosses occur in the Tree design, and may also be considered as the twelve points of the Zodiac, which happens to be the Expressional Symbol of Chockmah with which this card connects. The small square relates to the Elements. Again and again among all the symbology we encounter, we shall be told the same thing, namely to compare Right with Left, then keep a balanced Middle Way between them. It seems we just cannot be given this vital information too often.

There are seven main folds in the red outer Robe of the Hierophant, which indicate the seven levels or stages of the Tree rising from bottom to top. The bottom fold is very thick on the right side and very thin on the left. A coarse and a fine choice of paths for us to follow. The finer line is triple, and takes the Hermetic side of the picture, while the broader line is contiguous and travels in the Orphic direction. Although the Hermetic line seems more tenuous and difficult to follow of the two, the "broad way" is brought to a sudden stop with a clever device of lines that read "F 8" (Fate!). This means that the easiest appearing ways in the beginning are not always the simplest in the end.

The Hierophant wears white slippers to show innocence of intention when walking the Ways of Life with Wisdom. The dais on which he sits has a purple carpet with hieroglyphs to show how the steps of Life are to be taken, and the guide lines of black and white squares at each side. The purple carpet means we should walk on a basis of Might and Mercy blended together, while keeping between the lines made by our decisions of Yes or No at each side of the issue. All our lives we have to make a long series of these Yes-No choices from one end of our existence to the other, and here we see how we ought to make a walk-way through them.

Right at the front of the dais, where it falls to ground level, are crossed Keys left over right. Their handles have the Circle-Cross of Cosmos on them, because these are the Keys which are meant to unlock Cosmic secrets. The left-hand Key opens the Ways of the Right hand Pillar and vice versa. We might note that the left-hand Key has to be taken up first before the other will be freed. In other words, get over passions before intellect can be used effectively. There are ten small divisions on the shank of each Key meaning that all ten Spheres have to be entered in turn.

In the right and left foreground of the picture, we see who is waiting to pick up those Keys with the blessing of the Hierophant. Two dedicated Initiates are here represented as priests, the left-hand one bearing the roses of passion on his robes, and the right-hand one having the lilies of purity. Purity and passion have always been the twin Pillars of Life-experience through which we must pass along our Ways. If they are properly dedicated to the Cosmic Cause, they will carry us as far as any human needs to travel. The priest-Initiates are shown on the opposite sides of their respective Pillars here, because in order to enter the Inner Temple of Initiation we have to cross over diametrically like the Keys, changing positions with our Outer selves and so inverting our polarity from Earth-orientation to Heaven-orientation.

Each of these two Initiates has the Y cross pattern on the chasuble. The purity-priest's is plain gold, and the passion-Priest's is decorated with a dotted design. These crosses are not just for ornament, but signify the Golden Rule applied to Mankind, i.e., "Compare Right with Left, and choose the best Middle Way between them." Perhaps it may be remembered that this Y cross is a very old Magic-Rod pattern, and is still used by water diviners. With the Y right side up, it signified that the human who bore it was holding it open to Heaven for the guiding decision on whatever issue was being decided—a symbolic appeal for direction by the Inner Intelligence. Here, the priest-Initiates are asking for their dilemmas to be solved by the mediating Hierophant, so that they may proceed along their respective Paths with a Heavenly blessing on them. All of us have to do the same on this Path, where we ask our Highest Authority to crown our Ways with Wisdom.

Returning to the clue of the crossed Keys for a moment, we may observe that their handles are circular and their faces square. Squaring the circle is an old problem of Initiation, referring to forming a right relationship between Humanity (the Square) and Divinity (the Circle). This is precisely the whole problem of our lives which we have to resolve four ourselves with all the Keys of the Inner Kingdom we may find as we go along. The Human ends of the Keys have to be placed in all the locks of life and turned successfully in order for the Inner secrets to be revealed. The suggestion here is that Initiation offers these Keys to those who devote themselves like priests to the purpose of the paths leading to Inner Illumination.

It can now perhaps be appreciated how much there is to learn by systematic study and contemplation of well-designed and deeply thought-out Symbols like these Tarot cards. There is plenty more left in the Hierophant picture to discover yet, as those who care to continue its investigation should find out for themselves. Why, for instance is the back of the throne shaped as it is? Why is one sleeve of the outer robe gold-lined and the other not? Why do the fingers upraised in blessing point in the direction they do? The old ritual method of asking endless questions and then seeking answers is still the best way of working along Inner lines. Every Path has its own set of queries, but it is for every one of us to answer them ourselves with the aid of what Inner information we may obtain if we use the right keys.

The Hierophant shows us unmistakably here that we should be devoted to the Divine purpose of Life in every possible Way. Each Initiate of the Inner Way must sooner or later rise to the position of Priest-King, or ruler-Redeemer of their human selves. Until this function of Sacred King-Priest is fulfilled in us all, we shall not truly enter the Kingdom and gain the Crown for which we were created Children of Cosmos. This is the Path of Melchizadek, linking us with the highest point of Life upon the Tree if we walk it with Wisdom.

Originatively, we meet Divinity on this Path as AHIH and IHVH. The I AM, and I WILL BE WHAT I WILL BE. The first two Principles of Life. First BE, then be anyone or anything in conformity with the Cosmic Will which began that being. According to Inner Tradition this Fiat goes forth at the commencement of every Creation, and as the Will directs, so is the WORD uttered and I AM becomes WHATIAM. What indeed are we? We spend incarnations and aeons asking this answerless question which cannot be concluded until All become One in the Ultimate.

Divinity is termed the All on this Path. Everyone, everywhere, everything, and always. THAT which was, is now, and ever will be AMEN. The Absolute Whole of which we are individual integers. Our little personal areas of awareness will certainly not contain all THAT—and yet—does not a small seed contain the largest of trees? in that sense, we have within us the vital seeds which will truly grow into the Tree of All Life, if we know how to plant and cultivate them. Small, and relatively insignificant as we might seem, we do indeed bear the Seed of immortal Spirit in our secret hearts. Each of us has the ALL virtually within his soul.

All of us are points of the mightiest mass in Existence, and our personal progress depends on what degree and amount of that Mass operates through our individual instrumentality. Achievement of our proper working degrees with this Mass is the evolutionary task of all who claim Cosmic Initiation. The authority of anyone derives from whatever Mass or Group he personifies or represents. A King-Priest has the power and authority of all the people presented in and by his sacred person dedicated to that office. So do Initiates of the Holy Mysteries gain whatever authority and power they are able to mediate through themselves by the paths of the Life-Tree leading them to the Ultimate Power conferring on them the Crown which must be earned by Wisdom.

When dealing with the paths of the Tree, we should remember that they are not only linkages between the Sephiroth themselves, but also between the various levels of each Sephirah arbitrarily considered as Originative, Creative, Formative, and Expressive. Each Path should therefore be followed along these levels as we go, keeping the categories of consciousness in clear thought-streams the while so that all appears to flow freely in the correct channels.

Here, at the level of I AM becoming I WILL, we are at the initiating point of Existence where Being converts into Doing by Consciousness. This, of course, is the essential step we have to make at every point of our lives. I am—what will I do with me? On that first fatal step, every issue of our living depends, and once it is taken we cannot very well go back on it without continuing around the best course for returning it to the starting place back into the Nil from whence it emerged. Divinity has to do as much on Its scale of Life as we in ours with our Microcosmic mentalities.

It is exactly this faculty of engaging ourselves with Existence by decisive acts of Will which indicates our creation "in the Divine image." In God and Man alike, this is the highest ability of all, and hence properly placed at the top of the Life-Tree with AHIH and IHVH. Here, we must learn first and foremost how to use this unique God-given faculty on the Path between our maximum reach of Wisdom on the Right-hand Pillar, and the very apex of our awareness connecting with Divine Cosmic Consciousness Itself. If we only confined every effort of will to this channel, and let the effects proceed down along the remainder of the Paths in an orderly (or Cosmic) manner, we should be nearly perfect, and probably not humans at all. However, the meaning of this Path is quite plainly that we ought to dedicate the actions of our lives to the direction of Divinity within us at the beginning of their inception. The closer we can bring our consciousness into line with this particular Path, the nearer we shall come to working the True Will of the Word which brought us to Life in the first instance.

It is on this Path we must eventually realize our deepest Inner identity and relate ourselves from that aspect of awareness with all Life. Thus Will and Word become one, and I Am equates with WHAT-I-SAY-I-WILL-BE. Here, Consciousness conceives what it intends to become. Initiates of the Path have to learn that they should only apply the processes of their intentional consciousness to precisely what they mean with the whole might of their Will by the authority of Divine direction through them. That is the beginning of the Way of Wisdom, and the point of the whole Plan of Perfection. AHIH and IHVH hold the Keys of this Path between them, and will admit those uttering the right Word.

Creatively, we meet the Archangels Metatron (Near Thy Throne) and Ratziel (Divine Emissary) as they direct this level of the Eleventh Path. Tradition tells us that Metatron was once human in the person of Enoch (I, ME, a man). Metatron is the highest of the Archangels, being the "Angel of the Presence," who alone sees the Holy Countenance directly. Metatron personifies the very maximum aim of Mankind, and like Enoch, "walks with God" along this Pathway to Perfection. Where he goes, other ex-humans may surely follow eventually. His colleague, Ratziel, the Divine Herald, is said to proclaim all the secrets of Creation every day in his loudest voice for the whole world to hear—if it will. As might be expected, few humans bother to listen, and fewer still attempt to make sense of what they overhear.

As mere mortals, we are very limited forms of Life, and if we would achieve our immortal Identities, then we too must learn how to walk with God like Enoch-Metatron, and listen to the Voice of Divine Wisdom speaking through Ratziel from the heights within ourselves. Metatron tells us of our possibilities and Ratziel informs us Inwardly how we may achieve them. Together they initiate us into the Mysteries of Life and the Laws we must observe if we would ever rise to Hierophant rank therein.

BE AS THOU WILT WITHIN THEE is the Law of Life expounded by the Paths of the Tree. They are strictly Internal, and do not lead outside the Tree System except theoretically at the Highest and Lowest points. This is a very highly important consideration indeed, and if we tried to model ourselves on such a Pattern of Cosmos, life would better for all. To keep ourselves AS WE WILL, cosmated around our central Spirit, poised between the pivots of Divinity above us, and Humanity below us, all internal Paths of Power functioning properly, is the Qabalistic concept of spiritual health and fitness. Every soul has the Divine Right to be ruler of its own Cosmos WITHIN ITSELF. As soon as we start projecting our Will outside ourselves, then we encounter foreign energies and forces which we have to cope with as best we may. Yet, unless we make ourselves Rulers of what is WITHIN US, we have no right whatever to expect other Wills to fit in with ours. Divinity Itself must first Rule Within Its Being, and so must every soul within It who hopes to live by the same law of Light.

The difference between Chaos and Cosmos is that Cosmos is a Will-Directed outcome of Someone's efforts whether the Being in question is Divine or Human. The Hierophant-Figure typifies our highest aim of Will this side of Uncreation. What more might we WILL TO BE than King-Priests of Divine Wisdom? Melchizadek means "Ruler of Righteousness," and his legend also tells us that he was "King of Peace." We can scarcely set our True Wills at a higher objective than the "Peace Profound" all Initiates Will for each other.

Creation is a Work of Will, and no work of Magic is possible without developing degrees of Will to far greater extensions than most ordinary humans are capable of exerting. Break the Will of any Being, and they themselves become broken, as any despot knows. Destroy national Will, and whole Nations fall, as all politicians realize. Their problem has always been finding ways of weakening Wills in their enemies without damaging the Wills of the protagonists. Propaganda agencies of all types deal daily with this question. Will is the crucial factor of Cosmos, and one of the hardest Paths we have to progress in. We must not only KNOW, but also GOVERN ourselves with the Rod or Royal Will or Sceptre of Spiritual Strength. Until we hold that firmly, we have no real right to claim kinship with Kingship. Enoch and Ratziel have the Keys.

Formatively, we view this Path as an Extension into Existence. All Life Extends itself. It may even extend itself from one set of Dimensions into others, but extend in some manner it must. The Hierophant-Pontiff extends himself as a bridge between Humanity and Divinity. We all have to extend ourselves from the end of one Life to another, and we cannot even guess the Life-limits of our Ultimate Extension.

The Angelic Orders meeting here are those of the Holy Living Creatures, CHIOTh ha QODESh, and the Wheels, or AUPHANIM. The Holy Living Ones are the Four Life-Elements on the highest imaginable spiritual rulers of Elemental spirits at the bottom of the Tree in the Kingdom-Sphere of Malkuth. Both top and bottom Spheres of the Tree mirror each other as Divinity and Humanity are believed to do. The AUPHANIM, or Wheels, Rollers, Turners, are the Cycles of Life throughout the Cosmos. In the meeting of these two Angelic Orders, we have a summarized picture of the Life-Elements extending through every possible cycle of Time-Space-Event continua in Existence. Everything, as they say, "goes in cycles." Life turns Externally on its Axis, and our Living Wheel of Incarnation and Excarnation brings us in and out of this world as often as may be needed before we learn how to sit behind the steering wheel instead of falling underneath the crushing Rollers of the Manifesting Machine. We must either control our Vehicle of Life by Will, or risk injury if it runs away with us. In this case, the Hierophant is in the driving-seat. The Holy Living Ones are the Elements of Life in their purest state. We cannot imagine exactly what they are except by analogy. So far as we are concerned, they may be variants of a single underlying Cosmic Life-Frequency tuned to the "Ineffable" Name of God, or Ultimate Tetragram of Truth. They are certainly far removed from mere matter, even though our lives here on earth are remote evidence of their Inner activities.

If we will ever reach the top of the Tree, then we shall have to extend ourselves, and keep on extending. Having aimed at our point, then we extend physically toward it if necessary, and when we can go no further along this line, then we must continue extending ourselves mentally, then when another check is met, go on again extending our souls in the same direction, and when we come to another stop, carry on extending in Spirit. If we think of ourselves like a fireman's extension ladder, with sections of Body, Mind, Soul, and Spirit, this will make a nice analogy. We should never abandon a perfectly good aim if we fail to reach it by extending only one part of ourselves. What we cannot reach mentally is quite within the reach of spiritual steps. Those who refuse to investigate Cosmos beyond their merely mental range are losing invaluable experience of Existence. The initiated Qabalist simply goes on extending his Ladder of Light until a Way ahead becomes available, as it always does eventually. The CHIOTh and the AUPHANIM have the keys.

Expressively, the Eleventh Path extends into our perceptible Cosmos by a relationship between the Nebulae and our Solar Zodiac. The Primal Movement of the first Space-spinnings, and the ordered course of Cosmos our planet keeps in company with its companions round the Sun. Both are extensions of the same Cosmic Principle of Cyclic Light-Life. This relates with the physical quality of conduction, or passage of Power through Time-Space-Event conditions. In particular, we should consider the conduction of Consciousness throughout Cosmos. As the basic Energy of Existence, there must be universal conduction of its power-principles to a far wider extent than radio-energies are conducted through interplanetary Space. Every item of the Cosmos we exist in, including ourselves, is an Effect of Consciousness operating on so fast a Space-Time-Event scale of Dimensions that we cannot hope to appreciate Its real nature while we are limited by human capacities of consciousness. Even to become aware of Its Existence is sufficient to lift us considerably in spiritual evolution.

We ourselves must necessarily be conductors of Consciousness, since our individual and collective awareness are phenomena deriving from It. As yet, humanity is only hovering uncertainly on the verges of the most incredible Energy of all, Consciousness Itself. We have scarcely begun to realize the possibilities of this Greatest Potency, and it will need somewhat more Time-Space-Event conduction than we already control before we shall be in a position to use this Energy AS WE OUGHT TO WILL IN IT. The clues to its usage may be found in the nebulae and the zodiac. Both are cyclic. The spiral spinning of the nebulae produces world after world, life after life, indefinitely—a continuum of conducted consciousness. The cyclotron of the zodiac is the source of consciousness on a scale that keeps our planetary cosmos going around its solar nucleus. When we learn to behave likewise in ourselves OF OUR OWN WILLS, then we too will become adequate creatures of cosmos. There are the Energy-examples for us to follow in the Heavens all around us. They are constantly (like RATZIEL) proclaiming their spiritual secrets in a loud way for all to hear—IF THEY WILL. We have only to Listen in ourselves, and keep extending that faculty through different media until we hear something worth listening to. Because we are natural conductors of Consciousness, we are bound to get results, though it must be admitted that some souls are far better conductors than others on the deeper and consequently more important levels of Inner awareness. Improving our qualities of conduction through deep Inner Space is a major concern with Initiates of the Qabalah and all other esoteric systems. Technical details always become available to those cycling themselves correctly through Inner Time-Space-Event continua. Suggestions are likely to be received via the Nebulae and Zodiac Systems of Outer Existence. They have the Keys to this part of the Path.

So far, we only seem to have scratched the surface of this eleventh Path, though deeply enough to appreciate what lies underneath to be discovered by future travelers. There are yet another twenty-one Paths to be traversed on this "Lightning tour" of the Whole Tree. Everyone is at liberty to go back and explore every single inch at their complete leisure AS THEY WILL. To reach the Path as a whole, it is only necessary to "Think B." To reach it in the right way, the Hierophant-Symbol will grant access. For contact with the Path on different Levels, the God and other Names will sort these out. For the rest, individual noses must be followed. None of these Key-devices will work, of course, unless they have been adequately meditated and mediated by their would-be users. Ritualized and magical procedures for this purpose will be considered later in other works. For the time being, we had better continue building up solid ideas and images to construct a Magical Cosmos with, and so we shall plod dutifully along to the next path.

The Twelfth Path

SPHERE—LETTER CODE: Crown 1 C 3 Understanding
DIVINE ORIGINATION: AHIH—IHVH ELOHIM The One
ARCHANGELIC CREATION: Metatron—Tzaphkiel Specification
ANGELIC FORMATION: Chioth ha Qodesh— Distinction
Aralim
APPARENT EXPRESSION: Nebulae—Saturn Isolation
TAROT SYMBOL: HERMIT

This Path is the one of individuality by which everything and everyone becomes typified uniquely into what it is as distinct from the ALL. Its Symbol naturally enough is the Hermit-Solitary with his particular portion of Light, or Divine Spark which makes him a spirit as apart from Spirit *per se*. It is the beginning of differentiation, where Consciousness not only Knows Itself TO BE, but recognizes Itself by categorizing Its Energy, so that within the Whole, part perceives part, and I AM becomes WE ARE.

This is something we need to understand in ourselves. Our consciousness follows the same pattern in appropriately diminished scale, and we are always seeking otherness than ourselves to be conscious of, or making differences and distinctions in ourselves so that we realize we are actually living in a human body. How do we accomplish this? Only by standing apart from the action and being aware of it from a higher level. We can never understand anything or anyone properly from an equal level, but only from an "overlooking" position. Normally, we must undergo an experience, and then "think it out" afterwards from an overlooking point of time and co-relative information. Understanding is always a process of consciousness operating from a vantage position in relation to what is understood.

The Tarot Symbol of the Hermit, or Solitary, in the Waite

pack is of a most unusual simplicity. On the highest mountain peak of a snow-covered range stands the dark grey-cloaked Figure, almost majestic in its loneliness against the starless sky. The upheld right hand at head level holds a lantern in which shines a single six-pointed Star of Light. The Figure is shown in left profile, hooded and white-bearded. The left hand grasps a golden staff which is the same height as the Solitary. That is all. On face value, there would seem but little to interpret.

The mountain height typifies the isolation of individuality which is experienced at the beginning of our existence when we separate away from the One Life of All in order to become beings in our own right. It also shows the loneliness of living which must come to those high Initiates who have risen so far above the ordinary levels of humanity that they stand by themselves as self-supporting Companions of Cosmos raised to the peak of conscious understanding as they contemplate the Absolute Alone.

Though the Hermit seems to be white-haired and bearded, he does not have either an old face or white eyebrows as might be expected. There is something almost feminine about the cast of feature and the closer this face is observed, the more a possibility occurs that the Hermit might, in fact, be a young person of either age disguised, or an ageless individual who could appear as he pleased according to his mood of mind. Despite the Starlit lantern held aloft, the Hermit's eyes are closed, and head bent in an attitude of calm Inner contemplation and Understanding.

What is the Solitary contemplating? The Figure is wrapped up in a concealing cloak of its consciousness which covers it almost completely. Who knows for certain what is in anyone's mind except the Mindmaker? The grey cloak signifies the Middle Way between Black and White extremities of awareness. This seems dull on the outside to external viewers, but if we could see what this sober garment hid, the revelation might overcome our unprepared senses. To understand anything properly, we must get inside it and wear it like a cloak around us. Only by the feel of things and topics from the inside can we ever hope to understand them entirely. How shall we understand what we do not enter? Since Divine Names are suggested by the shading of the cloak, we may suppose that the Solitary is concerned consciously with sacred subjects.

Borne in the left hand of the Hermit is a staff of his own

height, which is the Golden Rule and the Measure of Man signifying the Middle Way of Life. If the Staff is considered as the Life-
Tree and divided into tenths, the Hermit's hand grips it at the
point of Understanding. With this Staff or Standard, he tests the
ground he stands on his by own measure of Mind.

Held high between head and heart (intellect and emotion) is
the lantern containing the Light which reveals all Ways ahead. It
is the six-point Star of Light that illuminates the Cosmic space-
points of height, Depth, North, East, South, and West. All the Directions of Creation controlled by one Supreme Source of Light-
Life Spirit of Cosmos. The lantern takes the form of an open Temple showing three visible Pillars. This is the Temple of Truth not
made with hands, and represents the degree of Enlightenment
we carry with us on our Inner Journeys. With this type of of Lantern, we shall see our ways through the Pillar-Pattern of the
Tree, and they will be made clear to us by the Light shining
through these and casting shadows of the Pillars as guiding
markers over the area illuminated. It might be expected that a
lantern of this sort would have a stout suspension ring at the top
to grasp it by, but on the contrary, we find that only a very thin
triple thread is provided for the Hermit to hold. Delicate indeed is
the link between ourselves and the Light of True Understanding,
and fine is the balance between ourselves and that vitally important point. We must learn from the Hermit how to keep it securely held, so that our grip on the only reliable Light of revelation will neither be broken nor slip.

The gray of the Hermit's cloak, and the gold of the Staff and
Star is reminiscent of the Alchemical "lead into gold" transmutation theme. This Path, leading between Saturn, the "Gray One"
of deep and dark Understanding, and the Crown of all Light, is
well represented by such a Symbol. None may *be given* this Understanding, but only the ability to gain it by themselves. That
tells the story here.

Hermits or Solitaries become so purposely in order to understand themselves, their fellow beings, and Divinity. Whether or
not they succeed, they follow along an inherent Pattern set by the
Paths of the life-Spirit projecting itself into Existence. This is the
Eternal Solitary in ourselves constantly rising above all else we
are, providing our sole hope of ever becoming higher than human
beings. We may think of this allegorically like a Great Light (Di-

vinity) which emits endless radiant particles (our Divine Sparks) into return-courses around Cosmic circles which enliven whatever they encounter on their way. As living creatures we each have such a Spark in us. Either we try to "follow it home," becoming immortal with it, or we do not attempt this, and consequently "go back into the melting pot" which holds the general mass from which we emerged as an entity in the first place. Either we will BE, or else we will NOT-BE. It all depends on what we Will. So long as we are aware to even the dimmest degree of this Inward Light we can scarcely be entirely lost. It was, and is, the deliberate refusal of humans to keep any willing contact with this Inner Light-Spark which constitutes the so-called "sin against the Holy Spirit which can never be forgiven." Spiritual suicide. Certainly none can be forgiven who no longer exist to experience anything at all. Even so, this self-destruction is no easy matter, or something accomplishable in a momentary fit of human temper. It depends on individual soul-states. For the great mass of mankind who are yet linked with Life via Group-Souls, it is relatively easy to reject any more specific individuation, and sink gently back into the "Great Mother" from whence they emerged into specified entity. For a highly developed and specialized soul deliberately to destroy itself is quite another matter, having much more terrible effects. Only a Solitary who is strong enough to survive whatever Life brings him in contact with is likely to reach a soul-state above average.

None except a soul who dares accept its own Divine Spark as itself will achieve Immortal Ultimate Union with the Supreme Life-Spirit. Who knows this more than Initiates of Light due to the strange state of Inner solitude they must accept as a Path-condition of Inner individuation. We all have to advance toward Divinity *alone*, just as tradition tells us that Divinity became Itself *alone* so that all other manifestations, including mankind, might be themselves Within It. The Hermit-Solitary has many lessons to reach upon this Twelfth Path, the most important being that of Living by the Light within each single one of us

The experience of solitude can transform a soul out of itself into another self again. We are alone in the womb and the tomb, yet all around us is alive in each case. Old-time mystics were familiar with what they called the "Dark Night" of a soul, when they felt utterly alone except for a tenuous hold on "That" which became the only Reality worth living for. This, and this alone, "saved" the soul in question. We must all have "something to hold on to," however we care to call this vital link with Inner Life. Be it a belief, a custom, a Principle, or even an ugly little idol, without our "One and only" to fall back on this side of extinction, we are indeed utterly "lost." The Symbol of the Solitary Hermit represents this thing for each of us, whatever it may amount to. For a Qabalist it is the Light-Spark of Divinity Within. No matter how terrible events of Life may become, every Initiate of the Qabalah must keep himself alive by this Light, even while going through the Doors of Death in search of it. The Hermit has the Key.

Sephirotically, the Path joins the Crown to Understanding. Who understands loneliness better than the Monarch of All, Whose Existence is unequalled? Just as the Supreme Life-Spirit is solitary Within Itself, so on much lower levels of life are we. None can live for anyone else in any way. We cannot eat, breathe, or BE for them. Whatever we do together, each life-unit is acting independently of the others according to whatever scheme it is accepting. Our criterion of growing up is when children begin to "do things for themselves," and when people recover from an illness we say they are "holding their own again." We must understand things for ourselves," if we are to evolve as creatures of Consciousness. Who or What is likely to understand our most intimate and individual problems better than the Ultimate Unique One Itself? The Great Spirit has always been known as One by Mankind. All Pantheons were considered as specific Aspects of One and the same Spirit. Each has its function as we have ourselves in the Life-Scheme. All of us are single particles of the Divine Body. Unless we understand this we shall not be eligible for crowning by a consciousness linked directly with Divinity.

Originatively, we meet here Divinity in BEING (AHIH), joining Itself in being ALL OTHER LIVES (IHVH ELOHIM). THE pluralised term "ELOHIM," sometimes translated as "Gods and Goddesses," indicates that I AM becoming WE ARE. To understand All, it is necessary to BE every single one. Only Absolute Divinity can accomplish this. In our lesser way, we too must BE every cell in our bodies, every thought in our minds, and every feeling in our souls. What do we mean when we say "This is me?" We mean our totality as a number of separate parts. We are All and All else is *Not*. Knowing and understanding ourselves as such is the Magnum Opus of the Mysteries. None should dare claim any understanding of Divine matters who are unable to understand their own Inner workings. If we do what Divinity does, and look for others in ourselves while we seek ourselves in them, we shall begin to understand what Life is about.

Since the Spheres on the left Pillar of the Tree, which we are contacting for the first time in a descending series of Paths, are reckoned as Feminine by contrast to those of the Right Pillar, the Middle Pillar being an ideal balance-line between both, we find on this Twelfth Path the first emanation of Divinity into Female polarity. This creates the Matrix-Concept of Intuition or "Learning from Inside." Just as a Mother brings forth life after life from inside herself, so does Divinity produce every separate life, including ours, from Within Itself. Everything points Within. Where else can Life come from?

Qabalism freely admits a Divine Mother Aspect of the Absolute, which made the System automatically heretical for orthodox patriarclialists. All our oldest religious beliefs were matriarchally inclined, and God-the-Mother was worshipped before humanity recognized fatherhood as a Divine function. The Qabalah settles this issue in its customary quaternal fashion by placing a Supreme Cosmic Consciousness as the Life-Spirit at the apex of All, then emanating a dual ray to each side of Itself which polarizes into Male-Father and Female-Mother Principle levels, equally aspected to each other and the Infinite One as Divine potencies. Simultaneously, the Life-Spirit projects another Aspect of Itself as the outcome, issue, or "Child" of its own projected polarities. We can see this scheme of Life on the Tree plainly enough. The Qabalistic "Holy Quaternity" is thus: God the Spirit, God the Father and Mother, God the Child. It must be admitted that this arrangement appears far more likely and natural than the somewhat forced characterization of the Christian Trinity, which had to be belatedly and lopsidedly balanced by the inadequate elevation of Mary to a "Mother of God" position.

A father may and should instill Wisdom into his family, but only the mother Understands them. That is the Divine quality we have to acquire on this Path to our greatest possible degree. Somehow, we must come to terms of Understanding with the Divine Mother of all Life, gestating in ourselves, as She does, the Seed of Light to be ultimately born as a Child of Divine Consciousness. Literally our new selves must come out of our old ones in this Living Way, yet however we change in emerging from ourselves, we stay with the same Spirit which begins our being. The Mystery of the Mother may only be entered by Initiates of the purest purpose.

Our physical sex-polarity neither facilitates nor prevents the Divine Mother Principle from acting in all of us. Whatsoever human soul seeks the Living Seed of Light within itself, and bears it faithfully until its time of fruition brings it forth into Life among us, becomes fulfilled as a Mother of the Word. Every Initiate of the Inner Way must sooner or later offer himself to the Spirit of Life, saying the time-honored formula: "Behold, I wait thy Word. Be it unto me according to Thy Will." Physically a mother needs to be young, but spiritual motherhood is the privilege of those old enough to fully Understand what this means. Spiritual children are best born of mature souls, and to prepare ourselves properly for this Path may take many incarnationary periods of living. The longer the gestation, however, the more remarkable is likely to be its issue.

On every Path, we must learn how to balance ourselves between the Principles marking its extremities while keeping contact with the Consciousness categorized by both. Here, we are still theoretically on the Supernal side of the Abyss, and while we are still humans, we shall only be able to Understand a very attenuated and remote representation of what Supernal Awareness amounts to. The fine filaments by which the Hermit holds his Light show this. Even a belief or inkling that such a Potency of Awareness Exists at all, marks a high development of human response to this call of Consciousness from beyond the Abyss of our ignorance and Unknowing. If we follow the Principles of this path they will lead us toward the Light of Understanding which gives us guidance across the Darkness we fear to face alone. Solitary as the Hermit seemed, he was only alone or himself, but not Within himself where Inward Illumination brought all to Life, nor yet Outside himself where the Star of Light revealed everything to be looked for in living. When Inner and Outer Light becomes equal, then we shall be able to enter that state of Light from which there need be no return, and live in Peace Profound forevermore.

Living on this Path, the Eternal I AM holds one end, and Everyone I was and will be holds the other. By our human standards of comparison, the entire Past and Future of Existing Life meet in everlasting NOW to form the whole chain of Cosmic events. It is as though we lived back with all our previous lives and forward with all our future ones until we come to a complete Understanding of everything our lives mean and all they are about. Looking at ourselves not as disconnected incidents of identity occurring at irregular intervals of evolution, but as continuous individuals of Divine duration in Cosmos. That is Supernal Understanding of Life, and if only we might reach the least fractional proportion of this during our merely mortal Earthlives, every incarnation will raise us higher and higher toward an eventual realization of this finalizing fact of Life. AHIH and IHVH have the necessary Keys for admitting us into this Adytum of Initiation.

Creatively, we make contact with Archangels Metatron and Tzaphkiel (Watcher of God). Tzaphkiel typifies the Eternal Observer in everyone. Whatever we do on any life-level has to be observed or "Overwatched" from a higher vantage. Sometimes we may do this ourselves, one part of us observing what another part does without apparently interfering with or influencing that activity to any marked degree. Divinity reputedly observes All that Exists, and without such supervision from the highest level of Spirit, Cosmos would discontinue. The Symbol of the All-seeing Eye is widely used in all Systems to denote the vigilance of our Omniscient Overlooker. Every police cadet is taught the use of observation, and intelligence agents of every country are most highly trained in the art. So also should be the Initiates of the Mysteries. To observe properly is to understand eventually, and this is its purpose. So many souls are singularly lacking in observant faculties, and it is only on this particular Path that these can be properly developed at sufficient spiritual depth to make the effort worthwhile. To be really observant does not mean simply noting a list of characteristics about anything and reciting these parrot fashion. It means to stand apart from what is being observed and then penetrate it perceptively from a higher angle as it were, so that the observer becomes aware or conscious of the objective along a steadily Inwardizing beam of illumination which will reveal all the realities which appearances would otherwise have hidden. This is how TZAPHKIEL teaches the art. We might term it Insight, for it is more of a feminine than a masculine gift. METATRON and TZAPHKIEL hold its secrets together, and they will instruct Initiates who approach them rightly on this Path.

Linked also here is the principle of Specification. What is anything? Animal, Vegetable, Mineral? The old parlor game is a fair representation of how Divinity or Humanity arrives at a categorical concept of what anything or anyone is to be in the basic nature. What singles anything out from the rest of Creation? Why should anybody be himself rather than somebody else? Does it really matter who we are? Have we any ability to specify what we Will become? All interesting queries to which Metatron and Tzaphkiel have the answers. The old catch-query: "If you could change yourself, who would you like to be?" has validity on this Path. We can and should specify what and whom we Will be, though it is unwise to be too demanding on these points, since, by the time they come within our grasp, we shall have discovered far better ideas to aim for.

Nevertheless, without adequate specifications, not even the most trivial piece of construction can be done, and when Cosmos is being constructed, its specifications should be very accurate and precise indeed, right down to the last individual atom, while at the same time containing a "constant improvement clause" so that evolution to a *ne plus ultra* degree becomes possible. We are faced with the same problems as Divinity in working out our lesser Cosmoi, so we might as well use the same procedure. Making spiritual specifications is a truly Magical art, and this Path is where it must be learned and understood. To have the ability of Will is vital, but to have the Understanding of What to Will is essential. Unless we know what to be, shall we ever become anything very much worth being? Perhaps the most important question in any young person's life is the portentous one of: "What do you want to be?" that decides future life-careers. How many of us really know the answers, dare to say them, or achieve a fraction of them? Divinity Itself had the same question to decide and specify at the commencement of Its Cosmic career. We shall succeed or fail with It. To specify ourselves, or choose rightly as we proceed alone the Paths of Life, is the lesson we have to learn with METATRON and TZAPHKIEL on this Twelfth Path of the Tree. They have the Keys.

Formatively, we encounter the Angelic Orders of the

CHIOTh ha QODESh and the ARALlM (Thrones) on this Path. The Elements of Life, and the Thrones or Basic Ruling Particulars of every life in Existence. Life and its individual location in the Time-Space-Event Circles of Cosmos. From a purely biological point of view, the Life-Elements of "Holy Living Creatures" are the male sperms, while the "Thrones" are the ova they fertilize. Out of millions of sperms in a single ejaculation, only *one* finally achieves "immortality" through a human egg in a maternal womb. The Tree of Life shows this plainly enough by its initial male plunge into multiplicity as All via the Eleventh Path, then singling this down to One via the female "Selection Board" at the Twelfth Path, which only permits the passage of souls in single file across the Abyss into incarnation—or out of it. Every soul-seed has to find its own proper "Throne" from whence to rule itself rightly. When this is reached, we are born.

How do we find our "Thrones" from a condition of "Unbornness" and become ourselves on Earth or anywhere else in Existence? From all possible thoughts, how do we discover what to think? From all we might be, why do we select what we actually are? How does each Ruler in us recognize their Right Throne? We shall learn the answers on the Twelfth Path. This is where the careful observation of TZAPHKIEL in each of us is needed, for it provides the important preliminary survey of any spiritual situation before Will is irrevocably projected past the point of no-return (the Abyss is this point on the Tree). Seed may pour itself outside a womb forever without raising further life, but once it reaches and fertilizes an egg, then, short of abortive action, the Throne of Life is irretrievably specified and the remainder of the process must continue. If we made use of TZAPHKIEL to any reasonable degree before launching into any course of Life, all would be so much the better for us. Once Divinity projected Itself past the Abyss, our whole Cosmic Life had to continue through its course of Consciousness. Let us hope piously that the prototype of TZAPHKIEL was both reliable and accurate. Observation before action is a sound principle to invoke at the commencement of every Cosmos, especially one involving human lives.

Associated with this Path is the idea of Distinction, or identifying anything as what it IS at its Point of Presentation in the Time-Space-Event continuum of Consciousness. If we had no faculty for distinguishing one thing from another we should never understand anything at all. To tell this from that seems so commonplace to us that we often fail to realize how vitally important such an ability is when operating on high spiritual Life-levels. On Earth we may know our hawks from our handsaws, but beyond this how do we distinguish Inner actualities from each other? Our first legendary step which lowered our present forms of life was our acquired ability to distinguish between the Principles of Good and Evil. This is like a child learning its Right from its Left so that it maintains uprightness and straightforwardness by remaining relatively balanced between both. We have to do just the same spiritually, and this is the Path where we shall best acquire the art. If we would really rule ourselves rightly, then everyone must find his true Inner Throne, and between the CHIOTh ha QODESh and the ARALIM, he may expect to claim it. They have the Keys.

Expressively we locate the Twelfth Path if we relate the Nebulae, or Primum Mobile Concept with Saturn. Not the actual physical phenomena themselves, of course, but what they stand for symbolically. Saturn has been sadly blamed by astrologers of old for human misfortunes, but the misfortunes of anyone might be attributed to his birth in the first place. The nine moons of Saturn are a human gestation-symbol, and "satus" means sowing, planting, begetting, origin, or descent. There certainly seems to have been enough sowing of human seed at the old Saturnalia festivals. Saturn signifies Fate, insofar that once Life is committed to any human womb, the incarnating soul is "Fated" to that particular family, their fortunes, status, nationality, and every circumstance connected with them. Saturn is the weight in the dice, so to speak, which determines the way they fall far the decisive years of a lifetime. Modern astrologers know better than to term Saturn a malefic. It is a determinant or isolator of basic individual characteristics which souls carry with them for the whole of their lives and even beyond. Not that Saturn, or any other planet, actually does anything to any soul, but the intrinsic spiritual state of individuals accord with the same Cosmic Patterns that relate points of Creation together, whether these points are planets, Principles, or even people. We are not ourselves because of planetary or star positions, but these are cosmically relatable to the Inner energies which result in the sort of soul we are. They and we answer a common set of Life-Laws. Astrology is a most valid art in the hands of those who appreciate this relationship. It is a question of judging an Inner Cosmos by the behavior of an Outer one.

This immediately brings up the point of our free-will and how far we can alter the Fate that goes with our lives. Our free-will outside ourselves must perforce be limited by the life-circumstances we have specified before birth. The more developed a soul becomes, the more selective of birth-conditions conditions it is likely to be. An average to less than average soul seems more or less indifferent to birth-status providing they just get born. In many cases almost anything will do providing they even get in edgewise. Free-will is sacrificed very considerably for the sake of becoming embodied again. Within ourselves, as Rulers of our Inner Kingdom, however, our free-will is virtually unlimited, and we can make ourselves AS WE WILL. In fact, we shall only alter our Fate by altering ourselves on very deep levels. With each life, we sow the seeds of the next one at this Saturn-stage. The whole purpose of Qabalistic or other Inner procedures which may be termed "Occult" is for Initiates to take their lives and Fates in their own hands and BE WHAT THEY WILL WITHIN THEMSELVES. Thus, and thus alone can we truly alter our Fate and "pay Karmic debts." The Tree-Plan and its Paths will show us how to do this most advantageously.

Linked with this Path on Expressive levels is the principle of Isolation. This does not mean any lack of companionship with Cosmos, but existence in such a pure state of being that any further alteration in the same direction would result in Non-being what anything essentially IS AS ITSELF. All our modern chemical advances have been possible through Isolation of the activating principles in various specific forms of matter and living elements. To cure a disease it is necessary to isolate its cause. To make anything, we have to isolate it from all else. To make ourselves we must isolate our own essentials from everybody else's. Any senior school-boy these days should know that the minutest imaginable particle or charge of what appears to us as solid material is really isolated from all others in a state of Space beyond our present comprehension. The same Laws apply in spiritual dimensions that operate physical extensions of them, except that these Laws extend limits in keeping with Dimensional changes. Just as a biologist has to learn how to isolate and deal with *ne plus ultra* types of living energy operating on physical levels, so Qabalists and other Initiates have to learn how to isolate and deal with their spiritual equivalents on Inner Extensions of the same Existence. This is the path for gaining that degree of Understanding at the Crowning Point of Life. Between them, the Beginnings of Life in Cosmic evidence through the Nebulae, and the selective seedings of Saturn hold the Keys of the Operation. Now the next path awaits adventurers into Life across the Abyss.

The Thirteenth Path

SPHERE—LETTER CODE:	Crown 1 D 6 Beauty	
DIVINE ORIGINATION:	AHIH—ELOAH va DAATh	The Omniscient
ARCHANGELIC CREATION:	Metatron—Michael Malakim	Awareness
APPARENT EXPRESSION:	Nebulae—Sun	Light
TAROT SYMBOL:	STAR	

This is the Path whereon Supernal Spiritual Life the Crown of all Consciousness emerges yet further from Itself, and crossing the chasm which divides the pure Principles of Divinity from their extended projections, links into the centralizing Solar Power of Harmonious Beauty which keeps Cosmos together as a whole. Omniscient Awareness enters Life as Light, so revealing the reality of Its Eternal Identity. This process is analogical to that of birth on our humbler and human levels of living.

Children ask with innocent intelligence: "Who was God's Mother?" and most adult hearers ignore the implication. Yet the Entity of Entities set the same Life-Pattern that we have to follow for ourselves in our distant degrees. On the Tree of Life, this "Gestation of God" is shown by the Supernal Sephiroth, where Life starts as pure Spirit, then projects through the Father-Principle of Wisdom into the Mother-Principle of Understanding, where it develops to the birth-point of crossing the Abyss into Light-Life Cosmos. If we follow this from Zero, we shall see that Limitless Light condenses itself into the First focus of Consciousness at Kether the Crown, issues forth into the second Sphere of Understanding where it waits until the instant of another Awakening, and bursts into shining birth again as the Sun behind the Suns of every living Cosmos.

The Tarot symbol here is the Star, and, of course, all Stars are Suns of galactic Life. We see this pictured as a golden-haired young matriarch in an early state of pregnancy, who has fallen to Earth while bearing the Waters of Life which are pouring out of their containers on land and sea alike.

Legend and science agree that Life came to this planet in some unknown way from the Star-colonies of Cosmos many light-years distant. This is indicated in the picture by a great Golden eight-pointed Star surrounded by seven visible lesser stars, one of which has fallen to Earth in the distant background representing the past. If we consider this lay-out carefully, it seems most probable that there should be ten smaller stars round the large one, of which we are only seeing seven, including the fallen one. That would show the Tree-plan of the three Supernal Spheres beyond our knowledge across the Abyss, and the seven remaining Spheres of which Malkuth as the "Fallen Sephirah" has come down to Earth.

The theme of falling is carried further by the naked Mother-Figure spilling her precious stream of Life to ground level. We realize that she has fallen, and is not just kneeling, by the way her right foot is poised in an overbalanced position above the water. The projection over which she has tripped appears near her left foot. We see her poised in the fractional interval just as she is about to fall in the pool herself. Light, falling to Earth, causes Life to spring up all around, as the red flowers indicate. They typify the various lines of blood from whence the different life-types descended until this day. Be it noted that there are two streams of Life coming down from the Starry skies. One is a single stream going into a common pool, and the other divides into a five-branched cataract for the five main human races, white, yellow, red, black, and brown.

On high ground, in line with the human Life-streams, is a small tree with a golden stem, three growing branches, and a very young pelican perching on the leaves as if considering the possibilities of a nest. Everything in this picture suggests Life in its very early stages on Earth. The pelican, of course, is symbolic of the offspring of Life from remote parts of Cosmos coming here to provide blood for its family of human fledglings, when a nest for them became established in the Tree of Life as its branches grew strong enough to support them. So was our arcane ancestry reputed to be linked with family Life in very far away homelands around other Stars than our present Sun. It is also likely that when our position on this planet becomes untenable, we shall have to go forth again on our Star-wanderings of Light-life.

The Star in the picture is eight-pointed. If we consider this against the background of the Tree-Pattern, it will fit only at Tiphereth, where eight Paths come together at the Solar centre. Our Soul here typifies the Solar Energy of the far Galaxies linking up with Life on Earth, so there seems no reason to doubt a good connection of the Tarot Trump with this Path. Eight is the number of the Quarters and cross-Quarters of the Solar Seasons which complete our Cosmic cycle. These old feasts of Life have been celebrated among us on Earth here in one way or another since time immemorial. The stars themselves in their courses marked out the chart of Cosmic Light which connected us here on this planet, however remotely, with our fellow beings in the unknown depths of Space. It was and is the Stars which bring Mankind the wordless message of assurance that we are not entirely alone here, cut off completely from every sort of Life elsewhere. Even though we cannot yet make material contact with the rest of our Cosmic relations living in other Solar Systems, the Stars tell us what we have always felt in the depths of our hearts, that we are Earth-exiles who will one day be re-united with the families of Life we really belong to elsewhere in Existence.

Between our stellar Life-sources and ourselves is the Abyss of interstellar Space which we must learn how to cross before we may hope to link up with Life beyond our human limits here. Light alone crosses this Abyss on material levels of living, and when we discover how to travel at the speed of Light, then transcend this velocity into other Dimensions of Life altogether, we shall hold the secret of "thinking ourselves there," and actually arrive intact wherever we intend.

This Path is the first Abyss-crosser of the Tree, and the Abyss of the Qabalah typifies somewhat more than a convenient crack in Cosmos for losing the undesirables of a Universe. It also signifies the point past which thinking about things becomes translated into doing them practically. The Supernal levels of conscious Life are considerations of Original Awareness, which may or may not go any further than their own Inner area. The Abyss is the boundary line of this area as it were. Once a Divine decision is made in favor of Creation, the Abyss becomes bridged into Creative Life-levels, and the process pushed one vital stage nearer completion.

We do this in our own lesser Microcosmic ways. We are always crossing what amounts to the minor cracks in the fabric of our lives, which sooner or later end up at the Abyss of Death we must cross by the Life-line of Light shining from the Star we follow for our spiritual safety. Legend says that we must cross our last Abyss of all by means of a Sword-Bridge or the balance edge of Divine Decision concerning our ultimate disposal. If we are worth retaining in the Scheme of Life at that level, we shall be included in the Divine Identity, but if not, then we shall be lost to Life in the Abyss altogether. Before that final and awful moment comes to us in actuality, it may be as well for all intending immortality to practice Chasm-crossing by minor methods, so that this will help conscientious practitioners to achieve the necessary perfection required for their ultimate ordeal.

When the Supreme Entity of Existence is ready for a further projection of Itself into Cosmos, It is "born" across the Abyss in a Star-like fashion. We should remember the Star-Symbol associated with the birth of Gautama and later at Bethlehem. Every soul is a Star properly speaking, for a Star is a Cosmic nucleus, a mass of radiant energy, and Light-Life in its own right. Poets have long likened souls to Stars, and a poet looking Heavenward often sees what astronomers miss. With this Extension of Existence, Spirit, properly placed at the Supernal Sephiroth, may be said to "ensoul" Itself. At its next main projection down the Middle Pillar of the Tree, It acquires "Mind," and with the last major move down to Its Kingdom, It "embodies" in what we know as "Matter." Here on the Thirteenth Path, however, we are at the Star stage linking the Supreme Light of Spirit with the Solar Energy the centre of every Cosmos. Stars *are* Suns. The Alchemy of the Tree is that from the lead of Saturn we suddenly switch to the gold of Sol. We might even make spiritual capital out of this by changing Sol to Soul by the addition of the Universal "U."

The Symbol of the Star is used in all esoteric Systems. It is even in common use to signify something special to be singled out for attention. A leading stage or sports personality is always a "Star." Everywhere it means the best and brightest of a type. We use multiplicity of Stars to show degrees of "betterness." The more Stars the better. How high does an Entity rate among all the Stars in Existence? Man has always looked instinctively to Stars for inspiration and guidance. They also offer us the hope that when this Solar system of ours becomes impossible for our sort of living, there will be opportunities elsewhere in the Galaxies. We are all Star-followers in one way or another, whether the Stars concerned are physical or not.

Without the Stars, navigation across the oceans would have been an impractical proposition, and if we believe in Astrology, those same Stars translated into Inner terminology will help us guide our personal vessels across the metaphorical Seas of Life on which we embark for an Earthlife. Stars make Cosmic sense of Time-Space-Events everywhere. We are now literally reaching for them from this planet, but unless we reach our own Inner Stars first, Outer star-travel will never bring us the Peace that was promised with a Star so long ago. This is the Path upon the Tree to seek that especial Star of Spirit in ourselves and learn to recognize its Light in all others.

The points of any Symbolic Star convey its significance. Initiates of Qabalah and other Systems have to learn the various meanings of Star-pointing, so that codifications of consciousness are possible under broad headings of stellar indications. Stars of all sorts are very major meditation Symbols, as all realize who have gazed at the Star of the Macrocosm in the center of a Chanuka minorah or the Star of the Microcosm over a Christmas Crib. There is no need to wait for annual occasions to contemplate Cosmic Stars, crowned by a Divine Diadem of Supreme Awareness in light. We can always find it waiting on the Tree of Life. The words of the old carol mention this:

> *Star of Wonder, Star of Light*
> *Star with Royal Beauty Bright,*
> *Westward leading, still proceeding,*
> *Guide us to Thy Perfect Light.*

What more charming description of this Path could there be? The Star that joins Royalty and Beauty as Divine Life proceeds into incarnation. The Light we must all follow in each of us, which will infallibly lead to the Crown of our Creation if we set our compasses by it. Significantly enough it starts at our end of the Tree on this Path at the Sphere of Beauty, Balance, Harmony, Poise, and Solar centralization. What better beginning can we make in the direction of Divinity than with a sense of

Beauty or "Right-Light?" We still speak of "Dazzling" Beauty, and the most brilliant of all beautiful wonders we may ever meet is the Star shining in every Light-seeking soul. Just as we stand on Earth and look at the Heavens to appreciate the Star-Pattern of our Outer Cosmos, so may those of Inner-vision look otherwise at our Earth to consider the Star-Pattern we make of ourselves as human souls constructing our share of Cosmos. Our Pattern may not yet be so perfect as our Heavenly model, but in our way we are trying to tell the same story.

Originatively, we encounter the Divine Aspects of AHIH and ELOAH va DAATh (Divinity of Knowledge) on this Path. The Keys to the whys and whats of any Path are usually in the Names attached to them, and this Thirteenth Path shows Life looking for Knowledge and Experience. It comes out of Itself to find out about Itself and All Within It. In the case of All-Being, this amounts to Omniscience, which is the associated Principle here. We get born for the same reason. To KNOW OURSELVES as the old Grecian Temples of the Mysteries so unerringly put it. What other reason would be sufficient to drag anyone out of a perfectly comfortable womb? The term "DAATh" really means knowledge gained by experience at first hand, and no sort of knowledge is much use to anyone if it cannot be incorporated into their individual Cosmos. Without our mechanical memory-banks of recorded human experience in books, Symbols, and by other means, none of our still very shaky cultures and civilizations would have been possible. Knowledge is the total of experience, and we on Earth are learning how to make the experiences of many available in concentrated forms to each of us who care to absorb this. Long ago, Divinity learned for Itself how to absorb the experience of every Life Within It, and so be omniscient as far as they were concerned. We have the same problem, however long we shall need to work it out for ourselves.

The one faculty allowing Man to rise above other creatures on this Earth and now above the Earth itself was an inherent ability for gaining Knowledge and passing the benefit of this down lines of descendants who successively added their own little by little until our present point was reached. Cumulative Consciousness, or our Inheritance of Light originating from a truly Divine Source. Man, as an Earth-creature alone, has nothing whatever to make him superior to others. Take away the single faculty of constructive learning by a cumulative and inheritable consciousness, and the last human would have been eaten millenia ago, thus sparing the other creatures much suffering and annoyance. Man, as Man, is actually a rather inferior sort of animal, but Man as a soul capable of carrying a consciousness of non-Earthly origin within him, is altogether different. If we should ever lose touch with this Inner Star, then we doom ourselves irrevocably. It, and It alone, makes us mean anything worth considering by Consciousness with a Cosmic Order of operation. We can only become what we make ourselves into by the Light of this Knowledge in us. Its Light alone is reliable enough to lead us over the Abyss of Darkness, Ignorance, Doubt, and even Death. What other Star may we follow with such complete confidence?

Divinity bursts into Being across the Abyss with a blaze of Light proclaiming its Presence as the Star of the All-Knowing. If we are to follow this example of Life as we should, then individually and collectively we shall have to make what are now called "breakthroughs" past many an Abyss into states of Stardom amounting to Knowledge which will proclaim Man at last as a worthy Companion of Cosmos. Until this is achieved, we shall scarcely be fit company for Heaven either inwardly or Outwardly. The sooner each of us achieves such spiritual status on our own accord, the better for all. Divinity had to accomplish the equivalent of this by Itself, and we have to do the same in terms of our Paths also. What AHIH and ELOAH va DAATh have agreed on between them, so must we in our proportions of their Principles.

To know what to be, and to be what we know is the problem of this Path. How many untold millions of parents have asked their children if they know what they want to be when they grow up? Does Man know what he wants or Wills to be when he comes of Cosmic age? It is vital to all of us that we *should* have some Inner knowledge of what we intend to become as specimens of spiritual Life, assuming we mean to live that long and far in the first instance. We shall not be compelled or coerced in the least into acceptance of our Immortal Identity. Man as Man is mortal and our personalities are perishable. Only the Spirit of Life Itself is truly Immortal, and insofar as we identify ourselves with It through transcendence of matter by soul and mind, so may we share Divine Immortality. Only a deliberate refusal to accept the responsibilities of Life at that high level by willing rejection of all that leads us there can doom us to utter disintegration of our identity at the end of our eon. This is a main aspect of the "sin against the Holy (Living) Spirit which is not possible to forgive." If we no longer exist to be forgiven, this has to be the case completely.

On the Tree of Life, this path must be paced and traced in theory and practice by every Initiate of Light seeking spiritual identification with the highest and Holiest Life of All. Though we may make but the least movement upon it while we are mortal, such would suffice to keep our contacts with it clear. AHIH and ELOAH va DAATh hold forth the Keys for us to claim.

Creatively, we meet METATRON again, this time in Heavenly partnership with MICHAEL (The Godlike). Metatron presents Archangelically the highest hopes of Humanity, and Michael is possibly the best known of Archangels to Mankind as Leader of the Holy Hosts of Light.

MICHAEL, the Solar Archangel, is the most glorious and spectacular Shining One of the Hierarchy. Every system of belief recognizes him in one form or another. To us, he is the Champion of Right and Light against every kind of evil, injustice, wrong, and corruption. With his Spear-shaft of light, he vanquishes the crawling horrors and enemies of Cosmos, thrusting them into the Abyss where they rightly belong. Michael personifies whatever is splendid, noble, and fundamentally good in Divinity and Humanity alike. No wonder he is unvanquishable! Probably the best legend of Michael is that he made a faithful promise before the Throne of God that he would befriend Mankind until the end of Existence, and champion the cause of Humanity throughout Creation while even the faintest spark of good remained alive in a solitary soul on Earth. He did not specify or demand vast amounts of good from humans before he concerned himself with their fate. The existence of good at all in any soul was enough for MICHAEL. He would fight for that soul with its spark of good as a physician fights for anyone with the slightest sign of life in him. Perhaps for that reason Michael also becomes the Patron of Healing in sickness. (Raphael, his colleague, heals hurts and wounds especially.)

In some old representations, Michael is seen standing by souls being weighed in the dreaded Judgment-Scales. One has the feeling that although such an upright Archangel as Michael would scarcely stoop to real dishonesty, he might frequently shine more heavily on souls who needed just that little extra to qualify for salvation! He is altogether the firmest Archangelic friend Man is likely to meet this side of Deliverance or Destruction. In fact, Michael might just make that difference. We may meet him on this Thirteenth Path of the Sun-Star.

Incidentally, making clear Concepts of Archangels. God-Aspects, or any other form of Telesmic Image is no idle pastime. If we construct these Inner Images well enough, the actual Energies they personify will flow into them and act through them from all sources of supply. Telesmics is really a Magical Art which should never be neglected. The Michael-Figure is well enough known for all of us to make for ourselves, and Energy of his nature does really activate the Michael-Concepts we construct in our own circles of consciousness, which is the true Magical way of Invocation.

Michael in each of us represents an instinctive sense of Goodness and Right which is bound to lead us along this Thirteenth Path by the Light he upholds. The Principle of Awareness associated here refers to the Inner Awareness we must inherit, acquire, or develop, which instinctively tells us the right way to take in Life through all its conditions. Unlikely as we are to meet souls who never make any mistakes at all in living, it is still possible to improve very considerably on our margins of error if we devote ourselves to the Metatron-Michael methods of this Path. They are the Creative Concepts we should study and seek to emulate experientially along these Inner lines of Light.

METATRON is the Archangel who leads us toward our most exalted ideas of Divinity. As the Angel of the Presence, he is responsible for helping us recognize the Holy Presence anywhere at all. How often in Life does perhaps some quite commonplace object or event suddenly work as a catalyst which opens up our Inner consciousness into an incredible and indescribable realization of direct contact with Divinity? Rare though this may be, Metatron's agency has been in operation. An event like that often alters the course of a lifetime. More usually we obtain such realizations in many minor ways rather than rare and impressive ones of maximum impact. Little and often is the best dosage of Divinity for Man to take, and Metatron makes our most reliable administrator of such a potent Elixir of Life.

While Michael protects us on this Path with his Lance of Light, and Metatron is mediating Patron of the Presence, we shall never be lost to Light or abandoned in the Abyss. It is well to remember that none are ever lost except those who intend to be. Obviously, no Initiates of Light who keep such Concepts as Metatron and Michael in their consciousness have any intentions of eliminating themselves from Life as spiritual entities. Therefore they are very good Concepts indeed for us to remain on friendly terms with. Between them, they hold the Keys of the Path at this level.

Formatively, the Angel Orders of the CHIOTh ha QODESH and the MALAKIM govern this Path. The Holy Elements of Life, and the Regulating Rulers. They should help us order our lives properly and so regulate our courses of consciousness that the act of living becomes well worth the experience. The associated principle is Relevance, and unless all our living affairs have relevance for us, and we learn how to relate what with which and whom in order to make good sense of everything, we shall be very mixed up and permanently perplexed people. With the help of the Chioth and the Malakim, we might be able to sort out our ideas and information so that these begin pointing the same way—in the direction of this Path. In doing this, these Angels are only fulfilling the function for which their Inventor intended them.

Even the newest student of the Qabalistic Tree notices that most of the Paths come together around here. As the Star pointed out, there are eight, so that all the Sephiroth except the Kingdom at Malkuth joins up with this one about Balance and Beauty in Tiphereth. Thus, these Paths represent the Cosmos of the central Sun related to the Nebulae in the distance, then the Zodiac, five planets, and Moon all focused on the tenth point of this Earth at base. To know the relevance of Cosmic points with each other and ourselves is the sort of Knowledge we should expect to gain along this Path. How are we to arrange ourselves so that we get the centers and circumferences of our individual and collective Cosmoi lined up Lightwardly? That, and many other queries like it, must be solved with the aid of the Chioth and the Malakim.

We shall meet the MALAKIM quite often in our present studies of the Tree-Paths—seven times more in fact, whenever we link up with the Balance of Beauty at Tiphereth. They are the

"Rules of the Game" we are supposed to learn before we attempt playing around with Life. All associative Life-entities must accept some kind of rules or code of conduct in order to live Cosmically together. The Malakim are the agencies whereby such rulings are determined and operated. Without them it would not be possible to follow any of the internal Tree-Paths at all. Life would have no Inner meaning for us, and we should see little sense in anything.

Even Divinity Itself lives by the Laws or rules of Life It lays down as a basis for ordered or Cosmic Being. To expect Divinity to deliberately break or suspend Its own rulings at the desire or decree of a purely human person is sheer insanity, and yet how many Magical mistakes and errors are due to such utterly presumptuous stupidity? Properly instructed and Initiated individuals in the Holy Mysteries are not concerned with such unintelligent inaccuracies. Their first interest is to learn the Inner rulings and Laws of Life which, though hidden from the majority of Mankind, are definite boundaries of conduct observed by the Consciousness behind Cosmos. Put into very simple instructions, this might read: "Find out the lines along which God lives. Then rule out a proportional plan inside yourself." This is exactly what the Tree of Life Plan stands for, and why Qabalists revere its design. For them, the Malakim represent the active agencies whereby all the internal scheme of the System is ruled in relationship to every external Principle-point except our mundane Sphere of Life.

The CHIOTH ha QODESh may be considered as the Elements of Holiness in Life, or those qualities which provide means for Divinity to live through every Life-form in Existence. In all of us, and indeed every living creature, there are distributed what might be called Divine Elements rather like chemical elements building up our bodies. Whatever these Elements actually are, Qabalists term them the Chioth ha Qodesh. According to their degrees and distribution in anyone, so does Divinity operate through them. How much God is in any Man? Only the Chioth concerned could answer that one. That is why we ought to ask the Chioth ha Qodesh and the Malakim for the Keys they hold to this part of the Thirteenth Path. These will open our ways to the utmost limits of Life even beyond Light leading to Perfect Peace Profound at the End of All.

Expressively, the Nebulae and the Sun are the apparent links with this Thirteenth Path. Nebulae are Cosmic beginnings, and Suns are Cosmic Nuclei of Energy around which a planetary System provides Life-opportunities for souls adapting themselves to the prevalent conditions. We certainly cannot live on Suns with our type of body, but it is just as certain we could not live at all without Solar energy scaled down to suit us. This applies to our minds and souls as well as our bodies. Human souls are in their degree "Suns of God," and should cosmate themselves round this Inner Light-Source of Spirit just like planets are cosmated round the Sun of their System. Deriving our distant supply of Energy from the most Abstract and Nebulous contacts we have with the Absolute, these must lead into our Center and there become an Inner-shining Sun round our Nil-Nucleus. Around this "Sun behind the Sun," all the particular parts of our beings which correspond to planetary forces have to arrange themselves in relevant rings or orbits within a Zodiac which marks the individual limits of our Cosmoi in spiritual Dimensions just as our skin does in physical ones. We, too, as the Ultimate Entity does, must make ourselves into Solar Cosmic Systems and live according to the Laws of Light. On this path, we have especially to learn about the conversion of Nebulic Energy into Nuclear Energy on a spiritually Solar scale.

The Principle associated with this part of the Thirteenth Path is Light. Its Laws apply to Inner Life as much and even more than they do within our Outer ones. The Holy Mysteries are otherwise termed the "Mysteries of Light," and everything to do with Light symbolizes Spiritual Life Universally. It is a pity that over the centuries Darkness has become associated with evil-doing, for this was not an Original Intention of the Life-Spirit in any way. Humans simply found night a convenient cover for marauding and murdering, robbing and raping, treachery and thievery, etc. By trying to hide behind the cloak of a beneficent Night to conceal their ill-doings, men have sadly stained this merciful mantle of manifestation. None have become evil by Night except Man and similarly inclined spirits. Besides, the Night is not Dark at all with its blazonry of Stars; one, it is said, for each soul in Existence. We just need special sight for Night-vision, and to live by the Light of our Inner Sun-Stars.

The terrible sense of Utter Darkness experienced by those

encountering what might be termed "Deep Evil" is really what might be called "Anti-Light," shining inversely in such a way that it has a cancellation effect on the Light of whatever Cosmos the unfortunate individual happens to be working from. It is not so much that any Light is actually extinguished *per se*, but that the soul in question becomes spiritually blinded in some particular area. "Anti-Light" is a very nasty weapon indeed, as those who have suffered its effect will testify. A dangerous weapon for its user also, because if it should be turned against them, it has the effect of doubling the intensity of whatever Light-frequency it otherwise "antis." Everything depends on the way it is directed. Michael, as Leader of the Hosts of Light, must have discovered this a long time ago, and is still using it to hold the "Powers of Darkness" in abeyance. We might do worse than humbly ask his assistance in coping with our own confusions.

The secrets of Light and those of the human Spirit go together. The entire Tree-Pattern is a tracery of Light-Life in relation to Truth. On this vital Sun-Star Path, we should hope to learn some of these secret matters in company with our Cosmic Companions who are engaged in their practical use in whatever Dimensions of Life they center their consciousness. What is the difference between a Nebula and a Solar System? When we find the Keys to that enigma on this Path we shall be ready for the next one.

The Fourteenth Path

SPHERE—LETTER CODE:	Wisdom 2 F 3 Understanding	
DIVINE ORIGINATION:	IHVH—ELOHIM	The Discerning
ARCHANGELIC CREATION:	Ratzie—Tzaphkiel	Experience
ANGELIC FORMATION:	Auphanim—Aralim	Definition
APPARENT EXPRESSION:	Zodiac—Saturn	Adaption
TAROT SYMBOL:	JUDGMENT	

Here we have the supreme faculty of Judgment as a direct link between the Principles of Wisdom and Understanding. True discernment defines all operations of Consciousness so that it becomes auto-adaptive throughout the extent of its Experience. Let it be noted well that this Path covers the entire length of the Abyss on the Supernal side of Life. This should be enough to warn every living being not to cross any sort of an Abyss without using all the Judgment of which they are capable by their combined faculties of Wisdom and Understanding.

During the meditative dissections of the Tree-Pattern, students of Qabalah usually discover a sort of "backbone" to it, consisting of the Middle Pillar connecting the four central Sephiroth, and the three horizontal bars joining up the others. By itself, that makes the "Triple Tau" design or, counting our Earth-level, the Four Worlds of Life. In this present System we are studying, the cross-bars of the Life-Tree are formed by Judgment as this Path, Justice in the middle, then Chance on the lower level. Lowest of all is whatever holds the baseline of the Tree in question, which is usually the individual considering it. Thus, the symbolic figure of anyone holding a Triple Tau before him indicates an upright Spirit contemplating the three bars to involving himself with Life unless the right conditions apply.

Three vital questions have to be answered by Initiates before proceeding along any Path of Life.

1. What is my right Judgment in this course?
2. Am I entirely justified?
3. Is opportunity favorable?

Once satisfactory replies come from Inner Intelligence concerning these points, the symbolic Bars can be turned safely on their axes and become sight-lines connecting the Initiate with the objective in view. Wise and Understanding Initiates always bar themselves in this way from action in Life until they have performed this Triple Tau rite in their Inner Temples, or at least stopped to ask the questions before tackling an Abyss. These three important bars to rash and unconsidered activities may be likened to the rails of a fence erected to save people from disastrous falls—providing they are heeded.

The Tarot Symbol of Judgment shows the traditionally yawning graves and reconstituted humans arising from them. The Angel of the Trumpet is giving the Call to Life above a dead world awakening into new and resurrected conditions of living.

Careful examination of the Angel-figure shows that it is a dual Male-Female Concept as most of the Waite images seem to be. Its wings are different on either side; so is its hair style of gold and red flames representing Light and Life-Blood. The cloud-effects, symbolizing a manifestation of some Concept from the workings of Consciousness (in this case Divine) vary on each side of the center line also. Placing a mirror at right angles edgewise from top to bottom of this card at center, and then studying the variations between the right and left hand pictures this will produce when viewed half in the mirror and half as the card to make a whole picture, provides most interesting information for those taking the trouble to do this and meditate upon the issue.

The Trumpet, or Tube of Life, indicates the means by which the Living Word is communicated from Heaven to Earth toward each corner of Cosmos, as the Banner of the Blood attached to it shows. This so-called St. George's Cross simply indicates the crossing of one straight blood-line with another in order to produce balanced and well-born types of Life. Without the least hint of snobbery, the symbology here indicates that only the finest and fittest specimens of human souls are likely to survive the selective processes of birth and rebirth leading to ultimate Life in finer forms of Being than merely mortal. There is nothing very extraordinary about this, after all. Life and evolution on Earth has always indicated that a long drawn out survival and selection of species is constantly going on. For what precise purpose and end we shall only discover for certain after we change our conditions of living into higher than human types of entity, or what would once have been termed "post Resurrection Life."

In this Tarot Symbol, the survivors at the end of human evolution who have been judged fit to live in better Cosmic circumstances than those of Earthlife are seen emerging from Earth as they rise toward Heaven. They are in families, showing that spiritual survival-strains are inherited characteristics, transmissible along genetic lines of Life. These are welcoming with joy their opportunities of Existence in their changed conditions of consciousness. In the foreground the woman reaches out her arms in acceptance, her mate places his hands together in the firm attitude of making a determined plunge into this new Ocean of Life before them, while the little child between them holds its arms apart in a worldwide and wondering gesture of friendship for everyone and everything everywhere.

That these people are living in what have been called "glorified bodies" is shown by absence of flesh-tints. They are all of the same race, if race, species, or other ethnological terms can possibly apply to those who have risen above mortal levels of Life. "Of one flesh," or whatever spiritual equivalent constitutes the make-up of our supra-physical vehicles, might describe their state of subsistence. At any rate, they are most certainly related to each other by the closest possible ties of family life and friendship that might be imagined. There are positively no aliens or enemies in this type of World of our post-Resurrective period, which will no doubt be the major distinguishing mark between our present planetary conditions and that almost unbelievable state of Cosmos which has been promised for those souls who survive until the end of our Earthly evolution.

To be really alive as conscious individuals in associative conditions of living wherein there are no hatreds, fears, suspicions, antagonisms, greeds, and all the other nastiness of nature which seems such an inherent part of humanity as we know it now, appears almost like asking for or expecting the utterly impossible. Yet all Inner Traditions assure us that such a state of what to us would be "super life," is actually a perfectly ordinary and normal way of living for those souls who have progressed past a certain point on the scale of spiritual development and so qualified for the "Second Birth" into a Life level beyond ours on Earth. In effect, they have been truly judged fit to associate with Companions of Cosmos in the same living-circles, and such is the significance of resurrection in an Inner sense.

There is a certain teaching to the effect that ideas behind the myth of resurrection are based on more scientific principles than might be supposed. It is a question of consciously constructing in our spiritual natures an automatic frequency-response to the characteristic "Life-Call" on higher than human levels. Just as there is a "Mating Call" or resonant frequency of forces between humans of opposite polarity which attracts their sort of soul into human incarnation, so is there a distinctive frequency of much finer types of force calling responsive Life types toward more advanced levels of thinking and living. That is really the "Trumpet Blast" which wakens the dead or deaf souls to Life, once their Inner Identities become attuned to its particular pitch, and follow it along like a radar beam guiding them infallibly toward their higher homelands. It is partly with an intention of developing and training our response factors to such important Inner frequencies, that Initiates of most Systems make use of sonic symbolism and chanting in rhythmical sequences calculated to open up our lines of conscious communication in those Divine directions.

Only the faculty of true and good Judgment poised between Wisdom and Understanding can possibly lead us to level living beyond the Abyss. This makes quite sound sense. Exactly how the "Last Judgment" presentation by the orthodox and established Churches took on its accepted ludicrous literal form is not easy to trace. The notion of long dead humans still attached to their decayed remains and past personalities, sunk in subconscious slumber until a single Divine Call awakes them all on Earth to a final reckoning and disposal, is rather insulting to an otherwise Intelligent Deity. There certainly has to be a Last Day for us in the sense that this world will eventually be uninhabitable for our type of Life-form. That is an inevitable conclusion, which our descendants must ultimately face. The horrifying point confronting us, is that instead of being a consoling few million years away, as it ought to be, we ourselves have made this possible in the alarmingly near future. Virtually any day may be the Last for everyone.

We all have a Last Day on Earth to come, one by one. Then we shall have to judge ourselves for what we actually amount to in Inner values, and fit ourselves in with whatever state of Inner Existence is compatible with our spiritual status. There is no question of condemnation or Divine animosity whatever. Simply a matter of belonging with the right condition of being for what we TRULY ARE AS AND IN OURSELVES. Nothing more complicated than that. Each soul disposes itself to its own category of fundamental consciousness. For some, this may be a terrible experience, and for others a wonderful one. For others again, an end to experience altogether. Whatever we really and truly are as human souls, that is our condition of Life when we have no bodies to hide in. There is no better or worse Judgment to face than this. It is quite serious enough.

Every judgment before any course of action is a Last Judgment, in the sense that what has been done is done. The more irrevocable the act, the more Final the Judgment. We make Last Judgments all the time, and if only we made them, like this Path, an issue of Wisdom and Understanding, we should be better Beings than we are. Judgment, after all, is an accurate estimation of intrinsic rightness as related with some Universal Standard. We attempt to raise such a Standard with moral, civil, religious, or other Codes and Commandments. The Standard of the Tree is its Middle Pillar, or most direct Light-Line between Divinity and Humanity. No less equivalent standards are expected of human souls. Without Standards, no army could ever fight, or for that matter, any organization continue in being. A Legion without Standards is lost. So are a people. By what spiritual Standards do we live? At one time the Mosaic code seemed sufficient for most humans, whatever System they subscribed to otherwise. How many souls still have any Standards today, and if so—what are they? From time immemorial, the duty of an advancing soul was to know and recognize the Standard or Standards they were supposed to follow. Just how many individual souls, if suddenly forced to declare their Standards of spiritual Life, could produce a satisfactory reply. What sort of Standards do most people set up in this age? Are they really worth any In-seeing soul devoting whole lives of service to them? Or are they just temporary labels destined for obliteration in the Universal scrap-heap?

A Qabalistic Initiate does at least know and recognize very plainly and clearly indeed the Standards of Life he follows even if he is personally very far from achieving them. The Tree of Life is about the clearest and most definite Standard of Living-behavior it is possible to imagine, once a combination of Wisdom and Understanding has provided sufficient Judgment to realise its value and importance. Given such a Standard, Life really means everything worth Existing for through all conditions and categories of Consciousness. This is the first Judgment the Supreme Life-Spirit had to make on Its "to BE or NOT TO BE" issue, and the Last Judgment It obviously made before crossing the Chasm into forms of Life we recognize. Deep in every human soul is the same Call of "Give me something to Live for," Something real, genuine, vital, and fundamentally acceptable by the Life-Spirit through each of us. Something to justify and make Life worth Living. We all ask this. Who finds it?

The Qabalist finds sufficient Life-motive in the spiritual values related to each other on the Standard of the Tree and projected everywhere in Existence throughout all levels of living. Being something that means everything, the Tree makes everything mean something to the followers of Its Paths. There is no more to ask of Life short of unliving altogether. What finer Standard could be asked for? No responsible Qabalist would ever claim the Tree as an easy Standard or Pattern of Life, but its practicability can never be denied by anyone who is steadfastly dedicated to living its Design.

To see the Principle of Judgment rightly, we must realize that it should never be confused with any sort of condemnation. The dictum, "judge not that ye be not judged," actually means "Condemn not, etc." No true Judge condemns, damns, or otherwise disposes of living souls. Once adequate Standards of Life are set up, and souls cosmate or congregate round them, the only Judgment required is whether or not members of that cosmic condition diverge too seriously from those Standards to make their upkeep a practical proposition among others in the same Cosmos. Is the structure around the Standard endangered to a degree of dissolution or not? The answer can only be Yes or No, and an estimation made of the degree of divergence from the

Standard. What follows on that Judgment is entirely a corrective outcome in accordance with the disturbance of balance involved. We are doing this all the time in minor ways. If we judge that our bodies are falling too far forward or sideways from our standard of uprightness, we automatically correct our stance before we collapse on the ground. That is constant Karma in action as a result of Judgment. The Judgment of the Life-Spirit Itself is only the same Principle applied on an infinitely greater Cosmic Scale. The closer our Standards symbolize those of Cosmos the better. The Tree of Life affords the best Standards we are likely to meet in the course of our Microcosmic lives.

Originatively, we follow this Fourteenth path from IHVH to ELOHIM. I AM and WE ARE. The Divine Father-Mother or Primal Parents of all Life projected past this point. Both Parents are needed to judge any Child of Cosmos fairly. We can scarcely hope to judge anything at all from only one angle of observation. Two eyes are needed to judge distance, and two points of approach are the absolute minimum for any sort of reasonable estimate to be made. The old adage of two sides to any argument is a useful truism. Here, we have indeed the "Mother and Father" of an argument concerning what Life itself is all about. The only hope of a solution is just—to live and find out. That is exactly what the Life-Spirit does through us. We have to do the same in our way. The "Last Judgment" will be made between these two categories of Cosmic Consciousness as to whether or not Life was really worth living after all, and, if so, should it be commenced again. To be or Not-to-be is certainly the Ultimate issue of Judgment in anyone's life.

Divine Judgment is no kind of retribution whatsoever, or a species of reprisal for past proclivities, and it was only so interpreted by mankind yet unable to rise above such reactions. Divine Judgment is that Assessment of Awareness which puts everything and everyone in its appropriate place within the Cosmos It controls. No more and no less. Since we have largely determined what we are by our own activities and Wills, the responsibility for such Judgment rests very much with us. For different results we must try different methods, but Divinity is scarcely to be blamed for our behavior. Once we can get away from our concepts of vengeful and retributive Deities, we begin to make good Inner progress. There need be no doubt at all that every soul will meet his or her due deserts in the course of Cosmos, though not according to our specifications or human Judgments made from very limited viewpoints. Oddly enough, human attempts at vengeance on other humans often have the effect of saving those individuals from far worse that they would have invoked upon themselves in the longer course of nature. The surest condemnation of any soul comes from Within itself. Ill-will and mal-treatment from other souls certainly causes damage to physical and deeper degrees, but these are compensatory, and may even pay dividends ultimately. The decrees of Divine Judgment, however, are irrevocable once the Final Fiat has gone forth.

For this reason alone, true Initiates never attempt to "curse" their enemies, or "ill-wish" anyone. They may, however, once they are absolutely certain that fundamental Principles of Right and Wrong are involved in some issue that affects them spiritually, apply the "Judica me Deus" clause in their conscious contact with Cosmos. This comes from Psalm 42, "Judge me, O God, and distinguish my cause from the unholy ones, deliver me from the unjust and deceitful man. What art Thou, O God, but my strength, why hast Thou repelled me? Why should I be sad while mine enemies afflict me? Send forth Thy Light and Truth. They have led me to The Holy Mountain and Thy tabernacles."

In other words and deeds, Initiates of Light direct their feelings of injustice not against those human agents associated with such a sad state, but straight to the Source of Judgment controlling Cosmos Itself. The Supreme Court of Appeal. As with an Earthly Court, this is a very serious and drastic step to take, for it will infallibly be dealt with on very High levels, and in the re-establishment of equilibrium between the plaintiffs and their accused before the Throne, drastic action may result involving the former to whatever extent they may be responsible for the latter's behavior. Only those with the clearest of consciences should dare invoke such a level of Judgment. Once a "Judica me" has been applied, it cannot be revoked. Only IHVH and ELOHIM have the Keys here. They are Discerning.

Creatively, this path is followed through the offices of Archangels RATZIEL and TZAPHKIEL. To Proclaim and Observe. Judgment must be proclaimed clearly and distinctly for all concerned with its course to observe its effects. As one authority remarked, "It is not enough that Justice has been done, it must be *seen* to have been done." The same applies to any Judgment invoking the action of Justice. Here, we must observe with Understanding and proclaim with Wisdom. Only so can we hope to make a proper Judgment on any issue. This Path is extremely plain and definite on that point.

The associated Principle is Experience, and without enough experience, who is able to judge anything effectively? How does anyone gain experience? By living and judging. The Circle of Cosmos. The Supreme Spirit of Life is naturally able to work by the experience of every single life within It, and we are also "made in the Image." As living organisms, we are, at any time of Our Earthlives, the sum of every experience undergone by every cell in our bodies, every thought that went through our minds, and every feeling we underwent in our souls. That is us. We can be, and usually are, much more than just that. By an ability to participate in the experience of other souls through various media such as writing, and other means of recorded awareness, we expand ourselves into a larger cosmos of shared consciousness. Others have proclaimed, and we have observed. Ratziel and Tzaphkiel Ltd. are in business. The more we share, the bigger the business grows. Nevertheless, there is much more to human experience than taking in other people's literary washing. It should be acquired on far deeper levels than these.

Individual lives though we are, right down in our spiritual depths we are connected with each other like every single tree has roots in the same earth. All those who have ever lived and died are part of us with the whole of their experience, including other lives we may have lived personally. Nothing is lost as Energy, but only altered in character. The Archetypes of Existence continue always. If we were able to draw deeply enough from this supply of what has been called the Collective Consciousness, there would be no need for each of us to go on plodding through the same material effectively dealt with long ago by others. We should be free from that necessity in order to devote our lives toward far more important objectives. This is the liberty of Life which each Initiate seeks for himself and every other soul besides. By linking their Life-Principles with sufficiently In-reaching connections of consciousness, Initiates of Light confidently expect to gain experience directly from the Spirit of Life Itself, however much this must be adapted and reduced to suit their individual capacities.

Why should any soul be limited to just one little Earthlife at a single point of Time-Space-Events? There is no real reason why any of us should be satisfied with this meagre ration of Existence if we say firmly enough to our Cosmic Controller: "Please, Sir—I want some more." On the other hand, why should we insist on going all through what everyone else has already accumulated for our benefit? The sensible thing for any soul to do, is take Life on from the point others leave off. It is a question of going deeply enough in ourselves to find the linkage with all the lives we have ever led and that others have lived in our Cosmic Company. This is the vital Inner Experience which Initiates of the Mysteries look for here. On the Tree of Life, RATZIEL and TZAPHKIEL have the Keys of this Path.

Formatively, the Fourteenth Path is administered by the Angel Orders of the AUPHANIM and the ARALIM. The Thrones, and the Circlers. Here we have an instant picture of Conscious Cosmos as Understanding remaining enthroned centrally while Wisdom circles around it in all directions to experience Life from every angle. Wisdom "goes out and gets," while Understanding "stays at home and receives." The Male and Female roles of polarized living. The Ins and Outs of Existence. The going forth and returning to itself of every Cosmic Circle.

The Principle linked with this section of the Fourteenth Path is Definition. All must be defined into what it is and should become. The definitions of every living creature is in its seed on all life-levels. Things are defined by description from every possible point, and this is just what the Auphanim are doing in conjunction with the Aralim. We might do worse than follow their example. Enthroning an idea, problem, or any unit of Cosmos and then running rings around it is a good way of gaining Wisdom. Staying still in the heart of everything and considering the courses of consciousness around us is an excellent way of reaching Understanding. We can learn both techniques on this Path, and they will give us the judgment we need to define Life in all its terms. How often do we approach any matter directly and come to what seems like a dead stop which annoys, irritates, or otherwise disturbs us? Many times a day, probably. Serious stoppages may hold us up for lifetimes, or impede our spiritual progress to very considerable extents. The obvious answer, as this Path shows, is to think and experience our way around whatever we have struck. A blind person defines anything by feeling all around its surface. A sighted person covers everything in view with a visual focal point and fills in the rest from imaginative memory-comparison banks of consciousness. Here we do just the same spiritually as an act of Inner Will. It makes all the difference between shutting the eyes, putting a finger on anything, then trying to guess its nature and, still with closed eyes, running both hands freely all over the surface of the object. This makes definition possible. Between Understanding Inside, and Wisdom Outside, all may be Known, Judged, and Defined to any degree of Existence.

Nor should we forget the function of the Auphanim as circular crushing-rollers originally intended for grinding grain or squeezing grapes. In that respect they equate with the "Mills of God," as they reduce what passes through them to basic materials ready for processing in other ways. If we use them properly, we shall work them with Wisdom in order to produce a worthy Bread and Wine oblation to enthrone on the altars of Understanding at the other end of this Path. The Aralim are just exactly that, for our Earthly symbolic altars should be intended and dedicated as thrones for a Deity who Understands the purpose of every ritual practice concerned therewith. Crushing rollers in older times also processed olives into oil which provided both a valuable nutriment and fuel for lamps which gave light for studying the Sacred law and fire for the sacrificial flames on Temple altars. Another example of Aralim-Auphanim partnership.

To this day we speak of "smoothing out" the difficulties in our lives, and that is typical of Auphanic procedures as we work with wisdom going over things again and again until they present a far more level and even surface for us to Understand by the Illumination shining from the altar-shrine we have dedicated to Divinity Within us. Life becomes quite a lot easier with the help of Auphanim if we use them to roll out the rough places on our personal Paths, yet without injuring the least feelings of other entities or crushing their souls to the slightest degree. The ARALIM and AUPHANIM between them will show us the secrets of this procedure if we ask them in the right way. They have the necessary Keys here.

Expressively, on this Path, we find the Symbols of Saturn and the Zodiac linked with the Principle of Adaption. The basic rule of Life every soul has to learn the hard way is the well known "Adapt—or Die!" Actually Death itself is an adaption or change from one set of Life-Dimensions to another, so perhaps the adage should be, "Adapt—and Experience." Adaptation certainly describes one noted definition of Magic in which it was claimed that Magic is the art of change in conformity with Will. For adequate adaptation, judgment is needed, and without that ability we cannot adapt ourselves properly to any arrangement of Life, for adaptation is not being forced or compelled by any external factors, but a deliberate auto-adjustment by the organism itself to suit changes of Life-energies affecting its existence, or for the purpose of initiating such changes on its own account. Circumstances may be such that the only possible adaptation is physical death which should be treated as part of the adaptive process. Everything depends on how the Will of an entity determines its reactive adaptation to Life. Our degrees of adaptability mark our measures as specimens of Mankind. The best adaptors usually make the best Life-types for any given condition of fatal Consciousness.

The Zodiac-belt is the practical Symbol of a complete course of Solar Consciousness. It covers an entire Time-Space-Event Cycle of adaptive Life to all the seasons and circumstances of a Solar system. If we see ourselves as Suns of our own Cosmic Systems, then we have the equivalents of Zodiacs around us also, and should adapt accordingly. Whatever "Birth Sign" we may belong to in respect of Outer Cosmos, we can progress through them all Inwardly at Will. It makes a very good "occult exercise" to take any chosen subject, set it up in ourselves, and then go around it like a Zodiac, experiencing and adapting ourselves to it from the twelve Zodiacal Sign-points, identifying with each in turn as we go. Most satisfying Rites can be built up out of this simple principle, and it does help adaptive abilities very considerably.

Old Saturn signifies the decisive factor of weight which tips the balance of Life one way or the other. In fact, if we think of this Path as being not unlike the yard-arm of a Balance, with the Middle Pillar of the Tree as its Upright, Saturn on the left as the adaptive weight, and the Zodiac on the right as the Scale on which the issue is read, we shall gain some good ideas about how to proceed here. It will also indicate how we ourselves are judged as creatures of Cosmos. There is a very great deal of information to be had out of this particular consideration. Saturn is not associated with Fate for nothing, for it represents our Last Judgments in any matter before committing ourselves to any kind of irretrievable activity. That might even be fatal in the worst sense of the word if our judgment is wrong. Saturn has only been regarded as sinister because so many people make such wrong judgments with such fatal results. The fault is ours, not Saturn's.

If we learned the art of relying on Saturnian stability and weight of Understanding before leaping casually over the Abyss of non-return into Life-action, our lives could be gauged far more accurately on the Scales of Cosmic Value. Saturn is not really an enemy of anyone. We have just not discovered how to make friends along his level. The legend of Saturn's "Golden Age" on Earth, due to his consort Rhea's understanding treatment of her husband, might still help us. It could be an idea to try the same methods that she did, providing these are brought up to date and adapted in a manner to suit occasions of use. This story should definitely be read and meditated upon by those intending to work this Fourteenth Path properly. Saturn and the Zodiac are the legitimate guardians of its Keys brought expressly into physical projection.

The Fifteenth Path

SPHERE—LETTER CODE:	Wisdom 2 G 4 Mercy	
DIVINE ORIGINATION:	IHVH—EL	The
		Beneficent
ARCHANGELIC CREATION:	Ratziel—Zadkiel	Constancy
ANGELIC FORMATION:	Auphanim—Chasmalim	Improvement
APPARENT EXPRESSION:	Zodiac—Jupiter	Cohesion
TAROT SYMBOL:	EMPEROR	

It is tempting to associate this Path with "G for Good." There is so much beneficence in it that a cautious traveller is apt to be wary in the presence of so many obvious advantages. The prevailing picture is one of a mercifully wise Overlord being constantly magnanimous for the sake of improving and keeping his cosmic Empire together—almost too good to be true from the human viewpoint of those conditioned to Life by experience in this world.

The Empire here, of course, is certainly "not of this world," but if Earth were the only world we ever expected to live in, we might as well abandon a search for any better living conditions, and such a course would mean spiritual suicide of the most hopeless kind. Either we admit the likelihood of an Inner Empire to which we seek admission and eventual full membership or we do not. If we do, and Initiates of these Paths can scarcely admit less, then this is the type of Emperor we shall have to acknowledge, and whose principles of ruling must be applied to ourselves. Matters are as simple as that. A straight Yes or No will solve this problem

The Tarot Symbol of the Emperor is relatively uncomplicated for a Waite representation. For once, the Figure is undeniably male, clad almost in the style of Charlemagne, and seated on a grey stone throne with rams' heads finials. His crown is tensided, and his scepter an elongated Ankh, or T-cross surmounted with a circle.

The background of the picture is an odd one, giving an over-all impression of regal red-gold, the lower half of which is so folded and creased that certainty of form is almost impossible. There is perhaps the slightest hint of heavily draped or concealed statuary, but, if so, the figures would be headless. Maybe "in-definition" describes what lies behind the Emperor's throne. If this applies, it would seem consistent with the ideas connected with this Trump. What else is an Emperor for, except to give rul-ings on unclear issues, straighten out and simplify complicated procedures, and bring hidden affairs to light? In that sense, the Emperor here might be presiding at an unveiling occasion when what lies in the background is about to be revealed to those ac-cepting his authority. On this Path between Wisdom and Mercy, we would believe that such revelations could only be beneficial, and if we are prepared to trust the Emperor, he will only show us what will be helpful in a kindly and pleasing way. There is noth-ing whatsoever frightening or formidable about the draped masses behind him.

The throne is gray, the shade of Wisdom, the finials of its arms being ram's heads, and those of its back ram's skulls. Rams, Sign of Aries, signify the opening forces of Life at the commence-ment of any cycle, and the determination to enter anywhere by means of sheer power brought to a head. In old times, battering rams smashed their way into sealed cities. Nowadays, their equivalents make "breakthroughs" in all fields of discovery. This last is the sort of ram to be associated with the Emperor's throne. The back of the throne being surmounted by skulls means that it is both wise and merciful to let the past die its natural death and be powerless to harm us while we uphold the dignifies of the Tra-ditions it taught us. The active rams' heads on the arms of the throne indicate that we should face our future with courageous intent, providing we act in accordance with the Symbols the Em-peror holds above each head.

The golden scepter which the Emperor holds with thumb up-ward (a will to Mercy) in his right hand, represents the principles of rulership he upholds. It is a T-cross surmounted by a circle, the proportions being that the horizontal bar of the T is a quarter of the vertical stem. Four to one, bar nothing in terms of odds. To be four times as upright as we are broad in terms of Life-proportions. As a Symbol, it stands for government of Life by a clear circle of conscience and consciousness through which all can be seen in proper perspective. In his left hand, also with upward pointing thumb, is a plain gold orb with only a very small sapphire at its top to indicate which way it should be held. This shows an Emperor should adopt an equable attitude to all his subjects but allow the quality of Mercy to decide any finalizing decisions.

The Emperor himself is white-haired and bearded to typify wisdom and dignity with benevolence. He is in full armor of blue steel covered with a scarlet surcoat to signify he is strongly and firmly clad with Mercy, any semblance of severity being but an external appearance. This is confirmed by his purple mantle blending both qualities together. His crown is composed of ten "Tablet of Law" type of plates, only five being visible, two of them bearing rubies and the others showing nothing except empty settings, probably intended for pearls. This is the Crown of Wisdom, which Solomon considered far more valuable than earthly gems. The ten "Tables of the Law" are, of course, the Commandments and the Sephiroth, or any decimal system of relationship with Divine Consciousness. It is summed up into a "topknot" of the "Endless Triplicity" type, the three-into-one theme being the Christian Trinitarian closure-concept of Creation, but also the triplicities of the Life-Tree layout as well. This reminds us that the Sephiroth are all tied together in threes in order to make sense as a single whole which makes the extra complete Concept.

With the Emperor on the Life-Tree at this point, we have to learn the Wisdom of Mercy, providing we fully realize the extent of each. It may not always be wise to over-extend Mercy, but it is always merciful in the long run to extend Wisdom. A true balance of power has to be achieved upon each Path in order to work it properly. Here the real quality of the "Emperorship" has to be acquired by whoever would be "Master of the Fifteenth Path." As usual, the Path-Principles must be applied in ourselves before they will work for anyone anywhere else. Everybody has to be their own Emperor—even God.

An Emperor, of course, is a King of Kings. One who rules rulers. An indispensible Powerpoint for any collection of Cosmoi intending to remain in confederacy together for their mutual benefit. There has to be some common control-point for even the smallest and most insignificant set of Systems with even the least idea of interrelationship. On this Path, we have to deal with the Emperor-Ideal for Entire Existence, and also for the well-being of every living soul. No less. How better could anyone choose to be governed than by Wisdom and Mercy? The Emperor is certainly an ideal Symbol for this particular Path.

Wise Mercy is scarcely an easy quality to define. Be it particularly noted there is no weakness whatever implied in this Path, or any acceptance of injustices, permission of malpractices, or condoning of social and spiritual evils suggested. Here is a *Wise* Mercy, not a *weak* or ineffectual one. It is most important to realize this. True Mercy and stupidity have no Path on the Tree at all. Mercy in this case is knowing and doing whatever is right and best in every instance of intelligent Existence. It is never merciful to permit the practice of evil. It is certainly never wise to do so.

We might remember also about this Path that it is one of the "Chasm-crossers." By its nature, this clearly indicates that whatever is not fit to be allowed across the Abyss yet could not be prevented from forcing itself past that point should be mercifully consigned to the depths forever. One is reminded of the old tale concerning a powerfully built Quaker traveling on a ship attacked by pirates. His religious principles forbade him to participate in the actual combat, but when one pirate singled him out for destruction, he hurled the man overboard, remarking calmly, "Friend, thee's not needed here." This applies exactly to this Path. Evil is unneeded in an ideal Empire.

Without excretory bodily functions we could not stay alive and healthy. Without their equivalents on spiritual scales, our Inner Cosmoi would be in danger of destruction and disease also. A constipated Cosmos is truly in a sad state, which it might be merciful to put out of its misery. The Abyss serves the function of a spiritual sewage system for the merciful disposal of all that would otherwise undermine and eventually corrupt the Inner Empire which the Constructors of the Life-Tree are endeavoring to establish. Those of us who are Wise try to follow the same Plan. Whatever is unworthy of inclusion in this Empire should certainly be dealt with as a Wisely Merciful Emperor directs. Even sewage has enormous value if reduced back to its originally pure Elements and made available for re-use. We live out of reconstituted sewage in this world, and life otherwhere runs along the same lines in different dimensions of being. We have to discover how to cross the Chasm like an Emperor, and we shall live like one also.

The principles of Empire, based on Wisdom and Mercy, are the best on which to base control of Cosmos. The alternative is a state of tyrannized terror which would be unthinkable in the type of Life intended for those who follow the Tree-Paths faithfully. Every soul alive should eventually rise to rule their own Inner Empires, and assume responsibility for their particular Life-realms. There are very many minor kingdoms in us. Every organ in our bodies is a state of its own with its peculiar purpose and function. Either all those organizations are loyal to the Individual in whom they are integrated, or they are not. Disloyalty means disease, discontent, disharmony, and eventually dissolution. This is so in the case of people, countries, nations, and entire worlds. In order to exist as a healthy and happy Cosmos, it is necessary to have loyalty and support from every In-group which counts as a "kingdom," toward the Empiric Principle of Government which co-ordinated them all. Whether this Principle is personified as the soul of a single human being, or a Head of State, or as a Divine Aspect, makes no difference except in practice. Somehow it should be seen and recognized as an Imperative Consciousness in which others unite for the sake of sharing supremacy as a state of being among them. That is what being an imperator means. It is a state which is reachable by anyone who has full command of himself, and it should be attained, as this Path shows, by merciful Wisdom.

However much modernists enjoy confusing vital issues, there is still only one behavior-control over human nature, summed up long ago as "Reward good, Punish bad." Pleasure and Pain are always the two Pillars between which Mankind has to develop toward Divinity. "Thou shalt" and "Thou shalt not" are the terms of all commandments. Here we have the "Reward" side of the issue. A System of Government producing such good results for all, that everyone accepts it gladly of his own will for the sake of its benefits alone. (Positively not of *this* world!) A Rulership that all within its realm realize to be essentially right, and therefore are satisfied to remain in its Empire. The bond throughout a state of this kind is Compassion—fellow-feeling, and this is only possible if the Head-Figure, or emperor, is universally loved and absolutely trusted. Such must be the Emperor of this path.

Originatively, we meet the Divine Aspects of IHVH and EL. "I Will Be" and "The One." "EL" is used in the sense of The, It especially, That in particular, This as distinct from others. It has always been customary to speak of the Head of any clan, tribe, or other human confederacy as "The" whatever they are. THE emperor, THE King, THE President, or THE anything. That is how "EL" is supposed to be understood here. THE Divine One. Looking down the Tree from the top, AHIH says "I AM," IHVH says "I Will Be," IHVH ELOHIM says "I Will Be All Those" and now EL says, "I Will Be This One in Particular of All Those." Life specifies itself in clearer and clearer terms as the Abstract approaches the Concrete.

Every thinking individual has asked himself the apparently unanswerable question, "Who am I?" This implies an "I" behind every "Me" who makes the "Me" into whatever the "I" wills. On this Path, we find the "Me" which the "I" projects past the Abyss on the Right Pillar of the Tree as a purely Beneficent Emperor. The Divine Benefactor of Good-doer (NOT in any sense a "Do Gooder"), Who may be relied on to do the Right thing always. The old time-worn question "How could a fundamentally 'Good' Deity permit the evident evils we all condemn in our experience of Life?" is not a very intelligent one. Deity does not permit evil at all. Deity permits *Will* and Will alone determines the Good or Evil of any issue, whether the directing Will comes from Inner Entities, or ordinary humans. To negate the Principle of Will would be to eliminate Life from Existence. Limited as our Will may be, we have the same choice of its use as a God. Who knows what Good and Evil really are except a Deity? Man is learning slowly. That is what we "fell" so far to find out.

On this Path Divinity operates as THE Beneficence. We must try and get away from nursery associations of beneficence with Father Christmas prodigality regardless of consequences. INVH Wills whatever THE Best or most Merciful Life-action. Mercy does not mean sparing any soul from anything they deserve if this will help their spiritual development and allow them to evolve into better types of being. Mercy means extending to a soul what is wisest and best for the good of that soul relative to its most direct links with Divinity. There is no point whatever, for instance, in punishing or inflicting any sort of treatment on souls which has the effect of alienating them from the Infinite. Corrective measures should not be a single degree past those needed to restore the course of a soul to its "Inner Light track." As humans, we have yet small knowledge of how Mercy works on a Divine scale. Sometimes it may look terrible to us as Death, and often what we construe as signs of Divine liberality are nothing but exhibitions of human prodigality. Divine Mercy can only be recognized by those who know what might be best for any given soul at that particular period, and who is on intimate enough terms with IHVH and EL to answer this?

Too much Mercy can be just as damaging as too much Severity, and over-benevolence may warp a soul as badly as over-deprival. The whole point at issue is that of balance. The Cosmic course of an inspirited soul is aimed at the Ultimate direction of Divinity, which in the Tree-Glyph is represented by the Middle Pillar. The Side Pillars of the Tree are those factors which keep us "on target" by relaying constant course-corrections as we evolve. Souls who can keep themselves "on course" while only relying on Divine Mercy for this principal purpose alone, are rare. Those who make no particular effort of their own Wills, and vaguely expect Divine Mercy and Providence to accomplish everything for them, are inviting some sharp course-corrections from Divine Severity. IHVH and EL can explain how they will always find a Right Ruling on this part of the Fifteenth Path. The Keys are theirs.

Creatively, Archangels RATZIEL and TZADKlEL govern this level of the Path. Ratziel we have been introduced to, but Tzadkiel is the "Righteous of God," or an Intelligence which not only knows what is right, but also chooses to do it.

The structure of the Tree, which, of course, represents Cosmos and Life in general and particular, is based on a binary code. That is to say, it always presents a double choice of issues to a determining Will which lead in turn to another such choice until a *ne plus ultra* is reached and an objective is either temporarily or permanently achieved. The real expert using such a system takes both offered alternatives and does his own computation between them, thus making a Middle Pillar of Progression for himself. That still keeps him in a binary frame working at right angles so to speak, because in deciding a course between alternatives, there is still a Right and Wrong course of action or inaction, depending on objective or Will. TZADKIEL, the Right-chooser, is the Inner Personification of an inherent faculty for making a series of right choices through any set of life-circumstances in all Dimensions of living. If ever Mankind needs a "Good Angel," Tzadkiel is the best Being to invoke.

This is the significance of the forked Rod Symbol, so often wrongly seen as an evil emblem. That is only because when driven to making decisions by the Eternal Dilemma (which is the binary code of the Universe), humans so often make the wrong choice which lands them in more trouble. No wonder such a fork is frequently placed in the "Devil's" hands, instead of being grasped, as it ought to be, firmly by its central staff, representing the deliberate decisions of an Initiate's True Will. Everything depends on whether we are poked around by a forked rod by another being like someone trying to catch a serpent, or whether, like the Wise Serpent, we coil ourselves sapiently around the center staff of the Rod in a Cosmic Solar direction. Tzadkiel provides us with the Wisdom to choose the Merciful outcome of any dilemma for ourselves.

How are we humans supposed to know the rights and wrongs of anything? Our definitions of good and evil apply only to ourselves. Some Cosmic-sized Being might consider it a good thing from Its point of view to wipe all human beings out of existence and thus clear up a lot of Inner irritation. We should scarcely think this a good idea, however much we might ruefully admit its possible justification. In order to discover this knowledge of the difference between Right and Wrong, or the correct Cosmic use of Will, is surely why we become human. It is a major Life-motive which has cost us endless incarnations to work out. An old esoteric tradition says that the minimum number of incarnations for achieving ATTAINMENT are three. One to discover What NOT to do, another to discover WHAT to do, and the last to decide with WILL, a perfect Path between them.

Inner Man has been visualized as having two Angels in attendance, one Black and one White. The Black one warns him against any course of ill-action, and the White one advises him what is best to do. After listening to both, it must still be a free decision of the True Will which ultimately determines the course any individual soul keeps. That vital Right is what we incarnate to earn each for ourself—the hard way! In this instant, TZAD-KIEL is the White Angel offering the good advice which we must only take if it is our own Inner Decision to do so. Nor should this Archangel be blamed if we have not heard his suggestions properly. He speaks in a very soft whisper.

His path-partner RATZIEL, is, to the contrary, a proclaimer aloud for those that have ears to hear. He usually speaks so loud and so long that the sound deafens us, and we do not have time enough in one life to catch the end of perhaps a single word he says. It has always been a tradition of practical Magic that Words of Power used in Rites should be very long drawn-out and loudly proclaimed. The Ratziel method. If he tells all the secrets of Cosmos, and we hear only one word in a human lifetime, it will take us a lot of evolution to become really Wise. Yet—that is the Way we learn the Laws of Spiritual Light. In the same way we have to learn the Inner Alphabet of the Tree. A Letter at a time, until we grow big enough to make Words of Inner Power from them.

The associative word at this part of this Path is Constancy. Being true to a cause believed in as Right. Unless we are constant to our causes and courses, we shall get nowhere worth arriving at in any direction of Cosmos. Constancy is our built-in auto-corrector extending throughout the Cosmos of Inner Consciousness in which we must live so that we can have Existence as souls in our own Life-right. Here, we have to listen for the background Sphere-Music of Ratziel's large-scale proclamations, and, contrasting this with the "still small voice" of Tzadkiel speaking in our conscience, make the "bleeps" which keep us constantly "on course" through our Inner Cosmic Journey to the Infinite. It is not unlike using a telescope and a microscope to arrive at accurate life-conclusions. Scientists do this constantly. So should Initiates of the Inner sciences make use of their con-science, or "with-knowing." Ratziel and Tzadkiel will demonstrate how to do this. They have the Keys here.

Formatively, we travel this Path in company with the Angel Orders of the AUPHANIM and the CHASMALIM. The Auphanim, or Circlers, we know, and the Chasmalim signify the "Bright and affluently Splendid Ones." Just the sort of Angels to deal with Beneficence. They also indicate the benignant power of Fire, or pleasing Light and warmth associated with hospitality and geniality. We can think of them as "Flames of Fusion" in the

sense of using heat Constructively and beneficially, as in thera-
peutic instances. They link with Life-warmth, or government of temperatures necessary for sustaining Life-forms in
their most favorable conditions of Existence. They may well be
thought of as agents of Divine Mercy for either providing suitable
living-climates or suggesting means of life-survival in otherwise
impossible places. This is not only so physically, but also, and
perhaps more importantly, in Spiritual Dimensions.

Between them, the AUPHANIM and the CHASMALIM
have to circulate what amounts to Spiritual "Life-Blood" through
the Cosmic System. Merciful and welcome warmth is not purely a
static energy, but a circulatory one corresponding in many ways
with the circulation of blood through our bodies. Blood must be
warm, or we die, though not too warm, or we become fevered and
still die. Our bodies have wonderful control-mechanisms for
maintaining this "Life degree," and our spiritual systems are entitled to no less. There is a correct "Inner temperature" needed to
maintain a soul in good living condition, and the Chasmalim are
certainly connected with the "warmth compensation" factor in
this respect. Should an Inner climate get too frosty and frigid for
comfort, they control the thermostat which should thaw us into
easier atmospheres of Inner Life. As this Path indicates, such
would be both a Wise and a Merciful act.

At this point, we meet the idea of improvement. Beneficence
is not only a maintenance of *status quo* but should be directed towards making the beneficed objective just somewhat better than
previously. This does not mean altering its nature out of all proportions, but assisting its evolution at the correct "rate for state."
All life has a natural rate for improvement beyond which its existence is imperiled. In the case of our Outer Cosmos, the Zodiacal
Cycle provides a standard reference for mundane Time, and the
Auphanim set the Life-rates in Spiritual Dimensions. Here we
see them working with the Chasmalim on this Fifteenth Path in
order to make sure that living beings are not improved or evolved
at a greater rate than they can stand with safety. The Principles
of improvement are that constant evolutionary changes must occur at a rate which still allows the Identity of the improving Entity to remain Itself. Any rate-acceleration past this self-safety
mark turns improvement into dissolution. This may even be necessary when improvement-response ceases in reply to spiritual

stimuli.

In order to determine this "improvability" factor, some of the old Mysteries made use of Mazes into which they introduced soul-subjects, much as a modern psychologist does with rats and other creatures. A Maze is a miniature ground-plan of a Cosmos with a central or other objective, which is only reachable after a series of dilemmas or "yes-no" choices have been successfully passed through. The Mystery-Mazes were, and still can be, wonderful training devices for spiritual development if they are properly arranged. A really well programmed Maze is a valuable asset to any Temple, providing skilled Initiates are available to set it up. Here, the Zodiac Circles and the Auphanim cycles can supply the basic Pattern of a Maze while the Right-setting Chasmalim may give the Right Light for guiding souls past all Dilemmas, or Cosmic computer-paths they are likely to meet with. They have the Keys.

Expressively, the Zodiac and Jupiter associate with this Path by the Principle of Cohesion. If we received all the benefits Jupiter was supposed by astrologers to bring through the Twelve signs, we should be theoretically satiated on every life-level. The most modern astrology is discovering that Jupiter is by no means the Great Benefic in the prodigal sense once attributed to that planet. Jupiter's blessing can often be likened to a diabetic person winning the prize box of candies in a raffle, while a chronic alcoholic gains a crate of whiskey with another ticket. True, the diabetic *could* give the sweets away, and the alcoholic sell the whiskey or exchange it for something else, but—? Jupiter's benefits are seldom any good to those who cannot handle them properly. To get any real value from them, the Right choice of action, or Decision of Will, must inevitably be made. Jupiter's gifts are unlikely to bring automatic blessings with them. They are all highly qualified by attached strings which need to be pulled very carefully. Pull the wrong one, and the benefit is liable to blow up in one's face.

A nice Maze-Pattern can be worked out with Jupiter and the Zodiac, by noting what effect the planet is said to have in each sign, and asking oneself "Yes-No" queries about all the points that come to light. A Quiz is really a Maze worked in theory, or consciousness put through a computer-circuit. In a sense, our lives are Mazes at the end of which we decide what we, in ourselves, really amount to. Do we cohere to our Cosmic Principles or do we not? A lot may depend on our answer.

Cohesion means that a number of separate units relate together for the sake of being something as a whole. Cosmos. The real benefit of being anything. The Mercy in manifestation. Cohesion is not compulsion, but staying in association because of an attractive force existing between all the integers. Cosmically, this is all our individual Wills freely extended among each other from a motive of Compassion (fellow-feeling) and Companionship. (Com-pan-ions, together-all-wanderers). This is the sort of contact which might be expected on the Fifteenth Path. Coherency signifies welcome clarity, and this is most certainly a benefit worth having to make any world livable in. The biggest blessing Jupiter could possibly bestow on any soul is the Mercy of Wisdom. Wisdom to make Right use of Will.

So many people have got in the somewhat mistaken habit of connecting Jupiter only with material largesse, that we are very apt to overlook the spiritual equivalents that are more likely to be available if we take advantage of them. Constant complaints are heard about Jupiter that, although a particularly good aspect of that planet occurred in someone's horoscope, he seemed to have no noteworthy luck on that occasion. No winnings, no legacies, no nice surprises, and in fact, his material circumstances might even be a little worse than usual. Rotten old Jupiter again! Such complainants have quite failed to look for Jupiter's luck in themselves rather than their affairs. Jupiter should provide a largesse of mind and soul which affords an Inner ability to deal with otherwise overwhelming difficulties. Jupiter is big, magnanimous, and, above all, optimistic. His main fault is over-optimism, which tends to encourage carelessness, and yet without optimism to some degree, there would be little incentive to do much in this world of ours. In every Sign of the Zodiac, Jupiter offers some kind of optimism and Inner buoyancy which should enable souls to tackle the problems of that Sign with confidence. That is his special personal gift which we cannot afford to refuse—optimistic self-confidence. On the other hand, if a soul is so greedy for this that he snatches far more than his fair share, then he should not blame Jupiter for what happens to him.

Jupiter's benefits on both Inner and Outer Life-levels are meant to be shared out in circles, as this Zodiac-Jupiter shows on the Fifteenth Path. The old adage about the trouble shared being a trouble halved, has to be matched with the equal truism that a joy shared should be a joy doubled. If Jupiter gives us no more to share than a smile and a cheery greeting, those will not only go a long way, but might quite well be productive of much more in the long run, as every ordinary salesman learns early in his career. On this Path, we are supposed to learn the art of gift-giving in a wise and merciful way. Not alone on material levels, but especially along spiritual lines. The right thing to be given the right soul in the right circumstances. Otherwise there is little point in giving anyone anything. Unwise gifts are a curse rather than a blessing, bringing little luck to the receiver or giver. The Zodiac combinations of Jupiter relationships should provide a useful "giving-guide" to those who work this Path with the care it well deserves. For the Keys of this process we must consult Jupiter in concert with the entire Zodiac Circle, where we shall learn when and how to give to whom what should pass between us on the Fifteenth Path.

The Sixteenth Path

SPHERE—LETTER CODE	Wisdom 2 H 6 Beauty	
DIVINE ORIGINATION:	IHVH—ELOAH va	The
	DAATh	Mediating
ARCHANGELIC CREATION:	Ratziel—Michael	Patience
ANGELIC FORMATION:	Auphanim—Malakim	Carefulness
APPARENT EXPRESSION:	Zodiac—Sun	Elasticity
TAROT SYMBOL:	TEMPERANCE	

On this Sixteenth Path, we immediately gain the impression of a Beautiful Wisdom which, for the sake of holding everything together in harmonious and balanced Cosmos, mediates all within itself by patience and care, stretching points as far as they will comfortably go while being entirely temperate throughout the whole process. A picture to inspire confidence in even the most timorous soul trembling before the Abyss.

The Tarot Symbol here shows a great Angelic Figure of asexual aspect poised between land and water in the act of pouring water into a wine cup. This Being's wings are purple to show the Severity-Mercury balance, its hair is gold and the head shining with pure light to indicate its motivation by the highest possible purposes, This is confirmed by the Great Name IHVH made by the upper folds of its white robe and the Solar Symbol on its forehead, plus the Lamen of Light on its breast.

The background of the picture is interesting. On the left is a pleasing green landscape with a very reasonable pathway leading between two jagged and dangerous looking mountains into a Crown of Light. This says plainly enough that those of temperate persuasions may expect a relatively smooth path through Life, passing between its mountainous problems safely into a Heavenly reward. To the right is a bed of yellow flags, or water iris. In mythology, Iris was one of the Oceanides, her particular mission being to sever the thread of life between body and soul for those having difficulty with dying. She also signified the rainbow, an almost universal symbol for heavenly hopes. Thus, the entire set-out of this Symbol speaks of moderate and temperate procedures leading to immortal Life in Peace Profound.

The Solar Symbol on the forehead of the Angel, and the IHVH of the robe, seem to locate very positively with this IHVH-Solar Path. The white square and gold triangle on the Angel's breast say quite simply: "Man, purify yourself and direct your thoughts to the Apex of Light Itself." The water pouring from one cup to the other is both a libation and a purificatory stream shown as four waves because of passing through the four worlds. Even the ripples on the water beneath the Angel are of the mildest kind, to indicate a minimum of disturbance in Life.

We are actually observing the Angel in the act of thoughtfully mixing water with the Wine of pure Wisdom for the benefit of those who would otherwise find this too strong for them. Most human beings cannot possibly drink such a potent draught neat, so it must be watered down to suitable degrees for us. Unless this moderation were made on our behalf, the resultant state of confusion, mental intoxication, irresponsible behavior and muddle would put us quite out of the running.

Wisdom is the strongest Wine of all. God help those who over-imbibe it into systems unable to mediate its influence. To them it can be the most powerful poison they are likely to encounter. Ultimately they may destroy themselves on this account, but seldom before they have done a considerable amount of damage all around them. Let the havoc wrought by an ordinarily violent and disgustingly drunken human in terms of mess, mayhem, and murder be imagined, then projected into Inner parallel states, and some idea may be had of the danger-liability from intoxication on those Life-levels. The possibilities are appalling. Yet even the most potent poison we can produce ourselves, such as prussic acid, may be safely and beneficially taken into our systems when diluted to the correct degree. Temperance is Wisdom making itself into suitable doses for all sorts of souls.

It is most unwise to demand more Wisdom than a soul can distribute through its system in a balanced and harmonious manner. Our history is crammed with horrible examples of disaster from such causes. Asylums, graveyards, battlefields, and every variety of human scrap-heap are piled with the casualties of over-stimulated consciousness. Attempts at force-educating, instructing, or exposing to wisdom, classes of soul quite unprepared or insufficiently developed to absorb such concentrated Inner Energy, are not only wrong, but very cruel and inconsiderate. Our modern society is suffering quite enough from such stupidity already, and there may well be worse to come.

The whole problem of education (*e-ducare*: to bring qualities *out* of someone) is how to classify and arrange tuition in order to get the best consistent results from the sort of souls who are in this process of being led out of themselves. In other words, how to temper Truth suitably for every category of consciousness exposed to it. If this is the principal problem of ordinary educators, it becomes magnified in the case of those responsible for managing the practical processes of the Holy Mysteries. Intemperate and unwise imbibing of Inner Wisdom can result in many fatal forms of spiritual intoxication. We have only to glance sadly at the terrible trail of religious insanities, misunderstandings, persecutions, and other human horrors through our history, to realize what happens when, to put it crudely, Man gets a bad overdose of God.

For this reason, the Inner Mystery Schools instituted systems of degrees, so that all entrants could be sure of evolving through their Inner education by a series of safe stages, each stage suitable for some particular point of expanding and extending themselves in compatible ways with the Cosmic growth of their souls. Thus was the progress of souls safeguarded by means of Beautifully Wise Temperance. Everything was made as pleasantly easy as possible for those with the Wisdom to follow this Path. Such Wisdom is not very common among ordinary humans, and so, if they insist on being intemperate, and getting themselves hurt as well as injuring others, they will be left to learn the hard and uncomfortable ways. It must be to them AS THEY WILL WITHIN THEM.

An enlightened Initiate only seeks whatever degree of LIGHT can safely be borne by the condition of his soul. Naturally there is a reasonable tolerance-factor, and this is decided by the particular temperament of an individual or group of persons. That is the degree of Temperance needed. The decisive point is that of BALANCE. How far can a soul extend itself safely without losing its own central control? To what degree may that soul maintain its Cosmic course-correction? That is the safety-margin which decides for everyone exactly how the energies of Inner Wisdom must be tempered in his particular case. Knowledge of this degree-factor is as vital from a spiritual standpoint as awareness of a blood-group on physical levels. This was what "Degrees" were supposed to mean in the genuine Mystery Schools. They were "Truth tags" or spiritual specification labels which clearly indicated the exact requirements of the soul-organism they protected. Since a soul is a living creation, the Degree-descriptions naturally altered according to its Inner Growth.

These Inner Degrees were usually ascertained by a series of patterned tests and "ordeals" on the lines of modern I.Q. and other suitability estimations. Once the true Inner soul-status could be recognized, that particular soul might then be dealt with fairly and honestly, treated properly, and provided with whatever facilities it needed for its best natural development. The Light of Truth was tempered to its most beneficial degree for the soul in search of it.

The lesson of this Path is unmistakably clear. We must learn how to relate Wisdom and Balance, or the Poise of Power by the use of Temperance. Not Abstinence, be it noted, but Temperance, the balanced and wise use of anything in Existence. The message might be interpreted as, "DO WHAT THOU WILT, but be CAREFUL." *Aude Sapere—sed Cautuus*. "Dare to be Wise—but carefully." It should also be remembered that this Path is another Chasm-crosser by its own technique. Since the Symbolic Bridge is along a Sword-edge, strict Temperance is a *sine qua non* for the task, the care comes in by watching the Line of Light reflected down the edge, and progressing along it with such caution that balance is maintained the whole time of the danger-period. This is the degree of care necessary to cross Cosmic Chasms by concentrated consciousness. Some Temples actually made physical Sword-Bridges, and trained their Initiates to cross them. Virtually the same degree of skill can now be developed by anyone driving vehicles in modern traffic—at greater risk!

Temperance is essentially an act of control directed by Will, normally for the benefit or welfare of some soul or souls. It does not in any sense imply narrow-mindedness, meanness, or senseless strictures on behavior or aims. One might say that another name for Temperance was Economy—avoidance of waste and un-necessary use of energy for achieving specified objectives. An in-telligent and sapient way of working as against the "brute force and ignorance" methods of the less instructed. Few qualities show up the Beauty of Wisdom like Temperance does. It is cer-tainly the valid Symbol for this Path. By developing Temperance, the Initiate discovers the secret of redirecting energies which would otherwise knock him off his Path, into valuable means of propulsion along that Path towards his Purpose. Temperance does not mean inaction, but the intentional direction of action. A drunken driver swerves from side to side, and an intoxicated walker lurches violently from right to left, because they can no longer control the energy needed to keep their vehicles confined to a sensibly straight or consistently curving course. So they come to grief. So do those who suffer from spiritual inebriation, because they cannot toe the line of this Path properly.

To be "God-intoxicated" is NOT a wise procedure, despite the enthusiasm of various Mystics obviously "hooked" on Deity drugs. All drugs are valuable when properly used for the right purposes on the Temperate Path, but Divinity is the most dan-gerous drug that exists, and should be rightly placed first on the entire list. It is small wonder that Deity is strongly proscribed by Socialist States, and discouraged throughout Democracies by far more devious and less obvious procedures, which are actually of much greater effect than the sternest prohibitions. An addiction to Divinity can call abilities and potentialities out of humans which no chemically based drug could possibly reach. Marx was mistaken in supposing religion to be purely an opiate. Spiritual stimulants have evoked energies from mankind that have brought about major changes in our civilizations again and again. Not all of them have been for the best at the time, and it is not impossible that former errors may be repeated on more fatal lines.

Experienced Initiates in the Mystery Schools are very well aware of these dangers. When one of their number showed any signs of becoming "God-intoxicated," they usually arranged some practical way of de-toxifying their companion before any serious harm was done. They were all subject to that hazard, just as atomic workers are liable to radiation damage. Outside these controlled circles, of course, it is not so possible to apply Principles of Temperance in the case of souls who are not directly subject to spiritual discipline immediately stemming from an Inner authority. Sooner or later the Laws of Cosmos must surely operate compensatory procedures, but the closer spiritual irregularities can be confined to their individual circles, the less contagion is likely to spread through the soul-systems they are liable to infect.

That is why this Path is so important. It is not that Divinity or any other Energy is dangerous to us in or for Itself, any more than the most potent drugs we can think of are likely to harm us when therapeutically applied. The danger lies in our own inadequacies and inabilities to make full use effectively of Temperance in these matters, and it is *within ourselves* we shall have to set up such a faculty with the help of the authorities governing this Path.

Originatively, we meet with the Divine Aspects of IHVH and ELOAH va DAATh. I Will Be, and the Spirit of Experience. A relationship of discovery in both directions, humanity and Divinity gaining knowledge of each other by experience of existence along each other's lines. This can happen as many ways as there are possibilities of existing, but in this case it is the guarded way of temperate caution, which may seem slow and usually unspectacular, but is structurally the most suitable for souls who, sensibly enough, see no good reasons for exposing themselves to quite unnecessary and unprofitable risks on their way up the Tree of Life.

The actual Bridge across the Abyss which human souls will have to take in their final stage of spiritualization to the Ultimate, is naturally the central DAATh-KEThER one, but the other Crossings show us means and methods of procedure in accomplishing this last Life-hazard. So far, we have seen the Chasm crossed by a sheer Life-leap, and a truly Royal road rather beyond the capabilities of most souls, though positively an example for them to emulate. Now we come to the Crossing by Caution, or feeling our way step by step, which is well worth considering. Our original Spirits may have leapt Lightly into Life across the Chasm between Consideration and Creation, but on our way back we are souls burdened with a precious payload of Life experience from every incarnation. This needs careful negotiation in some way. Here we have the bit-by-bit way of getting it across.

This particular Chasm-crossing is known as the Gate of Righteousness, said to be used by Inner Entities of Justification, and also by great Teachers and Messiahs, or Avatars, who came to Earth from time to time in order to lead us Lightwards. These last have all tried to teach us temperate and careful ways of Life. Gautama Buddha even entitled his particular system "The Middle Way," and spoke endlessly about the "mean" and the "norm." The Symbol of Christianity is Man with feet pointing to Earth, head to Heaven, and both arms outstretched to balance the Upright of the Centrally dedicated Being. The Sacrificed Sacred King is a major Magical Image of Tiphereth at one end of this Path. The "God who learned by sad experience—in Man!" Our Leader-Liberator into Light.

These Avatars or Great Souls, do not have a number of different "Messages" for Mankind, but the same fundamental Truth to tell each time in ways suited for various kinds of souls in different ages and stages of evolution. There *is* no "New" Message to be given, although new means of appreciation and approach to Truth may indeed become available. Those who are awaiting or expecting some "Great Teacher" of this "New Age" to come and deliver this world from the mess we have made of it ourselves are wasting valuable time and opportunities. The "Message of the Age" is very simply that after all the received Teaching and experience the human race has had over its last several millennia of Earth-Life, it is about time we learned how to be our own Messiahs and Saviors. The Message of this Age is the Message of Melchizadek, "Be Kings and Priests forever, Rulers of Righteousness, Princes of Peace, independent of purely human ancestry, bearing the Bread of Blessings and the Wine of Wisdom." The esoteric attributions of Melchizadek were Oil, Asbestos (Protection from Fire, an indestructible Wick for an ever-burning Lamp of Truth), and a Hive of Honey (the Sweet Food of Heaven and perfect provision for Life, plus all other significance). All these points alone afford sufficient material to make the Mystery of Melchizadek a very fascinating one indeed. We ought to develop it. It is the only "Message" we are likely to receive during our era.

IHVH and ELOAH va DAATh combine to find out what Life is all about in a well-balanced and reasonable way. Combining these "God-Names" usually provides interesting information. If, for instance, we take all the God-Names of the Spheres, and read them in sequence, they sound like Divinity describing Itself in very definite terms. The Names from 1 to 10 say, "I Am, and I Will Be, of All Divinities, the One Almighty Deity, knowing and Experiencing Every God, and all the Children of the Gods, because I am the Lord of Life and Lives, and Supreme Ruler of My Cosmic Kingdom." Perhaps more simply, "I AM ALL LIVES WITHIN ME." Whichever Points of Life we join up, there is therefore bound to be some Aspect of Divinity at each end to complete each other's Existence and make another Living-Circle. If, instead of seeing the Paths as mere straight lines statically placed on a paper diagram, we can think of them as circulatory force-fields working between Spheres, this will be a helpful aid to "Path working." Nothing to do with the Tree of Life should be imagined as flat, immobile, or in any way lifeless. It is essential that the Tree and all its characteristics should be imaginatively experienced as Living and Vital phenomena. The Tree must be brought to Life both Inwardly and Outwardly by whoever would operate its amazing energies. Until it lives properly in a soul, the Tree will be unable to provide many spiritual supplies. IHVH and ELOAH va DAATh can offer information here; they personify the Mediator Aspect of Divinity, and have the ability to relate anything and everyone together.

All that Lives must necessarily be Mediated by some common means of combining individual points of Consciousness, and an agency applying the Principles of Temperance between all factors of Existence may truly be regarded as Divine. On this Sixteenth Path, only a Divine Personification of Wisdom and Harmonious Beauty can be recognized as a satisfactory Mediator at this spiritual level of Life. We may scarcely do better than ask them their secret. They have the Keys.

Creatively, we travel the Path in company with Archangels RATZIEL and MICHAEL, who between them uphold the Principle of Patience. Who might we imagine with greater need for patience than a Being charged with instructing humanity in "Secret Spiritual Science," and another Being prepared to stand by the human race until the last fraction of good has been accomplished with it? If ever Beings stood in necessity of even temper, patient temperaments, and unlimited degrees of Temperance, Ratziel and Michael are those Archangels.

What earthly teacher could hope for success without pa-

tience? In a sense, Michael is related to the human race not unlike a Heavenly Probation Officer, and the task of that official is
trying to discover, encourage, and bring out even the least good
they can find in their charges. Probation Officers with neither patience nor Temperance are soon dismissed, if ever they were employed, in this world. Ratziel's job is giving out good teaching, and
Michael's task is finding souls good enough to make good use of it.
We think of Ratziel as an associate of the Teacher-Avatars on
this Path, and Michael as a celestial companion of the Savior and
Messiah Avatars. Together, they make up a team dedicated to
the Inner spiritual progress and well-being of human souls. They
are scarcely likely to become unemployed for the duration of
Eternity.

  This is the Path along which Inner adventurers have to acquire what they can of such Archangelic qualities as will rub off
on them from Ratziel and Michael. It may, and probably will,
take us many lifetimes to gain enough spiritual patience and intelligence to progress peacefully and temperately on our way to
Ultimate Enlightenment with good effect as we go. Nevertheless
some Inner agencies have got to be responsible for our guidance
on this difficult Path, and if we choose to know them under the
names of Ratziel and Michael, Ltd. they will gladly do business
with us on behalf of the Company they represent. If we can think
of common commercial concerns in this world under various
trade names, and deal profitably with the unseen corporation of
coordinated individuals behind these nominal Symbols, why
should we not undertake transactions of much deeper import
with Companies of Inner-living Entities operating inter-Dimen-
sionally under names registered and recognized in more than one
Life-state? We have certainly nothing to lose by trying, and the
Ratziel-Michael complex is undoubtedly a reputable and reliable
one.

  Those inclined to doubt the existence of Archangels might
ask themselves some questions along these lines. They will accept the existence of a human commercial or social Group-Entity
which may have existed several centuries for its special purpose.
The humans of its Foundation-period have died long since, but
others devoted to similar interests have carried the concern
along from one generation to another. Whether the Group is as
large as a Nation, or as small as a family business, it still goes on

for what it is, and develops its own entity much as souls acquire individuality as they grow up into mature beings. What we can do in our little ordinary human ways, is more than possible in fields of Inner Awareness and Conscious Energy where human lifetimes amount to maybe less than microseconds, and the whole of human intelligence would scarcely be sufficient to accomplish any significant activity. Scaling such types of Consciousness down to make useful contacts with ours proposes problems of what our scientific people now call "micro-miniaturization." Possibly there is a similar purpose behind other processes, and one leads into the other.

There has to be some kind of Entity built up from Consciousness specifically devoted to human evolutionary gains of wisdom through the ages, and it has obviously not yet finished speaking to us in terms that need some time to translate. Lifetimes generally. Why should we not apply the generic name of RATZIEL to that Entity? There must also be an Entity arising from all the Consciousness directed with the specific intention of saving the best in Mankind from the worst in us, even if this takes until the end of Time. Why should not MICHAEL (Like God) be the most suitable name we may use to make Inner contact with that particular category of Consciousness in Cosmos? Again, if we can relate these two Entitized Energies through ourselves to work the Sixteenth Path on the Tree of Life, why should we not benefit from this operation according to the natures of the Entities invoked? Ratziel and Michael know the answers to these questions here. They have the Keys.

Formatively, we plod this Path helped by the Angel Orders of the AUPHANIM and the MALAKIM. The Circlers and the Rulers. They abide by the Principle of Carefulness. We must not only think of the Malakim as Rulers in the sense of Kings, but also as Regulators, and rulers in the common term of measures, standards, and the means of drawing a straight line between any two points. A practical Symbol may be made from these two Angel Orders in the form of the Square and Compasses, making the Hexagram, or simply the open Compass placed on a basic Rule, making the Life-degree Triangle.

With the aid of Circlers for surrounding anything from Cosmos Itself to Its least particle, and Rulers for relating anything to anything in the most direct line of Light, we can Compass Cos-

mos with all the care in Creation. This is how a careful consciousness works. First contain, then rule. Go around everything, then
line things up. If the Auphanim and the Malakim can do this—we
can, most carefully. Care comes in degrees like most qualities,
and a high degree of care is usually associated with a high degree
of spiritual development. Care, however, is not timidity, but wise
and intelligent calculation of chance factors covering as much as
possible of any condition of Cosmos of Consciousness. To realize
what care means by the use of Symbols, we might imagine here
the Circlers describing the Inner equivalent of a containing globe
round any given point of Creation, and the Rulers taking the
measure and value of everything within that Cosmos.

We often say that we "Take the measure" of anything in a
metaphorical sense, and this is what the Circle-Ruler combination exists to do throughout Inner Life-Dimensions. Any schoolchild provided with a common ruler and compass is learning the
theory of work on this Path, and competent teachers normally
keep insisting on the care needed to accomplish it properly. Students soon appreciate the need for "watching points" literally in
setting, positioning, marking, and calculating the work done
with these simple, yet basically essential, instruments of art. Initiates have to learn the same things all over again with spiritual
counterparts in the Inner Mystery Schools teaching them the
trade-tricks of Inner Life, and they have to learn Circling and
Measuring with care, right on this very Path.

To deal with life in terms of ordinary Space-Time-Events, a
soul has to realize first that it exists as itself, and then that a
whole Continuum of Consciousness exists round it. The Circlers
help us to do this. Next, any relative points to ourselves anywhere in that Continuum must be measured and estimated in order to appreciate our position and its value to us and others. The
Rulers provide the measures of Space-Time-Events which make
this possible. So the better terms we come to with these particular Orders of Intelligence, the more precise life-abilities we are
likely to develop, which is a great advantage to any soul in search
of spiritual success.

It is easy to believe in angels, once we stop thinking of them
like fanciful fairies. None of the old Initiates ever thought of them
that way. Angels were, and are, agents concerned with specific
categories of Consciousness in process of Formation. Their own

forms are whatever happens to be most convenient for achieving the Will which motivates their behavior in that special way. It is *function* which primarily determines whatever form an angel-agent of the Divine Will may take. We sometimes use the phrase to some welcome individual, "Oh, you *are* an Angel!" and this is indeed literally true of them, or a part of them, for that moment in that instance. Whatever functions on this Path as a Circler or Ruler, *is* a Circler and/or Ruler at least in part for that purpose.

As a rule in esoteric studies, the designation "Angel" is broadly taken to signify agencies of categorized Consciousness which "live" apart from the human race, in the sense that they are capable of existence and function independently of human-ized Life. They were not specifically created for the exclusive benefit of human-based souls at all, but for the pure purpose of keeping Cosmos going as Itself. By no means all Orders of Angels are favorable to human life as we understand it on this Earth. Such Angels are no more "Evil" than radium or nuclear fission is "Evil." They are simply inimical to our type of Life-form because of their essential nature. Our wrong or foolish associations with such Energies do produce "Evil" as far as we are concerned, and we shall and do suffer accordingly. Man is to blame entirely for any evils he brings upon himself by ill-intentioned misuse of these "Angels." Divinity does NOT permit Evil, Man insists on achieving it for himself.

The whole idea behind the Qabalistic Life-Tree is to show us a practical Path-System for associating and working with those Orders of Intelligence which are most favorable to our spiritual status and progress as souls in search of Ultimate Light. If we re-fuse to work within these limits, and deliberately of our own Wills insist on contacting other classifications of Intelligence op-erating with specific Energies which might be described as "anti-Life" from our viewpoint, then we have no one to blame for conse-quences except ourselves. Those of the Life-Tree do their best for us, but even They do not operate outside their functional fields of force. Nor would we, if we listen to the Circlers describing, and the Rulers estimating, our most carefully chosen Cosmic course. We should ask them for such estimates. Those are freely given by the AUPHANIM and the MALAKIM here. They have the Keys.

Expressively on this Path we have the Sun and Zodiac, cou-pled by the physical Principle of Elasticity. If we remember the

Tarot Symbol to be that of Temperance, and note the root of that word to imply control of everything by the factors of its proper Time and Season, what could apply to Times and Seasons better than the Solar Zodiac?

An elastic state of matter is one which has a wide tolerance of expansion or contraction either side of its normal condition, and thus has self-recovering properties from stress distortions or variations imposed on it by contra-directed energies. The annual recovery of our Earth through its Zodiacal ecliptic could be fairly described as an elastic phenomenon, and so might the apparent "retrogression" of planets in the various Signs. Even the Planetary effects from the Sign-points of the Zodiac are "elastic" in nature depending largely on how individuals "bounce" from their impact.

We must have some elastic qualities in us to survive Life on this side of the Abyss. Brittle souls break easily and repair with difficulty, if at all. On the other hand, if we become too "bounce-able," we can scarcely settle into steady spiritual courses. The ideal degree of elasticity for any soul to seek is comparable to our Zodiacal Solar return rate that keeps our physical Life-System in Cosmos. Theoretically, to force us past Midwinter point would freeze us to death, and to push us past Midsummer would roast us with the same result. If we get no hotter than Cancer, nor colder than Capricorn, we shall live within reasonable Life-tolerance. To live our Inner Life within these degress of extremity will condition our souls to exactly the right degree of "Temper" necessary for spiritual survival through Inner Cosmic Life.

Just as steel is tempered by applications of heat and cold in precisely the right way, so is a soul. Our "Magic Swords" are really our own souls tempered to the right condition of elasticity which enables us to fight the Inner Battle of Life and come out on the winning side at last. Too much cold, and we break off the point—too much heat, and the whole blade crumples up at the weakest blow. A well-tempered Sword will survive all battles to be easily resharpened and pointed again. An ill-tempered blade is a bad liability for its user to depend on. That is one reason why a Sword is one of the Four Major Instruments in practical Magic. Its physical Symbology has so many vital spiritual analogies.

Between the heat of the Sun, and the cold of Outer Space, our Zodiac indicates the degrees of temper we should apply to our

Inner Life in order to succeed with our necessary struggles therein. Just as a swordsman tests the temper of a blade by springing it to a reasonable degree each side of its "truth," and noting its ability to recover, so have we to test ourselves the same way on spiritual levels. How far dare we bend ourselves from our Inner Truth, which points a straight Line of Light between us and Divinity, and depend on springing back to this Line every time by our own natural elastic temper? That is the test we have to pass before we shall be much use as Swords fit for any Inner purpose.

No hotter than Cancer, no colder than Capricorn. If we temper ourselves by those extremities, we shall not exceed the activity of Aries, nor the accommodation of Libra. Those are the Zodiacal marking points for a well-tempered soul. Astrological investigation of this process will pay for the time and trouble spent. It is always well to know just what we ought to do with ourselves, even if we cannot quite manage this in one lifetime. What human can? Still, if we are only able to get some useful ideas stored away in our souls deeply enough to last through the Life-change we call Death, and have sufficient left over to start our next Earth-life cycle with, we shall scarcely do so badly in the end. One good use of the Life-Tree is for supplying us with enough fruit to provision our discarnate periods and save the seeds to plant on Earth for a fresh growing when we get back again. Provided that the climate keeps somewhere between Cancer and Capricorn our harvest ought to be reasonable. We can always ask for the Keys of this work from the solar Zodiac, because this is where we shall find them on the Sixteenth Path.

The Seventeenth Path

SPHERE—LETTER CODE:	Understanding 3 J s Severity	
DIVINE ORIGINATION:	IHVH ELOHIM—	The
	ELOHIM GIBOR	Liberator
ARCHANGELIC CREATION:	Tzaphkiel—Khamael	Mutability
ANGELIC FORMATION:	Aralim—Seraphim	Variance
APPARENT EXPRESSION:	Saturn—Mars	Conversion
TAROT SYMBOL:	DEATH	

The characteristics of this Path suggest that Understanding must be reached concerning the necessity for inevitable Severity operating to the point of making irrevocable changes in Life by use of the Death-principle which, however, leads to ultimate liberation through all the alterations demanded.

The Tarot Symbol of Death is possibly the card making the deepest impression on those who consult the Tarot Oracle, or play games with the pack for fun or money. It is absolutely uncompromising. We may argue *about* Death till the end of Time, but no one argues *with* Death for the briefest instant. When Death says, "Come!" we go—and that is that. Whatever is born into this world by any Gate of Life must infallibly go through the Gate of Death. It is actually the same Portal, White on one side and Black on the other. We must "Go out by that same Door as in we went." There is no other way, and the alternative of remaining on this same Earth, bound to the same physical body for who knows how many millennia is too ghastly to contemplate for long. Death is our only and solitary hope of ultimate freedom from the necessity of being limited to flesh bodies as our sole means of externalizing ourselves. Without Death, how shall we ever attain Immortality?

In this Tarot Symbol we have the conventional black panoplied skeletal rider on a white horse. There is a quadruply knotted red plume on the helmet to indicate that our lives here are tied to Death. A skull-mask hides the rider's face because none of us ever recognize the real identity of the Releasing One. Four skulls and sets of cross-bones are on the bridle to mark that Death comes from every quarter. In his left hand, the Rider bears the measure of Life marked off into Life-years, from the top of which the black Banner of Doom flies outward to show that Death has dominion over all the Outer World. At first sight, the device on the Banner seems to be a ten-leafed white rose, but is actually a clever combination of bone-endings, with a circular cross-section of bone in the centre.

The foreground displays Kings and commoners alike falling before Death. Only a mitred Bishop still stands. There seems to be a hint of the Sacred-King sacrifice here, with an indication of innocent victims and an officiating Priest. We note that the stricken children are garlanded, and it was always the custom to garland the heads of sacrificial victims who were innocent of any offense.

In the middle distance is the lethal river which must be crossed, and a small boat with a red sail indicating a cargo of surviving souls is in the act of crossing. Behind this river we can just make out the edge of the fatal Abyss into which all lost souls must drift or fall. We do not see any sign of a bridge in the immediate vicinity, probably to indicate that few souls are called upon to make the Chasm-crossing very shortly after a Death-event. Once across the Abyss, however, the Gate-towers of the Holy City are seen, wherein all reside in Everlasting Light. These towers are remarkably similar to those found in the Lunar Symbol, which have entries at the top only because they are not meant for mortals to enter.

All this symbology adds up to tell us that we cannot use Death effectively until we learn to Understand it. Whatever we experience in Life, we all have to make our single file exit through the same Door of Departure. This is the point at which we discover that we are intrinsically worth neither more nor less than our own spiritual value. That is the awful Judgment after Death, our realization of just what we amount to in contrast to what we ought to have become. There are no evasions or excuses possible at this point, for we have reached our inescapable actuality at last. Our reactions to this revelation make no difference to any but ourselves, though these will determine the courses of our next Life-incarnation. We judge ourselves, and unless we truly Understand the precise degree of Severity needed to correct our Cosmic course, we shall condemn ourselves quite out of proportion to what may be properly called for. Those having no mercy on themselves need not expect it of Divinity.

Death is in no sense a punishment, but a process. Punishment, in the sense of vindictive retribution for personal offenses against arbitrary Divine decrees, does not exist in the Tree-Scheme of Life at all. Correction by sometimes drastic means is a necessity for re-establishing our balance as Deo-centric souls, but any over-correction is a regrettable wrong, and must itself be corrected. All ideas of an ill-tempered, intolerant, and vengeful Deity, behaving in a spiteful or repressive manner toward Humanity must be utterly eradicated from the consciousness of Qabalists, except perhaps as sad acknowledgements of human misunderstandings. There is no Image on the Tree even remotely suggesting such a monstrosity or distortion of Divine relationships with Man. Correction is not, nor ever was, punishment—but care. "The Lord correcteth whom he loveth," says the text, read properly. Strictly speaking, we should correct ourselves, once we care enough about our spiritual fate to be concerned as to what becomes of us. If we are utterly indifferent about the outcomings of our Inner Life, then we shall scarcely have cause for complaint if we receive indifferent treatment from that same source of energy.

It is no more easy to Understand the need for Severity than it is to Understand the necessity for Death, so the Tarot association on this Path seems quite justified. Maybe our concepts of Severity and Death are faulty to begin with, which would certainly interfere with our Understanding of these most important topics. Severity should be understood as neither more nor less than the degree and nature of Energy required to control the course of Cosmos either individually or collectively for the sake of the Spirit in, and unto Which, it is directed. We might as well say that a motor driver has to keep a severe control over his road behavior, or atomic workers must be severely controlled in precautionary procedures. When supplies become desperately short, there has to be severe rationing. Severity is safety by stricture. If Mercy is the accelerator of Cosmic activity, then Severity is the life-saving brake. The root of Severity should invariably stem from genuine love, or concern for Cosmic harmony. No other motivation is valid—certainly not in the Tree-Scheme. Severity is for keeping Life going in the best way for those living it, and for no other reason.

Strange to say, Death is also for keeping Life going the way it should. Otherwise, Cosmos could not circulate properly, and Cosmos is the circulation of the Divine Spirit through Its Life-System. The essence of Death is a separative state-change of Life. So is Birth. At birth we make an irreversible change, from the comparative safety and comfort of a womb, to the hazards and vicissitudes of this human world. If the prospect appalls us, we cannot very well give a shudder of fright, climb back into our parental womb and close up the placental portals again. We have to live here once the Abyss is crossed worldwards, and make the best we can of it. The same applies to Death. Until our souls grow too large for human bodies to accommodate, we shall go through the Birth-Death cycles of Life in our search for better methods of being.

It is not Death itself that humans fear, but the changes associated with it. If we really thought Death was the entire end of us, we should not be afraid of it, because there would be nothing to he afraid of. What we fear is becoming something or someone we would rather not be. It is the prospect of existence in life-states to which our inclinations have made us antipathetic which frightens us in connection with Death. Not Death, but Life threatens us, unless we have good reason to suppose we might improve our life-status during our discarnate existence. This, of course, depends entirely on our Inner condition of Consciousness and degree of spiritual development, which is precisely why we concern ourselves with subjects like these present studies at all. To direct ourselves toward Divinity with increasing ability and scope of Will, from Birth to Death and back again until we are capable of Cosmation beyond the limits of Earth-life, should be the prime purpose of our association with the Holy Mysteries, whether by Qabalah or otherwise.

Death is not something to be explained, but lived through. It is fundamentally an exchange of existence, whether for better or worse being a matter of individual experience. There are only two possible attitudes we can adopt to Death. Either we have reasons for supposing our individual and collective spiritual survival of a Death- change, or we have not. The more a soul evolves, the more likely it is to follow survival-paths, because its deep experience tells it instinctively of its own survival during many Birth-Death Life-cycles. Those who do not accept soul-survival are either immature and inexperienced at Inner Life, or else they have no individual Will to project themselves into Inner Existence past the Deathpoint, and are seeking Extinction for their own reasons. Whether or not they find it is their private affair. Failing either of these definite attitudes towards Death, the majority of humans drift aimlessly back and forth between the Birth-Death portals as a kind of tidal Life-flow that just keeps the currents of Consciousness going. One side of the Gates is much like the other to them, so they are apt to be somewhat indifferent as to their possibilities of progression to a finer state of spiritual Life.

If we can understand the necessity for severity, and the purpose of Death as an opportunity for changing ourselves into souls suited to better birth-opportunities than formerly, we shall learn how to tread this Seventeenth Path. As might be expected, it is a Chasm-crossing every soul has to make until we outgrow the need for "going over" in this way. At one time the Christian Church used to place great emphasis on the importance of dying while in a Divinely aimed soul-state, or what was termed technically a "state of Grace." This was not without reason and purpose. What they failed to make clear was that the action paralleled our pre-birth approach. Once we leap the Abyss either way, we are committed to some definite arrival-point in our changed condition of existence, and have to work our way forward from that environmental and inherited position. Hence the practicability in this world of relating individual souls with their Cosmic birth-data, or horoscope. The converse is true at Death. According to our soul-state as we make the Deathcrossing, so are we likely to pick up a suitable point for us to carry on our changed Life-cycle. The Church termed this condition "Purgatory," with unpleasing implications of soul-singeing and so forth, but the idea of this state being, like our present Earth, a Life-level of progressional possibilities seems sound enough. We simply continue ourselves in different Dimensions of Life. Nothing more remarkable than that.

In Earth-life, we have opportunities to develop ourselves so that when we are projected past the Death-point we shall find ourselves in a favorable soul-state. During Otherlife, we should still continue developing in order to plunge past the Birth-point into at least a reasonable type of incarnation. We should think of the whole process as an entire Cosmation of Consciousness leading up to an eventual Point where we shall be able to manage the entire issue AS WE WILL WITHIN US. After all, we are in the Birth-Death life-cycle to *do something about it,* and not just let everything happen without making any effort to KNOW WHAT WE ARE. Death may not solve any of our problems, but it does give us a chance to get a fresh grip on them, so we may as well see the phenomenon in its proper perspective from this Path. We cannot handle any problems at all that we do not Understand to some extent, and this is the Path where we may gain perhaps a degree or so of understanding about the Death-Door we all have to use in each Earth-life half of a complete cycle.

When we consider the Symbolic coverage of the Tarot, it seems oddly significant that no special Symbol is included for Birth. Euphemistically. the subject is indicated from many angles, but never given distinctive recognition for itself. The omission is obviously deliberate, and intended to set up trains of thought on this very point. Why make Death such a prominent Symbol, and Birth such an obscure one? There are quite as many reasons as there are Trumps. In this instance, we are supposed to realise that our birth is in itself the fundamental basis of our death, and we cannot very well look at one end of a circle without seeing the other immediately connected. To see our birth as a separate incident unlinked anywhere else is to divest it of all purpose, and this is the point the Tarot System means to make plain when it does not give Birth a special Symbol. It is joined to all the Symbols, and every one of them relates with it. Birth is Life-entry, and here we have entry to Life on other levels via the Death-Door. Intelligent Initiates grow into the habit of seeing Death and Birth as a conjunct Symbol, and never thinking of one without the other. That way, they both make sound sense and explain each other. That is only one of the many things we have to learn on this Seventeenth Path of Life.

Originatively. we meet the Divine Aspects of IHVH ELOHIM and ELOHIM GIBOR here. Though both these Names have feminine implications with pluralistic significance, we may fairly generalize them as "Of all Divinities, I will be Mightiest." Might in the Heroic sense of an absolute authority to whom ultimate obedience is obligatory. There is an underlying qualification which suggests, "Of all that Lives, I will be the Most of Might." We may immediately pick up the thought that in this world of living creatures, what is mightier than Death, since it takes all lives, except Love, which replaces them again.

In any collection of individual lives, one of them has to have an ultimate authority of some kind by the acquiescence of at least most of the others. However these particular beings are styled, their function is the same, whether they fulfill it well, badly, or barely at all, save Symbolically like a constitutional Monarch. They are an integrative catalyst, making it possible for Cosmos to maintain its structure by stricture. They make the "Thou shalt not's" practical so as to allow the "Thou shalt's" to bring maximum benefits among all those who share this Cosmos Willingly together. From the Tree point of view, this is the pruning and training, chopping and clearing of dead wood, which makes for healthy growth and valuable fruit. Unless decay is removed and converted into fertilising humus, it will eventually erode and damage the living Tree-System. This Path of Understanding Severity is where the Mightiest decision is taken of what to keep going, and what to throw down the Abyss for disposal. Some authority has to make this procedure effective, and, in the Divine Plan of Perfection, here it is upon the Life-Tree.

Sooner or later, we are supposed to discover exactly the same matters about ourselves, and apply the same process. There is the equivalent of an Abyss in the structure-system of every developing soul, and it is there to be used just as much as our bodily bowels, which serve a similar function for our physical Life-vehicle. Our spiritual Life-systems are not at all unlike our physical ones in principle, and if we abide by the same Life-laws on their different levels, we shall do well enough with ourselves. Here, we have to learn the workings of what amounts to spiritual elimination. Energizing spiritual "Food" must enter our souls, be processed, assimilated, metabolized, and ultimately converted to sewage which goes on its way through the Inner-Life System in Which we live as individual entities, so that it will supply fertilizing material for new fruit. A child's school-book explains the process physically and we only have to convert this information by

Symbolic means into spiritual instruction. This is real Understanding on this Path. All that remains is to make it practical.

How many souls have really healthy eliminative systems? If a man had no bowel movement for several days, he would soon be hammering on his doctor's door, yet the same person will suffer spiritual constipation for so many years that the accumulation of Inner poisons eventually materializes and appears as fatal physical diseases. We are constantly being told how beneficial it is to "get things out of one's system," yet who takes this seriously enough to make it as much a rule of spiritual health, as regular evacuations of physical excreta? Perhaps we do not provide ourselves with such attractive and practical sanitary facilities on spiritual levels as we have invented on physical ones. It might be an idea to discover equivalently reliable means of relieving ourselves spiritually. At one time, confessional boxes provided some kind of spiritual sanitation, but they are not as good as they used to be, like much else which has fallen into disrepair. Psychiatrists now get highly paid for acting as bucket-boys to wealthy clients with considerable spiritual sewage to dispose of. One is cynically tempted to think they earn the money in a most unpleasant way. A very, very long time ago, even poor people knew the secret of going literally to a lonely place, digging a small hole in the earth, whispering into it all the nastiness and unwanted matters that needed clearing from their spiritual systems, finally covering in the hole, and then going home with a wonderful feeling of relief. The principle of this practice works just as well as it ever did, with the same beneficial results. Either we learn how to clear ourselves effectively from spiritual waste, or we suffer the consequences even as far as Death.

The associated Divine Principle of this Path is that of The Liberator. We shall never be completely and entirely Liberated into Light until we are Absolutely Free from the slightest trace of whatever binds us into the Birth-Death cycles of Cosmos. Everything of such a nature has to be utterly eliminated from our spiritual Systems. Death is but a partial liberation, only freeing us from whatever we manage to clear from us during that part of our Life-cycle. Everything depends on our eliminative ability for clearing what used to be called "Karmic debts," with the greatest efficiency. There is no sense trying to do this any faster or slower than the safety limits of our individual Systems permit. This is where the point of strictly and severely keeping ourselves within reasonable bodily and spiritual bounds becomes very plain. Unless we become capable of imposing some kind of Inner discipline on ourselves, we can never hope to be liberated Lightwards. The only discipline that matters in Cosmos is self-discipline, and that is what we must acquire on this Path, if we would achieve its greatest possibilities.

No discipline is worth applying without Understanding. The Seventeenth Path ought to make this point abundantly clear. True discipline has nothing whatever to do with sado-masochism in the slightest, and anything of such a nature disguised as a discipline is only insulting to the intelligence of those who really understand what spiritual discipline means. Followers of this Path must be very careful indeed to discriminate between Understanding and mis-Understanding this vital matter. IHVH ELOHIM and ELOHIM GIBOR can explain this. They have the Keys.

Creatively, we follow the Path with TZAPHKIEL and KHAMAEL, the Watcher and the Burner. They associate with Mutability. Each Archangel is really a control on the other. If Khamael just burned everything regardless, Cosmos would soon become its own pyre, while if Tzaphkiel watched the same things inactively, Cosmos would become the most revolting heap of refuse in Creation. With the Understanding of Tzaphkiel telling the Severity of Khamael what to burn up, a nice balance of Life by the Death-door can be achieved to everyone's benefit.

The whole idea of the Purgatory state was, and is, to purge, or purify, by the Inner equivalent of Fire, whatever made a soul unfit for a better state of Life. This Inner Fire should not be thought of as a total destructor, but a selective heat-process not unlike a laboratory technique for applying exact degrees of temperature for separating out different elements from an impure mixture. The separation of spirit from a brew of mash is a good analogy. That should be the sort of spiritual equivalent encountered on this Path, where the cooperation of Tzaphkiel-Khamael types of conscious activity allow a soul to be refined into a better condition not only during its Death, but also its Birth-half of a Life-cycle.

There is nothing frightening about Khamael any more than the fire of a cremation-oven or a garden incinerator need frighten anyone. Besides, on this Path, Tzaphkiel is watching closely the whole time to make sure no mistake occurs. It is not unlike a factory belt arrangement where a selective eye determines which items pass for productions and which must go back in the melting pot. Nothing fit for further use will pass Tzaphkiel's observant notice. That is his specialty. He Understands. That is his Sphere. He and Khamael are charged with keeping the fields of Inner consciousness clear from unwanted growths of weeds and unnecessary accumulations. Since they have been created and conditioned for this work, they do it admirably. If their counterparts in us did the same, we would have so much the less to worry about.

The Archangels which really matter to anyone are not so much the Categorized Entities of Consciousness extending through Greater Cosmos, but the personal projections of these we are meant to make for ourselves in our own Microcosmoi. In a way, this so-called Magical process of making Telesmic Images is not unlike constructing a transistor receiver set for that particular station. The Tzaphkiel Image we make in our own consciousness will only be an Observant Watcher maintaining Inner contact with the Archetype of that nature already existing in what Jung termed the Collective Unconsciousness. Our Khamael Image should be specifically concerned with the controlled burning of what we should dispose of in this way alone. Put the two Images together, and we can work the Seventeenth Path with them. Practical Magic.

When things burn, they change from solids to gases, thus altering their nature entirely, or mutating. This is what happens here in effect via the Death-Gate. We change from one state of Life-expressions to a much more mutable one. Nothing is entirely lost, only changed, and that is what the Tarot Symbol should stand for. In conditions of nature, a dead body breaks itself up with reasonable rapidity and returns its chemical constituents through various channels of Life as fast as it can. The hotter the weather, the quicker the corpse disposes of itself in all directions. Life is claiming every bit of it back for re-use by every scavenging creature available, including the bacteria. Cremation is only a cleaner speed-up of this process. As the body turns to gas, its molecules scatter far and wide into an atmospheric grave, out of which they will find their way back to life through breathing creatures of all descriptions. That is the kind of mutability we would expect to find on this Path where the Tzaphkiel-Khamael partnership operates. We watch with Tzaphkiel, while Khamael burns up our bits which need brightening. It is like watching a piece of metal which has grown so corroded that cleaning is impractical, melted down and recast into a bright new shining product. Such would be a Tzaphkiel-Khamael sort of operation if it were conducted on purely spiritual lines.

When studying the Archangelic Intelligences of the Tree, it is, perhaps, as well to remember that when in combination with each other, they form up between them what might be almost considered as a mutually created entity. The Khamael of the Khamael-Tzaphkiel partnership, for instance, is a much milder type of being than the Khamael we meet in alliance with Michael. Each Tree-Being apart from its pure state in its own proper Sphere should be appreciated from whatever angle it is encountered by other types of entity. This will allow us to work the different Paths properly and fit ideas in with each other so that they will produce other ideas again of their own accord, just as if the Beings themselves were telling their own stories to us inside ourselves in terms of the Old Inner Tongue we all used to know once, and must learn to speak again if we are to be competent Initiates of the Holy Mysteries. Unless we hear the various inflections and nuances of the Tree-speech it will not talk to us very much, and so we shall have to listen for undertones very carefully. In the case of the Archangels and other Power-personifications on the Tree, we must see them from the viewpoints of three, four, or five others of their kind at least, except the central Beings, who have to be considered from not less than eight Path-angles. All these modifications should lead us from one point of Inner Life to another until we establish our Inner Identity to degrees long past the least possibility of doubt or denial by any part of our awareness. We shall KNOW OURSELVES FOR WHAT WE ARE WITHIN US, and the Voice of the Tree will indeed have spoken. KHAMAEL and TZAPHKIEL will tell us about each other here; they have the Keys.

Formatively, we tread this Path with the Angel Orders of the ARALIM and the SERAPHIM, operating by Variability. The Thrones and the Kindlers working together to accomplish the purpose of their combination. The Seraphim are often visualised as darts of fire, and signify the disruptive activities of that Element. As we considered their opposite numbers on the Tree, the Chasmalim, to be Flames of Fusion, so may we consider the Seraphim as Flames of Fission. It is interesting to note that the root of the word "Seraph" has a special side reference to anyone kindling a funeral pyre. Most appropriate on this Path.

The Seraphim are Burners in a sense like Khamael, but fulfil their functions on lower Life-levels. They have sometimes been described as brandishing Fiery Swords, and it was reputedly a Seraph which prevented Adam from re-entering Paradise in his "Fallen" condition. The Aralim, usually taken as "Thrones," carry the significance of strong and courageous heroes, supporters of a cause, and there is a side significance of a hearth, or that which supports a fire. So taken together, here we have an Angel Group who brandish Fire around where it may be needed to clean up corruption or act as a prophylactic, and another Group who act as hearths or upholders for this process. That certainly sounds the right sort of combination on this Path.

In such a connection, the old sacrificial altar-fires rekindle themselves in our minds immediately. The Symbolism is so appropriate. A stone altar, or "God-throne," with its Life-sacrifice of a body on it, being consumed by the Element of Fire, so that a Life-essence was shared between Divinity and Humanity. When the meat was sufficiently cooked to eat, the humans took their portion, then burned the remainder completely for the benefit of the unseen Divinity supposed to be the Provider and Presider of this banquet. The humans in their circle around the altar-fire considered themselves the guests of the Gods. A Chasm between Divine and Human understanding had been crossed by such Symbolic means, and everyone had died a little on one side, in order to live a little more on the other. A really beautiful, if primitive, form of the Mass. It certainly served Mankind for many, many centuries, and is even with us today in modified ways. Any modern funeral party partaking food together after the cremation of a friend or relative are doing as much. Symbolically, they are eating up their share of the departed from their circle, and hoping that God takes the immortal Fire-surviving soul. However they disguise or remain in superficial ignorance of the issue, this is precisely what they are doing. The same would apply had the body been buried. A funeral party consigns the body to its Earth-altar, and by symbolically eating up their share of the dead person, release the remainder toward Divinity with their pious hopes. By so doing, they automatically become what used to be known as "sin-eaters," or blame-takers for their late companion's misdeeds, so that, lightened by that amount, the released soul in that circle voluntarily sacrificed or "burned up" whatever tie he had with the departed which might hinder or burden the liberation of a Spirit into Light. If they had any ill-feelings or debts in connection with the dead, those must be burned or buried with the deceased. We even have the instinctive feeling today not to "speak ill of the dead." All that was likely to hold a human soul down to Earth must be relinquished by those who still retained their ends of the links. That was the real funeral sacrifice which helped the dead more than anything else. It still helps them—or would, if their Earth-remaining associates bothered themselves to such an extent any more.

With a sacrificial Fire, the rising smoke and sparks afforded the Symbology of thoughts and prayers arising to Heaven. The smoke dissipated into the atmosphere and was breathed by all as a kind of shared communion of hopes. The sparks rose toward the Light sources of Sun, Moon, and Stars, where Man instinctively knows his Divine destiny has always lain. By association with the outward sacramental appearances, humans attempted to undertake comparative Inner activity, and so accomplish on Inner Life-levels what had relatively happened Earthwardly. This may have needed some care and effort, but the results in spiritual satisfaction were well worth that expenditure. They still could be. The SERAPHIM and the ARALIM have a great deal to say on topics like these. They ought to know; they have the Keys to fit any variety of lock protecting these matters in the Holy Mysteries.

Expressively, the planets of Saturn and Mars combine to represent this Path, and between them symbolize the Principle of Conversion, or state-change. It would be difficult to discover what closer planetary association with Death there could be than a Mars—Saturn relationship. They typify the two main leads to Death—violence, and sheer old age with its ailments. The Sword of Mars and the Scythe of Saturn eventually account for us all, collecting us across the Chasm in never-ending harvests and holocausts. Not a soul have they missed since souls began.

The Mars of the Life-Tree is scarcely the stupid and blundering, clumsy Ares of the Olympians, or the viciously exultant War-God or Goddess of other Pantheons. The root-meaning here signifies Might, Power, Energy—that which is done quickly. Between the speed of Mars, and the slowness of Saturn, the death-rate has to be balanced out on this Path. Sometimes we die one way, and sometimes the other. The Life-Death Dance is quick-slow-quick-slow. Saturn tries to give us time to think of such serious subjects, and Mars favors the *coup-de-grace* system of parting soul from body. All they agree about is the necessity for such a separation. We may take which side we will, but until we free ourselves from their field of influence, our heads will roll before their weapons.

Since we cannot avoid the Saturn-Mars process which delivers us through the Doors of Death, we may as well bid for their best terms. It is also advisable to remember that what we call Death from our viewpoint, is a species of Birth on the other side of the same Door. Saturn is not only a Reaper, but also a Sower. With his time-measuring motion, he scythes the grain and casts the seeds for a fresh harvest. Saturn takes matured souls, Mars mostly dispatches the young. The old man dies in bed, the young in battle, but both die all the same. On this Path, we should hope to compromise with its Guardians in such a way that Saturn spares us violence, and Mars saves us from senility. We should think of their Symbolic weapons of Sword and Scythe meeting and restraining each other in a kind of Triumphal Arch, beneath which we may walk through the Door they guard in our own way.

Saturn and Mars are not purely concerned with Death, of course. Mars gives eruptive Energy, and Saturn gives Endurance. Mars is the Instant, and Saturn the Aeon. Between them, they not only limit our Birth-Death periods of Life, but our Death-Birth ones also. If we start dying the moment we are born, we begin being born the moment we die. Our Life Energy is convertible from one currency of consciousness to another, and what seems to us like a moment in one state of Life, may be a very long period indeed to souls living in other Dimensions. When we are young, we think in Mars-time, impatiently, and what does not happen instantly seems slow. The older we grow, the more we think in Saturn-time, and this is why most people are inclined to believe that time gets faster as we get older. So far as we are concerned, it does. The Time-secrets of Mars and Saturn may be learned on this Path, and how Life-time relates with Death-time. It is all a question of consciousness.

Even the Symbolic metals of these planets are characteristic here. Steel kills quickly, and lead poisons slowly. Steel is hard and bright with the spring and glitter of youth, while lead is soft and dull with the weight and grayness of age. The Mars-Saturn combination is a good illustration of young and old Life-energies bringing enthusiasm and experience to bear on common problems. If they operate as allies instead of adversaries, humans might gain all sorts of benefits through mastery of this particular Path. The sharp Severity of Mars, and the malleable Understanding of Saturn will get us through many an awkward situation. By analogy, it will shoot us across the Abyss if we use the fire and steel of Mars in gun-form to project the lead bullet of Saturn with sufficient force and accuracy. The target of Truth may be difficult to hit, but with enough Will and Skill, there seems no reason why good scores should not be made from this point of the Tree.

Using this same kind of Symbology, we might remember the magnetic properties of steel which make it the finest material for compass needles, and the weight of lead making it most suitable for plumb-lines. These ancient instruments tell us at all times how to find our way round the surface of the Earth, and how to point from the center of Earth to the zenith of Heaven. In a very primitive way, they possess the principles of an auto-pilot. On spiritual levels, this would amount to a built-in sense of direction toward Divinity which we might depend on to guide us faithfully through all the Birth-Death cycles we shall ever follow. To know how we stand and where to go is the best kind of knowledge for any state of Life we are likely to encounter. If a combination of Mars and Saturn can offer us that, we have every reason for being grateful to them, not only during Earth-life, but also Otherwhere.

Centuries ago, if a fighting man was absolutely at liberty to go where he pleased, yet was uncommitted to any particular cause or country, he sometimes drew his sword, invoked his Gods, and whirling the sword round his head several times, let it fly into the air to fall as fate decreed. Where the sword pointed, the soldier went. Older and less active folk used to melt lead and pour it from a height to either the ground or into water so that the arbitrary shapes it assumed might suggest some course of action or decision to them. The oracles of Mars and Saturn have settled many an issue in the past, however chancily. Although our faculty of Will is far too valuable for total submission to such erratic phenomena, we must always be prepared to accept guidance from the Inner Mars-instinct which impels us into action, and the Saturn-instinct which warns us against it. When the two are consulted in partnership, they can teach us what we ought to learn on this Path. We should not make any final decisions here until we have listened to both Mars and Saturn, then settled the issue ourselves with our own Wills. This should lead us reasonably from Birth to Death—and back again by this Seventeenth Path. Mars and Saturn may be relied on to open up this level for us. They have the Keys thereto.

The Eighteenth Path

SPHERE—LETTER CODE:	Understanding 3 K 6	Beauty
DIVINE ORIGINATION:	IHVH ELOHIM—	The
	ELOAH va DAATh	Enduring
ARCHANGELIC CREATION:	Tzaphkiel—Michael	Determination
ANGELIC FORMATION:	Aralim—Malakim	Continuance
APPARENT EXPRESSION:	Saturn—Sun	Pressure
TAROT SYMBOL:	THE HANGED MAN	

The configurations of this Path tell the story of the most Beautiful Understanding that can be imagined, which keeps the human soul suspended between Heaven and Earth. Divine knowledge and Experience lead to observance of the Supreme Life-likeness among all its supporters who are ruled by it, and even the heaviest and basest matter is transformed by the pure bold light of the spiritual Sun around which our Inner Cosmos is centred.

Here we meet the ever-controversial "Hanged Man" Tarot Symbol. Perhaps his significance becomes clearer if we call him "Suspended Man," for he is only hanged in the sense of being suspended between Heaven and Earth upside down from an Earthly viewpoint, depending from his gallows by a minimal noose round his right ankle. Circus performers frequently do this in order to make spectacular spins and free contortions at the end of their life-lines.

There are quite a number of interesting points to note about the Suspended Man. His sole attachment is to Heaven—not Earth—and although he is well aware of Earthly affairs, they seem all upside down to him, and he is not tied to them in any perceptible way. He may be bound in Heaven, but he is certainly free from Earth, and seems quite satisfied with his situation. In fact, the Suspended Man is very much a betwixt and between character. He is neither quite bound nor quite free; he is both right and wrong way up depending how one looks at him; he is neither an Earthly nor a Heavenly based being, even though he has Heavenly linkages, and could reach Earth with his fingertips if he wanted to. He is, of course, Mankind in a state of suspension between Humanity and Divinity, trying to maintain relationships in both directions while determining which way to go in the end himself. The condition of an Initiated Soul, in the course of spiritual development.

There is naturally an implication of sacrifice with this Symbol. Some of the old Sacred Kings were sacrificed by being tied to trees until released by physical death. Occasionally, to speed this process and save unprofitable suffering, they were indeed sacrificed this way with head downwards. Legend says St. Peter ended his Earth-existence so. Temporary head-down suspension is a fairly common practice among Yogis and other exponents of psycho-physical experiments aimed at inducing some kind of "God-sense" in the practitioner. Another old method of inducing an ecstatic state in anyone was the so-called "Witches' Cradle," sometimes no more than a species of rope net, similar to those used for loading ships, in which the victim was confined in a bound-up head-down womb position, suspended from a beam or tree-branch, then spun or swung round until disorientation with Earth-life occurred, and visions or "wild" experiences were undergone. It was hoped in this way to achieve "short cuts" to Inner actualities and informed Intelligence, but there is no-evidence that much of real value "came through" by these means. In cold climates, the suspension was occasionally carried out over fires burning all kinds of stupifient and hallucinatory herbs, such as henbane, etc. Undoubtedly, fatal accidents must have occurred on a number of occasions, which probably accounts for the rumor that Druids burned their victims alive in wicker cages. The shrieks and cries heard by unauthorized observers at a distance were the prophetic "utterances" of these unhappy people, which the organizers of such experiments tried to translate into comprehensible terms. Not a recommendable custom whatever.

The Suspended Man on this Tree-Path hangs between the Spheres of Understanding and Harmonious Beauty. He Understands because he is Poised and Balanced. His feet are linked to the Way of Understanding, and his head is full of all that is Beautiful in Consciousness. He depends on Divinity rather than Humanity and, to him, the Ways of Heaven are right side up in contradistinction to the ways and habits of human beings. He is learning to see Life from entirely another angle than average humanity accepts as normal. His normal vision is the "Inner opposite" of Earth events. Being a trained Initiate, he Understands enough to keep his own counsel concerning the Beauty of the Inner Life he is trying to lead. Others may follow IF THEY WILL emulate his example, but none are compelled or even urged to do so. All souls must be suspended from their own Trees. None other will serve. This kind of sacrifice should not only be a voluntary, but a solitary one at this stage of Initiation. Nothing but a single cord connects the subject to his Heaven-hold in his spiritual state of resemblance to Womb-life, neither in nor out of this world.

The depth of Symbology with the Suspended Man is fascinating. So much can be found so easily, it is Small wonder the Tarotists give it so great an amount of attention. One wonders, for instance, what might happen to the Man if his foot-cord were suddenly cut. Would he fall like Adam, or "walk with God" like Enoch? Does the cord represent our Life-links with Universal Life itself? Why the *right* foot? And why are the hands hidden? All kinds of interpretations might be put on these and other points by the simple process of asking and answering our own questions about them. That is what Symbols are for—to process consciousness. However we play with the Tarot on one level, it has to be worked with higher up.

The Suspended Man is the last Chasm-crosser we shall have to deal with on the Tree, so we may as well consider his crossing method carefully. This particular way across is that of Doom, Fate, or whatever we like to call the Cosmic Law of Happening generally termed "Karma," or the interaction of Energy variations through Inner scales and ranges of spiritual experience. This means that energies operating in any particular state of Life may and do affect changes of condition through other Life-states. In purely personal terms, the general implication is that our reactions to events in any life set up stress-alterations through Inner Dimensions which are most likely to affect our later living-conditions in future projections of personality. Note that it is not events themselves in terms of physically observable phenomena which bring about such results, but our Inner reactions to them.

We make our own Fate or Doom by our reactionary releases of Inner Energies because of our Life-experiences, or by intentional impulses of consciousness directed through a Inner Dimensions which have a determinant effect on our subsequent spiritual status. It is for this reason that the Hindu mystics advocated "non-attachment" so frequently, and Christian teaching attempted to promulgate the "Love for Hate" theory.

Put very simply, most souls tend to project ahead of themselves into their own Paths that which they will eventually experience in fact. Depending on what we think, imagine, believe, or otherwise convert into conscious energy terms at this present moment, so are we most likely to "walk into" the outcome of this at some future instant of our existence, even perhaps several lifetimes away. True, we can indeed alter our Fate as we go along, but only IF we Will such alterations with sufficient energy and skilled direction to ameliorate or change out of course what we have already sent ahead of us through Inner Space-Time-Events tracks. A very high degree of Initiated Intelligence is needed to effect such alterations with any remarkable results, because of their extremely complex nature involving maybe very many other souls. This is why many esotericists advocate a policy of "uninvolvement" while dealing with mundane issues with which there is no intention of remaining connected in later states of spiritual Enlightenment.

The Suspended Man has established ties with Heaven at the sacrifice of intentional involvement with Earthly concerns. Hence his hands are kept behind his back to avoid the temptation of interfering with what he should leave alone. Not that his nature is an interfering one, but he plans to make no move on Earth that is not indicated via his connections with Heaven. Thus, he crosses the Abyss by the weight of his own Inner Gravity Earthwards, and is hauled back by the help of heavenly agencies when his Life-mission is accomplished among Mankind. In a sense, he is like a diver sent down for some specific task to the sea-bed, and afterwards restored to his normal conditions of living by means of his life-line. The Suspended Man is a Heaven-Earth operative Initiate of a similar sort.

By suspending his purely personal Will and inclinations in Earthly affairs, the Man allows the Will of Heaven to work through him in order to influence other souls toward some valuable Cosmic purpose, or maybe avert an otherwise certain coming catastrophe. Human beings alone have scarcely such ability to concentrate Consciousness sufficiently and accurately enough to alter a Fate of their own making which is liable to affect them all adversely. Providing the requisite quantity and quality of souls capable of self-suspended Inner abilities is available, higher than human directions may be applied along human life-courses to alter or at least ameliorate the more disastrous likelihoods of destiny. Divinity does not intervene in human living except through human intentions and human energies, Inner or Outer. Insofar as Initiated human souls are able to suspend themselves so that their own Wills depend on Divine direction, then Divinity may be said to move Mankind in accordance with Its Eternal Will.

The Suspended Man is not necessarily supine and motionless at all. He is free to gyrate and move in any direction he will round the single pivoting point attaching him to his sole spiritual anchorage. If we can imagine such a theoretical point as being the Nil-nucleus of a Cosmos, it will show how a soul connected to it like the Suspended Man would be able to travel in any Time-Space-Event arc or complete Circle it intended. Given the auto-gravity set up by such a motion, it might direct itself as it Willed throughout its own continuum. Once the Suspended Man learns the acrobatics and manuevers made possible by his unusual relationship between Inner and Outer Cosmos, he may become a very dynamic soul indeed, turning himself into the mobile factor relating his particular pivoting-point with every other at all angles of Existence to it. By Fixity at one end of him, and Freedom at the other, he develops enough power to put in practice whatever purpose motivates his motion. It is always a useful idea when Tarot Symbols are being studied, to "bring them alive," and see what they will do with themselves within the framework of their setting. The depicted characters should be allowed to speak for themselves, tell their own story in their own words, go through their repertoires of behavior, and live their lives in our imagination so that we may learn from them whatever they have to teach. They have to become more than just painted pictures. If we treat them as such, that is all they will ever be. Once we give them a life in our own living, they will speak to us of their secrets soon enough.

The purpose of this Life-Path is Understanding Beauty. Perhaps we might call it the Appreciation of Being in the best possible sense. It is impossible to define Beauty objectively, but we may conceive it to be whatsoever has the effect of evoking the best and noblest reactions from souls capable of experiencing its Inner influence—that which brings us Inwardly into closest contact with the most Divine Reality we can reach, and is therefore the greatest Beauty available to our belief. The nature of this varies for all kinds of soul, of course, but its Principle remains unchanged. True Beauty may only be estimated by Inner effect, which is invariably the finest possible. Those who say unthinkingly that Beauty can associate with evil or disaster have completely failed to Understand Beauty in the slightest. That is what this Path is for, and they are obviously total strangers to it. For anyone to claim that true Beauty may be evil means they have evil inclinations in their own nature which they secretly admire and would like to consider beautiful if they could. A sad attempt at self-deception.

Who knows how to Understand Beauty? Who knows that Understanding is Beautiful. None can Understand love and appreciation of Beauty by any rule of thumb, manual of instructions, or computerized comprehension. This path is a direct matter between ourselves and the Divinity within us. It is all we have to "hang on to" or depend on which makes Chasm-crossing worthwhile. This is what the Suspended Man tries to tell us all—if we will listen. The least moment of truly deep appreciation and realization of genuine Inner Beauty is worth Eternally more than the longest winded and most sophisticated sermon ever preached—assuming that sermons could possibly be beautiful in the first place!

The Beauty set forth in the Tree of Life lies in its harmony, order, proportions, and relationships with all that Lives through Spirit or Substance everywhere in Existence. Thus it is natural to seek contact with the Principle of such Beauty at its heart and Point of Poise. Any Initiate of Life knows that true Beauty emanates from Within, and relates All as One. Therefore the Sphere of Beauty, Tiphereth, has to be the heart of the Tree-Glyph. The other Spheres are drawn out from that Point. If we thought of the Suspended Man as a kind of indicator freely pivoting round his captive-point, we could draw a Tree with him, or any other design which is Cosmically constructed. This means that all individual points of the Whole are relatable with a Single Point or Principle they hold in common. Again the Suspended Man speaks up to show us his Single Point of Dependency on Divinity. He is worth hearing on this issue. It is his specialty.

Imaginatively, this Path is governed by IHVH ELOHIM and ELOAH va DAATh. I Will Be all Lives, and I am the Knower. In order to Know All, Life must necessarily Be All. Ultimate Knowledge being the most Beautiful Concept of Consciousness, the Deity of All-Knowing equates with the Principle of Beauty here, and balances with All Lives that live to Know, and know how to Live. Very simply, "We live and learn." What else indeed is Life all about?

Real Knowledge is not just loading up memory banks with data. Any computer can do that, and acquire no more than a stock-in-trade. True Knowledge is the application of information in such ways that promote the perfection of both Knower and Known. For example, anyone may become rich by piling up money in a bank, but this fact by itself is of no value except to the miser's self-esteem. Banks do not pile up money, they apply it where and however they believe it will increase their own importance and power. Banks do not grow richer and richer by hoarding capital, but spending it in greater and greater quantities. If we apply the same Principle on spiritual levels from totally different motives, we shall get some ideas on the purpose and practice of Knowledge from the ELOAH va DAATh point of view, which is what we should travel this Path to learn.

To know two things affords the possibility of knowing three if we rub the first two together until they breed a third between them. This is how Knowledge is gained with the Tree-of-Life. Ten Concepts, or Conceivables, so called because they themselves will conceive other conceivabilities. By pairing them off in "Paths," and relating them with each other on Inner levels in order to make them breed, we will eventually produce all the Knowledge in Life we shall ever need. To increase stock and his own wealth, a farmer takes male and female creatures, puts them together so that they will reproduce their kind to greater extent—and his profit is made for him. A banker does the equivalent with his money. A Qabalist should do the same again in spiritual dimensions with the Tree. Breed its ideas for his Inner profit.

If we like to think of this in terms of sexual behavior and re-lationships, the comparison seems quite a valid one. The Tree is bi-sexual, like Life. It has "masculine" and "feminine" Spheres, relatable to each other by the "Paths." If we put a "male" idea into a "female" one with Love, seed-energy should pass through this polarized Path, and after necessary gestation, an issue should arise from this connection like a child of the union. It does. That is why the Tree lives, because it breeds, and has the ability to repro-duce and increase its own stock. To put matters plainly and crudely, a competent Qabalist organizes the sex relationships of the Tree on spiritual levels, and nourishes his soul on its fruits, besides being in a position to supply others from his surplus stores.

Each Path is thus a spiritual sex-relationship between two separate Spheres of the Tree, and if we connect them together in ourselves with real Love on Inner Levels, they will associate through us Willingly and wonderfully, ultimately making us the guardian of their "Child." All we have to do is become the actual means whereby the Spheres "mate" in the field of our conscious-ness. That is what Qabalists must learn if their Trees are really to live as more than designs on paper.

The practice is as simple as sex itself. There is a "Male" and a "Female" side, or Pillar, to the Tree, and a Medium, or Middle, Pillar by which each may be related with the other in various ways. The Spheres of the Middle Pillar are thus in the position of being "Male" to "Females," and vice versa. In effect, the Middle Pillar typifies the CHILD OF LIGHT unifying and directing be-tween Earth and Heaven all potencies and potentials of polarised Life. It is the prototype of the Perfect Being that is "self-sexual," balancing its polarities through Itself, and extending Itself AS IT WILLS around Its Own Existence.

It is interesting to note that the "Male" and "Female" Tree-Spheres only relate directly with each other three times at three different levels of the Tree. All their other relationships are via the Middle Pillar, or with their own "Sex." This has to be taken into consideration with our Path studies because it throws light upon every Path in turn. With each Path, we have the question of polarity to determine in order to discover what flows where, and what happens in consequence. Here, for instance, we have a

"Male-Female" relationship between Tiphereth and Binah. To produce issue from these, we have to penetrate Understanding by Beauty, and relate the two rhythmically with Love. Then await results. Had both the Spheres been similarly "Sexed," or polarized (which can only happen four times on the Tree), there would still be a positive-negative relationship possible which would produce results in terms of reaction rather than offspring. Nevertheless, the principles of productions from Sphere-contact Paths are the same, whether we regard the Spheres as "sexed" or not in the human sense of the word. Even in our world, relations between similar sexes other than physical are productive of issue on intellectual, emotional, and all Inner levels of Life.

The Path-Principle here is The Enduring. This does not mean merely long lasting or perpetual, but just what the word signifies—hardwearing, able to survive any degree of erosional stress. True Understanding Endures All, and Divine Beauty is quite beyond the slightest erosion by Man, though who among us is able to endure the Brilliance of such Beauty and yet live? By learning the Way of this Path, we also learn how to endure with ever increasing fortitude the incredible Beauty of the Inner Realities we shall be called upon to face in the course of our Cosmic Initiation. Beauty is not easy to live with, if we have no comparable Beauty in ourselves. We can hurt ourselves harder with Beauty than anything else if we do not Understand it. This is why such a market exists in this world for unbeautiful, inharmonious, and messy, inept products of modern inartisticness. So many souls are utterly incapable of managing better Inner material. A genuine revelation of Inner Beauty at its own face-value would shatter what already unstable sanity they have for perhaps several incarnations. Fortunately for them, they are spared abilities of realizing or recognizing it. Real bravery is called for to encounter Inner Beauty and endure it with spiritual advantage. IHVH ELOHIM and ELOAH va DAATh will help us develop this quality on their part of the Eighteenth Path. They have the Keys here.

Creatively, we meet our friend TZAPHKIEL for the last time in this Tree-trip, in company with MICHAEL, with whom we shall deal several times more. Their Watchword in this instance is Determination, a much needed quality in both an Observer and a Leader. We shall never be able to Understand Beauty until we discover how to Observe it properly, nor will we ever become truly Beautiful in ourselves until we learn from Michael how to look God-like from Within, as he does. Michael is a Revealing Light, but Tzaphkiel observes what that Light reveals. Together they make the ideal Partnership for this Path.

One of the chief issues they have to tell us about here is the essential Inner faculty of Contemplation, and its effects on Activity. Contemplation varies from Meditation, insofar as the latter practice is carried out mainly by the mind, and "middle" part of our Inner constitution (hence its name), whereas Contemplation is engaged in by our highest abilities of spiritual perception. So high, in fact, that from such a point we can do nothing whatever except observe and be impressed by what we experience at this remotest apex of our Inner awareness. To reach the top of this "Mystic Mountain" takes all the determination we can summon up, and places us somewhat in the position of the Tarot Symbol, hanging by a figurative thread over the Chasm between Consciousness and Non-consciousness.

At one time, Contemplation was recognized as so important in spiritual affairs that individuals spent whole lifetimes in its practice, and Ordered communities of all Faiths made it a major purpose for their formation. Now, in the West especially, we are in danger of losing touch with this vital Inner ability, because of the temporary suspension of physical and other activities needed before we can hope to achieve any success with Contemplative practices. We are made to feel guilty in making any attempt to reach Truth entirely from Within Ourselves, yet how else shall we ever find real Inner Freedom?—and obey the injunction of the Mysteries, "Know Thy self." Looking over the general outline of our modern mundane socio-political setup, it is easy to suppose the existence of some kind of a conspiracy to discourage or entice humans away from discovering Truth in the most obvious and accessible way—inside themselves. Most people are frightened about one main point—being found out! There is no question that if the majority of humans ever really found out the actual truth behind the shaky structure of their so-called civilized society, it would collapse in ruins all around them, probably leaving an even worse condition of helpless anarchy in its wake. Therefore the mass of humans must be kept deliberately confused—not, it must be admitted, entirely without their willing collusion. They know instinctively they are in no condition to KNOW.

We may be reminded here of the story concerning Satan in company with a fiendish friend, who observed a human being discovering a piece of real Truth. "Isn't this a bit awkward for you?" queried the fiend. Satan smiled cheerfully. "Not at all, my dear fellow," he replied, polishing his claws carefully. "I'm going to have Hell's own fun helping him organize it into what he wants." Man has grown up a little since this story was first told. We are quite capable of ruining the most perfect Truths for ourselves without any assistance from our Old Enemy any more. It is sad for even Satan to feel superfluous.

Michael on this Path has to supply us with courage to climb high enough Inwardly so that we can contemplate Truth with the Observation of Tzaphkiel. That courage is needed above all here, for without it we shall fall and injure ourselves terribly. Without Michael's support, the observant abilities of Tzaphkiel will bring us no benefits whatever and may even plunge us into very serious Inner perils. Hence the importance of paired Pathworking. It takes very great courage indeed to be a Contemplative. We sometimes say automatically that something is "too terrible to contemplate," and we are only telling ourselves the truth here, except that we ought to qualify it by adding "alone" to the sentence. We do not have to be alone if Michael is with us according to his promise. Who dares indeed to be alone in spirit when contemplatively seeking Highest Truth?

Actually, the word "contemplation" explains itself. A "Templum," from which the term "Temple" comes, was a special place set apart for observation because everything around it was clear. A hilltop, or a promontory on a cliff, was usually favored, though in the cities it might be on the highest building. The entire purpose of this place was for observation of auguries, or more properly ascertaining the Divine Will in any particular matter. Thus "Contemplation" really means, "With Observations of Divine Intentions." That is precisely what Contemplation should be for Initiates of the Mysteries, in the hope that ultimately our viewpoint will coincide with that of Divinity Itself. Unless a soul is prepared to learn the art of Contemplation, and how to apply it by methods appropriate to our times and customs, it need not expect to penetrate the Mysteries very deeply. Those who will not gladly sacrifice some of their living-time in this world for Otherlife Intentions, deserve no more than they offer, which is far less than they demand. To understand about Contemplation, we should enquire from MICHAEL and TZAPHKIEL. They have the Keys here.

Formatively, we work this Path with the ARALIM and the MALAKIM. Thrones and Rulers. Where should any King rule from but a Throne? We are back again Symbolically to the Suspended Man, with his fixed and free points. The Throne is a fixed point from which Rulership is supposed to extend all round in a Sphere or Realm—the longer the Ruler, the larger the Sphere. The Principle shared by the governors of the Path is Continuance, or "Unbrokenness."

If a Kingdom, Realm, or Sphere is to exist at all, it must necessarily have some one particular Point from which its government proceeds. Symbolically, this is the Throne, or Seat of Government, and the administration of Power from that Point is via the Rulers appointed for this purpose by whatever the Overall or Decisive Consciousness may be called.

Such a condition should apply to ourselves. Somewhere in each soul, ought to be a Throne, or Seat of Rulership in which we repose our faith and confidence, and from which we may rule ourselves in any direction. Behind all our doubts, indecisions, changes of mind or variabilities, there should be one deep-down Throne in ourselves which we can reach if we try hard enough, and appeal to for rulership in our lives. Moreover, this has to be a continual availability, because if our contact with this point is broken, we become what used to be called "unruly" and ungovernable, a dangerous state for all concerned, threatening a breakup of the personal Cosmos.

What can any of us find in ourselves as a Throne to hang on to with all our strength amid every adversity, and depend upon for reasonable rulership when we are in a state of suspension between all kinds of belief and know not which way to turn? Unless we find, and have complete faith in, some such Ruling Point in us, we shall be as helpless as the Suspended Man if anyone cares to knock him about like the punchball he resembles. This one Ruling Point, whatever it may be, is our sole link between sanity and madness. If that breaks, we break with it. Our Thrones are rooted in Understanding, and our Rulings in Beautiful Harmony, or Balance. We should remember this always. Our Inner lives may depend entirely on it, and this is the Path where we must discover it.

Without this One Link with Sanity and safety to fall back on when emergencies imperil our Inner spiritual balance, we are certainly at very grave hazard, but how may we be sure to find such security when all our beliefs may be blown to shreds by some Cosmic catastrophe which is perhaps confined to the Cosmos of just one soul? Supposing we cannot find any beliefs we consider worth holding on to in the first place? What then? The answer is rather an odd one, which is that we need not believe in this, that, or the other specifically, so long as we believe in Belief itself. That is what matters.

As an illustration, a distraught soul once cried to its spiritual mentor, "What shall I do? All my faith in everything and everyone is utterly gone. I believe in nothing whatsoever. Help me!" The strange reply in effect was, "Splendid! You have achieved a miracle of faith in ceasing reliance upon finite and impermanent formations of Consciousness, and have at last transferred your Inner allegiance to the Absolute. You believe in Nothing, the Great Nil from Which all emanates into Life. Keep your faith there unbroken, and all you can ask for will come forth. Once you can believe in Nothing, everything is possible. Inner Freedom is yours forever if you Will. Treat NIL AS YOU WILL, and It Will Be What you Will with It. You have believed in Belief, and that is the secret of Faith. Live in Peace Profound."

This may not be easy to understand, but it is well worth investigating with the help of the Aralim and the Malakim. Nothing alone can break the Faith of Whoso has Faith in Nothing. It is the firmest possible Faith in Existence, and everything emerges from it. Armed with such Faith we can believe in anything to whatever degree we Will, and it will work for us. Be it noted by Symbologists that the noose securing the Suspended Man to his Heavenly attachment is a diminishing Zero-sign of Infinite Nil. From this Ultimate throne, ALL is ruled. Gain this Point and— but the ARALIM and the MALAKIM prefer to give personal tuition about this spiritual Secret which, after all, is personal to each soul. They have the necessary Keys.

Expressively, this Path is represented by the planets of the Sun and Saturn-though the Sun, of course, is not really a planet, but a Star. The Combinative Principle here is Pressure. "God is Pressure" was said once, when a one-word description of the Deity was requested from an Initiate, and there could be far faultier estimates than this simple one. Pressure is cumulative Cosmos, or the Weight of Will. Perhaps we might think of it as Existence Expending Itself in Expansion. Certainly without it we should explode into the most revolting heaps of putrescent protoplasm. Pressure is a very delicately balanced life-factor indeed, and has to be meticulously maintained if we are to continue as conscious Cosmic creatures.

A combination of Sol-Saturn naturally suggests the old Alchemical Lead-Gold Aim, a most reasonable idea to ultra-modern physicists, but ultimate anathema to economists and politicians. From a spiritual viewpoint, the transformation of Saturnian lead into Solar gold, regardless of the Principles of Understanding and Harmony involved, would be a highly dangerous operation also. The Sun is a mass of pure Radiant Energy, but are we yet able to exist in such a state? Obviously not. What provides us with the best protection against radiation? Lead. As we are at present, we need the Shield of Saturn against the range of Solar Energy which destroys our living tissues. This is true spiritually also. Again and again, we are warned not to expose ourselves senselessly to Inner Light we are unable to absorb safely. Again and again souls insist on defying the Laws of Light-Life, and pay the bitter price of their stupidity. When did enormous accumulations of gold ever benefit humanity? Its critical mass is potentially as dangerous as plutonium from a different angle. Fairly distributed throughout Nature, gold and Light alike bring blessings to all. Concentrated to points beyond our endurance, their pressures break us in pieces. If the Alchemists had tried to turn gold into lead, they might have stumbled on very vital information indeed. Gold and lead balance each other's pressures to a Beautiful Point of Understanding on this Path, and there is yet much to discover with this process.

Astrologically, the Sun is reputed to represent the best of what we may expect in any life, and Saturn is supposed to stand for the worst. Though not strictly accurate according to modern Astrological experience, the Tree-symbology of this combination here may be taken as such in this instance. Between the two extremes, we are suspended on this Path. They are like the Principle of the Pillars in a horizontal direction so to speak, keeping us on a more or less level course between Heaven and Earth.

As an analogy, we may imagine ourselves set on a Starward journey, with the weight of Saturn as ballast above us, and the heat of the Sun as the driving power below us. As the leaden ballast slowly melts from Solar energy while we go along, we steadily rise at a corresponding rate, so that in the end we arrive at our destination in a reasonable condition, fully adjusted to our complete change of nature during the voyage. Without Saturn, the Sun would have blown us up altogether, and with no Sun, we could never rise with Saturn's weight at all. Together, they operate as a beautifully controlled process of living from one state to another.

These two planets also typify a normal lifetime, with a human soul suspended or stretched between both ends. (The Suspension of the Man may be either from a rescue rope lifting Heavenward, or a rack, pulling him apart between extremities. Everything depends on which end he releases first). At the Birth-end of Life is Sol, gay, lightsome, darting, irrepressible youth. At the Death end is Saturn, solemn, heavy, ponderous, indifferent age. Experiencing both, and all that comes between is the human soul, learning to deal with Life, and unable to avoid coping with all contingencies. The obvious thing to do with any life-cycle if possible, is join the ends together and make a resonant loop out of the ensuing circle. Youth needs the stability of age, while age needs the buoyancy of youth. If we can find means of applying Saturn at the Birth-end, and Sol at the Death-end of Life, we shall live far more evenly and effectively than might otherwise be possible. Naturally, this sort of Alchemy has to be carried out on spiritual Life-levels, but there is no reason to suppose such an idea either impossible or impractical.

To melt Saturn with Sol is easy enough in practice. A large burning glass will concentrate enough light to liquefy lead. This elementary form of laser will soon demonstrate the principle of light-penetration. We can do just the same with Inner Light as Outer, though it should be remembered we might get seriously burned by mishandling the energies concerned on Inner, as with Outer workings. It is a fatal mistake to assume that because we do not see, hear, smell, or feel any evidence of energy in operation, no danger exists, and so we can play around as we please. Only the right degrees of pressure should be applied to the operations of Inner or Outer living. On this part of the Eighteenth Path of Life, Saturn and Sol have the Keys we need to learn such a necessary skill in balancing our beings between the Beauty and Understanding of our lives.

The Nineteenth Path

SPHERE—LETTER CODE: Mercy 4 L 5 Severity
DIVINE ORIGINATION: EL—ELOHIM GIBOR   The Decider
ARCHANGELIC CREATION: Tzadkiel—Khamael   Exactitude
ANGELIC FORMATION: Chasmalim—Seraphim   Correction
APPARENT EXPRESSION: Jupiter—Mars   Compensation
TAROT SYMBOL: JUSTICE

This Path tells unmistakably the story of Justice and the principles of Compensation from every possible angle. Here, Might and Mercy become balanced. Fear and Favor are equated, and all is placed exactly as it ought to be in relation to the One Reality behind all the ephemera of Existence. The Sword of Mars is restrained by the Scepter of Jupiter, but on the other hand, Jupiter's prodigality is countered by the economy and reductive behavior of Mars. Between giving and taking away, we live along the margin of the Middle Line.

The Tarot Symbol of Justice is the obvious one for this particular Path. Virtually everyone accepts the Ruling Figure with its Sword and Scales. Sometimes the Justice Figure is shown as blind to signify its unbiased nature, but the Tarot Justice is not blind at all. Its vision is presumed to be perfect, seeing everyone and everything not as external appearances, but for actual Inner realities revealed by the Light of Truth. We have to try and imagine just what we would look like, if instead of being illuminated by ordinary daylight, we were shown to some impartial observer by the same Spiritual Light out of which our original entities emanated. How true or representative of that Light are we now? To what degree have we distorted and obscured it? Reflected it? Transmitted it? Only the Light Itself can prove this and, being Truth, it cannot lie. The Justice we are dealing with here sees us purely and simply for what we actually ARE, in contrast against what we ought to be as indicated by the Light-Life extended and expended through us. It then sets the "Stick and Carrot" system of Cosmic compensation into action with an intention of establishing a state of harmonious Balance among all parts of the Whole Whose integrity it must maintain.

True Justice neither rewards nor punishes. It corrects and compensates conditions of unbalance which would otherwise upset the courses of Cosmos to dangerous degrees. In a sense it is no more or less than a built-in auto-pilot keeping us all on our charted courses to Ultimate Perfection. It may not look this way to us when we are on the receiving end of its "stick" rather than happy munchers of its "carrots," but such is its function. Justice has but one aim. The equating of extremities by relating the point of poise between them with the Control-Centre of Cosmos Itself. It is governed by the Exigencies of Existential Equilibrium entirely. We cannot avoid or avert it. All we can do is alter our relationship with it, so that we benefit by the balance of any spiritual situation, rather than grasp at perilous profits from a dangerous over-accumulation of energies at any particular point of its Cosmic periphery.

The Scales of Justice are an easily understood emblem, but the Sword should not be taken purely for a punitive Symbol at all. As an instrument, a Sword has point, and unless the point of any issue is made abundantly plain and clear to us, we shall never recognize Justice anywhere. Moreover, a Sword has edge, and if we do not know to a hair's breadth the distinction between Justice and injustice in our affairs, we shall not conduct ourselves in accordance with Cosmic principles. Nor should we ever forget the symbol of the Crown or Circlet on the head of Justice. It represents the Eternal Equation or Circle of Equilibrium wherein all energies "get even" with themselves in the long run, and Justice is done when the end of an event-cycle meets up with its origin.

Probably a sense of injustice is one of the worst stresses we have to bear in this world. It is inherent in every soul to "get even" with what or whomsoever they feel has unjustly upset the balance of their Inner Cosmos, causing them suffering or inharmony in some way or other. This is a natural feature of our construction, and we shall not eliminate it without imperiling our very Identity and integrity. Our troubles arise in connection with it purely because of misunderstanding and misuse. We wrongly assume that the injuries or unbalancing influences we experience can be compensated by reciprocal reprisals inflicted on others. This, of course, cannot possibly be the case. No amount of punishment heaped on any number of souls will ever compensate for the least injury to a single individual. Such would only be revenge, which has nothing to do with Justice. Nor has true Justice any place for vindictive and quite pointless punishments. Real Justice is Compensation and maintenance of Balance among all Beings. What goes wrong in any unit of Cosmos has to be put right in that same state of its continuum.

The socio-political laws of most modern countries and nations are based on extremely unjust principles indeed, because no adequate mechanism exists for compensation of individual and collective injuries. An offender is sent to prison for breaking the civil or criminal code. How can that possibly benefit the community, or more particularly those individuals an offender has wronged? It may perhaps prevent further offenses by those inside prisons on those outside them, but it does not in the slightest way compensate or benefit such souls who may have suffered from the criminal's activity. Until we have evolved some satisfactory system for compensating the victims of criminal intentions, we have no right to talk about Justice. We may speak of our retributive and retaliatory power if we please, but those again are not processes of Justice, and should be classed as counter-attacks. Justice only exists where peace and harmony can be established among all parties concerned.

All this applies on spiritual levels. We should never make the mistake of confusing Justice with any form of retributive punishment or "Divine vengeance," neither of which exists in such a sense at all. There is cause and effect on every level of Life, and Laws of Compensation acting through Dimensions of Existence we cannot comprehend in our ordinary conditions of consciousness at all. Some call this Karma, and others the Will of God. It is Absolute Justice in the purest sense, and is Ultimately Infallible. To look at it from our very limited viewpoint and attempt to criticize, condemn, or otherwise challenge its ageless action, is a very unsound practice. We should much better be employed in studying its methods and attempting to apply these suitably scaled down for use in human living.

On the Tree of Life, Justice is shown on this Path which connects the Principles of Severity and Mercy. How else may we be truly just, except by a combination of these qualities? Again we have to avoid any association of Severity with Ill-will, malice, or spite. Severity is no more than restrictive or eliminative procedure applied entirely for reasons of sheer necessity to avoid evil effects. Mercy is the provision and encouragement of conditions favorable to good and kindly spiritual growth. Justice is the application of both these in order to obtain a condition of fully-compensated Cosmos. If we think of Severity as the weed-killer, and Mercy as the fertilizer, we shall have a homely gardening analogy.

We cannot conceive any true kind of Divinity without Justice. Humans instinctively seek compensation in all directions. Whether we believe this will reach us in some Heaven above, in another embodied incarnation on Earth, or simply hope to grab what we may in this life, we demand Justice for ourselves from the Life-Spirit, insisting that we achieve what we consider to be our "rights," as distinct from what we see as our "wrongs." In fact, we have no legitimate claims on Cosmos apart from compensatory energies needed to keep us in a state of spiritual balance directed toward Ultimate Union with Infinite Identity. Between experiential extremities of Mercy and Severity in every Way of Life, that is the only Divine Justice to which our existence entitles us. We are not entitled to claim vengeance on human enemies, enormous profits and possessions for ourselves, favors for our friends, or anything at all resulting in unbalance anywhere. These things are likely to happen, but only because of instabilities occurring otherwhere than in ourselves. Each soul has only the right to claim compensation within its own Cosmos. Its own necessities of Justice in itself, whatever these may be. Outside those limits we must accept those imposed by collective circumstances

Whatever we do of either Good or Ill which unbalances a person or situation beyond its inherent Cosmic rate at that instant, needs Justice to correct. Over-beneficence can result in as much loss of balance as over-severity and is equally wrong to apply indiscriminately. The only rules for spiritual safety we can reasonably adopt are similar to those needed for driving a vehicle along a road. In that case, we are proceeding along a Path toward an

Objective at a variable Velocity or Rate. These factors only remain in our control while we grasp the steering device, unless an auto-pilot is incorporated. If the vehicle swerves too much to the right we correct with our left hand, and vice versa. We control its rate with the accelerator, and its course with our consciousness. Provided we continue so, we shall arrive at the objective if no event occurs beyond the limits of our control. If only living were as easy as that! Yet those are the principles involved in spiritually directing ourselves toward Divinity by Justice. Employment of Severity and Mercy to the exact degree necessary to maintain our progress on our Path within the width of a sword-edge. Just that.

Humanity as a whole has not yet learned how to apply the Cosmic Principles of compensatory Justice. We are far too concerned with vengeance and insufficiently interested in re-establishing healthy and happy harmony among unbalanced conditions of Cosmos. We are too careful about our criminals and too careless about the victims. Our injustices cause disasters throughout our spiritual and social structures comparable to a driver's inaccuracies causing road accidents. For the same fundamental reason—we are not keeping our attention on the job properly, and our Intentions on the Objective of our journey. The only worthy objective of true Justice is PERFECT PEACE PROFOUND in all the Inner meaning of the phrase, and that alone should be what our Justice Symbol stands for at the Balance-point of our Life-Tree.

Originatively, this Path lies between the Divine Aspects of "The Almighty," and Power personified simply as "The One." ELOHIM GIBOR and EL. We may think of these in a way as Prohibition and Permission, Might and Mercy, or any complementary Energies whose combined efforts result in a state of Justice and Equilibrium. They can be termed "I Will" and "I Will Not," "Thou Shalt" and "Thou Shalt Not," or whatever makes most sense to us when we attempt to conceive Divinity defining the "straight and narrow" Light-Life-Line marking the Middle Way between Itself and ourselves.

We have strange ideas about Divine Justice and Mercy. Only too often we associate the former with extermination of all we dislike, and the latter with granting all our wishes as fast as we can think of them. We love the idea of a Cosmic Overlord doing all our dirty work for us. No Power thus amenable to purely human whims and dictates could possibly maintain our Cosmos in Manifestation for even a single second. Yet we are able to use our proportions of this Power for our own purposes, though far less effectively in ratio, because we have not yet discovered how to apply it along similar lines. Even if we assume the Existence of an Omnipotent Entity, someone invariably asks the time-honored catch question, "Can God make a stone so heavy that He can't lift it?" The answer to this question is more or less that this is exactly what Omnipotence would have to do in order to Be Itself. Impose Limitations within Its Own Unlimited ability. Cancel Its Own Commands. Will and Un-Will. Be Both Ends of Its Entity in Its Own Circle. Be and Un-Be at Once.

The distinguishing mark of true Cosmos is that it does not begin what it cannot end within Itself, or initiate anything Its own ability cannot control. It must contain Its Own Energies in Its Own Circle. Otherwise Cosmos would become Chaos. Assuming the theoretical possibility of the God-and-Stone query, we are faced with the issue that the God would not have created the Stone in the first place without Absolute Knowledge (or Omniscience) of Its Own complete capability of controlling that Stone throughout the course of its creation and endurance. The limitation does not apply to the Stone, but the God upon Itself. Humanity has not learned this lesson to a sufficient degree.

As children, we have been told often enough not to bite off more than we can chew, or start anything we cannot stop, but this homely advice is very rarely heeded, and so we live with all our troubles around us among everyone else's. If not entirely Chaotic, this is certainly un-Cosmic. Once the containing Circle of Cosmos breaks, its auto-equilibrating energies pour out through the fracture of its force-field and run wild at all angles until absorbed or neutralized within the next greater Cosmos capable of containing them. This process usually results in some disorganization or temporary disadvantage to the Cosmos successfully containing the disaster. If we on Earth were able to devote the same amount of energy toward our own Cosmation as we are compelled to spend containing and clearing up each other's disintegrations, we should undoubtedly be more advanced than we are at present. However, we are learning faster. We now have access to destructive energies that no human forms of Cosmos can contain. Nothing prevents our annihilation on Earth, except our own Wills against this event. Can our united Wills be strong enough to contain this danger? Have we at last answered our doubts of Divinity by making a Stone so heavy that we dare not lift it? If not, who is guilty enough among us to throw the Stone first at anyone?

So it is on this Path that the Mercy of EL and the Might of ELOHIM GIBOR keep Cosmos in control between them. Sometimes such King-Figures were shown with a Sword and a Rod. The symbology indicates that those who will not control themselves by the Life-Rule represented by the Rod, must be controlled by the Severity of their Life-System as signified by the Sword. If we do not contain our own outbreaks, we have to be contained by whatever next circle around us can absorb and equate those energies. On individual levels this is not a very serious problem except for the souls concerned. When large groups or nations are involved, results are far more catastrophic for everyone. Even so, we can only wipe out some millions of lives on this planet. If our containing Inner Cosmos of Spirit broke up, all Life everywhere would break with It. God cannot possibly be dead while even the least living creature survives. The Life-Spirit does not die. It IS or It IS NOT. In it alone are our sole hopes of ultimate immortality.

The whole message of this Path concerns the vital necessity for maintaining our balance along the edge of our Light-Life-Line by means of the "Might-and-Mercy" mechanism of spiritual steering. Probably our worst errors are made when we allow ourselves to deviate too much in one direction before trying to apply the corrective measure. This is a comparable fault to that of an uncertain driver who lets the vehicle go far beyond reason one way before frantically wrenching at the steering wheel and so over-correcting the course, so that the next swerve is to the opposite side, and thus the erratic journey continues until accident terminates it, or expertise develops sufficiently to make it successful. Once the driver gains skill in control, the lightest finger touch keeps the vehicle going in accordance with Will, because the opposite elements of correction are applied instantly at the very commencement of alteration from the determined Progress Path. This is the Cosmic "driving lesson" which ELOHIM GIBOR and EL are attempting to teach us here. If we want to learn the "feel" of controlling our spiritual vehicles on our Inner Way, we had better ask Them. They have the ignition Keys here.

Creatively, we encounter Archangels KHAMAEL and TZADKIEL, the Burner, and the Righteous of God, on this part of the Nineteenth Path. Their combined function is Exactitude. Here again, we meet a sort of two-power Selection Committee, one choosing what to save, and the other what to burn off. We may see the physical side of their work on any farm.

Spiritually, this Archangelic partnership operates in a similar fashion, deciding between them the exact demarcation line which should separate the goods and ills of any soul. This is a very individual affair, because what is good for one soul may not be so for another. Everything depends on whether or not that particular soul is keeping to the most direct Light-Life-Line between itself and Divinity. Tzadkiel is concerned with encouragement of energies which effect this, and Khamael attends to those which might prevent or hinder it. In a driving analogy, Tzadkiel keeps the driver's mind and attention on the ultimate objective and the Will behind the journey, while Khamael tries to stop the driver's mind wandering from this point by insisting on the possibilities of accidents, and the personal responsibility of everyone in charge of an automobile towards themselves, other road-users, and the families connected with everyone. In plain old-fashioned language, Tzadkiel stresses the benefits of right behavior, and Khamael puts the fear of God into those who willfully oppose the Laws of Life. One waves the carrot and the other shakes the stick. Both have the same aim, but from opposite angles.

We may sometimes be tempted to think how nice things might be without the attentions of Khamael, but in fact we should be doomed to destruction otherwise. Khamael operates our inbuilt warning alarm-system which tells us what we should do or not do in order to avert unpleasant incidents. Often this means drastic and energetic procedures or disciplinary measures on our part, which we may not enjoy at all. Everything depends on the point where we react to Khamael's promptings. Obviously the quicker this is done the better, and the same applies to reassurances from Tzadkiel, which, if listened to exclusively, would result in our reaching positions of over-confidence and false security that nothing but the loudest roar from Khamael could rescue us from. These two Archangels work not unlike the directional "peeps" on a course corrector. Those come in steadily from right and left in two different tones. If the vehicle or missile is on correct course, the "peeps" cancel each other and nothing is heard. Should it swerve too much either way, one type of "peep" is immediately heard which warns the pilot to alter course accordingly. The greater the deviation, the louder the "peeps." Therefore course correction should be carried out before the "peeps" become too clamorous.

Most of us might imagine that nobody could have too much of Tzadkiel's Merciful Righteousness, but this is much the same as an overdose of Khamael's Severity. Too much Mercy is just as diversionary as too much Strictness, and probably more risky in the long run, since it allows accumulations of pressure in opposite directions to very dangerous degrees. We all know about disasters that have occurred throughout our human history caused by violent and oppressive activities, but how often do we consider the degrees of disintegration due to unwise extensions toward Mercy which degenerates into indifferent toleration of unsatisfactory behavior (now termed "permissiveness"). There has probably been more harm done in this world by well-meaning "do-gooders" inflicting their intentions on others than by hordes of ravaging barbarians. It is a sad thought, but in Spiritual Dimensions there are certainly more wrongs wrought by humans in the Name of Right than for most other reasons.

Goethe makes Mephistopheles describe himself as being:

Part of that power—misunderstood
Which always Evil wills, yet ever worketh Good.

We might well paraphrase this sublime statement, and refer to Humanity in general as:

"Most curious creatures of Divine invention,
Who work their Evils with a Good intention."

We make so many of our troubles by stuffing our good works down the unwilling throats of those who never asked for them, do not want them, actively dislike them, or otherwise resent them. In doing this we only unbalance people and divert them from their Cosmic courses to almost hopeless degrees. This is entirely un-just and quite against the Principles of this Path. How are we to define Good and Evil in terms to suit this System? Only in the broadest sense by accepting Good as whatever helps to harmonize and balance souls in their own state of Cosmos relative to their Paths of Progression toward Divinity, and Evil as all that unbalances and Chaotifies souls away from this direction into conditions of disintegration and inharmony. Since these factors vary with almost every individual, and also depend on evolutionary and ethnical considerations, we dare not be over-rigid about requirements. Our only criterion is whether a soul, or group of souls, Cosmates or Chaotifies relatively to their Inner Integrative Identity. What Cosmates them is Good for them, and what Chaotifies them constitutes their Evil. How can we discover this all-important difference? Only from TZADKIEL and KHAMAEL. They ought to know, because they hold the Keys between them.

Formatively, we tread this Path with the Angelic Orders of the CHASMALIM and the SERAPHIM. They may be thought of here as the Flames of Fission or Fusion. The two opposing uses of the Fire-Principle, maintaining or eliminating Forms of Life in Cosmos. Together, they fulfill a compensatory role in the economy of existence. One gives to Form, and the other takes away. We can only alter the shape of things on any level by adding to or subtracting from them, and that is how the two Angel Orders operate here.

Physically, we can watch them work in the metabolism and heat-control of our bodies among other phenomena. Our heat-regulation mechanisms keep us alive within the relatively few degrees of heat our bodies are able to tolerate. The principles of the Chasmalim and Seraphim are in physical action all the time we live in human bodies. Seraphim tend to increase heat to cremation point and beyond, Chasmalim ameliorate heat right down to minimum need for life. We have to remember that the Angels are not infallible agents in themselves, and if they fail in function, faults occur which need correction. If Cosmos could not correct its own internal errors, It would disintegrate and so would we. Our bodies depend on this faculty of auto-correction in order to eliminate disease and remain healthy. So do our minds and souls, therefore it is just as well for us that the Seraphim and Chasmalim are active on these Inner levels.

Their operation often shows up in individuals as tolerance or intolerance. We are usually critical of intolerant people but over-tolerance is an equal error when it becomes sheer apathy and ineffectualness. Warm-hearted love is always welcome, but tepid love is a sickly affair altogether that stultifies souls exceedingly. It needs both the Chasmalim and the seraphim in combination to keep our spiritual temperatures at the proper degree compatible with our best progress. Here again, the maintenance of Cosmic balance is the only possible criterion. Suppose, for instance, that a fire was keeping an otherwise icy room tolerably warm. This illustrates the seraphim in the shape of the fire, and the Chasmalim in the shape of the ambient warmth. Naturally, a human hand cannot directly handle the blazing coals without serious injury. What would happen if the occupants of the room decided to let the fire burn down to a point where their hands could tolerate the coals with impunity? Since the fire would be out, those people would soon suffer the freezing consequences. The lesson here is that we should not inhibit the functions of Angelic energies to degrees which impair the abilities of their compensatory countertypes. Each has to act as a control upon the other so that we get the benefit of the balance.

From our point of view on Spiritual levels, this means we ought to cultivate the art of controlling the operations of the Chasmalim and the Seraphim ourselves with our own Wills. Not easy, perhaps, but we shall not be able to keep our Life-Systems properly balanced otherwise. It is very largely a matter of recognizing and reacting to their influences with sufficient response to restore equilibrium. As soon as we realize that we are drifting too much in either direction, we should invoke the opposite control to pull us back on course.

This is where ritual practice is a great help. For those accustomed to visualize and focus Inner forces into forms where they become amenable to Will, it is a relatively straightforward procedure to consider the Seraphim or Chasmalim as Entitized Inner energies fulfilling their specific spiritual functions in our Cosmoi. If, say, we find ourselves becoming over-biased in the direction of Severity, so that we are reaching stages of irritation, intolerance, impatience, and the like extremities, we can balance this out by "invoking" in ourselves the mild Force-Forms of the Chasmalim with their calming and cheering effects which incline us to take things more in our stride and let storms blow over while we shelter with the Inner comfort and consolation they afford. Conversely, if we realize we are becoming lazy, over-luxurious, and neglectful of our spiritual duties, then we "call up" the Seraphim in us to wake up our ideas, shake us into action, and generally prod us with their Flaming Swords until we guide ourselves back on our Cosmos-course again.

These imaginative exercises are no waste of time or merely childish games. They are Inner disciplines which really do operate energies inside us having definite effects in accordance with what we have imagined with Intention These effects will be initially confined within our individual Cosmoi, of course. Nevertheless, it is impossible for any soul to control outside itself what it cannot control inside. Therefore, that is where all Magic starts—inside the soul—and until we learn how to make Intentional use of these Inner mechanisms, we shall never grow very greatly as Life-Trees in our own right.

A fair analogy to use here is to think of the Middle Line or Pillar of the Tree as being like the direct Route we have to follow toward our Divine destination. The whole Tree and ourselves are aligned with this like a chariot, team and driver. KETHER is the guide-Light ahead, the next four Sephiroth are the horses, NETZACh and HOD the two wheels, and TIPHERETH the body of the chariot, YESOD its platforms and lastly ourselves are MALKUTH, the driver from the human end of this road, with the reins in our hands. To steer a straight spiritual course, we need both the Right and Left teams going equally, and to keep our course correct, following any curves or alterations which may lie before us, we have to vary our rein-controls accordingly. When we can drive our own Solar chariots successfully round the courses of our individual Cosmoi, we shall be able to enter them for greater events. Meanwhile we can learn control-techniques from handling Angelically complementary energies such as the SERAPHIM and the CHASMALIM. They have the Keys to this process on the Nineteenth Path at least.

Expressively, we face this Path along the line connecting Mars with Jupiter. Here indeed are opposites. War and Peace. Fear and Favor. Economy and Abundance. Keenness and Kindness. All the contrasting conditions possible between extremities of human circumstances and behavior. Both entirely necessary to the Life-process, though by no means to the degrees we allow them to overbalance in this world.

If we look at the pattern of Nature, we shall find that abundant supply is constantly countered by eliminative action which results in the survival and continuance of whatever Life-entities are most suitable for that particular type of Cosmos. From millions of seeds, how many gestate and grow into Life-frames? Fruitfulness and famine would follow each other faithfully, if we had not learned how to even out and compensate the natural variations in the vegetation cycles of the Earth, which also affects our own Life-Pattern, since over-population is no longer controlled by starvation to the degree it was. Human breeding patterns are fundamentally based on those of herd animals. Sexually mature males fight each other to death in order to gain females, just as the male sperms struggle for supremacy in the battle of embryonic achievement. In the next stage of selection, natural climatic and other causes such as diseases cut down the population again during infancy, more females usually surviving than males. If humans out-ate their naturally provided resources of food, starvation soon reduced their numbers to reasonable quantities until the vegetation and animal production had a chance to reestablish itself. All contingencies were provided for by Cosmos.

We have changed this Pattern to suit ourselves in accordance with an Inner Will we are far from understanding— but can we change the Pattern sufficiently and swiftly enough to cope with all the drastic deviations unbalancing us at this period of our history? Even two incredible world wars, and possible prospects of a third far more horrifying one, have not brought about a satisfactory balance of population-resource ratio. Worse still, the Inner Spiritual balance of Energies, where all our Life-affairs as soul-entities commence, is reaching an appalling state of inequilibrium. Just how this is likely to blow up in our faces is anyone's guess, but blow it certainly will, unless our Mars-Jupiter factors can be correctly co-related along the Line of Justice which should stabilize our Light-Life-Lines as individuals intending to share the same state of Existence. The English letter to suit this Path happens to be "L," and if we cannot work the Path successfully among us all, we shall discover the reality of "L with a capital H."

Mars represents far more than wars and aggressions. It stands for the survival struggle of every soul, and on Earth is simply a continuation of the seed-struggle to obtain priority of position with the human egg. Everyone alive in this world has won this battle at least once, otherwise we would not be here. Souls fight for the right to be themselves, and that is the fundamental reason for all wars. In order to accomplish this aim, they may demand the concomitants of food, housing, or the ability to follow some particular way of life, but the basic motivation behind battles of any sort whatever, is the Entity-insistence of individuals and identifiable masses of souls involved. To maintain or increase themselves on any life-level, they will grasp and grab what comes within their clutches, while if they feel their entities being threatened severely enough, they will start attempting to destroy whatever entities appear to threaten their own. This operates on the principle that if they are likely to lose their lives anyway, they might as well ensure that other humans do the same, so the struggle may be continued in other Dimensions of Life, thus providing the possibility of an active existence after physical death. The old Norse idea of Valhalla was simply a projection of human instincts to stay alive as souls apart from bodies, and this could not be imagined without the element of Striving.

To experience an identity sufficiently to make life worth living, a soul or group of souls must normally receive recognition of their existence from others to a degree which satisfies their demands for life-awareness. This factor is of vital importance, because it is a basic of behavior at this part of the Tree. Between Mars and Jupiter, souls cry for Love or Hate, Pain or Pleasure, War or Wealth, Charity or Chastisement—in fact, any extremities of experience—purely to convince themselves they are important enough to be a Life-Identity. Anything at all which makes a soul feel "I am ME" is more acceptable than denials of this insistence on existence which is our common basis of human belief. What we really fight for with the deepest possible motivation is our Sense of Identity.

It is impossible to avert wars in this or any world unless some satisfactory formula can be found which will guarantee the egoic integrities of the self-struggling souls seeking their expressed identities. First and foremost, they need to feel *themselves*. In human ways we try this in all directions—as people, families, occupations, associations, nationalities, or whatever gives us the feeling of "belonging and being" so that we realize we are actualities. Whatever threatens our Identification threatens us, and so we fight for its preservation. The deeper we believe this, the harder we will fight. Those who see their Inner identities in terms of national or racial characteristics will fight to maintain these with all their power, and indeed there is no reason why they should not if they are unable to adjust their entities to life apart from these very deep divisions of ethnical entitization. We are fundamentally entitled to BE WHAT WE WILL Within the Cosmos of Consciousness we have chosen.

It is quite obvious that whatever such a Supreme Formula might be that would save perhaps all of us from eventual destruction, its essential nature and constructions must very definitely be Spiritual rather than material. Physical threats and bribes only avert violence for uneasy periods of pseudo-peace. The same stimuli may equally be used to precipitate trouble. None may become Emancipated Entities, spiritually secure in their own continuum of Cosmic Consciousness, save souls able to rise far beyond the reach of being bought or frightened. Those who control both Mars and Jupiter in themselves, may truly be called "Just." We are familiar with the Buddhist formula "Convert Untrue Self to True Unself," which is intended to accomplish the miraculous shift in consciousness for us which will solve our self-problems with a single solution. Theoretically this may be so, but souls evolving through the Western Tradition cannot accept it in those terms, therefore it is impractical for us as it stands. We need sound spiritual assurances that far from giving ourselves up in any way, we shall become ever greater and greater souls beyond any human range of harm, having capabilities only limited by the extent of our own consciousness. We do not seek to renounce Self in the Great Nil, but realize It in that Complete Condition. The Western Formula is more like, "BE WHAT AND WHOM THOU WILT WITHIN THEE." If that can be successfully worked out, our war-worries would be slight. Actually both Western and Eastern Formularies amount to the same Ultimate State, but each needs its own suitable approach to the Absolute.

Whether our Humanity as a whole will succeed in discovering this Self-secret of consciously compensating the effect of Mars and Jupiter is something to be prayed for rather than assumed. If we are ever to live on this planet with relative freedom from fears of war and weight of wealth, balanced between poverty and possession along a Just Light-Life-Line, the secret of so succeeding will be learned on this Path of the Tree especially. We can scarcely over-stress the importance or necessity for prolonged investigation of this particular Path. It can mean a life-or-death difference for countless souls. Here, we have done no more than flick the lightest touch of consciousness across its most superficial structure. The need is for deeper and ever deeper probing with the strongest searchlight any self may shine from inside its own being. Once Mars and Jupiter can be held in balance by humanity and kept in their Cosmic Course, our Spiritual Way ahead is at least safeguarded. Every soul is responsible for working this out for himself, and those intending the Operation of the Nineteenth Path had better ask the Spiritual categories of Consciousness represented by Mars and Jupiter how to proceed. They alone hold the Keys between them.

The Twentieth Path

SPHERE—LETTER CODE: Mercy 4 M 6 Beauty
DIVINE ORIGINATION: EL—ELOAH VA   The
    DAATh   Mighty
ARCHANGELIC CREATION: Tzadkiel—Michael   Application
ANGELIC FORMATION: Chasmalim—Malakim Effort
APPARENT EXPRESSION: Jupiter—Sun   Powcr
TAROT SYMBOL: STRENGTH

Here we find Energy being used for the single purpose of controlling other Energies so that these work only for beneficent and beautiful reasons. Only a God-sized combination of experience and right intentions accomplishes this. It is the type of power exercised by an Overlord who is determined to keep everything in a state of strong order for the sake of all asking to live in peaceful prosperity among harmoniously harnessed strength. A good motto for the Path would be: "Peace with Power."

Although the guiding Life-principle of the Tree is an ultimate BE AS THOU WILT, this must never be interpreted to the least degree as any kind of license for bad behavior. The control of such conduct is encountered here. There are really only two ways anyone can behave: Inwardly towards himself affecting his own nature and Inner Cosmos, or Outwardly toward others, influencing those individuals into courses of action and reaction they would not otherwise have taken. Both these ways meet up in the end through what we might call a Karmic cycle of consciousness.

If anyone behaves badly towards others by his own Will or Intention, then the combined strength of those people is likely to be directed into corrective channels because of their multiplied Wills, and the ill-behaved individual is controlled for the sake of law and order among the whole community. Cosmos controls Chaotic effects within Itself to maintain Its integrity. On the other hand, if anyone is acting badly in a purely private capacity so to speak, directing his behavior into himself rather than to-wards fellow-humans, he comes up against another type of cor-rective control which is much more difficult to recognize or avoid. That is the control exercised by the Strength of the Life-Spirit It-self, acting along quite different Time-and-Event tracks from those humans use, but with far more certain results. There are two types of control: One by firm kindness in the case of those able to accept this method, or drastic discipline for those who defy well-intentioned direction. On this Path we are dealing with the first method, characterized by Mercy and Beauty.

The Tarot Symbol here is a powerful Figure of a probably an-drogynous nature but suggestive of Female polarity, shown in the act of quietly controlling the jaws of a lion. This is one of the only two Tarot trumps with an eternity emblem over the Figure's head, which in older packs is shown by the twist of a hat-brim. The other card is the Magician, which, if we connect the two, seems to signify that Magic is applied strength of Will in service to the Eternal Entity or Living Spirit.

Probably the old name of the card, "Force," suits it best. We hear a lot about "force-fields" today as descriptions of energized areas round specific sources of strength. Most esoteric Systems agree that there is only One Energy in Existence, and all the ap-parently different forces are adaptions of it according to Cosmic circumstances. Physical science seems to be tending to much the same conclusions. Theoretically, and in many cases now practi-cally, forces are convertible into each other's terms; as, for in-stance, the Magnetism-Electricity-heat-Light chain of energy events. Equivalent conversions are also possible along Inner lines of force-action, using processes of consciousness that are sometimes thought of as "Magic." This is the type of Force espe-cially summed up in our present Tarot Symbol.

The background of the card is a golden sky-field to show the idealistic level from whence the Concept comes. The only land-scape visible consists of pleasing green fields and hills, with a mountain peak in the far distance. Mountains usually signify heights of attainment or objectives possible with considerable difficulty. The message here is gaining ascendancy over Nature by means of effort. We should note in passing that no water ap-pears in the picture.

The dominant Figure of this Trump is clad in a white robe,

partly to indicate purity of purpose and partly to show its super-human character. Only one other Figure in this pack has a similar robe and that is Temperance, who is winged as well. Strength is not winged, and has brown rather than golden hair. This makes a nice distinction between the two comparable Trumps, because where Temperance is strictly a mediator and moderator in character, Strength, or Force, is directly applied from one level of energy to influence the issues of others on lesser levels. Both Temperance and Strength are modifiers of action, but where Temperance is conciliatory, Strength is mandatory in effect. Thus, Temperance is represented with wings to mean movement from one side of an issue to another, strength is depicted without wings to mean the taking up of a position and acting from thence. We are therefore looking at a Symbol which signifies the position of Strength we should adopt when dealing with Life along the lines of this present Path.

The Strength-Figure is girdled and garlanded with a chain of red roses and green leaves, these complementary colors indicating that passions should be held at a safe distance from each other throughout our courses of consciousness. There are two roses in the garland, the number of Wisdom, and six in the girdle, the number of Beauty, which makes another likeness between this trump and Temperance. Nevertheless there are four bunches of leaves sticking up from the garland on the head like horns, and horned roses have always stood for Strength, while four is the number of Mercy on the Tree. Mercy with Strength. Just above the garland, two or three little dots represent bees attracted to the flowers, and the Sweetness and Strength symbology of the bee and lion are highly significant with this card.

In contrast to the controlling Figure, the poor Lion looks rather a pathetic sort of beast. He is thin almost to emaciation, and his tail is between his legs in the subdued gesture of a submissive dog. He has no whiskers, and, as far as one can see, no teeth to speak of. Even his ears are drooping, and by the appearance of his front paws, he is about to lie down very tamely. Altogether the Lion presents a picture of exhausted energy finally yielding after a struggle with superior strength. Since a Lion is a carnivorous creature and in a sense Cosmos is cannibalistic, inasmuch as it eats itself to sustain its own Life, whatever controls the "mouth-function" of any Force governs that Force itself. This is what the Tarot Symbol here is meant to demonstrate.

There are a number of reasons why anyone would take an animal by the mouth in the way this card shows. The most obvious are to silence it, prevent it biting, examine its teeth, feed it, or simply pet and play with it. All these reasons apply here, and we should note the Lion is perfectly docile, responding well to its handler's intentions. Somehow, there is a kind of empathy between Beauty and the Beast we should try and learn something about.

Who is this mysterious Beauty, and what power has she over Brute Force? Today, she answers to the name of applied Science, though she was once called "Gnosis," which has a very similar significance. Hers is the quietly compelling Force of Cosmic Beauty and Harmony, keeping everything in its own kind of order by a compassionate Consciousness. If we want to see her at work, we have only to look around a room or Temple where we sit and watch what she does. We shall see little evidence of her activity on the surface, but as we go deeper and deeper into things, irrefutable signs of Force and Strength appear everywhere. The atmospheric pressure, for instance, without which our bodies would fly apart. Then the Force of gravity which keeps us in place. There is the electricity supplying us with light, heat, and services. The magnetic field of the Earth is present also, and a great number of other Force-fields of which we know little or nothing as yet. There are Forces constantly acting in and around us quite unnoticed by our ordinary physical senses, which keep us alive and aware of our objective conscious circumstances. That is the type of beneficial Force meant by the Tarot Symbol here.

We are shown that we ought to control our forces as the Gnosis-Figure governs the Lion from a higher level. If we learn how to hold our "Lion's mouth" with the "grip of advantage," we may also feed or starve our forces, prevent them from injuring ourselves or anyone else, examine their "teeth," or the effectiveness of their "bite," work silently or with a roar, and in fact do what We Will with our Lion's share of strength; always providing we do all this with a firm and kindly Knowledge in the Name of Beauty and harmony. That is real spiritual Strength, which must never be confused with violence of any description.

Strength of such a kind is not always easy to recognize. The Lion, with its roaring and rampaging, power of presence, and all other Leonine characteristics, makes himself seen and heard with a great Show of force, inspiring awe and fear mixed with admiration from his entire audience. The quiet and silent strength of the Force-Figure, controlling such commotion with a firm gesture of will, attracts much less attention because it appears unspectacular by comparison. This means plainly enough that we are supposed to bring all the power and performance of our animal passions into the control of our higher capabilities for handling these exuberant energies from spiritual standpoints. There are certainly enough legends of Beauty being the best bondage for Beasts and we might remember the tale of the Lion which broke the strongest chains easily enough, yet was led into willing captivity by a Beautiful Lady with a rope of Roses.

From another angle we might see the Lion as a "devourer of flesh," or our physical passions and lusts which tear us apart emotionally before we gain sufficient strength to hold them captive, or simply wear them out through sheer survival. We must remember the Eternity Symbol over the head of the Figure. If we live long enough, we shall outlast all human passions and lusts until they become relatively feeble enough to come into our control tamely and obediently. This means we have to identify ourselves with our immortal principles which will rise above and outlast every Lion-lust we shall ever live through. Yet the Lion is a noble beast associated with regal qualities, and we should respect, rather than despise or condemn the animal passions he represents here. If we take up our positions of Inner strength on firm grounds of faith and stay there calmly as this Tarot Symbol shows, sooner or later the Lion will come quietly to us of its own accord, lick our hands as it is doing in the picture, then lie down beside us or follow As We Will on this Path. So will the Lion lie with the Lamb, once we have the secret of holding its mouth with our hands in the correct grip.

As an interesting sidelight, if we take the two Hebrew letters for "hand" and "mouth" (I and P) and combine these in different ways, there are some revealing phrases. IPH means to be fair and beautiful like the works of God. IPI indicates the beauty or order of a King, and the loveliness of a woman. PI means simply "my hand," or that which effects an act. All these seem very much to the point here.

However we look at this Symbol. it always speaks to us of

Harmonious Power, or Cosmos folding in contented captivity the Forces which might otherwise damage its structure senselessly. This is the main reason why a Female Figure is shown to indicate that such control is not associated with any kind of repressive counter-brutality, which might be supposed if the Master-Figure were male. The whole point of the picture is that the Lion has at last recognized the superiority of genuine spiritual strength and submitted to this power because it knows it will only meet with the kindest care from those controlling hands. In old-fashioned language, we should say that our lower natures accepted the authority of our Higher Selves. Perhaps the Lion in the Tarot Symbol takes this eventual course partly because it has come to realize its finite and very limited force by comparison with its Controller. So, too, should our merely mortal principles acknowledge the Eternal Energy we must identify with if we intend Immortality for ourselves.

All this and very much more may be learned by contemplation of the Tarot Symbol for this Path, but unless we actually live out the significance of a Symbol as an experience, we shall never assimilate it as we should. Lions, like ourselves, live by eating, and Initiates of the Path have to learn how to "eat up" the strong meat of spiritual Symbols so that these provide us with the Inner Power we need for living toward Immortality. In the picture, the exhausted Lion is looking up trustfully at the face of the Figure above whose head is the Eternity-emblem. This is the strongest meat of all for Lions with the courage to face their Cosmic destiny. Fed with such meat by Merciful Beauty, any Lion-hearted Initiate of this Way will endure with Energy forever.

Originatively, the Divine Aspects here are EL and ELOAH va DAATh. Put together, these Names carry the significance of: "The kindly Way of Knowledge." As most of us have discovered for ourselves, Life has two ways of teaching us about itself, the sharp way or the smooth one. This is the Path of peaceful Power. Our best plan is to gain as much as we may from it while opportunity lasts, so that this will help us over rougher periods of living. A friendly Lion makes a more formidable defender than a tame dog, and the more power we obtain from this part of the Great Plan, the better condition our Life-systems will be in when we have to face the inevitable dangers and hazards which we may scarcely hope to avoid altogether as incarnate humans.

On the previous Path of Justice, we considered the "Stick and Carrot" principle of progression along our main Middle Path. Here we have the "Carrot" by itself. We have often been told that the basis of our relationship with Cosmos is a Love-Fear reaction. It is very confusing to a young mind when the old-fashioned phrase "Fear and Love God" is encountered, but this is exactly the two-pronged Rod of Power with which a soul relates itself to Life on every level. If we take the Chariot analogy of the Life-Tree, this Path represents the rein in the driver's right hand, or what we might call the "love-lead." How, after all, do any reasonable beings relate themselves with Life? By determining what they consider is good for themselves, contrasting this with whatever they believe is bad for them, and finally trying to steer some kind of a central course between both extremities of their Way. This knowledge of Good and Evil is the fruit of the Edenic Tree, and here on the Tree of Life, from which we hope to obtain our ultimate Immortality, we are dealing specifically with the Path of Pleasure as distinct from the Path of Pain.

We gain our knowledge of Life through experiences which we translate emotionally as Joy and Sorrow, rationally as Acceptance or Rejection, and spiritually as Integrating or Disintegrating. If we take it here that the EL-ELOAH va DAATh axis presents us with an acceptable Path of Joyous Integration with Divine Power the whole idea of this particular Pathway should be plain enough. It is the Sympathetic, instead of an Antipathetic, way of discovering our relationships with Divine Life Itself.

The question of leading importance at this point is whether or not it is possible to live in a constant condition of integrated joy and happiness with all the benefits of life and no disadvantages or sorrows. Could we continue existing in the sort of "Happy Heaven" most human souls would consider so wonderful? Can we avoid experiences of Hell or Purgatory altogether? The issue is not so much *can* we as *should* we. Both types of experience are really human reactions to the oppositional controls of Cosmic stability, and are only necessary insofar as they keep us balanced along the Middle Way, progressing at a reasonable rate toward our Ultimate of Perfect Peace Profound. A growing soul has to develop past the necessity for either agonizing in Hell or luxuriating in Heaven except to the exact degree of each which may be called for in the way of Cosmic course-correction. A Master-Soul of the Middle Way would thus partake of Heavenly or Hellish experiences entirely As Willed by the Divine Drive in himself. When a soul is able to use all experiences associated with Pain or Pleasure for the Single Purpose of achieving Perfection in Peace Profound, then the course of his Cosmos becomes clear ahead.

The Divine Aspects of this Path show what amounts to all our human ideas of Happiness coming true. Prosperity, abundance, conviviality, power available for every constructive purpose, ease, elegance, and enjoyments of all descriptions. The Spirit of Life luxuriating in Itself. Not idly, be it noted, but actively. This is a Path for participators, not spectators. Enjoyment comes through effort here, and it is essentially the effort of doing what is believed to be right. One might say for the sake of pleasure obtained from the satisfaction of a good job well done. As Scripture puts it somewhat smugly, "And the Lord saw that it was good." Here we have the complete self-confidence arising naturally from the knowledge that what has to be done is well within the competence of the craftsman.

If we could only live our lesser lives with the least degree of confidence in the Master-Craft Consciousness controlling Cosmos, how different everything might be for us. Lacking the powers of this Path, we continue to endure quite needless miseries and frustrations. It would help if we could reach even a feeble recognition of the purposeful Power behind our lives which combines the Principles of Compassion and Harmony through this Path of Consciousness. The only way we might possibly achieve some slight share in this Power is firstly by faith in its existence, and secondly by belief in our own entitlement of claim thereto if we are willing to fulfill the conditions required of us.

There is a subtle difference here which must be clearly understood, between levels of self-confidence at the Divine and Human ends of Existence. We should not impute to our purely human personalities powers and capabilities which are actually of a Divine degree and far beyond our present reach. That is where many serious mistakes are made by those who over-estimate their potentials because of excessive egoism. Our ordinary human selves have very limited and localized powers indeed. Behind these self-expressions, however, are much greater categories of Self, ultimately culminating in the great Self-Spirit of Cosmic Life. Our effective energies and practical powers while we are alive on this Earth depend on the degree to which the energies of this Greater Self are focused through the force-fields of our personalized projections. We are only great to the extent we are able to invoke greatness into us, as it were, from these larger lives.

EL, the special Spirit of anything, and ELOAH va DAATh, the Spirit of Living Experience, are the Divine dispensers of power upon this Path. How often have we heard it said that we should "enter into the spirit" of whatever activity is being advocated, and taken this old phrase for granted as a pure figure of speech? It is much more, being a literal instruction of how to live on this Path. The real strength of any Life-system lies in its spirit, and without spiritual strength we shall never survive as souls. There is no use seeking for real strength in Life from the various pseudo-sources we have set up in this world in a foolish attempt to hide our worst weaknesses from ourselves. Only a single Source of genuine Inner Strength exists: the Living Spirit Itself. If we learn how to make correct contacts with this Strength upon our present Path, then we shall become strong enough to deal with whatever Life offers for our experience. There is no substitute for such Strength whatsoever, and it alone will enable us to achieve anything of true value in our lives. We should ask EL and ELOAH va DAATh for the secret of this Living Strength, because they hold the Keys between them.

Creatively, we meet the Archangels TZADKIEL and MICHAEL in partnership on this Twentieth Path. The Righteous One, and the Godlike One. In his relationship with Tzadkiel, Michael is seen here as an upright Leader, setting a standard to be followed by all who recognize the rules of good conduct. Tzadkiel's job is to help souls realize that they should have some kind of spiritual standards to live by. Between them, they are supposed to guide us along the right lines of Cosmic conduct.

How is anyone to know the rights and wrongs of anything? Since human history began, no one on Earth appears to have had final words on such vital issues. No sooner does a set of standards become generally accepted by any section of humanity, than social or religious changes occur which alter the standards so considerably that dissents and quarrels eventually upset the rest, and in the end people merely sort out another set to maintain until the next break-up of belief arrives. What passes for right with one generation is condemned as wrong by another, restored in some other form by a third, and so we go on.

At one time, the Ten Commandments served as a fairly common Standard for Life-behavior among the majority of mankind under one form of belief or another. Whether these were kept or broken, they served well enough as a *modus vivendi* among most civilized communities, and at least their principles were observed by various Creeds. Now, there seems to be a rejection by modernizing Mankind; not so much of the fundamentals of the Commandments, as the format in which they appear. The swing is toward substituting Human for Divine authority. This is a complete reversion to "DO WHAT THOU WILT, etc." Yet without a Code of Conduct or Standard stemming directly from Spiritual Principles, how can Man ever hope to rise above merely mortal and material levels? It seems reasonably probable that a very large proportion of human beings have no special intention whatever of passing evolutionary points beyond which their consciousness becomes directed from material to spiritual values. They do not ask for individual immortality, or for that matter expect any advantages except those they are able to sequester for themselves during a single earthly lifetime. Their standards of life are purely concerned with social, political. and financial affairs. Regarding physical death as a complete finality, they consider this even negates any responsibility they might incur for their behavior during life. Such an attitude leaves a soul no way whatever to learn otherwise except the Hard Way, commonly called "bitter experience." Human history is too full of this altogether.

What really Spiritual Standards, apart from the Commandments, do people live by if they seek a Standard at all? How many souls could clearly see and state their Life-Rule if this demand were suddenly made on them? Most of all, how many actually use such a Rule to direct their course of Life in Cosmos of their own True Will? This means, before considering any particular course in their lives, deliberately applying their Standard-Code and determining what ways the proposed course fails to match up with the Standard, or fulfill its conditions. Then, having assessed the situation, acting in accordance with the Standards upheld. Relatively few souls of this period bother much with purely Spiritual

Standards, except as these coincide with social, monetary. or other material interests. Yet our amazing advances in the technical fields of science, engineering, medicine, surgery. etc., are mainly due to the exactitude of Standards maintained almost everywhere on earth in this way.

So precise are engineering Standards, for instance, that it is possible for factories all over the world to make but one part apiece of some complicated mechanism with such accuracy that, when the whole thing gets finally assembled in one place, it functions perfectly in accordance with the designers' original intentions.

Until our Spiritual Standards are observed with the same accuracy and precision as modern engineering or scientific specifications, we cannot hope to fulfill our Maker's Directions to any remarkable degree; especially if we have lost, cannot read, or do not agree with our spiritual Specification Sheets. Even the best engineer or technician can accomplish little of importance without a Project Plan and Scale of Standards.

The Project Plan for the Qabalist is the Tree of Life Symbol, and the Standard Scale is the Pillar of the Principles as defined by the sphere of Humanity at one end, and Sphere of Divinity at the other, with the remaining Spheres marking the Degree-divisions between them. With this decimal Rule of Life, an instructed Qabalist measures and calculates the courses of Cosmos to be constructed and kept according to Will. The markings on this Rule say quite plainly:

10.	MALKUTH	O Earthliving ones,
9.	YESOD	Be faithful to Life,
8.	HOD	Intelligently honorable,
7.	NETZACH	Emotionally emancipated,
6.	TIPHERETH	Wholly harmonious,
5.	GEBURAH	Dutifully disciplined,
4.	CHESED	Kindly compassionate,
3.	BINAH	Understanding,
2.	CHOCKMAH	Wise,
1.	KETHER	Single-spirited.

and
ULTIMATELY
You Will

000. AIN SOPH AUR   Live limitlessly in Eternal Light
 00. AIN SOPH   Beyond all boundaries of Being
  0. AIN   as PERFECT PEACE
                           PROFOUND
        AMEN.

That is the rule of Life marked off for the practicing Qabalist. How to fulfill and measure up to those general specifications is the life work of all accepting the Rule. Everyone has to adjust himself as he believes best in order to uphold his spiritual standards, and this, of course, means regular readjustments as he continually recognizes his divergences. MICHAEL, the Standard-Bearer of this Path, will show these up by the Light of Conscience he represents, and TZADKIEL, the Right-doing One, will help to distinguish what should be done in any circumstances, and how necessary alterations ought to be made in conformity with changing conditions. They have the Keys to this part of the Twentieth Path.

Formatively, the Angelic Orders of the CHASMALIM and the MALAKIM share this Path. They are the Warmers and Governors. Their combining principle is Effort. The Malakim (literally "ruling or governing principles") act as controls toward whatever other Orders of Angel they work in combination with. Being Solar spirits, they have the effect of balancing out the natural functions of the various categories of specializing spirits associated with different divisions of Cosmos. In this case they have such an effect on the Chasmalim. These cheerful and jovial Angelics are perhaps comparable to the pleasure gained from the rightness of anything. There is a natural enjoyment in feeling right which we all know well enough, yet at the same time do not care to experience at any severe cost to other souls. So many ways exist of being right, that we need not suppose this impossible unless others are wrong somehow. We can make right choices for ourselves, appreciate the rights of others for themselves, and not purely because we believe everyone else is wrong. Yet we can be so right that the extremity of self-righteousness becomes dangerous, and smug self-satisfaction threatens the balance of our Cosmos. This is where the Malakim help to counteract such conditions.

They do this in a good-natured way by trying to make us laugh or smile at our own mistakes, crack the crust of our pomposity with honest laughter, and see ourselves in the light of an amused awareness by which a higher order of Life than ours might view some of our less repulsive Earthly antics. The famous line of "seeing ourselves as others see us" applies if we think of "Others" in the Otherworld Entities. After all, the behavior of animals in Zoological Gardens amuses a great number of humans in the kindliest and most sympathetic way. Surely a great deal of our behavior must have an equivalent effect with Those able to observe us without our immediate recognition of them. For that matter, how can we be sure we are not kept under surveillance by souls like ourselves in far more advanced corners of Cosmos. It is not technically impossible that anything we do or say might be relayed to viewing screens in other Time-Space locations. Nothing but the good nature of such people would prevent them prying into our private concerns everywhere on Earth. That sort of good nature is typically Chasmalic.

If we could only "cut ourselves down to size" in spiritual Dimensions more accurately, by the aid of the Malakim-Chasmalim scissors, we might get into better Spiritual shape than most of us are. Do we have to take ourselves with such deadly and portentous seriousness, or pretentious solemnity, in order to realize our importance? What sort of a God would enjoy the sound of a lash rather than a laugh? Only a Devilish Divinity would be pleased with pain. Holiness and Happiness are really inseparable in the true sense, and how can any being Love without Laughing?

Anyone with real confidence in his ability for some special reason, is normally cheerful and calm in that direction. Grim deadly earnestness is frequently a sign of incomplete confidence. This is true in Spiritual Dimensions also. If we are uncertain or doubtful along spiritual lines, we usually get horribly earnest and self-righteous in that particular way. This is characteristic of humanity faced with insecure spiritual positions, inclusive of strong elements of doubt and Inner indecision. Attitudes of gloom, dejection, or other abnormal insistence on "sin," "punishment," "guilt," and the like, are all evidence of human mistrust in Cosmic compassion.

Those who sincerely feel that with help from Inner Sources they could tackle and eventually overcome whatever spiritual difficulties or deficiencies they may have to cope with, have every reason to be quietly cheerful about their prospects—more so if they hear the Chasmalim offering encouragement during the worst moments. Chasmalim do not lie and say there will be no difficulties or bad situations to face. They tell the truth, and assure their hearers that no matter how bad things seem, there is good on the other side of the situation somewhere. Were it not for such often illogical and unlikely Inner assurances, uncountable souls would certainly perish very miserably. The comfort offered by the optimistic Chasmalim is frequently all that provides souls with enough incentive to survive.

The measure of the MALAKIM and cheer of the CHASMALIM should get our souls into reasonable shape if we form ourselves in the ways they outline. As Formators, that is no more than their job. Besides they have the Keys here.

Expressively, this Path is worked with a combination of Jupiter and Sun. The astrologically minded will probably equate this with great wealth, prominent position, and all kinds of "success stories." This could be very far from the spiritual situation here. What is indicated as an ideal for achievement is the acquisition of sufficient spiritual strength to use all forms of material resources and advantages for beneficial purposes, uncontaminated by greed, lust for power, or the usual failures and errors of human beings with the possessions of Pluto, and the soul of an unequated egotist.

The aim here, is purity of purpose and incorruptibility of intention. Be it remembered that the traditional metals of Sol and Jupiter are gold and tin, two untarnishables.

It is positively not the accumulation or gain of riches and renown that apply on this Path, but the achievement of a soul-state beyond becoming unbalanced by such responsibilities. In other words, a soul fit to be favored and trusted with powers and positions which might very seriously affect maybe millions of lives. Whether or not an individual soul actually acquires or inherits such doubtful advantages in this world is not so important as that the soul should be worthy to administer those estates if elected for this purpose. It is the Inner state of readiness for responsibility which counts. None should wait until born into powerful positions before learning how to manage affairs from that angle. So much trouble in this world derives from entirely unsuitable, unstable, and quite unready types of souls obtaining positions of authority and influence from which they are willingly or inadvertently able to cause great damage all round them in the political, social, and spiritual fields.

An instructed Initiate of the Qabalah prays that he may never be able to wield powers beyond his degree of development on this Path. Instead, every spiritual effort is made to gain those true qualities of the Life-tree which alone bring any soul into a state of worthiness to be entrusted with the Energies of existence and their symbolic counterparts in material currency. The very first necessity an Initiate should pray for is fitness on all levels. Powers and position are purely secondary considerations if, and only if, these might serve some useful purpose in the Plan for Perfection.

A query probably arises here on the possibility of anyone being properly prepared to handle powers or positions in material actuality without the experience itself in earthly terms. The answer is that correct and adequate spiritual development does eventually result in souls becoming fit to do whatever the Will or Intention initiating such development has designed. This happens all the time on Earth in lesser ways, when individuals are put through colleges and training schools in order to condition them for some particular form of employment or service. Those institutions cannot possibly impart a fraction of the spiritual experience and Inner training necessary for soul-development into anything like an ideal state of being for fulfilling very high spiritual standards. Nor does it seem that many modern establishments of earth mean to turn out much more than competent technicians controllable by manipulated pressure from artificial socio-economic structures. Unless some satisfactory equivalents for the Old Mystery Schools of Initiation are successfully instituted again on Earth, the spiritual future of humanity is not likely to be a great one in terms of very wide reference.

These Spiritual Schools of the Mysteries were intended for the training and production of souls fit to take places of senior responsibility in the Cosmic Sense for human relationships with Divinity. This would also entail the assumption of Earthly offices and estates calculated to further this main motivation. The ancient Office of Sacred King is an example. Those operating the structures of such Schools for Souls realized perfectly well that many lifetimes or generations might be needed before souls could possibly reach a state of essential rightness or qualification for the particular position they were meant to fill. Spiritual maturity is only arrived at through full cycles of Inner Seasons corresponding with the Solar cycles of Earth, though extended much deeper into Existence. Inner Cosmos works on very different Time-tracks to the one we are living at the moment. The complete transactions of a human lifetime may only provide the barest alteration in the spiritual "genes" through which another incarnation becomes possible. It was a major aim of the Mystery Schools to offer spiritual Training Systems which produced the best results with the least wastage of effort over the fewest incarnations consistent with the finest qualities and characteristics of souls possible.

Looking at our present world, it is cynically tempting to ask why such Schools have failed. In fact they have not failed, but simply not yet succeeded. Relatively few souls are willing to offer themselves life after life as candidates for training through such a streamlined, disciplined, and sometimes stringent program, which only the most dedicated of all are likely to remain with from one end to the other. Most people prefer to take their chances with the general Stream of Life and get what they can out of it for themselves. Nevertheless, once any soul has been attached to the Inner Mysteries, he is bound to carry something of the spiritual qualities obtained therefrom around with him, and so disseminate these through Cosmos. Eventually those souls usually complete full circle, and return to their Schools for the purpose of continuing their training. No effort made by Initiates of the Inner Mysteries is ever wasted. There is certainly a current need for intensifying these efforts if humanity as a whole, or even selectively, is going to survive the next few generations with genuine spiritual success.

This is the Path of the Tree, where all that is represented by the Sun and Jupiter must come to balance, on which we have to learn how to cope with plenitudes of power, prosperity, and all that goes with governing positions. When we discover, like the "Lady in the picture," how to control the Lion's mouth which would otherwise devour us, we shall be free to use this Path AS WE WILL. Perhaps the Lion stands for "animal appetites," sheer greed, or a dog-eat-dog attitude. Whatever it means, each soul has to encounter it for himself here, and grow strong enough to conquer and subdue it so that the Lion obeys the Lady's intentions. The Keys of this operation are held by Solar-Jovian hands and that is where we should collect them—if we Will.

The Twenty-first Path

SPHERE—LETTER CODE: Mercy 4 N 7 Victory
DIVINE ORIGINATION: EL—IHVH SABAOTH   THE
    Merciful
ARCHANGELIC CREATION: Tzadkiel—Auriel   Tolerance
ANGELIC FORMATION: Chasmalim—Elohim   Security
APPARENT EXPRESSION: Jupiter—Venus   Compatibility
TAROT SYMBOL: EMPRESS

On this Twenty-first Path we have the impression of Compassionate Victory, and a rulership by love and affection rather than any suppressive or authoritative means. A spirit of tolerance prevails here which is in no way due to the slightest weakness, but because those who are proper to this Path are also compatible with each other. Feeling secure in mutual affection, all entities here live together in a happy condition of trustful love. What else might we expect when Jove and Venus agree with one another?

The Tarot Symbol of the Empress is seldom given the attention she deserves. She means so much more than just beneficial government by a loved ruler. She is usually equated with fecundity, because of all the symbology about her: ripe grain, trees, flowing water, and the suggestion that she herself is pregnant. True enough, but of greater importance still is the fact that she represents only the best type of fruitful life. Her concern is not so much with quantity, as with the highest possible quality of everything to do with the fertility factor of Existence. That is her Realm and Empire which she rules by the Right of her own example. From our point of view, she is the rule of Nature in Mankind which eventually enables Man to govern Nature by her own Laws and obtain maximum benefits.

This triumph is shown in the Empress-Symbol by the laurel

crown of Victory beneath the starry diadem indicating her Heavenly Nature. Some believe we triumph over Nature, but we do not—we triumph with her, which is quite different. The Empress does not represent our failures in Life, but our successes. She stands for all we have done, and will do yet, in the way of becoming better and better beings. Her Royal Arms are shown as a heart with the sign of Venus on it. On the Tree of Life, the heart obviously links with Mercy and Compassion at Chesed-Jupiter, and the Venus sign with Victory at Netzach-Venus. This is plainly her Path. Some cards show an eagle on her shield as a Royal emblem, which has also been taken as a Phoenix to indicate the eternal renewal of Life in improved ways from old forms.

The Empress displays herself seated very comfortably and easily. Cushions indicate this in the Waite pack. Common sense alone tells us that the more we learn from the Empress concerning the secrets of Nature and their development, the greater our standards of comfortable living will become on all levels of life. What might be her suggestions for gaining such knowledge and ability? If we look at the Symbol long enough, it will be seen that she is holding up what seems like a short scepter, as if to draw attention to the object. Several interpretations of it are possible, but the one which makes the most sense is that the scepter consists of a clear globe mounted on a graduated stem. Its essential symbolical message is "See and Mark—Study and Measure. Find and Focus." It should also be noted that the general shape of the scepter is like a Keyhole. The Empress might as well be saying: "Unlock me, and enter the Inner Empire of Natural Existence." She could scarcely speak more clearly. The actual Key in this instance is not visible because the Empress is probably sitting on it. When she rises to greet souls on this Path, the Key will be available, but Royalty does not usually rise except for equals, or highly privileged people. If we cannot be the first of these, we may yet become the second.

The Crystal Globe signifies clear and carefully focused concentration of consciousness directed toward whatever we would learn. Intensive and Intelligent Interest. In or concerning what? No less than the whole of nature and its workings. The Empress is surrounded by natural phenomena, and these have their Inner spiritual equivalents. We see the external products of Internal energies. Growth, maturity, technical ability, refinement, and many other qualities are represented, all bound together with the greatest attraction we know of—Love. The Empress says again: "Love and Learn. Love Learning, and Learn Loving." Only sincere and deep spiritual Love unlocks the ultimate secrets of Nature. Venus opens what Vulcan shuts. The Mirror of Venus reveals all sorts of Mysteries in its magical surface, which in old times would be of highly polished tin on copper, the metals of Jupiter and Venus.

It is said Love laughs at locksmiths, and this is entirely true in the spiritual sense as well as the physical. We must love the Nature of anything or anyone in order to enter them. Love is the Key of admission to the adytum of any arcanum, human or otherwise. Hence we are told to Love God for the simple reason that such is the only way any Entity of Existence can possibly be entered, enjoyed, or united with. No Love—no Life.

The Empress deals with Love on a Royal basis, in the best and finest sense of the word. She would not even understand the application of such a wonderful word to the sordid sex-scufflings of sub-humanity scarcely risen above emergence from animal life-levels, and insulting sexuality in ways no true animal would ever dream of. To the Empress, Love is of noble birth altogether, being of Divine origination, and without Divine Love, no life should enter Earth, any more than entities of Earth should enter the Inner Kingdom lovelessly. This does not mean the Empress symbolizes sexless love. Far from it. She is, however, the antithesis of loveless sex. For her, this is the saddest and most senseless occupation (one might say preoccupation) in the world. She would not allow this in her Empire, where none live without Love.

One of the most serious deficiencies in the English language is a lack of "Love-words" to indicate degrees and types of Love from highest to lowest, and also the antonyms to these expressions. There is therefore no single verbal symbol we can apply to the Empress-type of Love encountered on this Path. It is Love on such a splendid scale that relatively few humans are able to conceive its actuality or even believe it really exists. Yet it does not necessarily imply wealth, ostentation, spectacular display, or any merely vulgar possessions or material advantages. The Empress-scale of Love is essentially spiritual in quality, being a natural inherency of the soul to become its noblest among all that is most highly cultured, developed, polished, and of great ex- cellence. We may think of it as the victory of what is best in a soul over what is worst in it. The survival of good taste over bad. This is not a question of money at all, but entirely of Inner attitude. It is easily possible to find better taste and appreciation together with finer Love in circumstances of physical poverty, than amid the most expensive circles. The converse may equally be true, and well-ordered wealth contrasts favorably with ill-disposed poverty, plus lack of even elementary Love. Everything comes from Within, and any disposition of Outer effects is only indicative of the soul-state arranging it. The Empress-soul presides over an Empire of Elegance from one end of its Existence to another. It reaches from the flowers of the fields to the stars in Space. Elegance is Eternal.

Another main point the Empress represents is what used to be called quite plainly "good breeding." Otherwise intentional production of high quality humans. Once people were either "well" or "ill" bred. This depended on genetic characteristics being carefully chosen and related. Originally, it had nothing to do with money or social status, but was meant to indicate facilities for incarnation among advanced souls capable of leading others by the light of their own achievements. They became what was later termed the "ruling Classes," but unhappily history has shown up their failures rather than emphasized their successes. They did not fail quite as badly as many nowadays might like to suppose. Despite everything, they managed to get something of their evolutionary characteristics into humanity. Perhaps the last relic of their activity is traceable in the custom of *droit de signeur,* or the breeding of one offspring of lordly stock in each suitable peasant family. Scarcely an ideal practice, but it did have an effect of spreading selective strains over a widening field. Since the act was usually unmotivated by genuine Love, however, results were scarcely satisfactory by spiritual standards. The Empress now has to solve the problem of selecting the best breeding strains among the various categories of humanity and eliminating the species that are degenerating or unimprovable beyond low levels. Unless this can be done effectively and within reasonably few generations from ours, the Empress-method will fail to control Chaos, and much more stringent measures must apply. It is better to work with the Empress than against her.

Man has never abrogated a single Law of Nature. We have
only learned to take full advantage of them, and so relate them
through our consciousness that they respond as we choose to select patterns for their behavior. This is material magic. We can
work eventually in Spiritual Dimensions by selecting a Symbolic
Soul-Pattern, and operating Inner Energies through them. This
is Spiritual Magic, which we are concerned with in these studies,
and the Laws of Nature still apply. The Tree of Life Symbol, and
its associated Magical practices, show a sincere attempt to bring
all the best of Existence together in the finest possible System of
Spiritual selection and specification. It is therefore quite in keeping with the Empress-ideals of this Path. The more we ask her in
the ways she suggests, the better we are bound to become because of what she brings out of us. She holds the best of our Inner
ancestry in her capable hands. We might as well reach for the
Key she offers.

Originatively, we walk this Path with the God-Aspects of EL
and IHVH SABAOTh combined as the Merciful one. In particular, IHVH SABAOTh signifies "I will be Everyone." A "One and
All" relationship. There are many ways this may be taken. Some
assume a kind of Universal Uniformity in which all individuals
are equals, being as it were replicas of each other in a state of
what can only be imagined as Cosmic Communism, or Absolute
Monotony of Manifestation. If Divinity has nothing better to offer
Humanity than a species of Holy Homogeny, then there is neither point nor purpose to our individual conditions of entitized
consciousness through soul-states which we call "ourselves." Yet
every Faith, Tradition, and Spiritual System has a "One and All-
ness" theme between Divinity and Humanity as a basic belief.

Not so long ago in human history, major religious ideologies
were used as compulsive formularies to be forced upon unsuitable sections of Mankind in order to artificially absorb their identities and energies into spiritual subservience within this field
controlled by unscrupulous manipulators on either side of the
Veil for their own ends. The same process continues today except
that political and commercial ideologies have taken the place of
religious ones. Fundamentally, this amounts to "soul-stealing"
on most shameful scales, and Qabalistic principles and practice
totally oppose such Inner oppression. It is a basic belief in
Qabalah that every separate soul has an inherent responsibility

for relating itself with Divinity and other souls in its individual way and Will deriving from Inner contact with Divine Life Itself. All that Qabalah does is supply a system of Symbols and encourage souls in arriving at a "find-it-yourself Faith." It does not insist on uniformity of belief or practice as an imposition upon any soul whatever. On the contrary, an initiated Qabalist considers that every distinct soul, whether from an individual, cultural, familial, or ethical viewpoint has its own unique contribution to offer Cosmos, without which Cosmos is incomplete.

This is a highly important consideration, and we must give it a little detailed attention. It means that individualism is essential to Inner Entity, and that our characteristic distinctions of ancestral associations, races, codes, etc., have the highest value in making up the components of a common Cosmos. It is our differences from each other which are so absolutely necessary for promoting unity among us all in Spirit. If all colors were identical how could a picture be possible? If only a single note existed, no Symphony would ever be heard. Were there but one letter, no literature could be written. Without all the Elements, Matter would not Manifest. Life is One, but It consists of every single individual entity that will ever live. All living for One by themselves.

Every unit of Energy that makes up our material Universe is individual, free in its Space orbit like a soul in its Inner equivalent. If all our Earth-energy "collapsed," and "fell together" as it were, our planet would diminish to very small and insignificant proportions indeed. We are what we are because we are collectively "WE" as Life-units in mutually acceptable association. To lose our identities is to lose our lives altogether, and our souls are the seats of our individualism. Loss of soul is entire loss of entitized life.

We differ from each other on Earth, just as the Spheres differ from each other on the Tree, yet such differences are essential to produce the Plan for Perfection. We are different sorts of people by necessity, because it is exchanges of Energy which produce Life, and without differences there can be no such exchanges. Nothing but our differences from one level of Life to another keep us alive at all. The Symbol of the Waterfall in the Empress-card indicates this. No flow—no Force. Attempts at reducing human souls to uniform levels of enforced flatness is little short of mass spiritual murder on a very subtle scale. Such programmed processing is aimed at producing personal powerlessness over large Life-areas, and concentrating energies almost exclusively in the hands of clever controllers. Perhaps this may be necessary to some extent as a temporary measure for a brief period during present history, but the dangers to the Spiritual structure of our Cosmos are desperately serious. The application of spiritual anesthesia is an exceptionally hazardous operation, only justified for the gravest reasons. To stupefy souls with no other object than taking advantage of them is a blasphemy against Being Itself.

Initiates of all Inner Systems are only too aware of what is happening among humanity during our present era. It is hard to keep Inwardly awake, and decidedly difficult to work in conditions of confusion not unlike the mud and semi-darkness obscuring the working world of a deep-sea diver. Even with well-designed equipment and training, the task of clarifying and reconstituting the dangerously confused and disordered currents of immediate human Inner consciousness is formidable in the extreme. To some extent, it may be compared with the improbable job of repairing and rewiring some highly complicated and semi-burned out electronic circuitry while the main power is still connected. One serious mistake might easily electrocute everyone and destroy the apparatus as well.

In this world, we have evolved into very distinct species, races, and types of people, for definite purposes concerned with our particular Cosmos. Each has its own function to fulfill in its own way which none other could achieve exactly in that fashion. Every soul has something to say for itself that no one else is capable of uttering. This is indicated by the old legend of the True Divine Name being unutterable by Man, because it consisted of as many letters as there were human souls, and each soul had to find its particular letter and then utter it together with everyone else. That is the meaning of "I will be Everyone." The Life-Spirit has not yet been everyone, and we have scarcely begun to find our own souls before we are in real danger of losing them again.

As far as a Qabalist is concerned, whatever helps to relate Life through individual souls or whole racial ethnoi with the Single Living Spirit according to their particular spiritual specifications is in keeping with Cosmos. Whatever attempts to depersonalize, uncharacterize, or force evolving spiritual structures into artificial and unnaturally controlled confinements of consciousness from sheerly assimilative motivations is utterly wrong. Souls should never become spiritual sausage meat to supply someone else's life-larder.

To this extent, a sincere Qabalist is a sincere racialist, believing that every human race and species has its own Ethos of absolutely unique character with its priceless gift to offer the entire world. Genocide, or destructive compulsion of any race into denials of its individual Ethos, is not only a shocking moral wrong, but if successful, would deprive others of that essential contribution to Cosmos. We might remember here the story of the Three Magi who came of three races, the White, the Dark, and the Medium, like the Pillars of the Tree. They brought entirely different gifts to the same spirit, and their Symbols could translate into modern terms as Wealth (Gold), Work (Myrrh), and Worship (Frankincense). It might also be remembered that these were gifts freely offered by willing love, and not extorted from the Magi, or forced by them upon reluctant recipients. In that entirely free offering and acceptance lay the spiritual value and wonder of those unforgettable gifts. If Humanity as a whole ever learns how to give and take each other's Inner gifts in the same Magical Spirit, it may well be supposed that a Second Coming, when Divinity comes forth from everyone, is imminent.

That is the message of this part of this Path. How all must learn through themselves and their Ethnoi, their best and finest ways of serving (giving to and taking from) or exchanging energies with the Single Living Spirit. Unless we find this ideal "One and All" relationship among us on this Earth, and work it successfully, even the "little that we have" may be taken from us. To discover more about these vital issues, we must ask that Unique Spark of the Universal Spirit in ourselves which is represented here as the EL-IHVH SABAOTh relationship. There lie the necessary Keys.

Creatively, this twenty-first Path is aligned with Archangels TZADKIEL and AURIEL. Right and Light again. Auriel the "Light of God" as an archangel of Earth, and Custodian of the special "Spark" of Divinity that every human entity is entrusted with as an evolving soul. The Inner Light of everyone. Just the sort of archangel we would expect to find at this point of the Tree.

Auriel?

If we were reminded of the Magi in the last part of our present Path, we are brought to mind of the Star here by Auriel. He represents the Hidden Light in ourselves we have to discover and follow in order to reach the point where the Divine Spirit "comes to Birth" in our souls by the "Virgin" part of our Inner beings which only Divinity may inseminate with Its essential Entity. The Incarnation Myth tells the whole story to those who understand its symbolic speech. The Incarnating Divinity comes out of a Virgin Womb into the semi-dark Cavern of our deep Consciousness amid the peaceful animals of our obedient instincts. The Incarnation displays Itself from a manger of animal food, appearing thus as the sustaining One of Spirit, who is offered for the Divine nourishment of all Mankind. This Symbolism is confirmed at the end of the story by the Flesh and Blood commemorative and consecrating Covenant of sacramental Bread and Wine. Then the Light hides in Darkness again, and the entire Creation-cycle repeats with the Resurrection.

In olden days, one of the few ways of safeguarding a lighted lamp or small flame when exposed to weather outside a house, was to put it in a large earthenware jar while being carried around. That is a Symbol which explains Auriel's connection with Earth. Our bodies and beings are seen as the pot, fashioned as Divinity is said to have made Man from "good red Earth," and Auriel appears as Guardian of the Inner Flame. Break the pot, and the Flame rejoins its principle of Fire, from which all Angelic bodies are supposed to be constructed. Also the Flame is formally invisible to anyone looking on the outside of the pot, although heat is discernible to those who touch it. In the same way, we do not actually see much, if any, evidence of divinity in other incarnate human beings, but if we ever come close enough to touch them in reality, we shall feel indications of the Inner Flame quite unmistakably, providing we understand where these come from. The only angle from which the Flame may be seen is directly from above, or the Heavenly Viewpoint. An ancient proverb said: "The place of deepest darkness is always immediately under the lamp" for that reason. Generations accustomed to modern ease and electricity miss the point of so much of the old Wisdom, but they are not yet wise enough to replace it for themselves.

Following this analogy, it may be wondered what eventuates if the Flame goes out before the pot is broken. The same happens on spiritual levels as physical ones when soul and body separate. A body does not disappear in a flash at death—unless atomized. It decays over a period until nothing but clean bones remain. If Spirit and soul separate irreversibly, the soul also decays just as unpleasantly as the body, though usually for a much longer period and with more risk to spiritual health than putrefying corpses are to physical well-being. Such are the "shells," or "Empty ones," about whom repeated warnings have been issued so frequently in connection with necromantic practices. If artificially animated for malicious reasons, these filthy fabrications may be the means of severe spiritual infections. This explains the aversion to death and morbidity among all genuine Qabalistic practitioners and their dislike of what may be called "dealing with the dead." This does not refer to Inner Spiritual contacts established with the surviving souls of entities sharing the same Cosmic Circles whether embodied or otherwise. Since in such cases Spirit and soul are even more closely united than when in incarnation, prohibitions for contact on these high levels would not apply. The "dead" referred to are spiritually dead as well as physically and they must on no account be used for any form of "Magic," but should be decently disintegrated through the Inner equivalent of Earth-absorption similar to inhumation, or reduced to Elemental energy by Inner Fire like bodily cremation.

Auriel and Tzadkiel between them work for the victory of loveliness and pleasantness over ugly and horrifying entities or events. We can see how green vegetation and flowering plants try to cover the ravages of war made by Man on Earth. Sooner or later the unhappy memories of life fade out and the best impressions remain. Beauty lasts longer than beastliness, but it succeeds more slowly. "Truth takes Time to Triumph" might be the motto of Auriel and Tzadkiel. In comparison with other Pathworkings, this particular Path may seem extremely slow and leisurely. Nothing happens in a rush here, and everything evolves at the rate required for its best improvement into the finest its species can produce. This is where really selective strains are sorted out and separated from those of perhaps more rugged construction who will serve the Cosmic cause better in other categories. Thoroughbreds from mongrels in fact. Both types are needed and have their proper places in Existence, and all souls eventually have opportunities for evolving As They Will. It is the

Immortal Spirit in humans which is "equality before God," and not the soul, which is what it makes of itself. We are not "all equal in the eyes of God" as souls and individual entities at all, and never were—or will be. It is our difference from each other which makes us valuable as a Whole. Every one of us must find and fulfill their own function, however many lifetimes this may take. It is for AURIEL and TZADKIEL to help us bring out the best in ourselves on this Path. They have the Keys.

Formatively, the Angelic Orders of the CHASMALIM and ELOHIM appear as partners of the Path. This is the only position on the Right Hand Pillar where the Elohim are mentioned as a single species, and the word is always liable to cause confusion. Here it is taken to mean "gods" in the sense of personified ideas of Divinity held in the consciousness of every soul. Everyone has their own concepts of Divinity to some extent, even if the outer symbol is no better than their bank balance. Whatever anyone believes is bigger and better than they are, and in respect of which they align their thinking, living, and especially Willing, becomes their "God-Symbol," or "Cosmic Key," through which they relate their lives with everything and everyone else. Some souls manage this with a single Concept and may be termed monotheists, while others prefer a lot of minor Concepts and become pantheists. Those indifferent to Cosmic contact-Concepts usually describe themselves as atheists, but this actually means a verbal quibble to disclaim acknowledgments of their "gods" as such. Whatever people govern their lives by, amounts to their "gods," however poor and inadequate these may seem to others. The monetary-mechanistic "gods" of today are only modern extensions of the bribable-animistic "gods" which were accepted in the past. Mankind does not change as much as he flatters himself he does. The "gods" of crude and greedy people have the likeness of those souls. Archetypal Man may have been created in the Divine Image, but Earth-Man has to reflect that act by creating his own ideas of Divinity which will place him—wherever he rightly belongs in Cosmos. Those are the "gods" we are dealing with here, and very important to us they are.

Souls become what they make of themselves by means of their "gods." If these are no more than the usual personified motivations of purely materialistic character, then the souls accepting them will never rise higher than those levels until they change their Concepts. We never grow greater than our "gods," and our spiritual evolution depends on our "god-growth." When "gods" become "Gods," men are on the way to becoming "Man." Nevertheless, we should not utterly despise the "ground-gods" in use by so many millions among humanity. Selfish, stupid, clumsy, and even barbaric as they may seem to souls of more advanced spiritual culture, those crude creations of human cupidity and cunning are absolute necessities to the sort of soul which nothing finer will reach in nobler terms of reference. No souls should be condemned or blamed for attachment to their primitive power-personifications while they have not the ability to grow beyond their lower levels of Inner Life. Any wrong involved consists in refusal to "grow up with the Gods" and eventually attain Inner adulthood. Sooner or later, we have to change the "Mickey-Mouse" currency of our childish Inner consciousness for Credits based on beliefs backed by Divinity to ever deepening degrees of value.

To an initiated Qabalist the God-Concepts of the Tree Spheres are not fossilized out-of-date bygone beliefs, but evolving entitizations of Eternal Energy Itself. They are alive! Though their Principles are changeless, their personifications change to keep pace with Cosmos. The "Gods" of the Life-Tree are *growing* "Gods," and they grow as our souls should. Given enough lives, we have opportunities of growing up with them, and becoming also immortal. Once we arrive at a stage of making clear God-Concepts, and relating ourselves rightly with these, we shall be able to walk this Path in company with the Chasmalim and Elohim.

The Angelic task here is to formulate the very best and finest God-Concepts possible, while realizing that these have to change with our Cosmic rate. In fact, the entire process is one of refinement analogical to the way a pure product is developed from crude and contaminated material. In effect, we commence with mixed-up and inaccurate ideas about Divinity, then, during our relatively slow seasons of spiritual growth, we refine these steadily until the Inner essence of unalterable Truth begins to appear. If we ever arrive at the Absolute of this Essence, It and we become Identical, for it is the real "Elixir of Life" which does not confine Existence to one little mortal body, but permits Living through the entire Life-Pattern as everyone or anyone, always,

AT WILL. The Chasmalim and Elohim are trying to teach us how to "grow into God." No less. Most importantly, they are attempting this Ultimate Life-lesson by the kindest, nicest, and most welcome ways possible. If we cannot or will not benefit from their methods, there are others to deal with us as we deserve—much less enjoyable. As Kingsley pointed out, those unfit for the sweets of Mrs. Do-as-you-would-be-done-by, have to endure a birching from Mrs. Be-done-by-as-you-did. So we had best gain all the goodies we may from the former before the switches of the latter catch up with us. The CHASMALIM and ELOHIM will help us steer the best path between extremities. They have the Keys.

Expressively, the Influences we term Jupiterian and Venusian exert a common control on this Path. On low levels, no doubt, these might be claimed as Sex and Money, the main interests of such a percentage of Mankind. They may indeed represent these motivations to those whose spiritual standards are no higher. It must be recognized that Sex and Money do in fact mean "God" for countless souls unable to relate themselves with any other integrating factors of Cosmos. While souls are unwilling to seek Victory on wider and more important spiritual fields than physical sex and amassment of material wealth, they are best left to occupy themselves with such activities for as many lives as they need to grow out of this elementary soul-stage. When they learn how to make both Money and Sex into valuable services toward their best spiritual interests, they will begin to realize the true purpose of this Path. It is the old question of which is master or slave. Love worked with Will is indeed the Law of Inner Life.

Sex, at bottom basic, is a biological reproductive function common to even the lowest cellular creature. As our highest possibility, it is a spiritual faculty which enables us to establish polarized relationships with Divine Entity and achieve Ultimate Union with the Life-Spirit. As the *Gita* says: "Higher than Indra may thou lift thy lot—or sink it lower than the worm and gnat." Everything depends on how the Life energy is employed. Sex and soul are inseparable, but it is essential that we discover how to make the former serve the latter, rather than sink into a sense-servitude we have no will to liberate ourselves from.

Money at bottom may be about the surest means of holding souls in subjection to their worst inclinations if they are willing and eager to sell themselves for illusory and ephemeral gains, or so desperately driven by sheer oppressive poverty, that they have temporarily lost the spiritual strength to fight for Inner freedom. At the other end of the scale, credits, in keeping with spiritual rather than social standards, enable every possible advantage of Inner and Outer Existence to be made freely available for souls to relate themselves with Divine Reality. Money is not the "root of all evil." The correct quote is, "The *Love* of money is the root of all evil." Diverting our faculties for loving toward merely monetary objectives is the evil we must obtain Victory over on this particular Path.

Jupiter means so much more than money, and Venus stands for far greater varieties of Sex than purely biological behavior. Material millionaires may easily be spiritual paupers, and the most doggedly incessant sexualist be utterly devoid of any love or satisfaction whatever. To learn the secrets of this Path, we must learn how to feel incalculably rich with the gold of a sunset, and rejoice in our sexual relations with the shining Sun itself. As the counterbalance to this Inner extension of experience, we must come to realize the true value of money as being neither more nor less than what it will do for us and others in the best way of spiritual service, and only seek sexual experience of any sort for the sake of directing ourselves toward Divinity. The issue concerned here is one of applied realization.

It is perfectly possible to deal with money even in very small and ordinary ways in order to impart an intention of doing this in the Divine Name. It is equally possible to make each sex-motivated act into an impulse leading our souls towards Ultimate Light, rather than waste the whole energy of the act in petty and unsatisfactory personal pleasure. So amazingly much may be done for our best and truest Spiritual benefit by means of Sex and Money, that it is heartbreaking to see these inestimable resources so shamefully ill-treated among Mankind. It is not that prodigious quantities of either commodity are needed by anyone, but only that available supplies are used in the correct way as learned on this Path. A minimum properly applied is of far more value than a maximum recklessly squandered.

Unless humanity discovers and practices the finest Inner techniques of using Sex and Money for genuine Spiritual ends, our Earthly stage of evolution is not likely to improve very greatly. Such an achievement will be a major task for the next few generations, and it is to be hoped they will succeed where their predecessors failed. So many attempts have already been made and also made a mess of. Earlier generations tried donating Wealth to Temples and practicing religious sexuality with dedicated individuals. The Temple was supposed to do good with the money, and the prostitutes do good with their tension-tortured clients. As we know from history, the whole scheme was a failure because of human inadequacy to apply it properly. It remains for future incarnations of humanity to perfect the Sex-Money-Spirit System that will bestow the blessings on our souls we may expect from this particular Path. There should be enough for everyone who will ever exist.

Ask anyone why they are so concerned with Sex and Money, and they will probably say it is because they are seeking satisfaction therefrom. Satisfaction in its true sense, however, is a purely Spiritual state, and no amount of material incidents or accumulations can possibly give real satisfaction to any soul. No more may be gained that way than imitations and illusions of achievement which, having no great Inner depth or reality, soon pass by, leaving a discontented soul still snatching at shadows. It is not that sex and money are any more or less wrong than other living-incidentals, but we have not yet found out how to use their Principles so as to satisfy ourselves on the very deepest levels we can reach. These lie far beneath the usual surface of human consciousness, and it is only there that we shall ever reach a genuine and lasting state of entire satisfaction with our Life-affairs, especially about Sex and Money.

Sex is infinitely greater than a reproductory romp. Why should we assume that such is the only way of practicing it? Why need we deprive ourselves of opportunities for un-physical sex relationships with the Life-Spirit otherwise than in human bodies? Whatever we can do in physical terms, we may also do spiritually with considerably enhanced effect. This definitely includes Sex. In fact, really satisfactory sex-relationships are only possible if the spiritual factors involved are fully fulfilled. On bodily levels alone, sex is simply an insatiable repetitive impulse. We have to grow into physical puberty before we are capable of organic sex, and there is an equivalent of this on Inner levels of Life, where we have to reach a state of Spiritual potency when we become capable of Sex as a normal act of relationship with Divine Love. There is nothing peculiar about this whatever. It is simply an extension of our existence into other than material ways of living, even though we are still bound by the same fundamental Laws behind all Life.

There are Spiritual equivalents of Money (or, more properly, Credit), too. We can exchange currencies of consciousness among each other in much the same way that cash is dealt with on Earth, and practically all the fundamental principles of finance we are familiar with in Earthly practice apply Inwardly as well. There is a very important difference, however. Earthwardly, as we know, the controls of Finance, and consequently all humans affected by it, are kept within a relatively small circle of governing individuals, whose first concerns are naturally their own interests, combined with whatever policies they claim to represent. Spiritually, this is impossible. No governing interests can ever sequestrate spiritual capital entirely for their own purposes, no matter how much they might like to do so, or put up an appearance of doing. Every soul has the right to be as Inwardly rich as they Will, if they care to Work for their Inner Living. Unhappily, work seems even more unpopular on Inner levels than on Outer ones. Material poverty is bad enough, but how so many souls appear to prefer living in such degrading conditions of abject spiritual squalor remains the secret of their own indifference. Perhaps Jupiter and Venus may solve this mystery. They have the Keys here on the Twenty-first Path.

The Twenty-second Path

SPHERE—LETTER CODE:	Severity 5 P 6 Beauty	
DIVINE ORIGINATION:	ELOHIM GIBOR—	The
	ELOHIM va DAATh	Destructor
ARCHANGELIC CREATION:	Khamael—Michael	Dissatisfaction
ANGELIC FORMATION:	Seraphim—Malakim	Reduction
APPARENT EXPRESSION:	Mars—Sun	Dispersion
TAROT SYMBOL:	BLASTED TOWER	

The Twenty-second Path presents a picture of active Power eliminating from existence whatever threatens the spiritual Beauty of Cosmos, or might endanger the Balance of Being beyond limits of safety. It is essentially the act of a protective device such as a fuse or safety-valve and most certainly not due to any form of Divine vengeance or punishment. Perhaps our best way of thinking along this Path is to consider it as an entirely necessary precaution against pressures and stresses developing in the spiritual structures of Cosmos to degrees of danger which might otherwise explode us into irredeemable Chaos.

The Tarot Symbol of the Blasted Tower has a great deal to tell us here. Its original title of the "Maison de Dieu" (House of God) was an old euphemism for a madhouse, the mad being considered as in "the care of God," since humans know not what to do for them. Tied in here also is the Tower of Babel legend, of insane human ambitions and presumptions being blasted by the Heavenly Powers challenged by avaricious defiant mortals.

This Symbol is one that virtually explains itself a glance. An unstable structure has been built on very inadequate foundations. From its pinnacle (or Crown) its builders have obviously intended to set up their position of power and domination. Although they have lifted themselves above the reach of other humans, they have also made themselves all the more vulnerable to

Heavenly energies. In this case, a Lightning-flash disintegrates the Tower, and hurls the builders back to Earth where they must either learn better techniques, or endure a sharper lesson next time. We should take careful note that it is the Tower which is destroyed rather than its constructors, who presumably may escape with whatever losses and injuries they have deserved.

We might well ask why it seems necessary to destroy the Tower. The answer is because it amounts to a monomania rather than single-mindedness, sheer egoism instead of self-sufficiency, and a static impedance to the free flow of forces which should be circulating in a Cosmic manner. In other words, it represents a pile-up of insanity, inharmony, and unbalance; to a point where nothing but a breakdown will restore something like good order once more. This happens all the time in nature, and the sooner such obstructions are dealt with, the better.

The Tower, in this instance, is only wrong because it is built of the wrong materials, in the wrong place, and for the wrong reasons. A Tower as such is not necessarily a bad thing, but if fundamentally constructed for anti-Cosmic reasons, it automatically invites eventual destruction on itself. How many souls build themselves into towers of pride, arrogance, and other structures of spiritual superciliousness which are bound to collapse sooner or later? How often do humans attempt to make purely selfish piles of material or other energies which time alone would topple? A tower of Uranium would not be very high before it blasted its builders to pieces. Simply heaping everything together for the sake of towering temporarily over other humans is an insane act on any life-level, and that is why it will be ultimately blasted.

Why blasting in particular? Why not some less drastic means of correction? That is certainly possible on reasonable levels, but as the Symbol of the Tower shows, when conditions of unbalance mount up fast and high enough to shake the Crown of Reason on its seating, and result in sheer insanity to a dangerous degree, then nothing but a Blast of Light will serve to equalize energies again. There is simply no alternative under the circumstances, and if no such Blasting occurred, we should live in even more insane conditions than develop among us in this world already. In fifty short human years we have seen the tops knocked from many Towers and their replacements will also fall if they suffer from the same structural defects. Heaven help the heads those Towers are likely to fall upon.

The Tower is, after all, a Symbol of rising pressures and tensions without adequate relief or reasonable means of compensation. This always means trouble in the end, and a blow-up of some kind if nothing else can clear the congestion. It will be noted the Tarot Tower has no door, and the impression received is that its builders have sealed themselves in with no means of exit except by leaping or being hurled from the top. This is symbolic of many situations on various life-levels which are best avoided by spiritually sane souls, and immuring ourselves in Towers without safe escape facilities is a very unwise procedure. For those who seek sex-symbolism everywhere, the Tower may be considered as an erect phallus with no means of releasing its tension apart from an ejaculation into space instead of a surrounding vaginal channel. Though this may seem an unproductive act in a physical sense, it may yet be quite a necessary one in order to release dangerous emotional and Inner tensions. There is a widening knowledge concerning the ill-effects of sexual stresses on the human character, and evidence is appearing in favor of dispersing these by convenient methods where more complicated or advanced ways of dealing with them are impractical. Similar principles apply in other fields of working with forces.

There are four main courses to take with arising energies typified by the Tower. We can apply them, convert them, store them, or simply discharge them. Unless we have discovered the secret of Inner immunity from action except by Ultimate Will, we are otherwise compelled to deal with the energies affecting our existence in one or more of those four fundamental ways. Usually it is a question of dissipating energies through all of them according to circumstances and abilities. With any given Energy, we normally apply what we can, convert another proportion, store some more for later use, and release or discharge the remainder. Everything depends on our capabilities and capacities for disposing of energy through ourselves. Primitive people are only able to apply, convert, or store relatively small proportions of Inner energies, blasting off the remainder in wasteful or destructive ways because they have no other inclination or facilities for dealing with excess energy. As we evolve, we utilize our energies more, and blast off less, although such discharges are likely to be increasingly deadly in ratio to our improving proficiency. The aim of Initiates should be to learn the secrets of the Tower whereby the Lightning-flash is reversed, and instead of the Flash from Heaven blasting the Tower of Human Tensions, excessive and unmanageable energies are flashed from the Tower back to Heaven and Entities better able to handle them than mere humans.

Once this secret is discovered and made practicable, the Tower will function as it should. Instead of rising to a height of potential where energy is increasing at a much greater rate than it is dissipating, and so needing a direct blast from Divinity to restore matters, an automatic discharge from a slightly lower level than such a fatal one will come into operation whenever danger threatens. In effect, we must build spiritual safety valves into ourselves so that Inner tensions and pressures which we cannot safely dispose of through our own normal channels are flashed straight back to their appropriate Cosmic categories. For individual souls, this means a state of competent harmony to live in, and among groups, or better still, Nations, freedom from warfare and most of the troubles stemming from explosively dangerous situations. Provided our Towers do not rise faster than we are able to discharge excess energy from their tops, there is no real reason why we should not raise them as high as Heaven Itself if we Will.

The figures in the Tarot Symbol are being hurled down from their Tower, because they neglected to direct their mounting surplus of Energy back toward its Divine Origin, presumably intending to corner this for personal purposes they had not the spiritual stature to control within themselves. We must be careful not to make the same mistake if this may be avoided, and here on the Tree of Life is the Path we ought to follow very carefully for that reason. Once the purpose and project of any Path is known, its exploration and degree of Enlightenment becomes more or less of a routine matter—providing we stick to it. There are certainly valuable lessons to learn on this Twenty-second Path, and we should apply ourselves to the Categories of Cosmic Consciousness concerned, for all further information.

Originatively, the Path-Governors are ELOHIM GIBOR and ELOAH va DAATh. The Almighty and Omniscient Aspects of Divinity. That which Knows and Does what must Be Done. In relation to what? In this case relatively to Cosmos. That is the decisive factor. Whatever threatens the essential structure of Cos-

mos past a certain degree of danger must be destroyed or neutralized in the most effective way likely to safeguard the continuance
of the Cosmic structure for its intended purpose. We can see examples of this action almost anywhere. A submarine commander
making a snap decision to slam watertight bulkheads shut,
knowing that some members of the crew would perish, but the
rest of the men and the ship would be saved. A headmaster deciding to expel one corrupting individual for the sake of the whole
school. The action of any soul sacrificing itself for the salvation of
others. Wherever a relatively minor catastrophe may be deliberately applied as the only sane means of averting a far greater one,
we may recognize the ELOHIM GIBOR and ELOAH va DAATh
combination in action. Where else would instinctive knowledge of
what to do in emergencies derive from?

Not that the Powers of this Path are confined to emergencies
only. The apocryphal tale of Moses and the Angel illustrates
Path-procedures here very nicely. In this legend, Moses is
granted the privilege of watching an Angel of this Path at work.
In human guise, the Angel commits what look to Moses like several unjust and criminal acts, including arson and murder.
Moses accuses the Angel of being a fiend or Agent of Evil mas-
querading as an Angel of Light. The Angel metamorphoses into
its Heavenly form, and sternly speaks to Moses concerning the
Divine Will behind each act. Innumerable greater evils had been
averted, and a train of future benefactions laid by the Angel's activities. This was only possible because of Divine Knowledge directing Angelic acts with absolute precision and determination.
No human being could possibly have had such Inner information
or authority, nor are humans sufficiently advanced spiritually to
operate on such scales themselves. Ultimately Moses became
convinced of the Angels *bona fides*, and realized that Divinity
knew best how to manage Its own affairs, while we struggle along
with our feeble imitations of Its behavior.

We would do well to remember sometimes that in our Cosmos we are only back-seat drivers in the vast majority. It is so
easy to criticize and condemn what appear to us like Cosmic calamities and cruelties of vast proportions. Millions of humans
perish, and we find sadness, sickness, suffering, or miseries of all
kinds on Earth. Oppressors flourish, while inoffensive and gentle
souls remain in servitude. Why? Man has always asked himself

this vital question, yet never dared to answer it truthfully. All our social and spiritual disasters are brought upon us collectively by ourselves, and individuals partake of these according to the degree of involvement. We allow obvious evils to accumulate to degrees when only explosive or destructive outbreaks of Inner Energy will temporarily dissipate or change their course. What else are wars, revolutions, and other such terrible blots upon human history, than culminating explosions of energies concentrating in human beings as hatreds, greeds, malice, and all the other Inner factors of spiritual insanity. Are we not already mounting toward future flashpoints which will make previous ones appear like damp squibs by comparison?

We have no Cosmic right to let ourselves reach intolerable degrees of social, economic, or spiritual tensions, and then demand that Divinity should promptly get us out of the impasse we have reached on the tops of our Towers. ELOHIM GIBOR is not sometimes termed the "Lord of Battles" for nothing. Usually, the most we may hope for are minimum casualties through the calamities we have invoked on our own heads. Nuclear fission has altered our future for good or ill in this direction for the remainder of our history on this Earth, be its duration long or short. We have reached a point on the Twenty-second Path where we either discover its more advanced Inner secrets, or explode ourselves beyond recovery on this life-level. This would certainly imperil our subsequent spiritual evolution, so we had best seek alternatives as fast as we can.

About our only practical hope of short term dealing with dangers of ultra-disastrous explosions on spiritual or physical levels is to ensure an adequate provision of relatively low-degree flash-points. Humans unable to convert their energies into constructive channels must be given opportunities for releasing the worst in themselves by less dangerous means than devastating global warfare. Otherwise there will be no avoidance of such a culminating calamity. The basic overflows of uninitiated mass-humanity are into the two pools of Sex and Violence, as every journalist knows, and this fundamental fact cannot be ignored, disguised, or evaded in any way. There is no use whatever trying to substitute tea and sympathy or sweetness and light for the S and V demanded by the multitudes. Sex and Violence must be supplied to meet these urgent demands, and offered in reasonably harmless forms which are also effective releases for otherwise unusable or reservable energies. On this Path we must seek safe methods for exploding Human hatreds, and all tensions leading to inevitable violence.

It is utterly impractical telling average humans to "love their neighbors and all be good souls together" while their inclinations are directed toward stamping on their hated neighbors with spiked boots! One might as well throw water on a burning house with a teaspoon. The best plan in such cases is undoubtedly some kind of substitute violence through which antagonisms can be effectively voided. Humans need hate objectives to demolish with released fury sometimes, in order to bring themselves back to sanity. Let it be the work of initiated experts (or Adepts) to find means for humans to blast off their spiritual steam safely. Conventional "Christian forbearance" is quite useless in the face of fundamental ferocities deep enough to destroy us all if explosions cannot be adequately arranged on minor scales.

All this applies to individuals, of course. Every one of us must learn on this Path how to direct his dangerously mounting energies producing spiritual symptoms of rage, resentment, hatred, and the like evils, safely along the ELOHIM GIBOR—ELOAH va DAATh Line of Light. Initiates of this Path Know how to Blast Beneficially. The Keys of this Operation are here.

Creatively, we walk with KHAMAEL and MICHAEL. The Godlike and the Burning One in partnership. They have a tendency to make us dissatisfied with imperfections and injustices, so that we seek to eliminate these from our Life-Schemes. Divine discontent might well describe the combination of Path Archangels found here.

There is a good reason for Divine discontent. It helps to deal with situations in pre-explosive stages, providing proper action can be taken. It informs us that things are not as they should be in relation with Cosmic Harmony, and we ought to take appropriate measures accordingly. We may think of it as a last warning before the worst happens. Actually, the four worlds of this Path may be considered as a sort of "four minute warning" before the bang comes. The originative level gives warning that a possible blast may occur. The Formative level should inform us about the nature and location of the danger. This Creative level tells us that imperative action is necessary if serious effects are to be averted. Once the expressive level operates, we know that blasting is inevitable, and all we can do is seek what salvation we may. If we listen to Khamael and Michael in time, they can advise us how to escape with at least a minimum of damage.

We know that Michael sets the Standard, as it were, for the required state of spiritual Harmony or Beauty to keep Cosmos in healthy condition, whether for individual souls, or the Single Soul we all share. Naturally, there is bound to be an average fluctuation from the mean of this condition which is normal enough, but unbalance in excess of such a factor must necessarily cause concern for its safety. If this concern ever reaches Archangelic proportions, then things are indeed getting serious. Khamael may be able to burn up the trouble successfully, but if he should fall, then his fire becomes the lighted fuse to ignite an explosion on much deeper and more serious levels still.

All this happens in ourselves as well as Greater Cosmos. The longer and deeper our hates, fears, greed, and resentments continue to pile up their Interior Towers in us, the worse is likely to be our eventual breakout if tensions are unrelieved. History alone shows this with monotonous regularity. We even say "it burns me up" of ourselves when we experience deep Inner frustrations. Our Hells and Purgatories are visualized as slow "burnout" processes, rather than eliminative explosions. If only we could burn up the energies of our own evils as fast as these arise, our spiritual metabolism would stay in a healthy state, and this is exactly where Khamael can help us most—if we obtain his cooperation.

Since we are human beings, we have to cope with human imperfections, and these certainly include all the emotional and spiritual factors likely to cause structural damage to our souls and physical health explosively. We should only be foolish to deny to try and hide from this fact, and the best course is to deal with it sensibly, by working out operative schemes for handling these energy-exchanges in ourselves to our best advantage. Different types of soul need various sorts of systems, but the fundamentals are naturally the same. First we must know and recognize our necessity for ridding ourselves from damaging Inner tensions. This knowledge and experience derives from the Sixth Sphere of Harmonious Beauty. Secondly, we must discover means for controlling, consuming, burning, or blasting these inharmonies out of us before they rise high enough to cause Inner harm likely to last several lifetimes or affect our descendants. These procedures are to be found in the Fifth Sphere of Severity. Thus we walk the Twenty-second Path between the two Spheres.

A Qabalistic ritualist, for instance, would devise special Tiphereth-Gevuric rites aimed at releasing and expelling spiritual pressures from his own Inner Cosmos through appropriate channels to Nil potency where they simply merge into Undifferentiated Universal Energy. A Christian ritualist would probably offer up a Mass in which the unwanted Inner pressures were sacrificed directly to the Divine Spirit personified as a Christ of Comprehension.

A non-religious individual might "work off his feelings" in a variety of ways, from excessive physical exercise to writing abusive letters. Some people feeling sufficient personal aggrievement might even retaliate with a sharp punch in the face of whomever they believed responsible. Rapid temporary relief of tense feelings may perhaps prevent apoplexy, but it must always be remembered that such is only a surface measure, and the great need is for clearance and dispersion on deepest possible levels. There is not much point in clearing up the surface of a personality from evidence of tensions, when ill-effects have penetrated deeply into the soul and are continuing to mount up underneath everything else. One might as well attempt to cover dry-rot with a coat of pretty paint. Only deeply and truly worked clearances are effective, hence the necessity for real Inner action. Khamael and Michael have the Keys to this between them.

Formatively, the Angelic Orders of the SERAPHIM and the MALAKIM lead us along the Path. The Serpent-Fires and the Rulers. To use an electrical analogy, we might think of the Seraphim as the glowing heat from a fire-bar, and the Malakim as measuring instruments which inform us about upsurges of current likely to burn the fire out. If the Malakim can be arranged into thermostats which automatically control the current, so much the better. Once we become as proficient in spiritual engineering as we have with electrical equivalents, then we shall live in greatly improved Cosmic Circles. It seems a pity that a humanity so skilled and advanced in manipulating natural energies for pleasure and profit is still so primitive and stupidly inefficient at applying the same principles to far more important Inner spiritual structures and forces which constitute the essential realities of Cosmos and consciousness.

Unless our civilizations become adequately equipped with equivalents of Seraphim and Malakim for reducing the rise of Inner temperatures into useful channels of heat and power, we shall doom ourselves to destruction. Human souls will only bear just so much pressure before they break up or break out. This being well known by governing authorities in the past, periodic excesses such as Saturnalias and other relaxations were permitted and even organized. The "Bread and Circus" coercion of the Roman population is too well known to need comment. When the Christian Church managed to suppress the older Pagan methods of relief from frustrations and hatreds, it had little to offer in exchange except religious warfare and persecutions of other Faiths. True, the Devil was offered as a hate-target, but few souls took him seriously enough. They could so easily perceive more evil among the Church authorities.

It is very doubtful if the modern palliatives of TV and Social Security will provide deep enough outlets for mounting human tensions. All the signs are set for trouble ahead. Many of them seem idiotic, such as the dreary protests by bearded and unkempt incompetents concerning matters on which they are both ignorant and indifferent. The basic motives of these feeble and futile demonstrations are attempts to assert evidence of identity, something which would be done far better along Inner lines, rather than outer bad behavior. Nevertheless, no civil or legislative authority in the world today can afford to ignore such plain pointers to discontentment and rising pressures among modern humanity. Both individually and collectively, people need Malakim to take the measure of their intensifying insanities and Seraphim to dissipate these degrees of dissatisfaction with Life before worse conditions supervene. It remains for those who make far-reaching decisions to find some solution. There must be more scientific methods than global warfare, and less puerile ones than banner waving or screen watching.

Every soul is responsible for making his own Malakim-Seraphim contacts for relieving this Inner pressure due to ill-temper and other influences threatening sanity. Simple souls might find a hearty expletive sufficient for most minor needs. The Inner mechanism of this is straightforward enough. Something has caused a sharp rise of emotional or other Inner tension. The individual experiencing this promptly reacts by consciously directing as much surplus force as possible toward some Inner category of Existence considered capable of absorbing and neutralizing it. If successful, this action should leave the souls concerned feeling in a far better and more normal condition, having actually transferred at least the bulk of unbalancing energy away from themselves. There is one important proviso to this. The individual must implicitly believe in whatever category of Inner Entity has been invoked. It is no use sharply calling some Name which has no meaning or importance for the user, nor is there much point in specific references to parts of the human anatomy or its natural functions. This merely aborts an otherwise magical act into a stupid and ineffectual expression of frustrated incompetency.

The forceful invocation of a Divine Name or similar Inner Category of Consciousness to deal with an emergency of emotion or an otherwise unbearable accumulation of tension is in no sense a blasphemy or an offense but a direct cry for help which deserves an immediate answer in the form of reduced pressure. Far from "taking the Name in vain," it is being taken very much to the purpose. Experienced Initiates formulate their own lists of Names for use in various contingencies, from relative trivialities to the most deadly dangers. It is highly important that no Name is used outside its field of reference, such as the most revered and reserved Names being applied in all and sundry instances. Great Names are only to be invoked for great causes, and so on down the list. Once it becomes clear where the Names apply, they may be used effectively. Practicing Qabalists will naturally work this out through normal ritual procedures. The MALAKIM help set the scale, and the SERAPHIM determine the degree of heat to apply in any operation of this nature. They have the Keys thereto.

Expressively, this Path associates with the Sun and Mars. A powerful combination! It may be noticed that the four diagonal Paths on the Tree linking Tiphereth with the immediate external Sephiroth are all concerned with actualities of Force. We have Force itself and its control by conservation, between Chesed-Tiphereth. Netzach-Tiphereth is connected by the Lovers, which means energy applied in doing what we enjoy and want to achieve. Hod-Tiphereth links with the Chariot, or Force in process of change and motion from one state to another. Here, between Tiphereth.Gevurah, we have Force in a condition of a burning expiration, where otherwise unusable energies are returned to Neutral again. We might almost think of this action like a four-stroke Engine of Life going through the "Suction-Compression-Ignition-Exhaustion" cycle. Quite a reasonable analogy, in fact. It may also be compared with a heartbeat.

For a human or mechanical engine to keep healthy, it has to expel its over-plus energies into appropriate fields. Solar energy over-supplies us with life-force the whole time, but if allowed to take its natural course, would also apply controls to excessive life by encouraging epidemics and other means of reducing over-population among the various life-forms, each species of which preys on others. Thus does Mars keep down surplus livestock on Earth. We have not only upset this natural ecology through our evolution, but we also destroy our own species through warfare. Unless we speedily find satisfactory substitutes for war, our planet will be in deadly peril from its population. Mars has a definite function to fulfill on this Path, and if we do not realize this fact and make constructive use of it, the consequence to civilization will be very serious.

War is not so much an insanity in itself as the climax of insanities leading to such a disaster. In a strange way, war is a desperate and violent action of people, already tortured by Inner tensions and pressures, to regain a level of sanity through sheer exhaustion. Just after the completing climax of war or sex, we arrive at a momentary stage of relatively sane and sober spiritual balance, which seldom lasts long enough for us to have a reasonable breathing space before new reactions begin building up more trouble. Once again, this is because we have not cleared ourselves deeply enough in a spiritual sense to fully exhaust our systems from needs of war or sex. Though such deep clearance is beyond the ability of average humans, the forms of sex and violence necessary to clear their insanities back to reasonable levels may certainly be improved from old forms of expression.

What this world needs to safeguard future civilizations is not the imposition of high moral standards on masses of human beings utterly unable to conform with these because of inadequate spiritual developments, but some socially acceptable amenities for sex and violence, whereby those seeking such reliefs from Inner inbalances can "get these out of their systems" without endangering themselves or causing offense to others. It is imperative that some such schemes be made practical for the sake of everyone's safety on all life-levels. Shocking as this may sound, it is nothing but plain sense. To pretend that humanity has entirely risen above such primitive needs is sheer cant and rubbish. There are periods when even evolving souls become so tortured through tensions that murderous mayhem and savage sex seems to be the only way out of their Towers of Terror. Rather than allow this to explode with disastrous damage, surely it is better to release such perilous pressure through contrived channels which afford relief without intensive destruction? It is simply a question of discovering and constructing those channels, and that is what we must tread this Path to learn.

It may be considered a bad thing to apparently encourage activities of violence and sex among humans, but exactly the reverse is intended. The aim should be to release pressures in containable and controllable ways, so that ultimately these reduce to easily manageable proportions. Once a sufficiently deep spiritual reactive point has been reached, and contact with Inner Zero established, souls automatically seek finer forms of expansion through fresh Cosmic cycles of consciousness. If excess energy is successfully negated through channels arranged according to Cosmic principles. Life will be maintained in a properly balanced condition of being, and this is precisely why we should travel the Paths of the Tree in order to gain its Fruits of Experience.

The gold of the Sun and the steel of Mars typify so much of our life on Earth. At bottom they may signify greed and death, and at top, Perfection and power. There is no compulsion on souls to be satisfied with the worst when they might have the best for a little extra effort. We are in no way doomed to continue with our old-fashioned forms of Sex and Violence if increasingly better and improved methods of these actions open up for us along far more satisfying spiritual lines, as indeed they will. That is the vital secret this Path has to teach. The transmutation of Violence typified by the Iron of Mars into Beauty and Balance of the Golden Sun for the Ultimate good of all those who learn the process. We do not eliminate Violence from our Inner Cosmos, but project it properly by this Path so that it will not eliminate us from Outer Cosmos. Souls must learn how to work this Operation in themselves before it can be extended into wider practice on Earth. The alternative is too terrible to leave much choice. Either we find out fast how to follow this Twenty-second Path, or—!

There is far more to this Path than release of repressed energies, of course, but in view of its individual and collective importance at this period of world history, that is the aspect principally dealt with in this instance. Mars and Sol together signify either an ultimate Atomic explosion, or Nuclear Energy harnessed for Universal Harmony. The choice between them is ours. Let us hope for a Cosmic rather than a Chaotic decision. All the necessary processes will be found on this Path where the Keys are held jointly by Solar and Martial spheres of Awareness. May our guidance thereto be good.

The Twenty-third Path

SPHERE—LETTER CODE:	Severity 5 Q 8 Glory	
D1VINE ORIGINATION:	ELOHIM GIBOR—	The
	ELOHIM SABAOTh	Tribulator
ARCHANGELIC CREATION:	Khamael—Raphael	Suspicion
ANGELIC FORMATION:	Seraphim—	Testing
	Beni—Elohim	
APPARENT EXPRESSION:	Mars—Mercury	Friction
TAROT SYMBOL:	THE DEVIL	

This Twenty-third Path shows us the elements of friction and experience of life by trial and error which is part and parcel of life at even Cosmic level. It portrays action by disagreement and uncertainty of purpose, rather than by meek acceptance of precept. Here, doctrines and dogmas concerning Divinity are defied rather than denied, but such defiance stems from a need for a new and original approach, rather than from any actual aversion to Supreme Spiritual Authority. A soul on this Path insists on learning from his own errors and by his own misfortunes, no matter how much these hurt. He will deliberately risk all kinds of injuries for the sake of knowledge, and is quite prepared to suffer the consequences. In a way, we might say it arouses the "Devil of perversity" in all of us. Not work to any sort of evil, but to drive us along Paths of experience we either cannot or will not tackle on higher levels.

The Tarot Symbol of the Devil is not, nor ever was intended to be, synonymous with any personification of Pure Evil. Tiresome, irritating, troublesome, and mischief-making as the Tarot Devil may be, he has no direct connection with the deadly cold and utterly disintegrative Principle of Chaos which Qabalists recognize as Anti-Being and Evil in the worst spiritual sense.

The function of the Tarot Devil is mainly that of a Tester, having the effect of bringing all our latest faults and weaknesses to the surface so that we can deal with them for ourselves as they become evident. This has real value, because unless we find and rectify our structural deficiencies on spiritual levels, we cannot very well progress to higher kinds of Inner Life where those very faults would injure not only ourselves, but other souls in close contact with us. Here we meet the sort of Devil who brings out all our very worst characteristics so that we become painfully aware of these, and sooner or later come to realize something will have to be done about them. A hard way of learning perhaps, but a necessary one if we are unprepared to seek others.

Perhaps the Devil-design of the Waite Tarot pack, faulty as it may be, has the most esoteric information to offer in comparison with other packs. It is roughly based on the Goat-figure of Eliphas Levi, but minus a great deal of the significance contained in that illustration. Instead of light between the horns, the Waite Devil has the inverted pentagram of anti-Man. This immediately informs us that our Devil here stands for everything likely to hinder our spiritual progress. There is no suggestion that we shall be prevented from making progress, but only that we shall find obstacles to overcome. With the five points of the Star, the two down-curving horns, and the triangular face, we have the idea of "ten trends to baseness." This, of course, carries the significance of our failures to achieve any or all of the Sephirotic qualities necessary for our spiritual development. The whole card is full of indications that downward tendencies bind mankind to the consequences of his "Fall."

Maybe to emphasize this "downwardness," the artist has depicted the Devil-figure with a grim, down-turned mouth. This is an ideographical error, for the mouth should have the suspicion of a sardonic smiling grimace, showing a natural reaction to the stupid antics of Mankind falling into all the old traps and mishaps connected with his lower nature. Instead of staring straight forward, the eyes of the Devil should have been glancing down at his not entirely unwilling victims. That he himself is a creature of blind impulse, darkness, and ignorance, is shown by his bat-wings, the black background, and his attempt to extinguish the Torch of Truth by inverting it.

Part of the key to this card appears with the figure's right hand. This is shown as being divided into forked fingers, the thumb pointing at the Devil himself. The sigil in the palm said, in effect, "I am the old Confuser." The divided fingers, of course, signify dissension, disagreement, antagonism, enmity, and all other sources of pointless strife between souls. The thumb indicates the cause of such squabbles, and also that no attempt is made to control them. When the thumb is disassociated from the fingers, this indicates non-control by Will. In other words, unless we are prepared to solve our disagreements and divisions by exercising our Wills, we shall continue to suffer the ill effects of our contentiousness. An interesting thought here is that the Devil's sign is converted to the well-known benediction gesture, by closing the thumb over the tops of the tips of the last two fingers and keeping the first two fingers upright and together. This shows the circle of control by the Will (thumb) over the lower nature (last two fingers) while the higher faculties (first two fingers) unite and point to Heaven. Thus, the "Curse of the Devil" can be converted to the "Blessing of God," by subjection of our lower selves to Will, leaving our higher natures free to seek spiritual identity with the aid of Divine direction.

The lower part of the Devil-Figure shows a mass of hair indicating incoherency and lack of meaning, ending in Harpy's legs and claws, showing that we become easy prey for the nastier side of our own natures. One main thing is lacking. The erect and twisted phallus. Actually, this could scarcely have been added to the figure at the period of its publication and it was expected those using the Tarot pack would have enough imagination and insight to supply this detail for themselves. There seems no valid reason nowadays why this important feature should not be restored. A distorted phallus implies that sexual difficulties and malfunctions are frequently a main or central feature of human Inner sufferings, and how true this is can be testified by millions of souls. It also brings to mind the old adage that "A standing penis has no conscience," indicating the relationship between sexual and criminal activities. Most of us know only too well the connections linking sex urges and dissatisfaction with what might be termed anti-social behavior.

This Tarot Devil is squatting (in a defecatory position) on a black altar. Thus the oblation on the altar-top is likely to be of an excremental nature. So do we also pour out our filth and corruption in the way of loathsome and slimy writings, art, actions, and every kind of obscenity on the altars of acceptance we have raised among our so-called "permissive" society. It is not the actual nature of the excrement which makes it offensive, so much as accepting or attempting to pass off this ordure as a perfected product. Men worshipping their own muck are a disgusting spiritual spectacle, and until they raise their Inner eyes from the midden to the Mountaintop, they will rise no higher themselves. While they delight in "devil-dirt," they are unlikely to notice very much of a nobler nature. We must free ourselves from fecal matter before climbing to finer concepts of Cosmos. So the Devil of the Tarot informs us while testing our capabilities in this direction.

In front of the dark altar is secured a ring-bolt which serves either as a handling grip for moving the massive stone, or a shackling ring for tethering sacrificial victims with insufficient strength to drag the altar from its place in primeval sludge and mud representing the absolute dregs of Creation. Chained to this ring we see two strange creatures. They are human, yet horned to show their herd-animal level of life. Their heads are garlanded in the manner of old animal sacrifices, showing they must freely offer their animal natures in the sacrifice of renunciation, if they would be liberated from their linkages. They are loosely chained around their necks, and could easily remove these false fetters if they really wanted to. As the chains are, the creatures would only hurt themselves if they struggled and plunged about violently in witless panic. To obtain freedom easily, they have but to stand still, bend their heads, and slip off the chains. If they are prepared to kneel, then their task will be easier yet. As matters stand in the picture, the naked male and female beings seem witlessly awaiting whatever might happen to them.

An interesting cycle of events has obviously just begun. The Devil in his down-plunging attempt to extinguish the Truth-Torch, has set fire to the male creature's tail. This burning stimulus makes the male shield himself behind with one hand and reach for the female with the other. She reaches for a grape from a bunch growing upside down at the end of her tail, and this is the unlikely fruit she proposes to offer her partner. The message here is clear enough. Untrue promptings from "the Devil" trigger off sheer animal lusts on lowest human life-levels. Such lust can

never be satiated except for short intervals like links of a chain.
The female half of a lust-partnership only offers fruit from an inversed cluster—otherwise intoxication which drives men to even
wilder excesses. Unless they learn the secret of quenching the
fire in his tail with the juice of her grapes, they are doomed to continue their senseless cycle of activity while their chains hold
them captive to the Ring on their enslavement to the altar representing their own baseness which, be it noted, is the same height
as their genitals.

There are endless conclusions and ideas to draw from this
Tarot Trump. We see our worst inclinations at work, driving us
toward all sorts of perhaps desperate courses, because we have
neither the wits nor the will to stop and seek the secret of release.
That is the lesson we have to learn on this Path, and the Devil
will cheerfully drive us along it until we find out how to escape his
clutches. Be it remembered that once we discover the way to remove our chains it might be a good idea to shackle the Devil's
claws to his own altar, so that he cannot fly after us and drag us
back to bondage. Why waste good chains when they may be put to
such a profitable purpose?

Originatively, the Twenty-third Path is operated by the Divine Aspects of ELOHIM GIBOR, the God of Might, and
ELOHIM SABAOTh, the God of Multitudes. Perhaps some today
might interpret this as "The Power of the People" or the "Might of
the Masses," but wise souls know well enough that this form of
energy can be destructively dangerous unless controlled by
clever caution. That, as our Tarot Symbol would remind us, is
"the Devil of it all." Any advertising agency knows methods of
manipulating the "Mass-Mind," and most politicians seek sub-
tler ways of maneuvering the "Mindless Masses." Every expert
on processes of human consciousness realizes that incredible energies are connected with the Primal Powers behind the multiple
manifestation of Life termed "Mankind." Everyone tries to live
and survive as a soul-self. Here we find a picture of pure power
(ELOHIM GIBOR) activating every living soul with sheer determination to stay alive as a self among all others (ELOHIM
SABAOTh). Insofar as others assist that individuation they are
welcome, but if they threaten it, they must be resisted. This is the
Path of people fighting to be themselves regardless of moral or

ethical issues. Survival by selfishness, perhaps, or the innate need of Life to which we are driven by the "Devil" of self-interest.

Self-preservation is essential for the continuity of human life on earth, whether individually or ethnically. A human being under threat of death will naturally fight in self-defense, and races or nations feeling their ethnical identity in peril resort to warfare rather than lose their "Group-Soul." In this way is the "Devil" concerned with human hostilities. Greed and Fear are the basics of our battles. On the other hand, extensions of these drives into the higher level of identity Improvement and Cautious Conduct, are essential to our evolution. It is a question of converting the chains binding us to our "Devil" into a harness with which we may drive the "Devil" As We Will, instead of being relentlessly driven by what amount to diabolical dictates.

After all, the symbol of the Devil presents us essentially with a test of our determination and ingenuity, two factors entirely necessary for self-survival. According to the Tarot Glyph, we might go so far as to slip our shackles from our necks and chain the Devil to the altar Ring-bolt. What then? How turn the tables and control the monster? Two major acts are needed. First, for the male half of the human team to boldly grasp and get possession of the Torch of Truth. Since the Devil's hold on Truth is not likely to be a very firm one, this is a perfectly possible action. Once armed with the Torch, the Devil may be held off while the second act is performed by the female partner. This is discovering and unlocking the secret of the Ring-bolt, which is "lewissed" into the Stone, and not irremovably binded in. As Masons should know, a "lewis" is a simple lock-device whereby chain-rings or other tackle can be attached to heavy stones in order to move them. When the correct Key to this is used, then the whole Ring becomes free. Both male and female beings must now grip the Ring in a right and left hand partnership, and if the male threatens the Devil sufficiently with the Torch, that Light-fearing Being will turn about so that the humans now have a controlable Beast in their hands. Applications of the Torch to the Devil's hindquarters will make him move fast enough. Just two precautions are necessary to remember. The humans cannot control their Beast while facing each other in fornication, but they must remain side by side as equal holders of the Ring. Nor dare they release their grip on the control-Ring itself. This allegory has sufficient material in it for very many meditations on this path.

Together, ELOHIM GIBOR and SABAOTh signify the element of trouble encountered by all in their search for self-sufficiency. What human ever went through a whole life with no trouble at all? Difficulties and tribulations of some description are quite normal events of life, and what really matters for us is the way we react to them, survive through them, and learn how to rise beyond their reach. In the old Mystery-dramas, this was shown by frequent challenges of the Initiate from figures disguised as various monsters and trouble-makers armed with symbolic weapons quite capable of inflicting token injuries on the adventurer. Sometimes a mysterious "guide" would accompany the Initiate, whispering passwords or suggestions for avoiding or overcoming the obstacles on the Path. Ultimately, the travelers would be left to discover solutions of their difficulties by themselves from their own Inner sources of information. All this was very sound psychological conditioning which might be classed as "soul-training." Properly carried out, it enabled humans to cope with every sort of life-problem they were likely to encounter. People with "built-in" capabilities for tackling troubles are more likely to survive than other less prepared types, which gave Initiates of the Mysteries a distinct advantage. There is an old adage that we are never tested beyond our strength to resist temptation. This really means that the force exerted upon us by the elements of any spiritual situation may be utilized for its own control if we learn the secret of this Inner maneuver. Just as an expert in judo uses his opponent's strength to negate itself harmlessly to his own person, so may an Initiate of this Path use Divine Might through himself to counteract whatever forces may be obstructing the free flow of this Energy. Since all spiritual Energy is from a Single Ultimate Source, we should learn how to relate ourselves with It so that It will straighten out distortions of Itself arising from faulty human adaptations. The solutions of our problems have to be somewhere within the terms of their proposition. This is the Path where we must link our individual fractions of Inner strength with the massed might of all that would prevent our progress if we made no effort at equating the combined energies through ourselves. ELOHIM GIBOR and ELOHIM SABAOTh will tell us the secret. They have the Keys.

Creatively, the Powers of this Path are dealt with by Archangels KHAMAEL and RAPHAEL, the Burner and the Healer of wounds. They typify the purgative and restorative processes of life between which we adjust ourselves until we acquire our necessary balance from both. Life is a hurtful and a healing experience, and we partake of those two portions until they unite in a Middle Way of management, where we control both from a common center. Khamael sears, and Raphael soothes us on spiritual life-levels. Providing they operate evenly, we shall come out quite well for their attentions, but unnecessary healing action causes as much trouble in its way as excessive hurting.

Raphael could not be a Healer unless a Hurter existed also. A Hurter is not a destroyer or eliminator, but one who inflicts a remediable injury for some specific purpose. Khamael is here seen as a Hurter, not for any malicious reason, but strictly in accordance with the Laws of Life in order to cause changes in consciousness and Cosmos which are necessary for some legitimate reason. Khamael does not hurt us for the sake of hurting, but to obtain reactions from us to our ultimate advantage. Nor would he hurt us at all unless Raphael were ready to relieve us on request. Why then, should any suffering be necessary?

Suffering, or the sense of being hurt, is in itself an experienced reaction of a sentient soul to an applied stimulus causing a disturbance of consciousness beyond the normal change levels of calm comfort. We suffer, because we are moved from our mean positions of personal existence at a much greater rate than we can adjust ourselves to *pro rata*. Suppose, for instance, we are burned in a second or two to a degree needing weeks of recuperative healing to normalize. The total amount of pain and suffering endured will be quite considerable by our standards. Now suppose again we possessed the unheard of faculty for restoring damaged bodily tissues to normal almost as fast as an injury were sustained? We should scarcely notice the same heat-stimulus that would incinerate the flesh of another and "ordinary" human. The extent of any hurt, therefore, depends on individual or collective ability to absorb and neutralize stimuli which would otherwise unbalance the sentient part of our Life-spectrum to a dangerous degree. The less sensitive we are, the more it takes to hurt us, but on the other hand, the better we can react hurtful stimuli back into Zero, the less we shall need hurting. This calls for a little explanation.

By our reactions to physical, mental, and spiritual stimuli received during our life times, we build ourselves into what we are and toward what we hope to be. The more responsive we are to these stimuli, the more rapidly we should put ourselves beyond their reach except As We Will allow them to influence us. Our ultimate aim should be to Zero all stimuli so effectively that we react with none of them unless it is our True Will to do so in whatever way and degree we choose. Such perfection lies beyond mortal capability, but at least some small proportion of it is possible for advancing Initiates of this Path.

The less sensitive humans are, the more they have to be hurt before they will make any moves in requisite spiritual directions. This is a regrettable truth, but most necessary to realize. Nothing but really hard and brutal knocks are likely to obtain sufficient reactions from low-grade lives to make them climb higher on the evolutionary scale. Hell is the only way for so much of Mankind to seek Heaven. Just how hard some souls need hurting is a sad thought. There is no merit whatever in bearing pain stoically and stupidly without intelligent Inner response. Nor are we supposed to enjoy being hurt, or think that the more we endure on Earth the happier we shall be in Heaven. We cannot buy ourselves an instant of Heaven with a millennium of Hell, and no amount of Earthly misery will guarantee the least reward of Eternal bliss. There is no Inner point in our pain at all. That is simply a side-effect felt by ourselves from an original stimulus having far greater value than making some miserable mortal suffer. We do suffer, simply because we have not yet learned to interpret such stimuli on higher levels. If we could actually do this, our sufferings would cease, for they are solely in ourselves, and not sent as such by any Deity—or ever were.

Khamael's duty to us in Life, therefore, is to provide stimuli which burn us into action because they hurt, and Raphael should show us how to take the sting out of such experiences while still undergoing them if a useful spiritual purpose is served. The Sword of Raphael is only raised in our defense, but if he has to prod us away from danger with its point, or bar our rush toward disaster with its edge, then we ought really to be thankful for the minor cuts we receive as tokens of rescue. Better a broken nail

than a broken neck! Given a chance, Raphael will heal the most
wounding or injuries, but if we kept hold of Khamael's flame
while yelling for help, Raphael would reply sensibly enough, "I
cannot start my healing until you take your stupid hand out of
that fire!" We must initiate the process by our own wills.

Thus it is that a useful watchword for this section of the
Twenty-third Path is "Suspicion," which means taking nothing
for granted at face value. It does not imply that we must attribute
evil intentions everywhere, but purely that we must learn to recognize hidden dangers concealed behind apparently innocent fa-
cades. Nothing but our own experience linked with those of other
souls can guide us here, and that is where Khamael and Raphael
help us by connecting us Inwardly with the deep consciousness of
those who travel with us on this Path of pain-peace. If we share
the findings of fellow-souls on this virtually universal Path, we
might be able to avoid maybe some of their sufferings, and the
only real use of suffering is making us discover how to avoid or
transcend it. Once we suspect a possibility of injury ahead, we
shall be in a position to either prevent or profit from it. When we
become good enough friends with KHAMAEL and RAPHAEL,
the former will remind us with his flame to invoke Raphael instantly, and the latter will prod us gently along the Path while
urging us to be suspiciously wary of Khamael's too tender
touches. So we shall stay more or less in the middle of the Path
and perhaps be grateful to the Keepers of its Keys.

Formatively, we meet up with the Angel Orders of the
SERAPHIM and the BENI-ELOHIM. The "Serpent-Fire," and
the "Sons (Children) of Gods." As far as human beings are concerned, we might call these our "Temptations" and "Self-Glories"
on this Particular part of the Path. We have in ourselves that
touch of the "Old Serpent" which keeps stinging us into all sorts
of antics concerned with various aspects of Self on lower levels
which we think might be the antidote to this deadly bite. The Serpent stings us, and says perhaps in effect, "Get rich and dominate
others. That's the answer to my bite, and I shall go on stinging
until you achieve this." Later, maybe, the Angel of Death reminds
us quietly that it was not the answer at all, and the Serpent waits
knowingly to meet us again in rebirth. It was all experience, and
eventually human souls have to pass this part of the Path with

impunity. Both Seraphim and Beni-Elohim will help us if we know how to employ them.

The mechanism of this "Serpent-biting-tail" cycle is interesting. Deep seated impulses from the "Fire-force" elemental energy of our "Collective Consciousness" act on individual souls somewhat like a non-fatal snake-venom. They irritate, initiate impulsive and irresponsible actions, hallucinate, and otherwise induce very irrational behavior in souls unable to neutralize such toxins by the "anti-bodies" in their spiritual systems. In an attempt to rationalize or cope with this Inner state of toxemia, consciousness produces all kinds of suggestive images as cures or curbs for such a condition. Few, if any of these, are likely to be of more than very temporary relief, for they are only distortions of the "Beni-Elohim," or "God-Children" which we have to absorb as controls of the Seraphic influence. So all our unequated and unneutralized energies pass back again into our subconscious Serpent-cycles, and the tail-biting goes on relentlessly until we make our Serpents swallow their tails back to Zero instead of constantly gnawing them.

We should not think of the "Seraphic sting" as an evil of any sort, for the "Serpent-bite" is a great benefit to souls capable of converting this otherwise poisonous product into life-stimulating serum. This can only be done by using the Beni-Elohim as antibodies. From our viewpoint, Beni-Elohim are projections of the God-images we should like to resemble or become as personalized individuals. We all see ourselves as this, that, or the other kind of person in a state somewhat larger than life, yet still attached to Earth-existence in a sort of idealized way. Ourselves as we would let ourselves become if we had our own way unopposed by other Wills. Not necessarily a noble, good, highly spiritual, or wonderful sort of soul at all. Possibly quite the reverse. Just what we want for ourselves regardless of how we obtain it. Obviously the finer and better types of Inner image we produce for ourselves, the closer these are likely to approximate the Beni-Elohim in their highest forms, which is what we should be aiming for. It is the task of the Beni-Elohim on this Path, to help us find and focus our forces upon the best Self-images we hope to evolve toward and attain, while the Seraphim keep stinging us along on our search.

Everything depends upon what we demand or Will on this Path. The Seraphim are likely to sting us in any case, but the Beni-Elohim can only provide us with images constructed from our own sources of Inner supply. If these are inadequate, or we do not ask to become any very special sort of person, then the fault is ours, not theirs. Once we firmly insist on becoming nothing but the best specimens of our sort, the Beni-Elohim will comply by offering suitable suggestions, though they never make us adopt any of these against our Will. When an image reaches us of which we approve, it remains for us to accept this, and instruct the Beni-Elohim to convert all energies received from the Seraphim into constructing this image in "our own likeness" for our Inner life useage as a vehicle of our spiritualized consciousness. This they will do in partnership with other "Inner contractors" engaged on different sections of the same project.

Between them, these two Angel Orders have the effect of testing us for what we are worth as souls capable of deciding our own destinies. Those higher than human Beings who watch and wait for self-selective souls to achieve life-levels where they may be admitted to the conscious Company of Inner Cosmos, rely on the Seraphim and the Beni-Elohim for initiatory processes on this Path. Hence the prayer section of the Paternoster: "and induce temptations not in us, but set us free from evil." When we not only take, but welcome, every test of Life, because we have risen above making ill use of them, we shall indeed be free from our worst evils—those deriving from ourselves. The SERAPHIM and BENI-ELOHIM will help us turn trials and temptations into quite remarkable Inner opportunities if we approach them properly along this Path. They have the Keys.

Expressively, the Path is represented by Mars and Mercury, or Ares and Hermes, depending on how the same two personifications of War and Wit are seen. We may think of them as Strength and Skill, or Power and Performance. Anything suggesting the ideas of massed right and individualized intelligence. Ares was shown as a rather stupid God, while Hermes is the most rapid and brilliant thinker of them all in terms of instinctive intelligence, not to be confused with the pure wisdom of Athena. If we look at the four other Sephiroth directly connected to Geburah, and therefore controlling its action, we should note that these are Understanding, Compassion, Balance, and, in the present case,

Honor. Surely the four most general factors needed to avert bloody warfare among Mankind. Here we are presented with an Hermetic possibility of finding honorable solutions to conflicting human problems which will be acceptable to all contestants.

We are already familiar with the mass-effect of Martial energy building up blindly until explosions shatter structures unable to withstand them. Now we must consider Hermes in his capacity of Herald or Mediator between dangerously disposed explosive elements. It may be that his sharp wit and rapid reasoning will suggest ways out of otherwise disastrous spiritual situations. Hermes is usually able to see most feasible escapes and avoidances from pile-ups of power and pressures for which Mars would find no solution except sanguinary ones. Hermes is frequently our surest savior from war, if we may rely on his services. When Understanding is insufficient, Compassion absent, Balance upset, and everything seems set for calamitous conflict, Hermes from Hod leaps lightly in with convincing reasons why both sides would do better for themselves without war. Perhaps he whispers to one likely belligerent, "Don't destroy these people, they are your best customers." And to another, "Why fight them? Fleece them instead." Hermes is full of low motives when dealing with people incapable of appreciating higher ones. Frequently his sordid suggestions succeed where finer ones would fail entirely.

Not that Hermes is ignoble by nature at all. To the contrary, he has the ability of persuading us with his silver speech to put our lowest activities into the highest sorts of Inner service. He will cheat us into complying with the Cosmic Circle of Divine Consciousness which he represents, if he can. If we cannot accept the truth about ourselves, he will tell us a consoling lie, so long as this helps us out of a temporary hole and takes us to a better position for facing Inner factualities. Sometimes only a most unlikely Hermetic hope holds some struggling soul above the depths of destructive despair until they manage to gain a firmer footing for faith. The inventiveness of Hermes is possibly described by the schoolboy definition of a lie as being "An abomination to the Lord, but a very present help in times of trouble." A fair test of Hermetic influence is that it works ultimately in our best interests, however expediency may distort its appearance.

Hermes carries his own Key-Symbols around with him, and of course his caduceus is our Tree of Life in a stylized form. The serpents were once long fluttering ribbons from whence our flag of truce derives. While both belligerent parties held an end of a ribbon each, they were supposed to be bound by the most sacred Emblem of a Rod upheld by the mediating Herald (or Hermes) toward Heaven Itself. To obtain a peaceful solution to their problem, it was necessary to circle around still holding a ribbon-end like Maypole dancers. This ultimately brought them to a stop in close contact with each other and Hermes when the ribbons had twisted to the base of the Staff. Once antagonists and mediator were literally in such a position, conciliation became a very near certainty, or at least a most reasonable probability. The principle of this practice applies as much today as it ever did in the past, or may save us from in the future. Hermes has always tried to stop humans hurting each other by tricking them into mutual tolerance—and why not, if this works where solemn warnings are utterly wasted?

Physically, this part of the Twenty-third Path is reminiscent of friction, the normal concomitant of maladjustment between two or more interacting factors. Friction may also cause the fatal spark initiating a devastating explosion. We may be reminded perhaps that fulminate of mercury is frequently used in modern detonators. Friction is always wastage of energy unless it can be converted into practical purposes serving a main issue. Hermes might be termed in modern time the Patron of "Technology," and we may as well see him in this light. From where else are we likely to obtain the "know-how of changing" spiritual frictions into direct drives toward Divine ends? Only the equivalent of Hermes in ourselves will teach us this life-saving art. How do we turn antagonisms into amusements and hates into humor? Only Hermes knows, and he will only tell us if we gain sufficiently close contact with him on this Particular Path.

Who but Hermes could manage Mars amiably? It takes a mountebank to gentle a giant, and Hermes can play such a part if he has to. Here, he shows us how to overcome irritation with impishness, ferocity with fun, and laugh a lot of the lumps out of life. We cannot be murderous and merry at the same time, nor stupidly savage and sympathetically smiling at once. Hermes has the happy knack of dealing with Mars' most deadly blows in a diverting way that saves us from their fullest force. Without this very faculty of what was miscalled "war-humor," far fewer of us would have survived the last Earth-shaking thrust of Mars' spear. We had to learn the practices of this Path the hard way in the fastest time, for the sake of our souls and our sanity. May Hermes save others from even worse possibilities. The Keys of Escape are here on this Twenty-third Path to be found by all who sincerely seek them.

The Twenty-fourth Path

SPHERE—LETTER CODE:	Beauty 6 R 7 Victory	
DIVINE ORIGINATION:	ELOAH va DAATh—	The
	IHVH SABAOTh	Loving
ARCHANGLIC CREATION:	Michael— Auriel	Enthusiasm
ANGELIC FORMATION:	Malakim—Elohim	Suiting
APPARENT EXPRESSION:	Sun—Venus	Attraction
TAROT SYMBOL:	THE LOVERS	

Here, on the Twenty-fourth Path, we encounter a very pleasing picture indeed. We find ourselves experiencing all the delights, dilemmas, and the difficulties connected with not only sexual love and attraction, but also with whatever appeals to us emotionally along similar lines. All the magic of sex-stimulus is here, with its enthusiasms, impulses, satisfactions, and disillusionments. It would be a miserable life for a human who attempted to bypass this Path, even though it has its own bittersweet taste which few of us ever escape. Unless we learn to walk the Path here with impunity rather than immunity, we shall scarcely be fit company for our fellow souls who follow it life after life in search of its secrets.

Emotional empathy, classifiable as sexual, or for the sake of sensual satisfaction, is an integral part of our Inner structure that we dare not deny or dismiss disgracefully. Here, we must come to favorable terms with it, and live in triumph with its finest possible effects upon and within ourselves. All the needed Keys for such a wonderful spiritual success should be found among the Path-symbols. Certainly the Tarot has a lot of suggestions to offer.

The Waite version of this card probably tells us more than most other packs. It may be fashionable in some circles to sneer at imagined "Victorian sentimentalism" in the Waite Tarots, but

the fact remains they have an incredible wealth of relative symbology concealed among their designs, which is usually missed
entirely by casual commentators. When examining Waite Tarots, It is best to use a good magnifying glass and a lot of long looking. Even so, much may be missed unless careful meditation is
brought to bear upon their meanings, and like all useful symbols,
they are capable of interpretation on many levels.

In this instance, the Lovers are represented by nude male
and female figures to right and left of the frame respectively. Behind the male is a Tree of Light bearing twelve flames, and behind the female is a Tree of Knowledge with four fruit and a Serpent coiled three times round the trunk. Both the flames and the
fruit are irregularly arranged on their Trees, and the theme is to
signify the often irrational and uneven nature of human attrac-
tions to each other or anything else in existence. We are most in-
consistent in sex-oriented affairs of our emotions. Our desires are
rarely reciprocated as we would wish. Here the man is gazing at
the woman, and taking a step towards her, but she pretends she
has not noticed this, and has taken a step back while she gazes
above his head as if awaiting a finer sight. He needs her Knowledge, and she needs his Light; she will get burned if she throws
herself at his Tree, and he will be bitten by the Serpent if he tries
to snatch the fruit from hers. Their problem is how to accept each
other's gifts without hurting themselves. How many lovers solve
that enigma?

In the background behind them is a peaky purple mountain
suggestive of breast and phallus, and signifying the rising of passions and desires. At the base of this erection, lying in broken and
uncertain ground, can just be seen the mouth of a presumably un-
fathomed hole. So does spent passion drain away through the
cracks of its crumbling grounds, and lose itself in its elemental
basis. Here we see symbolized the sharp surges of emotion to the
skies followed by a fall-off of interest down to the very dregs—the
ups and downs of any love-life in fact. Be it noted that the summit
of the mounts is level with the sex organs of both figures.

Dominating the top center of the picture is a strange and supernatural Being. Its main character is Solar, as depicted by the
Sun-Disc above its head which is directly crowned with complementary red and green flames, suggestive of horns and leaves,
both connected with fertility meanings. Again this Being seems

vaguely irregular, until perhaps it dawns on viewers that it is bi-sexual in character, the wings being different, the hands differ-ently disposed, and middle and ring fingers of the left hand being crossed over the man (to wish him luck? a cynic might ask), while the right hand is extended encouragingly over the woman as if to impel her forward with a friendly pat. The robe of the Being is draped for a male on the left and a female on the right. Finally, the whole of this Being is materializing or emerging from a cloud between the heads and hearts of the humans as though coming out of their beclouded state of rapture and illusion. What they imagine they see in those clouds only they may have any idea. Probably much the same as the rest of us.

The huge central Figure on this card represents whatever strange Power or Entity brings lovers together, or makes us want other people or things for emotional purposes. How often do we know why others appeal to us so strongly that we need them with such intense and unutterable longing? Why is it we seem to want those who feel no need for us? The slightly smiling Spirit behind us may know the reason, but we might never discover it. People often say of lovers, "I can't think what he/she sees in him/her," and the inexplicable mystery continues. In actuality, we do not see things in other souls at all during this initial stage of attrac-tion, but are looking at our own Inner ideas of what we would like that soul to mean for us. Thus the Figure in this Symbol signifies the idealized Inner identity which she is looking for in him, and he in her. This does not mean that they both see the same sort of Image, or even that because one sees an Image the other must see anything of the sort whatever. We frequently find that some soul sees another in a most wonderful or beautiful way, but is not seen in return as anything but an ordinary and uninteresting individ-ual. If only the two souls could meet each other half way in the Image of their Inner Love-likenesses, life would be very wonder-ful for them while this lasted.

Though the wings of the Love-Figure in this Symbol are male-female, they are both the same color—rose red, the tradi-tional color of passionate emotional love. This indicates the "lift" we obtain from the experience, and its superphysical character. Nevertheless, the Being is robed gracefully in violet, the mid-color between red and blue, showing that our passions are best clothed with compassion and mercy. The ferocity of the blazing

Sun which sets the Being's head aflame with desires and intentions is tempered for the naked humans by the softness of the pearly clouds with roseate reflections. Unless we had some similar means of cooling our sense-urges, we too might be burned beyond recovery by the Solar sex-drives that impel us into reckless activities in search of relief.

Altogether, this Tarot Symbol is a splendid piece of imagery, covering every salient point concerning love on emotional and sexual levels. It does not attempt to moralize or dogmatize about the subject, but simply points out the operative principles involved so that those who follow this particular Path may Work as They Will upon it. To succeed as an Initiate of this Love-Path does not mean the achievement of numberless physical sex-incidents, but the acquisition of ability to live in the Spirit represented by the central Figure at will. In this way, the emotional experiences of the Path which are necessary to soul-development, will not depend on the behavior of other humans or literal possession of material objects, but on the deep Inner interpretations reached by direct contact with the Path-Spirit itself.

Why do we fall in love with another soul or any form of life-manifestation? Only because we believe we have found a means of fulfilling a need in ourselves which has resulted in a spiritual or Inner discrepancy demanding compensatory action. If a soul were entirely self-sufficient, rebalancing its Inner deficiencies directly from spiritual supply-sources, it would not need to look for those energies on physical levels. Since we are souls who have in the majority fallen far from our original Inner purposes within the Divine Design of Life, we shall have to do the best we can in the way of working along the Paths of Return connecting us with our commencement and completion through the Circle of Cosmos.

It should be realized before we attempt to follow this Path properly, that all our emotional love-needs are essentially spiritual or nonphysical in nature, and no amount of purely physical sex or material possession will ever supply our Inner-deficiencies of that kind. It is most important that this realization be reached and grasped first, because it is the main Key of this Path, and without it no lasting success can be hoped for. For many, this may prove an almost insurmountable difficulty and others may feel it instinctively yet hesitate to admit the possibility of spiritual realities being more potent than physical ones. No intellectual argument will get anyone anywhere in this direction. All must find or fail to discover the veracity of the matter entirely in their own beings. The Tarot Symbol shows humans finding their greatest fulfillment not in their bodies at all, but in the Spirit behind and above them.

Our human bodies and material facilities are in themselves Symbols through which we may derive sexual, sensory, or any other impressions of Inner importance. If we can extract sufficient spiritualized energy from our experiences with these Symbols to help us construct our Inner Identity satisfactorily within its Cosmos—well and good for us. If not, then we shall have to continue in our lesser courses until we arrive at some kind of an answer. At least if we know roughly what we are looking for, we are more likely to succeed in our search, so let us ask the Powers of the Path themselves.

Originatively, the Divine Aspects of ELOAH va DAATh and IHVH SABAOTh govern the processes of this Path. Divine Knowledge of Life, and the Divinity we would all be if we could. Our experience of Existence through Emotion. Our love-life, if we like to put it that way. Without Emotion and Feeling of any kind, what are we? Certainly not a soul of any sort. To be entirely deprived of any finer feelings is a terrible Inner malady and the most noticeable symptom of psychopathic illness. On the opposite hand, if we cannot govern the energies of emotions at all, we shall suffer every kind of Inner torture. Clearly we should build ourselves into beings having not only a full range of emotional abilities, but also possessing complete control over their actions and effects on us. LOVE UNDER WILL, as the Mystery saying goes. In the Tarot Symbol, this is shown by the entirely calm face of the central Figure, suggesting a state of Inner exaltation absolutely under command of the highest spiritual faculties. The folding of the robes over the breast is indicative of a heart, so that the entire arrangement speaks of emotions and feelings being gathered up together for the sake of providing a most acceptable and wonderful form of spiritual service.

Another interesting consideration displayed by the Tarot Symbol is an entire absence of condemnatory or deprecatory sentiments in connection with sexual and emotional activity. There are no implications of "sin," wrongdoing," "shamefulness," or other such charges leveled in any way against the humans undergoing their emotional experiences. Neither does anything encourage them to abandon any restraint and plunge wildly into exhaustive orgies of emotional unbalance. Everything indicates they should be confidently and completely happy and serene in their love-experiences once they are able to enjoy these fully on Inner Life levels. The whole design of the Symbol in this instance reveals the outline of the Tree of Life glyph. The Light above is the Ainsoph, the head of the Figure Kether, its wings Chockmah and Binah, its hands Chesed and Geburah, the heart Tiphereth, the Trees of Light and Knowledge Netzach and Yod, the mountain Yesod, and the Earth Malkuth. The cloud might represent the veil of Paroketh, but there seems to be no sign of the Abyss, unless the throat of the Figure counts as such on account of an association with swallowing. The two humans, of course, are the Male and Female Life-Principles seeking a Middle Way of meeting.

As Divine Aspects for the Originative section of this Path, ELOAH va DAATh and IHVH SABAOTh signify not only the sort of God we would all like to be in ourselves, but also the God-Image we look for in others. In an old children's version of a Christian catechism, the child is asked why the Deity brought his soul into this world, and the rather touching answer is something like "To know Him and love Him in this world, and to be happy with Him forever in the next." Such might indeed be a very fair motto for this Path. To know and be happy with the Spirit of Love in this and every world of Life. We can only succeed in this, if we truly fall in love with the Spirit Itself manifesting by means of other humans.

We suppose we fall in love with another human soul, or materialized objective, but we really do nothing of the kind. What we have fallen in love with is the image in ourselves which we have built up around the physical focus they have supplied. In these initial stages, we are not in love with another human being or material object at all. The love-attraction exists between our own Inner individuality and the entirely un-physical Concept which has its reality not in the other person, but in our Inner Cosmos. It is the Concept we desire so ardently, and not the other human being insofar as he or she serves for a means of contacting this Concept consciously. We are really only interested in our love-objective because he or she seems to materialize those Inner actualities we are seeking for our spiritual satisfaction. Perhaps he or she is treating us in the same way, and our human friends think we are in love with each other. We may be in love *through* each other, but this will be *with* the Spiritual Concept we need to fulfill our Inner lackings of Love-life. Being only poor little human creatures, we seldom manage to make or meet much of the Love-Spirit in each other, and after disillusionment sets in, we are apt to blame each other very unjustly and unkindly for being unable to hand us God on a plate so to speak. But then, we humans usually blame others for our own failures.

It may be most unflattering and perhaps even humiliating for souls to realize that others are not initially attracted to them for their own sakes, but for the sake of the Love-Spirit sought through them. If souls are wise, seeking Light and Knowledge in each other, as the Symbol suggests, they will try and personify in themselves the Love-Spirit needed by others. Should they succeed in this, energies released through this Inner Image will sooner or later center in themselves as a soul and self. This will result in the truly deep, and one might say Divine, Inner satisfaction which cannot possibly be derived from activities limited to purely physical levels of life.

Once it is realized we are looking for something far beyond physical and material existence, we can adjust our Love-lives accordingly. We shall not expect or demand that we find true fulfillment of Love from physical objective sources as such, and therefore these cannot disappoint us any more. Instead, we shall use whatever physical foci seem most suitable, as a symbolic means of making spiritual contacts with the Inner actualities which alone offer the sure fulfillment resulting in our Cosmic contentment and a state of Spiritual serenity because we have balanced our True Beings.

There was something of this idea behind the ancient custom of temple prostitution. The girls were not supposed to be offering their own bodies to worshippers, but placing those bodies at the disposal of the Goddess with Whom the worshipper sought the closest contact he could feel through performance of a sex-act. How far this worked is doubtful in the extreme, but the theory is not entirely without merit, being applicable through a much wider field of possibilities. There is a distinct likelihood of the basics behind this old practice finding future usefulness through considerably modified forms of expression.

Physical sex is only one type of energy-expression along this Path, after all, and its extensions through other Dimensions are quite amazing to say the least. As we advance spiritually, we shall have to manifest our Emotion-entities through a range of expressions few people might recognize as sexual activities at all, although in fact they are just that very thing. Emotion and sex are tied together with the True Lover's Knot which cannot be undone except by Divinity Itself. Take emotion and Love away from sex, and what is left except a cold, calculated, and cruel chemical event closer to Chaos than Cosmos. Loveless sex is the saddest and most degrading behavior a human soul may indulge in when failing utterly to walk this Path. ELOAH va DAATh and IHVN SABAOTh are the only Divine Entities likely to help us just here. They have the Keys between them.

Creatively, this Path is controlled by the Archangels MICHAEL and AURIEL. The God-like Leader of Light, and the Light of experience in Life. Again we find the same theme of living in order to discover divinity through life-experience along emotional levels. Michael presents here the God-Being Image we look for all our lives in other souls, and never find because such perfection is far beyond mere mortals in their present conditions of Cosmos. Nevertheless, the longer we look for Michael among our fellow humans, the nearer he is able to approach us. Auriel reveals to us by his type of Light on this Path the deep emotional experiences we need to alter our spiritual structures into closer approximations of the Inner Cosmos we should create for ourselves.

The activities of intellect alter the mental side of our consciousness, but it is only the action of emotions and feelings which affect our souls, impelling us to behave badly or well as individual beings in the courses of our own creativeness. By our dual usage of intelligence and emotions, we build ourselves into the Temple for the Holy Spirit "not made with hands." As we soon discover, the energies of emotions can hurt us very badly in soul and result in our doing all kinds of things which our intelligence would never sanction for a moment. These twin aspects of our awareness were actually meant to be compensatory controls for each other, so that we gain the best from both, and this is where

Auriel tries to help us on this Path.

Auriel's Symbol is the Shield, and that is exactly what we need in spiritual terms so that we escape serious emotional injuries which might inflict severe soul-damage calling for much unnecessary effort in reconstruction. Unless we have some form of protection from emotional injuries in this world, we should soon be very sad psychic wrecks. Imagine a human organism trying to live in this world without its skin, and this will convey some idea of the problem. The Inner task of Auriel is to provide us with the equivalent of a spiritual skin-shield through which we safely absorb and convert energies from emotional fields of force which would otherwise be too much for our Inner sensorium to deal with. The fine adjustment of such protection is a delicate affair, because a sense-shield must not be too thick for necessary stimuli to reach us, or so thin that it is easily penetrable by every carelessly flung item of emotional import. To grow an Inner skin-shield successfully, Auriel needs very close collaboration from every soul attempting to cultivate this essential asset of Inner living.

The Symbol of Michael being the Rod or Spear-staff, shows that we should always take the measure of the emotional energies we direct toward other souls. Do we intend simply to touch them with the end of the staff, or wound them with the thrust of the spear-point? If we hope to reach others by the former method only, in order not to hurt them, Archangel Michael will have to show us just how to use the Rod of our Intentions, carefully measuring out opposite number's ability to absorb or withstand our projections of power. We might also ask their personal concepts of Auriel to protect them from any inadvertent or thoughtless thrust we could accidentally make. It might be well to bear in mind that the Michael-Auriel team in any soul counter their own counterparts in others, but the will of the individual decides the issue for that individual. If, for instance, we absolutely insist on using our Rods for hurting other souls, no Archangel or anyone else will prevent this decision, but there is nothing to stop Inner Intelligences from suggesting to others how best to hit back if they really demand retaliation. By and large it is best not to play these Inner war-games. Everyone gets hurt badly for no particular reason except pointless and profitless personal revenges with no benefits to anyone.

The object of an Initiate when dealing with this section of the Path should be to set up an emotional control-point, worked by Michael and Auriel. Thus, we shall neither hurt other souls, nor be hurt by them through emotional exchanges. Once set free from apprehensions or injuries on this life-level, we may proceed happily along with ever finer spiritual issues. So many souls become helpless victims of their emotional upheavals that perhaps life after life is wasted in this futile spiritual scrimmage. Emotions exist for us to experience As We Will in order to become our True Being. A religious soul might say that emotions are for helping us grow God-wards. Certainly not for us to wallow in and cause casualties with.

Hence the immense importance of learning how to enlist the aid of Michael and Auriel here. No soul can really grow to full size if it is afraid of emotional suffering all its life, or conversely spends its time thinking out ways of hurting others. Nor will any soul grow properly if it is so devoid of emotional capacity that it has scarcely any faculties for feeling at all. We should be able to feel and love As We Will, not expecting returns for these outputs through other souls, but from the Inner Ones who may best be able to reach us on quite different levels of Life. Once we are able to gain confidence in the ability of Auriel to safeguard our emotional sensitivities, then we can really afford to love and emote in a fearless Michaelean way. This is an example of the "perfect love casting out fear." MICHAEL and AURIEL will teach us how to do this here. They have the necessary Keys.

Formatively, we encounter the Angel Orders of the MALAKIM and the ELOHIM on this Path. The Rulers, and the God-forms. How are souls to measure or rule what forms of Divinity or Gods they have in them? Only by their feelings for the degree to which they experience any kind of Divine activity in themselves. Most Faiths and beliefs attribute feelings and emotions to a Supreme Spirit expressing Itself through living beings. The question is just how far does anyone actually feel such a Spirit in him, and what form or forms does this feeling take? We all think we are some kind of a God, however this idea may be wrapped up and labelled. Here we find the God-forms, or Elohim, which we should like others to recognize in us so that emotions will be aroused and we may enjoy exchanges of love on this level. The Malakim determine the measure of this operation in ourselves, and inform us of our stature or shortcomings relative to others.

What makes us look for love in sexual or any other terms through another soul? Only a deep Inner necessity driving us toward Divinity by closure of Cosmic circuits between our two points. We are seeking specific spiritual objectives through that other soul, and they seek their particular needs through us. Can we, or can we not, personify and present a form-focus for those Inner energies to each other? Are we able to mediate in Elohic manner the sort of God-formations that others are looking for in us? That is the whole purpose of this Path. No other human souls are likely to regard us lovingly unless they see in us, or believe they see in us, the kind of God they are aiming for. The more we resemble or act in the image of such an Inner Being, the more we shall mean to those needing contact with that type of Cosmic Concept. Basically, they want something we have, and if that something is an Inner Image which helps them live happily and valuably to everyone, so much the better for all connected to those Circles.

It is natural for all souls to expect love from others for the sake of themselves, but—just what *are* we? The Law of Life says that we may BE WHAT WE WILL WITHIN US. So why should we not make ourselves into whatever God-form we are able to assume with the help of the Elohim? We do not have to be any one form forever, any more than we have to live in one physical body for longer than its lifetime. Therefore, if we learn how to present ourselves in "God-like guise" for the benefit of other souls, everyone will be so much the better off.

This does not mean that we shall be hiding behind any sort of a false front in order to conceal all our spiritual deficiencies. It means that we are trying to project ourselves into a finer and better presentation-pattern on Inner levels and this effort is surely incumbent upon every soul with the slightest interest in its own Inner evolution. How shall we ever advance as individual entities of spiritual structure, if we do not attempt to modify ourselves more closely toward the original Divine Design behind our beings? The Elohim are capable of suggesting many ways in which we might work upon this project, and the Malakim will size up our chances and estimate our needs in this direction. They make a good team once we find out how to cooperate with them.

All Path-workings demand patience, but this one certainly

needs forbearance to its very limit. The Keyword here is "Suiting," and this is just what we must do in matching up a God-form in ourselves to suit the spiritual necessities of others, as well as find what suits our own Inner scarcities. Knowing what and how much to look for is essential, and it is the function of the Elohim and Malakim to tell us these details as clearly and concisely as possible. Most souls blunder around rather blindly with only the vaguest notions, if any at all, as to what they expect or need from others for their own fulfillment. Consequently they experience very considerable trouble and dissatisfaction with what they encounter during their lives. Initiates of this Path first find out precisely what they need in spiritual forms or emotional fulfillment with the help of both Elohim and Malakim, then they go looking for this objective. It may be that they do not meet with their exact requirements for a lifetime or more, but the knowledge that the experience must eventuate according to the Will Within Them, keeps initiated souls flowing freely along this Path for as long as they Intend. They have learned that what they ask from their Inner needs here must come to them sooner or later, because that is the Law they have invoked.

Heaven knows how much we need to love and be loved in order to become really worthwhile Entities in our own right. This is the Path of Life where the art has to be learned, for the management and application of emotional energies is indeed an arcane art which Initiates of this Path must master. A soul with skillful mastery of its Inner emotional opportunities enjoys a range of experience far beyond the beliefs of more ordinary people still tossed wildly around by the waves of their sensual seas. Once the aid of the ELOHIM and MALAKIM are enlisted, life becomes much easier. They have the Keys of human passion-problems here.

Expressively, this Path is governed by Sol and Venus. Beauty and affectionate Love. Two qualities our world always seems sadly deficient of. Venus is usually associated with sexual forms of emotional energies, but the expressions and activities these energies connect with on physical levels are even wider than Freud supposed. Virtually almost anything on earth is convertible to some kind of human sexual value. The symbols with which we relate our sexual needs with the rest of available creation are almost beyond enumeration. Whether we realize it or not, we are capable of sex-intercourse in any one way or another with an incredible variety of objectives. Anything under the Sun we might imagine. To suppose that sex is purely a reproductive or stimulatory process between creatures of opposite biological polarity is to take a very narrow and limited viewpoint leading to great loss of Inner opportunities.

From the occult point of view, sex is a matter of personal polarity resulting in a spiritual state of soul-bias which determines whether we are male or female in character. Spirit in its pure condition is sexless, and we only speak of "Male" or "Female" Principles of Cosmos in order to compare or contrast Inner polarities of power with our states of sexuality and the symbols concerned therewith. The dichotomy of sex becomes increasingly pronounced through the Principles of Soul, Mind and Body in that order. The sexes are thus at widest divergence from each other in Body, closer together in Mind, closer still in Soul, and unifiable in Spirit. Since each individual strives to implement his own Inner Cosmos from emotional energies experienced in relationship with another soul, it is fair to consider that all such contracts between souls have a sexual implication to some degree. As long as we are sexed beings, our human dealings with each other must necessarily be sexual to the extent of emotions and feelings involved, according to the nature and character of these energies.

Since our widest sex-differences are physical, these are normally the most obvious preoccupation with our objective awareness in this world. Dealing with emotional energies through physical sex-action is one of the most pressing and difficult problems humans have to tackle in this world. Isolated sex acts can no more result in emotional satisfaction and stability than a few sporadic and varied occasions of eating could keep a body fed and properly nourished. If sex acts affect a soul no deeper than a transitory physical stimulus and satisfaction, that soul will live in a starving spiritual and emotional state. This is why purely commercial sex available from vendors is nothing but a very poor stop-gap in place of the required reality. It is the feeling and emotions fed into a soul which constitute the deeply satisfying element of sex, and if these are absent or insufficient, there cannot be any genuine Inner value obtained.

The soul is nourished (or otherwise) by emotional energies in a very similar way to the body being nourished or damaged by food and drink. With sufficient and correct diet of physics and emotional comestibles, both body and soul will flourish. It is unhappily much easier to feed the body with food than the soul with feelings, so it is little wonder we have such ailing souls in this world. The emotional needs of everyone differ widely, and even if they knew just what these were, how might they obtain steady supplies? Money buys food, but who can buy love and affection? Here on this Path we have to learn how to maintain ourselves in a healthy condition of balanced emotional nutrition derived from all sources of supply available to Initiates who have Inner access thereto. Those able to solve sexual shortages of energy and problems of practice in neat and natural ways suggested from studies of Solar-Venusian systems of procedure. Each must find his own most suitable methods, but the principles apply to all.

The rule to remember on this Path is that sex-motivated energy-demands on Inner and Outer life-levels are inversely proportional to each other. The more our emotional necessities can find fulfillment for us Inwardly, the less insistence will be directed toward Outer activities of organic genital character. Nevertheless, the urgencies of psycho-physical sexual needs have to be recognized and regulated just as much as any other state of natural imbalance such as hunger, thirst, oxygen-lack, or the like. Here, we are up against a whole conglomeration of ingrained customs, morals, conventions, and inhibitory factors which complicate an otherwise clear issue. Many of these restrictions are quite sound and sensible social observances, but a large number might well be dispensed with to the benefit of future generations.

The good sense of this matter is that if Inner and Outer sex-serenity may be achieved by methods satisfactory to those concerned which cause neither harm nor offense to others, there is no valid reason why these should not be effectively employed. This was the reason why old-time circles kept their sex-customs which suited them entirely within their own numbers. Whatever they did therein was no more than their wills allowed, and no one outside the circle need be affected. So long as that rule was observed, all went well, and trouble only arose when unwilling souls were annoyed or outraged by attempts to inflict alien or unsuitable practices on them.

How much misery has been caused among humanity by the

supposition that sex is shameful in itself, and only defensible on procreational grounds, Heaven alone knows. Physical propagation of species is but a biological use of sex. Fundamentally, the finest purpose and usage of sexualized emotional energies is for the evolution and fulfillment of soul-entities seeking their Cosmic completion in Spirit and even beyond. The sex-creation sought by each soul is his own. We can help each other through these cycles of attraction, and should discover such possibilities along this Path. After all, the test of the matter is simple. Are individual souls helped, improved, benefited, made happier, or otherwise into better beings by means of their sex interests and activities? If not, why not, and what may be done to obtain favorable results? That is what this Path is for. To become better and more evolved entities because of anything we work in sexualized ways.

With this exalted aim in view, sex-satisfactions are obtainable through every sense-gateway we have. Beauty and Love come to us by so many Cosmic channels. The sight of sunlight on the curve of a hill, the scent of roses and sound of bees in a secret garden, the touch of a water-lily leaf. All those symbols and countless others of this nature are sheer sex experiences, no matter how they are called. While we are sexed creatures we shall find sex everywhere in as many ways as we will. Once we align ourselves properly along this Path where Venus meets the Sun with an embrace of entire emotional fulfillment, sex difficulties will start disappearing into the Love-Light we shall recognize around and within ourselves.

Sex secrets and their satisfactory employment are the perquisites which Initiates of this Solar-Venusian Path expect. The Keys are all here to be found by those with enough initiative to investigate for themselves the principles of their own Inner polarity, then apply those Keys to the gates of opportunity as these become available. No matter how often this Path has been explored, fresh experiences always await enterprising souls seeking wider and more wonderful visions by the Light of Sol and Venus, the brightest planet of the Solar System. Those luminaries hold the Keys for all true Lovers to grasp who have a reach extending beyond their bodily limits.

The Twenty-fifth Path

SPHERE—LETTER CODE:	Beauty 6 S 8 Glory	
DIVINE ORIGINATION:	ELOAH va DAATh—	The
	ELOHIM SABAOTh	Moving
ARCHANGELIC CREATION:	Michael—Raphael	Versatility
ANGELIC FORMATION:M	Malakim—Beni—Elohim	Coverage
APPARENT EXPRESSION:	Sun—Mercury	Mobility
TAROT SYMBOL:	THE CHARIOT	

Here on this Path we are among affairs of intelligent movement and travel on all Life-levels. Purposeful journeys are made in soul, mind, and body to cover all sorts of contingencies. This is travel that not only broadens the mind, but the whole of our beings. The natural movements we all make in search of living experience, from the slightest flicker of an eyelash to the flight of a soul round Cosmos.

This is the Path of "go getting" not so much in the sense of abstract Mystical Quests, but for the sake of satisfying the rational enquiries every entity must make for himself in connection with his curiosity concerning the Cosmos he lives in. One might almost call it "An intelligent soul's search for reasonable relations with reality." As the last Path deals with emotions and feelings, so does this one deal with intelligence and thinking. The major factor here is mind and head rather than soul and heart, though of course we should always remember these two human principles must exist side by side as level partners and never as rivals or competitors in the fields of our consciousness.

The Tarot Symbol of the Chariot here is a controversial one. The Waite version closely resembles that of Eliphas Levi, but has a number of subtle differences. Though the fundamental figure of a triumphal car with a victorious warrior drawn by two sphinx-like creatures is common to both, the Waite picture presents somewhat more arcane symbolism than Levi's. Nevertheless, Levi boldly calls the Symbol "The Chariot of Hermes," and we shall do well to bear this in mind while we think about it, because its nature is essentially Hermetic, and therefore most properly placeable upon this Path between Hermes and the Sun.

We first note that the Chariot itself is cubic, and so more connected with rationalism than romanticism. At its corners are the Four Pillars of Reason we need to support our theories about everything under the Heavens indicated by the starry canopy. The structure of the car gives an impression of extreme solidity and weight, which seems to tell us that every precaution should be taken against being overturned or upset on our Inner and Outer travels. The wheels are broad to show that a wide grip is needed for traveling safely on our cosmic courses. Altogether the Chariot is a remarkably robust and unbreakable vehicle, as soundly constructed as the minds we need to travel from one end of life to another and beyond these limits without injury to our intelligent entities from the experiences and difficulties we shall infallibly encounter.

The symbol on the front of the Chariot is very interesting. Levi depicted an Indian lingam on a nipple-shaped shield, surmounted by an Egyptian winged disc. This was to signify constant fertility and nourishment of a conscious entity traveling toward Truth. The Waite card appears superficially to follow the same scheme, but on careful examination the shapes of these symbols convey a rather more cunning idea. The winged disc has the universal meaning of a motivated mind or consciousness soaring along empowered by the Will and purpose within it, but the shield and symbol shapes suggest not sexual but scientific equipment. The outline of the shield is that of an old-fashioned spinning top driven with a whip, and the symbolic object in the middle is another type of top having a gyroscopic nature. One might virtually consider this as a representative symbol of a built-in auto-pilot, steering the car wherever it ought to go for the sake of the traveler it carries.

As any average schoolchild knows today, it is the principles of gyroscopic control that keeps ships, aircraft, and space vehicles steady on their courses, but when the Waite card was designed, gyro-control of vehicles had not come into use except possibly for torpedo stabilization, a fact probably quite unknown to the designer. Spinning tops were very ancient, of course, and it was fully realized that only their rotary momentum kept them in dynamic balance. After all, our planet is an enormous top, and the Cosmos of our Solar System depends on the same principles. So does the Cosmos created by our mental and rational faculties. Our reason is balanced by the motion of its own dynamism which derived from the efforts we make to keep it going, just like children kept their tops spinning by skillful use of a whiplash. Tops had to be persuaded rather than flogged, because any over-enthusiastic lashing knocked the top hopelessly out of course and it crashed into senseless whirling until it fell down altogether. To keep a top going successfully, little and light stroke were needed at relatively frequent intervals, and that is so the best way keep our reason revolving steadily around its own axis.

If we apply all the principles connected with spinning tops and gyroscopes to constructing a control instrument for the rational part of our consciousness on Inner Levels, we shall learn the main secrets of the Hermetic Chariot. It is, of course, our metaphysical vehicle for taking our intellectual awareness anywhere we Will throughout Inner Dimensions. With it we may go where we please in Inner Space, provided we are not excluded from entry by other intelligences for their own reasons. Not only must we have skill and experience in driving our Chariot along Inner highways, but we also have to have a driving license as well. Much practice will be needed before we obtain permitted entry to Inner areas accessible only to initiated individuals and entities. This is the proper Path of practice where we shall learn how to direct and control the courses of our mental motors so that we will be welcome travelers among the worlds where other minds occupying various vehicles keep their courses in company with ours.

The motive power for the Chariot derives from a pair of sphinx-steeds, one black, the other white. They hold between their front paws the ends of their own tails, the black beast's being turned clockwise, and the white beast's tail counter-clockwise. They are not visibly harnessed to the Chariot at all, the assumption being that they are clutching the shafts along with their tails beneath other bodies. There are no reins attached to them. In the Levi card, they are shown looking rightwards, like the Charioteer, to show the intention of keeping to the Right

Hand Path. In the Waite card, the casts and the Charioteer look straight forward to indicate that the vehicle goes wherever the attention is directed.

These sphinxes are the endless enigmas of life we follow in our chariots to obtain answers. They can only say "yes" or "no" to all our queries, hence the tail-clutching eternal circle sign, and the nay and yea of black and white. The faster we chase them the faster they run, pulling our Chariot with them. They will only stop when we learn the Magic Word to command our consciousness. There are no reins because the beasts do not respond to forceful restraint, but to intelligent instructions—once these are forthcoming. Otherwise they pull us around as they please until we discover how to direct them. When we know the right words, they become docile and obedient. Sphinxes are feminine creatures to denote natural curiosity and the word "Sphinx" derives from a root meaning "The Throttler" or choker. We still have the slang phrase "to be choked," meaning frustrated, and to "choke off," meaning to stifle someone with stiff or silencing critical vituperation. This compares with the effect that living-enigmas have on most of us. We shall not breathe easily until we learn how to avoid their stranglehold. In the case of the Tarot Chariot, the dangerous paws of the Sphinxes are fully occupied with the shafts. As long as we keep our vehicles closely behind them they will not release their hold. The Chariot has no brake except the driver's indifference.

This Charioteer is a fascinating figure. We meet an armored male wearing a crown of Victory laurels around a circlet of Light with an eight-point Star. This reminds us at once that anyone intending to make reasonable sense out of living-enigmas needs to be well-armored to withstand the blows and shocks they are sure to encounter. On the breastplate is a Square Symbol to show the necessity of ruling all angles of life rightly and precisely so that they relate with each other into a balanced design or plan to be followed. The eight points of the Star in the Circlet of Consciousness are the points of the Inner Cosmic Compass. By this we realize that we must be prepared to go anywhere in Creation by means of our Chariots in search of the spiritual secrets we seek.

The pauldrons of the Charioteer are made like faces of the new and old moons. The right-hand face is cheerful to show our enjoyable and amusing intellectual expenses, and the left-hand is serious for opposite reasons. Between the two we must arrive at a middle meaning, while we continue to bear the burden of them both on our broad shoulders. The Chariot, in fact, is a Solar and not a Lunar Symbol at all, except insofar as the Moon reflects the light of the Sun, but since the search for enlightenment must continue by day and night alike, the Lunar association is not inappropriate.

A rather strange discrepancy occurs in this Waite Tarot version. A Sword was distinctly specified as being held in the Charioteer's right hand, and a Sword is indeed the proper emblem for this Path, yet the figure is shown holding a flame-tipped Rod, and wearing a sword-belt to which no sword is attached. The flame-tipped Rod naturally signifies inspired intelligent guidance, and the Rule of Reason with which the vehicle should be controlled. On the other hand, a Sword signifies keen flexible mind very much to the point, having fine edge, polished wit, and other sword-like qualities. There is a possibility that the substitution of Rod for Sword was made because a Sword might be construed as indicating aggressive tendencies, whereas the Charioteer has nothing to do with aggression whatever. He may be keenly competitive, racing his Chariot against others, but his attacks are only directed against ignorance and stupidity. We have to remember that this card in particular was designed just after the Great War of 1914-18, and no doubt a Sword was felt as an unhappy reminder of recent disasters. Undoubtedly a Sword is the correct emblem for the Charioteer to bear. It may be noticed that he holds no whip in his other hand. His driving is done with corrective consciousness rather than compulsion or cruelty. No need for a whip when the Will impels from Within.

Around his waist, the Charioteer wear an apron covered with hieroglyphs. The apron is a symbol of Hermes, being not so much a genital covering as a large pouch in which were all the plans and secret documents relating to the task in hand. The driver of the Chariot here has complete instructions and information for his journeys on his person. So has any soul who knows where to look for them. They are written in our genes in spiritual script. We can only read them by instructed Inner sight.

When we look closely at the drive in his Chariot, it almost seems as if a slight error in the plate has left an unaccountable gap between his lower body and the edge of the Chariot. This is not a mistake, but extremely subtle symbology. It gradually dawns on the initiated observer that the body of the Chariot is actually a Cubic Stone, out of which the top half of the Charioteer's body appears. This Stone is the Masonic Ashlar representing our rough and ready state which we have to square up, finish, true, and polish by our intelligent workmanship upon ourselves. The appearance of Man from Stone symbolizes the whole story of evolution, and speaks of the sacrifices we have had to make in the cause of Mind over Matter.

Although we have far from exhausted the contents of this card, we need yet to take a brief glance at the background. It must be noted that the Chariot is not on any sort of road, but is upon a field on the edge of a river flowing between two cities. The city on the left is fortified, while the city on the right is not. The open field is, of course, the area of intellectual awareness which anyone occupies at any given moment, and the water indicates a flow of consciousness between the guarded areas of the Inner Mind which contains the precious secrets we seek, and the state of open-mindedness we must keep in order to have an Inner habitation worth living in. Between our Inner Citadels and Inner cities, communication should flow in steady streams of clear consciousness like the river depicted.

All this is purely the surface symbology of this most significant Tarot Symbol. There is much more to be deduced on deeper levels still by those who care to continue delving. For the present we must follow our Path through the Four worlds.

Originatively, it is ELOAH va DAATh and ELOHIM SABAOTh that govern this Path. Divine Knowledge and Divinity in Everyone. Here is the Divine drive in us that makes us seek Knowledge for ourselves despite all opposition. The Glory of Knowing. The instinct to investigate. On low levels—cunning. On high ones—comprehension. A mid-meaning might be intellectual enquiry, while on a very grand scale we may consider the moving force here as Cosmic Curiosity.

The old proverb says, "If the mountain will not come to the Prophet, then he must go to the mountain." This is where we meet that very principle in practice, as travel in search of truth. The Moving Deity motivating Itself in all of us to go and search for the solution of Its own problems. It is almost as if the Ultimate Intelligence enjoyed setting up spiritual problem-situations as chess experts do for the sake of the intellectual exercise obtained in solving them. We are tempted to think of the lines:

'Tis all a checker-board of Nights and Days
Where Destiny, with men for pieces, plays ...

Which may be so in the case of many souls who make little or no attempt at directing their own destinies, and simply drift along in life just as they are pushed by every external force around them. As we evolve, however, we are expected to seek solutions for our various situations in the most natural place—within ourselves, and that is the type of travel we must learn on this Path.

Throughout our conscious lives on all levels, we are confronted by one problem or enigma after another. Those are the Sphinxes we have to deal with and harness to our Chariots. Once our problems become resolved and we equate their energies through ourselves, they are no longer problems but assets of experience amounting to Life-knowledge. It is our unsolved problems that bring us trouble and difficulties through our open-circuited concern with them caused by lack of knowledge or ability to reach their solutions. It is not so much our problems themselves that worry us and make our lives miserable, as our deep-seated fears that they are insoluble by us, or a fundamental lack of confidence in our own capability of ultimately arriving at a satisfactory state of affairs. When Fear obscures Faith, we lose touch with Knowledge, and drive ourselves into all sorts of dangerous situations quite unnecessarily.

If, say, we were told with absolute certainty at bad or difficult times of our lives, "Yes, your situational problems are indeed serious, but if you steer yourself in such and such a way for approximately so long, adopting this and that course of action, you are bound emerge all the better for your experience in the end," we should tackle the problems with determination and confidence, following through the worst of ways until successful solutions were reached. Human souls can face all kinds of horrible situations and problems with courage if only they can see their way clearly ahead through these to something worth arriving at, ultimately. It is blindness and ignorance of the way ahead that panics even brave souls traveling through the various fields of Life. If only we might achieve complete confidence in our ability to drive through any situational problems of Life with spiritual safety and emerge with a bonus-benefit of valuable Knowledge, we should be good Cosmic Charioteers, which is what we have to learn on this Path, helped by ELOAH va DAATh and ELOHIM SABAOTh.

This danger of becoming blind to our situational hazards and our clearest course through them is shown the Tarot Symbol by the canopy of the Chariot. If the curtains fell across the face of the driver, he would be blind and unable to steer his vehicle properly. As the curtains are, they have been divided in the middle along the Median Line, and secured to the front Pillars of Reason in order to leave the driver's vision ahead unobstructed. We must do exactly the same for ourselves by holding the curtains of our confusion firmly apart before our Inner vision by means of reason, so that our way ahead becomes perceptible. Yet even if we fail to do this promptly enough, we should still be able to rely on our "auto-pilot" system for keeping our course until we are fit to take command of our vehicles again.

ELOAH va DAATh is Divine Knowledge. ELOHIM SABAOTh is Divinity in everyone experiencing Life. Somewhere in our Cosmic depths of being exists our share of THAT WHICH KNOWS, and THAT WHICH IS WILLING TO KNOW. If the two connect themselves together through us on this Path, the energy-circuit will be complete, and somehow we shall know in our ordinary consciousness this vital Inner event has occurred in us. That knowledge alone will give us motivation for continuing our journeys into spiritual Space. The conviction in our consciousness beyond doubt that Something concerned with ourselves as an integral part of us Knows where It is going, and where It intends us to go with It, will carry us anywhere in Existence. It may be difficult to arrive at such a conclusion, but that should be our first destination on this Path.

Our most important journeys are Inner ones. There is no use visiting every place in this world physically if we do not take our minds with us. Furthermore, our minds are capable of travel experience quite apart from our bodies. An imaginative invalid with well developed faculties for Inner exploration travels far more widely and to better purpose than someone who covers thousands of miles each week thinking of nothing except commercial cares of material concerns. Apart from survival necessities, the best reasons for bodily travel are to provide the mind with more opportunities for excursions into Inner Dimensions, thus becoming more experienced and knowledgeable entities. Yet by itself travel is only moving our bodies around so that sense impressions via our brains supply our minds with unfamiliar stimuli to which we react on deeper than average levels. It is the newness of the stimuli which evokes responses from us causing expansive or other changes in our Inner Cosmoi. If we took the time and trouble to learn the art of Inner travel along this Path, we could explore quite new Inner territory and areas of existence which would provide us with sufficient spiritual stimulation to enlarge ourselves enormously. Why do we not travel inside ourselves more often? We might go to the ends of the earth and come back with nothing worth having, yet journey inside ourselves for less than half an hour and return with the keys of a whole new life. On the Originative levels of this Path, those Keys are held by ELOAH va DAATh and ELOHIM SABAOTh, so we had better ask them for permission to enter their Inner Kingdom.

Creatively, Archangels RAPHAEL and MICHAEL control this Path. Raphael is Hermes under another form, and is patron of travel and intelligent enterprises. The staff of Michael supports all souls seeking Light, and the broad brim of Raphael's hat protects them from being dazzled or burned by rays too strong or direct to bear comfortably. Furthermore, the Sword of Raphael serves to protect travelers from attack, or clear paths overgrown with entanglements. The same Sword will cut a way through the Dark Forests that symbolize the Unknown obstacles we shall have to penetrate in search of the secrets concealed in the Castle of Inner Consciousness which the Forest surrounds. All this symbology should be built into the imaginative journeys we must venture on this Path leading to knowledge.

Constructive imagination is essential in all magical work, and one of the standard exercises is to set forth on "Quests" entirely through Inner territory in search of some definite "Grail" or realizable Inner objective. This exercise is not at all comparable to the drug-induced "trips" which precipitate souls into wild worlds of Inner experience derived from contacts with projections of consciousness from all kinds of sources in haphazard fashion. The Inner travels taken by true Initiates of this Path must be fully under control of their Will working through Reason the whole time. Charioteers of Inner Space must always be in control of their vehicles. Drunken driving is no more welcome in other worlds than in this one and, though the penalties may be different, there are Rules of the Road to be observed just the same. "Driving a vehicle while under the influence of drugs" is against the laws of more than this one material world. Offenders usually get dealt with in both cases, depending largely on the degrees of danger involved, especially if other souls are endangered.

Legitimate and conscientious travel into Inner Dimensions while in control of one's vehicle by Will with Reason for some sound purpose is to be encouraged along this Path by every means. Operating Mind apart from Body is an essential technique to be developed by those intending to achieve a condition of entity independent of physical incarnation. Like every other form of activity, there are right and wrong ways of doing this. The decisive factor between these extremities is the motive behind the method employed. All our journeys ought to be properly motivated and prepared for before entering Inner Space travel, just as much or more so than in the case of physical trips. Even the most spontaneous Earth-traveler has to buy tickets, study itineraries, make bookings, and take some sort of luggage or the cash to buy necessities. To make situational excursions into Inner Space we need a prepared mind like a departure point, faculties of projection like a vehicle, a reserve of mental assets like travelers' checks, and, in fact, the Inner equivalents of every travel-adjunct on Earth. The only main difference is that there are no travel-agents to arrange everything for us to exchange for money. We have to arrange our own transport entirely. Moreover, although we are free to travel anywhere we like solely within ourselves, we shall need passports if we mean to pass through realms pertaining to other mental regions under the control of conscious entities other than ours. There are all sorts of important matters to learn in connection with mental travel, and this is the Path to learn them.

When we first begin to make serious excursions into Inner Space, it is always best to do so in company with an experienced companion accustomed to these conditions of consciousness. Here on the Hermetic Path, we may be reminded that Hermes was also known as a "psychopompos" or "soul-conductor" who led discarnate entities through all difficult ways of the Otherworld. Initiates on this Path wisely await a rendezvous with their Hermetic or Raphaelic Inner companions before attempting to explore unfamiliar depths of Inner Dimensions—even in themselves. In fact, we can get more lost and bewildered in ourselves than more other places, because nobody else is likely to look for us there for quite a long while. Eventually our yells for help will be heard, but we may be in a very sorry condition when rescued. It is far the best idea to travel this Path in company with Inner companions who not only know the way they travel themselves, but are able to suggest useful ideas to us also. In actuality we shall travel no one's Path but our own, yet encouraging advice and admonitions from elsewhere will provide us with invaluable assistance. Eventually, perhaps, we may do the same for others in our turn.

Before making any intentional Inner excursions in search of information and knowledge beyond average boundaries of mental limitations, it is a good thing to invoke the company of Inner associates on this Path who respond to the Raphael-Michael frequencies of imaginative energization. Mental imagery and constructive conceptions of these Archangelic Types will send out modulated mental signals recognizable by those able and willing to answer calls of this nature. Though we must always drive and control our own Chariots by our own efforts, no sensible Initiate of this Path will proceed without Michael-Raphael contacts, any more than an airliner captain would become airborne without radio contacts in all necessary ways.

Between them, MICHAEL and RAPHAEL are a versatile pair, affording us mental contact with the rest of creation once we learn the procedures for dealing with them. They have accompanied us under many names and disguises so far along our Main Path of Evolution, and one way or another will be with us until the end. Meantime we should make every effort at personal extensions and excursions into Inner Life in company with those who belong to the "M and R" line of travel. They have the Keys here which should eventually open our ways into wider and wider Inner Fields until we are qualified to drive our Cosmic Chariots by ourselves, yet beneficially for all else in Being.

Formatively, we pursue this Path with the Angel Orders of the MALAKIM and the BENI-ELOHIM. The Regulators and the Children of Consciousness. They help us formulate and arrange our Inner itineraries in regular and recognizable patterns. Without them, we shall not make much sense of what we encounter Inwardly, or be able to form consecutive and repeatable processes of our Inner travel-trains. Objective consciousness is not much use by itself unless it can be formed into processional patterns and sequences that make meaning in the mind of the entity employing this energy. This is where the Malakim and Beni-Elohim combination come together for that very purpose.

They give us coverage over the field of our life-consciousness and also in those Inner fields we have thoroughly explored along this Path. In a way, they are our "mind-children" and the order these keep in our memories and mental capacities for containing impressions derived from intelligent contact with stimuli received from all levels. They also enable us to cover fresh fields of Inner awareness by giving us means to formulate and put in place our own output of intelligized energy. If we need to think fresh and foreign kinds of thoughts, these Angel-orders allow us to construct and categorize such mentalizations into formations and sequences where they will fit in with our existent minds and memories and come within our rules of reason. It is their job, if they function properly, to reject any mental impression that might endanger our reason and its balance. Later on, if circumstances alter, they might accept that very impression on our behalf because we are then able to accommodate it beneficially. In this most important way, the Malakim and Beni-Elohim together help to keep us sane and reasonable beings. If we refuse their services and defy the laws which offer them, we have only ourselves to blame for the consequences.

A mind, like a vehicle, can only operate successfully within its safety-rates and performance factors. In the case of us humans, these amount to equivalents of the Malakim and Beni-Elohim, and each individual being has his own specific coding. To employ our angel-agents properly, we must keep them going at a reasonable pace all our lives, yet never drive them to an extent where they fail to function and our reason becomes unbalanced. This depends a lot on the rate we travel through new mental territory, or simply go so far with our lives and then keep drifting around and around over the same ground until it becomes so much churned Inner mud. True, we have to do our routine runs, but we should try and extend their scope for the sake of our evolving entities, providing we do this consistently with reason.

To use our Chariots and their angelic maintenance crew advantageously, we should never stop learning and exercising our minds in making more progress along our Inner Paths. For a Qabalist, the Tree-plan is a learning-program by itself, and at the rate of, say, a single Path to study each day or week, would supply enough work for a whole incarnation and more. This is why the Paths are sequential as ABC, and can be rated in accordance with individual ability to follow them. At first this seems slow and laborious like any other study, but after a while our mental vehicles pick up speed, and we may go as fast as we will, though our pace should always be deliberately controlled to match our speed of thought in assimilating and realizing at least some of the salient points covered. That is where the Beni-Elohim and Malakim are able to help. They point things out and precis them up for us if we give them a chance, virtually packing the souvenirs of our trip in the back of the Chariot so that they may be examined and considered at leisure later on.

The great advantage of the Qabalistic Tree with Inner traveling is that the Tree provides a reliable road-map from one end of the Universe to the other. Once we know how to read it, we can climb into our mental chariots and drive around all its Paths happily for the rest of our lives and more. Only the major roads are marked on the traditional Glyph, but of course there are innumerable side roads and by-paths waiting to be discovered, besides incalculable virgin territory as yet unexplored by human intelligence. Still, when learning to drive, it is best to remain on highways where help is readily available. Here is the place at which we pick up our driving instructors qualified in Hermetic schools of thought. They show us how to think quickly and efficiently enough to control our vehicles along our Inner mental motorways, and MALAKIM-BENI-ELOHIM combination will help us to observe the rules of the road and manage all our information concerning it. They have the Keys.

Expressively, this Path comes under Sol-Hermes control. The Golden-Mercurial force-flow. The Sun provides the Force, and Mercury the flow. Our Life-energy in this Solar System derives from the Sun, and Mercury is its proximal planet absorbing its most intense energy. Since Mercury is naturally the fastest planet around the Sun, completing its course at roughly four times our speed on Earth, it is well associated with the most rapid messenger of our Inner Cosmos—Mind itself, traveling with the speed of thought.

Even translated into common commercial terms, the gold of the Sun provides the motivation for the movements of Mercury in search of marketing facilities. Trade and travel go together for the sake of gold all through the ages. The experience gained in the fields of commerce has served mankind in far nobler spheres. Arts, literature, science, intellectual achievements, and every Hermetic benefit known to us arises from our attempts to gain something for ourselves in exchange for extending our intelligence into what might be called the market of conscious commodities. Here we buy the products of brains and borrow the services of other minds in order to enhance our own positions as living entities. Those of us with mental talents offer these for hire on differing scales of remuneration. Using a golden standard of some kind as a metaphorical measure, we exchange our mental energies and abilities against needed commodities available from other entities. To know the best current rate of exchange, we have to do considerable traveling in search of information. The Chariot must take us a long way yet. Even though a man at a desk with a telephone may not have moved physically from his chair, minds and messages from very many miles may travel along the communicative channels of this Path before a decision is made that moves his material body in any direction.

What do we usually seek most frequently from other beings like ourselves? Intelligent contacts of a communicative nature. Mind meeting mind and making the most of this. If anything, we tend to insist rather too much on intellectual experience as the criterion for acceptance of consciousness. This is liable to cut us off quite considerably from contacts with Inner intelligences if we are unable to operate our intellectual processes in metaphysical areas. That ability was and is precisely what the so-called Hermetic Mysteries are mainly about. Exchanges of intelligence according to the rules of reason accepted by human entities using brain based minds as mortals, and inntelligent beings independent of physically focused existence, yet capable of mind movements translatable into our terms through mediative symbology.

There is no use whatever in our expecting such types of entities to speak to us in English or any other Earth-language. We must be prepared to evolve quite a different method of communication and style of Inner speech which will only translate back into approximations of original meanings into our terminology. This may not make much sense on purely face-value, and only instructed initiates would be able to grasp the purport of much that "comes through" Hermetic channels. The Caduceus Symbol provides a useful Key with its crossings of the Serpent of cyclic consciousness in diminishing proportions until they become small through for a human mind to handle. When small minds make contact with larger ones, this problem always arises, and energies have to be reduced in ratio accordingly. Conversely, they must be increased in amplitude when directed from us toward intelligences covering far wider fields of awareness than ours.

The Solar side of this Path tells us quite plainly that we have everything under the Sun to think about and exercise our minds with. Apollo, the Sun-Deity, has always been regarded as the beneficent patron of harmony and healing in addition to all liberal arts, and the Chariot is his special symbol. While our Solar System lasts, Apollo throws light upon all its Mysteries, and what more brilliant reflector than Mercury? As quicksilver, Hermes responds with more sensitive expansions to Solar rays than other metals, and the combination suggests fluctuations of mental workings when modulating the energies of applied consciousness from a radiating source of supply. If we learn how to make our minds as responsive to rays proceeding from the Inner equivalents of the Sun as ordinary mercury acts thermically, then we shall make mental movements worth following. A Hermes-Apollo combination indicates that thought and the speed of light are the constants of both Inner and Outer Life-states leading in and out of each to conjoin Mind and Matter into complementary conditions of consciousness.

This is a very interesting point. We cannot live physically any faster than light, or mentally any faster than thought, and the two principles come together on this Path of the Tree. Out of Light is made our material Cosmos, and out of Mind is made our immediate Inner Cosmos. Our work and experience with one should enhance our entities in the other, and so this proves in fact. Hermes and Apollo in partnership offer us the best business opportunities between them that any intelligent human being is likely to encounter anywhere in life. Together they stand for what every Initiate of the Mysteries in general seeks. Illuminated intelligence. No matter how far, or for how many lives we must travel in search of this very acquisition, our journey will not only have been worthwhile, but also imperative.

What more valuable asset can we possibly possess in our explorations of Existence than an active, lively mind, ruled by reason and inspired by imagination? A mind guarded like one of the cities in the Symbol, so that unwelcome thoughts are excluded, yet open like the other city, so that valuable ideas are encouraged to remain in residence. The river of consciousness between the two carries passenger traffic, and the Chariot of the Sun handled by Hermes covers all possible areas of awareness. The power of Apollo and the persuasive pervasiveness of Hermes together will take travelers anywhere in Cosmos. When Means and Mind meet in harmonious relationship anything is likely, and this Path is that meeting point. The wealth of Apollo and the wits of Hermes supply us with travelers' checks cashable by any bank of consciousness, and passport to any part of the Universe. It is well to form a good friendship with this Olympic pair, because they have the Keys to Cosmic citizenship which most of us covet.

The Twenty-sixth Path

SPHERE—LETTER CODE: Beauty 6 T 9 Foundation
DIVINE ORIGINATION: ELOAH va DAATh—   The
   SHADDAI el CHAIM   Omnipotent
ARCHANGELIC CREATION: Michael—Gabriel   Brilliance
ANGELIC FORMATION: Malakirn—Ashim   Clarity
APPARENT EXPRESSION: Sun —Moon   Radiance
TAROT SYMBOL: THE SUN

Here we are upon the central Power Path of the Middle Pillar. If we take the right and left edges of the Tree-Glyph from Kether to Malkuth as the two external Pillars of contrast, we may note these have four Paths apiece while the Middle Pillar has but three. Eleven in all. Eleven other Paths interconnect these making the Twenty-two. This particular Path being, so to speak, the "center of the Middle" is very properly a Solar one, since the Sun is central to any Cosmic System. The Nil-Nucleus from which all energy derives, has become manifest as Light and Life. Potential has become Power, and None becomes One. Every energy we observe or consider with our consciousness comes from this single Source. More remotely above us on the Middle Pillar, we thought of Light-Life Energy in association with the Stars, or Suns of Space, extending to the ends of Existence. Now we must think of the same Energy somewhat nearer home, as the centralizing factor of our lives on all levels as inhabitants of this Solar System and Its Inner Cosmos.

The Tarot Symbol of this Path is not an overloaded one with any of the known packs. It must be admitted in the case of the Waite pack, usually top-heavy with significant and sophisticated symbolism, the Sun card has noticeable deficiencies in both design and draftsmanship. Even the artist's monogram of PCS

(Pamela Colman-Smith) looks slapdash and untypical of her usual neat and close style. A number of minor faults occur which give the impression of hasty or casual work rather than the deliberate subtleties met with elsewhere in this pack. Nevertheless the basics of the Symbol are all present and awaiting consideration.

The Sun-face itself in this instance has the somewhat dualized male-female expression either instinctively or intentionally arrived at with the Tarot Trump characters of the Waite cards. This makes sense, because although the Sun is frequently thought of as a typically masculine phenomenon, it belongs more properly to a force-fusion of both "male-female" polarity principles expressed as pure emissive energy. We must remember that all the Spheres except Malkuth meet in the Solar Sphere of Tiphereth, which holds their natures together in common. We must therefore understand the Sun-symbol to represent esoterically the Power of the Life-Principle in practice, and thus in the case of biological life, both Male and Female polarities combined as commencement and completion of the entire Life-Cycle. In a sense, we may see the Sun as a constant Cosmic copulation which conceives, creates, then cremates, and ultimately reconceives every life-form. Essentially, the Sun is Male-Female in the act of emitting new Life and absorbing old. It is the sign of our birth-beginning by which we are condemned to die, and our death-ending by which we become doomed to birth again. While we live under the Sun, we shall not escape its spiritual or seasonal cycles.

This particular Sun-face is obviously intended to have twenty-two rays, eleven straight ones for the Pillar-Paths, and eleven with four waves in each for the interconnecting Paths. Only twenty-one are shown, the card numeral occupying a clear space at the top, while an abortive attempt at the missing wavy line appears to the right of the numeral. The quadruple waves in the rays show that the Paths should be taken through the Four Worlds, just as we are doing in this work.

The lower part of the card displays the "Walled Garden" motif, now recognized as a fundamental archetypal symbol deeply rooted in human consciousness. The Solar nature of this particular Garden is shown by sunflowers appearing over the wall. There are obviously six of these (the number of Tiphereth), but only four are visible because of an obscuring banner held by the foreground Figure. The Wall itself appears as a series of stone courses most likely twelve from ground level, of which eight are actually in the picture. We may think of these as suggesting the twelve Zodiacal divisions of the imaginary "Cosmic perimeter wall" around our Solar System. Alternately, we might consider the four visible sunflowers as the four major points, and the eight stone courses as the sub-points of the Cosmic compass. In any case, the symbolism of Sun-centered Cosmos appears clearly enough.

A Walled Garden is a highly important symbol for all of us. It conveys the idea of an enclosed area of cultivation intended for the benefit of those who keep it in good condition. We are all "walled-gardens" to that extent, and even if we were living in a public Paradise, what would matter most to everyone would be their own private interpretations of this within their personal "Inner Walls." These are our secret "Gardens of the Soul" where we live our individual Inner lives among the spiritual surroundings which suit us best. Whether these "Gardens of Inner Growth" contain but a single soul, or embrace the whole of Existence, we may consider them as enclosures of Evolution, or the Cultivation of Cosmos. The "Wall-principle" is one of protection, preservation, exclusion of evil, privacy of purpose, and for a host of reasons concerned with confining areas of awareness and consciousness within calculated boundaries for perfectly good and sound intentions. Everything and everyone has walls of some kind, or we could not continue in individual being. In this present instance, we are concerning ourselves with the unseen but very appreciable Inner Walls that define the immediate boundaries of our lives as distinct entities, having responsibilities and rights within these areas for the practice of what might be called "Cosmoculture."

The cultivation of Life is a major Key to this Trump. All five Kingdoms are represented. Divinity by the Sun, Humanity by the Child, Animal by the Horse, Vegetable by the Sunflowers, and lastly Mineral by the Stone Wall. All the materials of our evolution related with each other by the same Banner of Being. Everything under the Sun on every life-level. This is where they may meet and recognize each other as Companions in one and the same Cosmos, yet remain complete individual cosmoi in themselves. Surely the Sun is the truest symbol of a common causation, creation, construction, and completion behind all life-types in Cosmos. The ancients realized this when they used the Solar Symbol as a faith-focus and prayer-point. They must have felt that the consciousness they were able to direct Sun-wards would automatically distribute its energy among all that existed, and that the Spirit behind the Sun they saw was indeed the Lord of Light-Life.

The centralizing Figure in this card is a naked child (which could be either sex) seated on a horse, and holding the staff of a red banner disposed in four waves. There is quite a wealth of symbology in this grouping. The Child, of course, is the evolving Soul of Humanity which entitled light-seeking entities to be known as the Children of Light. The arms of the Child are widely held in the gesture of universal embrace, to show that no human soul is excluded from this category except those who refuse to enter it of their own wills. A happy smile on the Child's face indicates how warmly welcome are all souls who claim their highest and holiest heritage.

Simple as it looks, the diadem on the head of the Child tells quite a story. It consists principally of the Six Precious Drops of that mysterious Blood from which all of us are supposed to have descended. Each drop is surrounded by a golden aureole of light. Here we have the ideal Light being converted into Life by means of consciousness. The Six Drops of Blood are representative of six major human groupings, *viz*.: the White, Black, Yellow, Red, Brown, and Olive skinned races. They also indicate the six points of any living being: head, feet, front, back, right and left. Even in Christian symbology the Six Drops may be associated with blood from the Five Wounds and the Crown of Thorns. All symbols connected with continuance of Life through direct blood ties with Divinity.

Rising from the diadem is a single feather from the tail of the legendary phoenix, that Fire-Bird which renewed itself from its ashes and lived by drinking its own blood. This creature is a form of the "Sky-Bird" who reputedly bears the Sun around our Earth on its back. The first shaft of light in the eastern sky at dawn was the appearance of its crest. Then it soared aloft over the world with the Sun in Splendor turning its feathers to sheer golden light. At the end of the day, it dived beneath the Earth giving a last display of brilliance with its crimson tail. The final "tail feather" of the Sun-Bird seen in the darkening sky of Night was a promise that the Bird would return next day with the resurrected Sun to gladden the hearts of all true worshippers. Sometimes a stray feather from the Bird actually fell to earth, and if a human was fortunate enough to find it, he could always obtain light from anything by touching it with the tip of the feather. Great caution was needed, however, not to incinerate oneself also by misuse of this marvel.

So here is symbolized in the diadem of the Child alone, our promised resurrection in Light and Life throughout eternal Cosmos. In the symbol of the Phoenix we have to remember that only one Phoenix existed. Each new Phoenix was the same one over and over again, rising out of its previous incarnation, just as we are supposed to do. In physical life we follow the seasons of the Sun through the year and in non-physical life we must follow the spiritual seasons of the Sun behind the Sun until we are led back to birth or beyond to Becoming.

The left hand of the Child grasps the Spear-staff upholding the Fourfold Life-banner. The Spear-staff belongs to Michael, Archangel of the Sun, and the banner is scarlet to indicate both blood and warmth, two life characteristics which are a common bond among all living creatures, even so-called "cold-blooded" ones. So the original meaning of the Scarlet Banner was associated with warm friendship and family ties of blood among mankind. When it floated freely from its Staff stuck in the Earth, it blew around the Circle of the Winds over those inhabiting every Quarter of the world. Hence its four folds, meant to show humanity coming together from the Quarters to the point of Unison where the Staff stood indicating Heaven. Unhappy political and historic associations with the Red Flag have debased the value of this once noble symbol except for those able to appreciate it on purely aesthetic levels.

The naked Child of Light is seen mounted on a horse, usually a white one, though in this instance intentionally gray to indicate a middle course between the Black and White Pillars of Life. The head of the beast points to the right of the card. This shows it about to commence the Sunwise circuit of Cosmos. The animal, of course, represents pure Solar Power amenable to control by its growing human rider. One point is important here. The horse is really a mare, or female of the species. The White (or, in this case, gray) Mare, is a familiar occult symbol. It may be difficult for moderns to realize just how important horse-breeding was for humanity in bygone days. Wealth, power, trade, travel, social and political status, in fact the rise of civil strength and establishment of nations, depended on the possession and deployment of horse-power. It still does in a symbolic manner. The old Gods made mares fertile on Earth, and the sign of the Solar stallions in Heaven meant success and prosperity to sun-worshippers in this world. We should not forget the Ceres-Demeter association with "marehood." The same sun that ripened the corn increased the horse herds whose quality depended on good grain also. Horse and human alike reaped benefits from the harvests their combined efforts produced in partnership with Demeter.

So much stemmed from horses, that it is no wonder our ancestors linked them with Divine providence. Nations without horse-power, like the Aztecs and Incas, perished. The mounted man became superior in all ways to the foot-man. Nobility and horses went naturally together. The very word "Knight" stems from "a noble horseman," and "Chivalry" meant a horseman's code of honor. Man could not have climbed to any of his civilized positions today without the assistance of his faithful, if sometimes shockingly abused, horse. Hence the horseman-Sun symbolism of this Tarot trump. We might also remember here the use of mare's milk as a food among Asiatic tribesmen and its reputation for assuring longevity and fertility. Wealthy women of high social standing would even bathe in this expensive fluid, since it was supposed to make them beautiful, and Tiphereth the Solar Sphere signifies Beauty in a shining harmonious sense. Altogether the symbological arrangements of this Tarot card are quite satisfyingly Solar, despite deficiencies of draftsmanship and lay-out.

Originatively, this Path is presided over by the Divine Aspects of ELOAH va DAATh and SHADDAI el CHAIIM. Divine Knowledge and the Lordship of Lives. What can be a better motive for living than to gain knowledge, or a more practical way of gaining knowledge than living? Here indeed is the Path of Enlightenment through Life and living toward Enlightenment.

The term "Lord of Lives" here is not meant in reference to the Supreme Life-Spirit Itself, but to that special Aspect of the Life-Spirit which is concerned with reproducing entitized energies of Life through biological processes and their spiritual equivalents. In regard to us humans, this means our incarnation, lives on Earth, and excarnatory existence as separate souls until we achieve sufficient Enlightenment to grow beyond the necessity for living in physical bodies. We shall always be alive while we exist as entities, but as we evolve from one type of life to another, so will our conditions of life and consciousness alter accordingly. Each Life-type has its own final degree of Enlightenment beyond which an experiencing entity passes into a more advanced state of soul-determination-if it so Wills. Once we cease being humans, we begin anew in Otherlife, and the vast majority of us are nowhere near such a state yet. Death does not release us from humanity—only Enlightenment will offer such liberation, which may seem wonderful to us as we are now, but is really the bottom of another Life-Ladder in different conditions of consciousness. The Lord of Lives is our spiritual superior in all these affairs of Life-change.

Why do we live as we do? What are we living for? Why live at all? How many countless millions of times have humans asked themselves questions like these and obtained no satisfactory answers. The only sensible reply might be, "I know that I live, and I live that I may KNOW." If the natural follow-up query is, "What would you KNOW?" the response can only be, "What I Will." Life is so that we may learn how to live in accordance with the Laws behind Life. We should neither crave nor condemn Life as we find it, but learn to control its course in ourselves so that we find the Middle Way which leads straight from one type of Life into another by the shortest and best route. This is the Path for discovering such a secret.

How do we do this? On physical levels we do it by condensing all the knowledge gained in one lifetime into our genes so that this will transfer to our descendants who will add their knowledge until we come around again to collect our bonus. What of those without physical children? Such people, naturally, have influenced the minds of others in one way or another, and through those and other channels affect the genetic patterns through which Earth-life perpetuates. It is on Inner levels these vital changes are made. One way or another, we are all making contributions of consciousness toward that Inner Store of knowledge which will enable us to live on successively higher levels of Life as we progress along the Paths of Light. We may suppose our thoughts and processes of consciousness are purely private, and so within our limits they are. Once they extend outside our limits into areas of awareness available to others, thoughts become the common property of any Intelligence able to reach them. There is no copyright on consciousness. Only a natural disinclination inherent in individuals to go very far beyond their own life-limitations, and an unwillingness to attempt such extensions. Perhaps the first thing Initiates of this path must learn is never to cease learning. Who ceases Knowing ceases Living. There is no age limit for learning. Even if someone working this path knew they would die physically in a day or so, there is still Life-Knowledge to be gained for both use in excarnation and for storage in the Universal Mind in case of rebirth.

Again it must be emphasized that the Knowledge implied on this Path is no mere matter of intellectualism or emotional adventuring, but the achievement made by every living entity through both Mind and Soul as a combined life-experience in consciousness. As such, it is our individual and collective contributions to Cosmos—what we have actually done and become in ourselves because we live. Most especially it is what we have gained and grown into through each life which has enhanced us as entities, improved as individuals, and so provided a sort of spiritual surplus or "profit" as it were, which supplies not only personal benefit, but extends to others also. This ability to contact and "draw upon" the deep reservoirs of Collective Consciousness and Knowledge is a secret to be learned on this Solar Path. It links with the greatly distorted "Doctrine of Indulgences," which postulated an available surplus of "Grace" from the good works of saints which ordinary mortals might borrow from, so to speak. It also ties in with the "Akashic Records" or Cosmic compendium of all that has taken place since Creation commenced. It is a sobering idea indeed that every thought and deed of humanity is on permanent record in the banks of some unimaginable Cosmic Computer—yet we must face that very question on this Path, and learn how to live with it.

The Divine quality of this Aspect-combination is Omnipotence. The Power behind all Life. The Power with which anything at all could be done providing there were a Will applied to that purpose. Power, by itself, does nothing. Will, applying, does everything. The Omnipotence of Divinity means that all the Energy in Existence may be applied for any purpose which conforms with the Will of the Ultimate Entity. The conditions imposed by such a Will determine the Life-laws behind our beings, and we cannot go beyond them, though as entities in our own rights we have scarcely started on our way toward attainment of our own Inner potentials. Being made "in the Divine Image," we have the same faculty of directing all the energies within our existences AS WE WILL. As we live, so should our Wills become conditioned by Knowledge until we really learn to be omnipotent in ourselves, or use all the Power within us for the purpose of whatever we intend TO BE. The vast majority of people rarely learn how to employ the barest fraction of this Power for even the slightest reason. Power and Knowledge both come together on this Path of Life, and ELOAH va DAATh and SHADDAI el CHAIIM have the secret Keys we need here.

Creatively, we meet the Archangel MICHAEL for the last time on this Tree-trip, in company with Archangel GABRIEL (Jivrael). The Perfect and Potent Archangels together. Gabriel is potent in the virile, fertile, and Life-producing sense, and his Cup-symbol is also the Cauldron-Cornucopia-Grail from which the Stream of Life pours freely forth. The Rod of Michael in the Cup of Gabriel should scarcely need explaining. Gabriel outpours all the concepts and ideas we need to gain Life-Knowledge, but it is the touch of Michael's Rod which selects and arranges those we should adopt as our "children" in order to live with them in the best Light. On this Path we have to do more than "come to Life." We have to achieve brilliance in the art of living so as to shine with the Inner Illumination which might be expected between the Solar and Lunar luminaries on the level of Michael-Gabriel.

We speak of ideas and of individuals being "brilliant," and this is exactly so when they are enlightened from within by the touch of Michael's magic Rod. Nevertheless no amount of Michaelian prodding would raise anything to light unless it could respond to such a stimulus. It is still Gabriel's job to present suitable material for Michael's attention. Here we have the "resurrection from the dead" connection with Gabriel. On purely physical levels, this is the continual rebirth of living entities on Earth reappearing under the Sun. By no means every entity reaches rebirth. Even when reborn, relatively few entities become suitable for more than mediocre living at the most. Yet from every point of our planet, individuals show signs of occasional or consistent brilliance which demontrates their obvious Inner linkage with somewhat higher than average human consciousness. In Qabalistic parlance, Gabriel has called them to Life, and Michael raised them to Light. They have heard and responded to the proclamations of this Path.

There is no need for us to wait until we are physically dead before answering Gabriel's Call to Life. His constant cry of "Awake and Live!" may be heard whenever we listen for it in spirit, and applies even more to Inner Life than Earth existence. Our resurrection should not be thought of as some remote and improbable event due to occur perhaps at the end of this Eon, or maybe at the beginning of another incarnation. Our real resurrection is a continual awakening to finer and finer forms of Life on all levels, and should be a permanent process of our Cosmic evolution. If we listen properly to Gabriel's Calls, we shall resurrect ourselves from one moment of Life to another for as long as we Will endure Eternity. Of course, if we also intend to make our lives mean anything, or keep rising in ourselves toward Ultimate Light, we must look to Michael for leadership as well. Neither Gabriel nor Michael will do our work for us but they are responsible for creating an urge within us to live and learn. The rest remains with us and our determination to travel this Path.

The Fire and Water of Michael and Gabriel present a picture of Power in action of Life in Expansion. Our element is the control of the other. Fire unmoderated by Water would cremate Creation completely, and Water uninfluenced by Fire would be the Life-inhibiting Ice of Ultimate Unliving Immobility. Working in balanced harmony together, they produce the expansive energy we recognize as motivated and mobile living. The aim of Initiates on the Path (as usual) should be to regulate this Power-passage through themselves so that the Elements equate each other as nearly as possible. Here we are on the Fire-Water combination of the Cosmic Circle, and thus have to mediate both Elements in our own natures until we gain control of the center-point between them. Work with the Magical Images of the Archangels concerned will prove of great help, providing we remember that no Archangel or Element is an *antagonist* of another, but a control co-operative. They assist each other's action by affording a natural counterbalance which keeps them safely concerned with Cosmos. Gabriel may provide us with the Water of Life, but it is Michael who must stir it into currents of consciousness and tides of thought which will carry us from one end of this Path to another.

The Rod of Michael and Cup of Gabriel typify in one sense the Ray of Light which originally shone upon the Waters of the Deep and so brought forth Life. It is most probable this was a literal fact at the commencement of biological life on Earth. The Sun shining through Air upon Water cupped by Earth. Once more we are reminded of the "Sun its Father and the Moon its Mother" quotation. Light and Life, again, for the sake of Knowledge. There are phallic-vaginal interpretations here also, but we should never make the mistake of supposing these are the be-all and end-all explanations of everything under the Sun. Sex will get us into this world, but it will not keep us living here as individuals with other life-needs, nor will it get us safely out again. Gabriel calls us to Life here, but Michael looks after our life-interests in other states of Existence than Earthly ones. While our cycles of living alternate between incarnation and disincarnation, it is just as well for us to make friends with Archangels who operate on both sides of the Life-scene.

Besides water, a Cup can contain oil, and when the Cup of Gabriel becomes a Lamp with an unconsumable wick, typified by asbestos, which is kindled from the burning Rod of Michael, the Mystery of this Path will be made much clearer. Float this Lamp upon the Ocean of Life so that its Light enables a course-control to be kept in accordance with Will, and the symbology is more explicit still. This is where we may learn how to become such a Lamp, and MICHAEL and GABRIEL have the Keys of this Knowledge between them.

Formatively, the Path is served by the Angelic Orders of the MALAKIM and the ASHIM. The Rulers and the "Souls of Fire." Ashim also signifies those who are fit and proper beings to found families, and this has an important meaning here at the Sephirah of Foundation where the Lord of Lives rules and the Potent Archangel persuades entities into incarnation.

If only perfect people emerged into Earth-life in every birth taking place in this world, we should obviously have long since evolved far beyond the need of embodied existence at all. As matters stand, there is a definite limit to the occupation of this planet by humanity, and life-entities who have not learned how to adapt themselves to nonphysical living beyond incarnatory levels will cease as auto-existence or egos. Apart from those truly noble souls who have no actual need of incarnation but remain associated with this world out of sheer compassion, or from a sense of duty toward Divinity, the rest of us are here for the brutally simple reason that we are not yet fit to live in better Cosmic conditions. We can only live for relatively brief and indistinct intervals out of our bodies, and then must return in search of more experience in order to evolve our Inner entities to a point where we shall be able to live dependent of physical manifestation.

Inner Tradition says we "fell" into this state of matter and so have condemned ourselves to an unnecessary series of sex-births on Earth, until we can climb back a Life-level beyond any need whatever for such materialization. This does not mean that sex-polarized principles automatically cease outside manifested matter, only that more selective and intensified use may be made of them quite apart from their applications in connection with organic living by Earth-bound entities. Be that as it may, we are faced with the problems of discovering how to live as ourselves without any human incarnations on Earth—or ultimately going out of independent existence altogether. This is where the Ashim are meant to help us make ourselves fit for excarnate life, and the Malakim teach us what rules and measures we should adopt for this vital purpose.

One particular teaching suggests that the Ashim are rather more than Angels, being the "justified souls" of ex-humans who have risen beyond rebirth. If so, they would be the very type of Intelligence best suited for the work of guiding others along the right lines toward achieving the same objective as themselves. If not, and they are simply Angels like others, conditioned and constructed for this particular purpose alone, they are still the ideal agents for our instruction and Enlightenment upon this Path. Their job is to facilitate our ascent on the Ladder of Life and the Tree thereof, so that instead of being as we are now "Earth-based," we shall become able to "found ourselves" upon the next Sphere of Yesod and descend no lower than that Life-level. Maybe it is significant for the whole of Mankind that humanity has physically reached the Moon, which is the material Symbol of

Yesod the Foundation. This may be an outward sign for all of us that our Inner liberation into Light is becoming more possible for everyone intending such an equivalent spiritual step toward Inner Space.

Here also for the last time on our Tree-descent we meet the Angel Order of the Malakim directly. They are the agents through which we learn at this point how to regulate and rule our conduct of consciousness, so that we live according to proper Inner Life procedures. Once we descend below this Sphere to Malkuth, we only make contact with the Malakim of the Middle Pillar through the mediation of the Ashim. Ascending the Tree, of course, this is our first living experience of the Malakim as immediate Intelligences. The Tree-design indicates clearly enough that we must raise ourselves from entirely mundane conditions of Earth-life to the Sphere of Inner-life Foundations before we can expect definite and direct contact with the Angelic agencies of good Inner-life government as represented by the Malakim. While we are still Earth-incarnating entities, we are obviously unable to do this on a Greater Cosmic Scale, and so must make this move first within our personal conditions of Cosmos, climbing the Life-Trees inside ourselves. The first steps along any Cosmic Path have to be taken from the Zero point within each of us, and our last steps will enter the infinitely greater Zero behind our beings forever, thus closing the Cosmic circuit completely.

Between the ministrations of the MALAKIM and the ASHIM we should reach a clarity of consciousness upon this Path which will show us very plainly how to proceed along all the ways which yet lie ahead of us. It is really the First Enlightenment experienced by Initiates who achieve the ability to realize clearly and distinctly the actualities of Inner Life and their own plan of participation therein. Having established themselves in the spiritual Sphere of Foundation by means of sheer persistent Faith and repeated efforts to rise beyond Earth-base, an incredibly wonderful vista of Life in New Dimensions via the Paths of Attainment opens up before them. The Ashim have introduced the Aspirant of the Middle Way to the Malakim, who in turn will help open all the other ways of Inner Cosmos to which they have the Keys. Life entities who succeed in ruling themselves with the same controls kept throughout Cosmos by means of the Malakim are entitled to ask for Keys at any Portal-Point in Existence.

Expressively, this Path is perpetuated by our two greatest luminaries of the Sun and Moon. Light and its returned reflection forming expressed evidence of the Light-Life circle of entities and events on Earth. There can be no darkness or ignorance of body, mind, or soul, for those living between Sun and Moon. We might term such a state, "Revelation by Radiation." Yet no human could live in those conditions without a radical change of construction in themselves, or some very reliable sort of protection. As we are, living in human Earth-life form, we may no more endure concentrated Inner states of Light and Knowledge than we would dare expose ourselves to a laser beam—or even to prolonged ultra-violet light. Again and again and yet again, Aspirants to the Inner Paths are warned never to seek more Inner Light than their degree of advancement allows them to bear safely within limits of their own spiritual structure. Again and again are those warnings ignored and needless suffering invited or inflicted upon silly souls. The story of Icarus has no meaning for them. They are like moths drawn to their destruction from lack of discernment. Bewildered by the Moon and burned by the Sun, they fall back to Earth fluttering helplessly.

This Path should be approached from below with the care and adjustment of a diver cautiously coming from th depths, or an astronaut fully trained and equipped to proceed Space-wards. To attempt this Path without adequate training and conditioning is more than folly, it is madness. We can see evidence of this in every tragedy of idealistic insanities, religious mania, and all the aberrations vaguely and inaccurately attributed to "dabbling with the Occult." Blindness of soul and madness of mind are all too frequently a result of over-exposure to Inner Light upon this Path. Perhaps matters are even worse because those who insist on pushing themselves up to this point without sufficient preparation cannot very well be prevented from making such a stupid mistake. Human entities have an inalienable Right to Light which will never be denied them even if this leads to their destruction.

There is an old saying: "Whoso would live safely in the Sun must first learn to endure the Moon." This is the best possible advice for guidance on this Path. To live in greater Light, we should first adjust ourselves to the lesser, turning ourselves steadily around like the Earth on its axis so that Inner Light gradually around like the Earth on its axis so that Inner Light gradually dawns upon us in a natural way and we adjust ourselves to its revelations normally. Once we are accustomed to living in the Light of Inner Day, then we shall tend to behave like responsible citizens of Cosmos. It is difficult enough to deal with the uncertainties and distortions of Lunar Light, as we shall see later, but such is the first duty and task to which the attention of sincere Aspirants seeking Initiation by this Path is directed. They are told: "Reach for the Sun by the Moon," and if this instruction is followed out faithfully, Initiates will surely be led to Light as fast as their degrees of tolerance will allow. It is scarcely possible to over-emphasize the importance of such very elementary and commonsense proceedings. The surest Foundation for all Knowledge is commonsense, and this useful commodity is often sadly lacking among those who plunge wildly along Inner Paths with reckless abandon. The same people would not venture outside their homes without all sorts of preparations from every angle, yet they will charge around fields of Inner consciousness without even bothering to take their wits with them. Then they wonder why nothing seems right for them. It seldom occurs to them to train first and equip themselves for Inner Life with at least some of the care and effort they need for ordinary day-to-day living on Earth. This is the difference between an Initiate and an intruder into Inner Dimensions. The Initiate is trained, equipped, and prepared to live that sort of Life. The intruder is not. On this Path it is easy to tell one from the other.

There must be few people alive today who are unaware of the dangers arising from overdoses of radiant energy, or conversely of the necessity for that very energy in correct applications for the maintenance of life itself. This part of our Path here deals with that very matter. The right intensity of Inner Illumination for humans aspiring to Higher Life. It concerns moreover the conversion or transformation of that Radiance from Solar to Lunar species of Energy. We might think of this in terms of an electric transformer which converts the potentially dangerous main current to low-power electricity so that it is quite safe for children to use when playing with their trains and other games. For the sake of spiritual children, Solar Inner Radiance must be converted to lower-powered Lunar reflections, and this is the Path on which such a change should be made. No one is guaranteed safety in

Cosmos, but at least all should be offered opportunities for accepting it.

When we are living as humans on Earth, our childhood beliefs and imaginings will eventually become adult knowledge and experience. Providing the transference is gradual and reasonable, we shall grow into well-balanced and conditioned Children of Cosmos. So it should also be with our Inner evolution from spiritual childhood to maturity, which is likely to take rather more than a single human incarnation. If we are truly wise, we shall turn on our Inner axis from Lunar to Solar Light at a normal and natural rate. It must be remembered this is a Middle Pillar Path, and therefore far more difficult than other Path types. Very many entities indeed can manage the climb as far as the Lunar Sephirah, but when it come to facing the overpowering brilliance of Inner Radiance from the Solar Sphere, it may well be wisest to follow the Right or Left Pillar Paths so as to approach the Sun behind the Sun at another angle. The most fatal mistake possible is to be so blinded by conceit as to wrongly assume a spiritual superiority and fitness for Solar status which, in fact, is not so. At the Lunar end of this Path, we have a junction with two others. Unless we are beyond need of either because we have equated them in ourselves, it is neither safe nor sensible to continue climbing toward the Inner Sun by the Middle Pillar. This is the great decision which has to be made by Initiates at this point of their Path-progress. No one can make it for anyone else. Perhaps the soundest guide for settling the issue is to see in what manner the Light appears to reflect from other entities. If they appear all wrong or unacceptable, then the ability to mediate Solar Light correctly has not yet been achieved, and it is advisable to proceed by other Paths for a while. If the very worst characteristics in others can be observed quite plainly and yet they appear as beings who merit Divine Love for the sake of what might be rather than they are—then the Solar Light has been sufficiently well reflected in a Lunar way for a relatively safe progress along this Path. It is well, however, to make absolutely certain of this Key first. Sol and Luna hold it between them here.

The Twenty-seventh Path

SPHERE—LETTER CODE:	Victory 7 V 8 Glory	
DIVINE ORIGINATION:	IHVH SABAOTh—	The
	ELOHIM SABAOth	Disposer
ARCHANGELIC CREATION:	Auriel—Raphael	Opportunity
ANGELIC FORMATION:	Elohim—Beni-Elohim	Happening
APPARENT EXPRESSION:	Venus—Mercury	Alternation
TAROT SYMBOL:	WHEEL OF FORTUNE	

The Twenty-Seventh Path is the third and last which directly connects the two side Pillars of the Tree. It does this between the Principles of Victory and Glory, providing a straight linkage from Soul to Mind or emotion to in intellect. This gives rise to very considerable fluctuations of force, and makes the effect in Existence we term "Chance," or uncertainty of events. Without this factor, however, life would scarcely be the phenomena it is, especially on our levels. Higher up, toward Absolute Divinity, we found the Pillars of the Tree equated by Justice and Judgment, but here, closer to mutable Mankind, we discover that so-called Chance decides a great deal of our destiny, although, in the long run only to the extent that we allow it to act upon us without our attempting to gain control of its effects upon ourselves.

This Path is likened to the Wheel of Life and Death, or Drum of Destiny, into which all living entities are thrown like lottery tickets and spun around together in their various worlds and orbits until they either make sense of each other and allot themselves to their proper categories of consciousness and Cosmos— or lose their chances of Life so often that they are eventually eliminated altogether. In a way, this is a kind of sorting system which roughly determines which entities are worth passing on to higher states of Cosmos and which are not. This issue is not de-

cided by what actually happens to us during the changes and va-
garies of a lifetime, but by what sort of reactions we make to
these, and how we interpret them Inwardly, which causes our essential natures to change for better or worse as we evolve. On this
Path, we have to learn how to use the chances of Life in order to
make an Inner best from every Outer opportunity. This leads to
an ability to set up Inner insistences which will eventually bring
us favorable Outer chances.

The Tarot Symbol is naturally the Wheel of Fortune. In principle, a revolving wheel bearing inscriptions which decide those
issues of fate and fortune that people are unable to determine for
themselves. It obviously applies only to factors in our lives over
which we have as yet no direct control or influence. For most of
humanity this means a very large proportion of their affairs, but
as we progress and develop ourselves, we should become able to
ride the Wheel with ever-increasing confidence and skill. It all
depends on our alignment with the Wheel. If we are at the bottom
it crushes us, but if at the top we can skip its surface lightly for as
long as we keep our balance. Our problem on this Path is rising to
the top of the Wheel—then maintaining our position there or getting off altogether.

Taking this Tarot Symbol as a whole, we note the Wheel
proper in the middle, and four Archetypal figures of the Human,
Eagle, Lion, and Ox, at the corners. At their highest Life-level in
Kether, these "Holy Four" are the Living Elements, or "Holy Liv-
ing Creatures." At lowest level in Malkuth they are the Four Elements of Air, Fire, Water, and Earth. They characterize the Life-
qualities we need throughout our entire existence in order to be
properly balanced and soundly constructed entities of Living
Cosmos. Astrologically, they align with the Signs of Taurus, Leo,
Scorpio, and Aquarius, and combined together they make up the
Kerubim or winged Sphinxes. They are major Power-aspects of
Life in an elementary way, and therefore are present in mixed
proportions, however our chances in life are presented. Each
creature is represented as enthroned upon a cloud, and holding
an open book. The Lion and the Ox are writing their books, but
the Human and Eagle are reading aloud or preaching from them.

Clouds symbolize consciousness in the process of formation
and dissipation, or the raw material out of which we manufacture
our thoughts. They also symbolize screens between a seeking

consciousness and its objective; obscurity, and lack of clarity. It all depends on whether the Sun is on our side of the clouds or not. Here, the figures are golden to show they are being observed by Inner Light, and the clouds mean that our Life-origins are obscure to us, being formed in the Divine Consciousness as we bring imaginative pictures to life against the clouds of the Sky-Heaven above us. The figures are enthroned on their clouds because they are "Creatures of the Holy Throne," or very close indeed to the Original Impulse of Intention which commenced Living Creation. Their "books" are, in a sense, computer banks of every single item of consciousness connected with their creative categories. The Lion and Ox (Fire and Earth) inscribe in their books, and the Human and Eagle (Air and Water) inform from theirs. The records and basic patterns of all Life are indeed implanted in the genetic elements from whence Life comes in the first place. So much shows that Life is the principle background and underlying meaning of this card. Now for the Chances of Life in the foreground.

The Wheel of Fortune appears as a circular disc with a Circle-Cross at center, subdivided into the Ouarters and cross-quarters of Cosmos. This is only to be expected, seeing that the Fortune of Life must necessarily occur during the orbiting of Earth around the Sun both literally and metaphorically. The rim of the Wheel is inscribed with T A R O and I H V H alternately. IHVH will read either way, but TARO is inscribed reading from left to right, and that is the way the Wheel revolves, despite any assumptions to the contrary. IHVH is the Divine "I will be as I Will" Fiat which is the Ultimate Settlement of any argument. Whatever we do with our Life-chances, Divinity will utter the Last Word which finalizes the First Word, and the Wheel of Fate will stop altogether. It is well to be reminded of this when we consider how the Wheel spins for any of us.

Derivations of the word "Tarot" or simply "TARO" have been guessed in all directions. The most probable and suitable meaning would seem a Semitic root "ThAR" signifying an outline, or go around, to compass, mark out, delineate, etc. Understood in this way, the Taro would thus be a symbolic marking out and delineation of Life, its Laws, and all Cosmic connections throughout, which is in fact just what Taro is supposed to be. The addition of the important Zero to the root enables it to be Latinized into

ROTA which has much the same meaning, and of course the Zero Cypher itself is symbolic of the Cosmic Compass. If we want to be fanciful and make anagrams of TORA, the traditions and teaching of the Holy Law, and ARTO, the art and skill of anything, no harm seems likely to the spiritual sense of the word at all.

The Wheel is fourfold. First the Rim with its inscription which engages with externals, then the spoke-space with symbols on four spokes, next the simple eight-socket Hub, and lastly the invisible axle-hole. It is not mistake that no axle has been shown. The theoretical Dead Center of any wheel is the motionless space in the metaphysical middle of its atomic structure. To remind us of this, the Wheel of Fortune is depicted without visible means of poise. Literally we do not know on what our Fortunes turn, and so no attempt has been made to illustrate this vital pivot of events. It may be anything—or Nothing.

How the Wheel turns is another matter. Its elemental energy is shown alchemically, in the lay-out of a Magic Circle Mercury points above, Salt to the left and sulphur to the right, while the sign of Fluidity points below. The alternate activity of Fire to expand Air in a closed container of metal representing Earth, which is then cooled by iced water, makes a good picture of a simple Elemental Engine. All engines work by Elemental energies one way or another in successive alternations. Even a Wheel of Fortune does not work by itself but has to be driven by some kind of motive power. At a first glance we might accept that its inner Elemental energies alone kept it going, but then we notice the strange Creatures operating around the rim like beasts around a Cage-wheel. The faster the Wheel revolves, the quicker they must move to keep their places.

There seem to be three Creatures attached to the rim, a Sphinx, a Serpent, and an Hermanubis. Later it may dawn on observers that there are really four Creatures, since the last character is a composite of two Concepts, Hermes and Anubis. Let us take them in their order. The female Sphinx is at the top of the Wheel and is sky-colored to show that she belongs to the Universal Element which is certainly the basic Enigma of Existence. Her right arm is invisible, and her left bears a Sword over her shoulder. This is the decisive Sword that stops the Wheel in whatever notch it engages with and settles fortunes in momentary accordance. Her nemyss, or headdress, is black and white striped to signify the alternations of "Yes-No" ideation which lead to the last click of this Cosmic Computer. Her tail is well between her legs and pointing forward to indicate the eternal chase of the tails every query that was ever asked since Enquiry itself was born. Although the Sphinx smiles her inscrutable smile, her hind feet must still keep in step with the revolving Wheel, and in fact add to its motive power. To topple the Sphinx, the Inner Engine of the Wheel would have to race the rim faster than the Sphinx could go. She looks like she will be staying where she is for a long while yet in Greater Cosmos.

Next we have the Serpent, who is colored yellow to show its association with Light. Both Sword and Serpent will be very familiar to practicing Qabalists, and this particular serpent has actually got ten bends in it of increasing variations which identify it with the Tree-Serpent, contacting each Sphere in turn as it climbs around the Sword Plunging from the top to bottom of the Middle Pillar in a single straight line. This is not the Serpent of Eternity, but that of Eden who literally stung Mankind into seeking Knowledge for themselves instead of accepting everything as it was without question. Thus, the Eternal Question of the Sphinx, and the Serpent that stung us into asking questions are well associated together on this Wheel. Somehow the artist has managed to convey a really cheerful and carefree expression on the face of the Serpent as its darting tongue seeks a target for its irritating fangs in the foot of poor old Hermanubis who apparently hangs on the Wheel by one unseen left hand.

Hermanubis himself, or itself, needs a few thoughts. It is two beings together, Hermes the clever and Anubis the faithful. This dual concept seems to have started in Egypt, but variations of it are known elsewhere. Anubis by himself has been described as the faithful companion of Osiris and Isis, wearing the head of a dog, and bearing in one hand a caduceus and a palm branch in the other. He was thought to be emblematic of Sirius, the dog-star, which gave warning of the approaching inundation of the Nile. He is naturally well-known as the Watchdog of the Dead, just as Hermes had the job of Psychopompos or "soul-conductor." Together as Hermanubus they typify an intelligent creature that "follows its nose"in the direction of Divinity. The natural instincts as humanity to find and follow the trail of Truth leading to Light.

A number of points almost leap up for recognition like a faithful hound here. The caduceus and the palm branch certainly align this Trump with the Path connecting Glory (Hermes) and Victory (Venus). There is an esoteric legend that Earth-life came originally from the direction of the Dog-Star, and we are related with Life-types in the quarter of the Greater Cosmos who provided our remotest ancestry. Be that as it may, the Hermanubis on this particular Wheel certainly stands for ourselves in a state of humano-animal struggle with the chances of events and conditions around us. The poor Creature is not traveling freely with the Wheel, but has its back to the rim which it attempts to push itself along by its feet. Its eyes are closed, and it has not yet developed a mouth or nose. Thus it only keeps itself going at all by blind endeavors of touch. Be it noted that the Wheel is not lifting Hermanubis up in any way, but is actually pushing him down. All the rises Hermanubis (or Humanity) can manage on this Wheel are due to his own efforts. If he falls too far pack, a sharp bite from the Serpent will speed him up again. Such is Life at the bottom of the Tree.

How like an average human condition this Symbology seems. Blind, mute, and unable to smell out our Inner trails, we valiantly struggle along with our Wheels of Fate. Sometimes the Sword of Decisions held by the Eternal Enigma stops the Wheel favorably for us, and frequently not. Meanwhile the Wheel looks as if it is giving Hermanubis a badly bruised bottom. An old Arab proverb says, "Sometimes you have the World beneath your feet– and sometimes you slip and it kicks you in the backside!" The only hope that Hermanubis of this Wheel has for better life, is to exceed the speed of the rim and arrive at its top, usurping the place of the Sphinx and seizing the Sword which stops the Wheel at Will. Then, providing Hermanubis keeps pace with the Wheel beneath his feet, it can revolve merrily again. Be it noted that although the Dog-head is shown without nose or mouth, it has ears very much to the point. This seems to indicate, "Listen to everything, wink at a great deal, smell as little as possible, and say absolutely nothing at all." Not bad advice, either.

It is probably by intention that the Sword which controls the Wheel points at the Eagle of Scorpio, that sign so well known to astrologers for producing people devoted to Occult matters. This may be a hint for Hermanubis to grow wings as the simplest way of reaching the top of the Wheel. However Hermanubis (or Humanity) contrives to reach the Top-dead-Center of the Wheel, it is certain that the Sword is the vital Key of control. The Sword means Decision. To use it we must push the point of our consciousness into the rim of the Wheel so that one side of the edge or the other decides this from that for us. Relatively few souls seem able to make positive and life-altering decisions for themselves, yet such is the secret of our Wheels of Fortune. When we are able to make clear-cut decisions with the Sword or the Sphinx and solve the Enigmas of Life thereby, we shall make our own fortunes, and the Wheel will remain revolving at our feet as long as we need it. All this and much more is to be learned from the Symbology of the Tarot of this Path. The Divine Aspects and Intelligences will teach us the rest if we listen with ears like Hermanubis.

Originatively, the Path is governed by IHVH SABAOTh and ELOHIM SABAOTh. The God-Being who would be everyone, and the God-Being whom everybody intends to be. If both sides ever became one and the same, Evolution would end and Eternal Entity endure, but we have no need to concern ourselves with this indefinite event here. What is more to the point for us, is finding the balance between emotion and intellect upon this Path so that the Divinity we feel and think about in ourselves makes contact with us through our consciousness, and we shall be able to stabilize ourselves and retain control of our Inner Concepts.

This is the Path where we have to reconcile the apparent antagonism between Mind and Soul, not only in ourselves, but in relation to everyone else. Both Divine Aspects are pluralities inclusive of unspecified multitudes, and here we are all thrown together to sort our ideas out and round off each others' sharp corners. When humans are pushed together in one pile, there are likely to be violent reactions just like an atomic compression, and every thought and feeling combines in order to influence the issue towards an outcome. By and large, this reactive process evokes both the best and the worst in humanity, eventually causing a change of nature for good or ill which is likely to affect the humans concerned for a very long time in quite marked ways. Any war will prove this on a large and drastic scale, or any quietly ordered and unspectacular community living in a much milder, but firmly effective, way. One might compare war conditions to an atomic blast, and disciplined community life to a controlled atomic pile, but both have the result in common of altering humans Inwardly for better or worse. Community life may warp a soul worse than a war, while war might bring nobility of mind and soul out of individuals which would not have emerged otherwise. Everything depends on individual reactions because of mass pressures.

On this Path we have to become what we make of ourselves on account of close contacts with other humans in the chances and fortunes of our common lives. The Divinity in ourselves has to accommodate Itself to Its being in others, and we must come to terms with each other's lives all round the Circle of Cosmos, or as it is represented here, the Wheel of our Fortunes. When we are able to reach a state of balance with Life on this relatively low level, we shall rise to conditions of entity where we are strongly and definitely individual enough to evolve away from the mass-average of Mankind and live in our own spiritual structures in the company of other advancing beings. Many entities are cast into the Mills of Fortune, but comparatively few emerge in a polished and perfected condition. It is no use supposing that the harder anyone is, the better their chances of survival will be. Hardness makes for brittleness, and thus is most breakable. Those who flow through the Mills uncrushably usually come out intact and in a much refined condition of being.

Only when we recognize and respect Divinity in others by the Light of Divinity in ourselves will IHVH SABAOTh and ELOHIM SABAOTh equate along this Path and make more fortunate the lives of everyone. It is the old injunction of loving God with a whole heart and fellow humans as oneself. That is the message and motto to follow here. We have chances every day in this direction, but how often do we take them? We tend to think of Chance and Fortune as applying only to material advantages, but in fact the Inner Wheel of Fortune has less to do with money and free gifts than literally Heaven-sent opportunities for spiritual gains and achievements. Perhaps not so attractive to Earth-focused eyes, but far too valuable to be overlooked by those with awakening Insight seeking other than material advantages.

Now it is possible to appreciate the anomaly of Hermanubis' position of the Wheel of Fortune. He is facing the wrong way for his best chances of surmounting it. If he could turn Inward and face the Wheel, he might then use his hands and feet properly for climbing it by getting a grip on the letters of the Names. In other words, he must get his nose to the grindstone and work a push-pull action with all his power. It needs the Hermetic instinct in us to direct us like a faithful hound along the Trail of Truth. Hermes belongs to the Sphere of Intellect at Hod, and the Hound belongs to the Sphere of instinctive feelings at Netsach, so there seems little doubt of attribution here.

What are we really looking for on this Path? Divinity in every chance or apparent accident that happens to us, and the best way through them all to the Ultimate Union we must each achieve by ourselves. Here the Hound-symbol comes in again. Some commentators connect Anubis with the Pole Star as well as Sirius, and somewhere we need an Inner Star to steer our spiritual courses by, and the Hermanubis factor in ourselves will recognize this Light in Darkness if we let him point it out. If we put our thoughts and feelings together and, facing our Fortunes Inwardly, commence our hunt for the highest facilities Humanity has to offer, Hermanubis will faithfully lead us Lightward toward the answer to the Sphinx's riddle.

Others will be doing the same thing, and it is easy to feel antagonism and frictions on the abrasive Wheel of Fate that binds us together whether we like the experience or not. Nevertheless, it seems intended by the Will working the Wheel that we should modify and adapt each other's thoughts and feelings during this inevitable process until something acceptable to all parties is produced. How long it will take Humanity as a whole to manufacture this ideal medium is anyone's guess. Not only must it suit everybody in general, but it must also fulfill the need of everyone in particular, and this is an unreasonable demand of Humanity in our present state of development. Initiation along this Path seems likely to be an individual affair for an unpredictable period yet.

The Divine influence here is well called the Disposing, for we have to alter our dispositions very considerably in relation to Divinity and each other through the Chance dispositions Life makes with us in Cosmos. It is our behavior in re-asserting ourselves that matters, for this is the criterion deciding the extent of our elevation on the Wheel and degree of free choice we shall gain for another determination of Fortune. There is no "luck" whatever about the issue, but only pure skill in play. Almost as though we were cast down like pieces upon the board of objective Life, but being living pieces, we are responsible for picking ourselves up again in the right way. IHVH SABAOTh and ELOHIM SABAOTh know the rules of this Life-play and how to find Fortune on this Path. They will show us the Keys if we ask properly.

Creatively, we meet archangels AURIEL and RAPHAEL here. The Light of Divine experience and the Healer-Teacher. We must remember that Raphael equates with Hermes, and aligns with the Element of Air and Symbol of the Sword, while Auriel bears the Shield-symbol of Earth, and like Anubis has the Pole Star as his Light attribute. Again we find the symbology of the Wheel of Fortune in the Shield of Auriel, and the Sword of Raphael to check its revolutions. How often is the sword of our wits sharpened against the grinding Wheel of Life? What lights are kindled from the sparks struck out of our steel? Only Auriel and Raphael can answer our use of their facilities.

Another Hermetic figure we meet on this Path is Hermaphrodite, because the Path conjoins these two Concepts of Hermes and Aphrodite, the Goddess of sensual love and affection. Aphrodite, as Nature, is essentially nearer to Earth than Heaven. It is the turning point which decides whether our sense-experiences will lift us up like foam into the sky, or plunge us though the waves of passion down to the Earth beneath. So does the shield of Auriel offer us attachment or liberation from, Earth, on how it is handled. Managed expertly, the Hermetic-Raphaelic way, our most sensual Earthly experiences can elevate us toward Light. Hermes knows the trick of making Aphrodite intelligible, and she knows how to make Hermes lovable. So, too, does Raphael stir up and brighten Auriel's solemnity, while Auriel increases Raphael's accessibility. Their partnership confers endless benefits on those learning to equate the Elements of Air and Earth through themselves.

All our lives, the chances, circumstances, and opportunities we encounter in this, and other worlds, confront us with problems to be dealt with as best we may. Almost invariably a conflict arises in ourselves between what we think and feel concerning every affair. If only our rational thinking and personally involved feelings came to one and the same point of decisive actions. Life would be a simpler matter for most of us. In some instances time is on our side and gives us a longer chance of adjusting the ends of this Path within ourselves, but, as often as not, decisions of some sort have to be made in split seconds which may affect the remainder of our incarnations. Everyone knows the terrible strain of these dilemmas. Here are two Archangels who personify the power in us of coming to at least satisfactory compromise conclusions with whatever Fortune flings at us in the way of living. Auriel will teach us to screen our sensitive feelings with his Shield, and Raphael will show us how to probe every possibility in and behind any situation with his Sword of keen and pointed intellect. If, with every chance of circumstance we met, a "flash invocation" was sent toward these Archangel partners, we should find ourselves balancing the issues between thoughts and feelings far more easily. They are the Archangels who enable us to recognize opportunities in even our most unlikely chances, and suggest methods of how to use them.

In one noteworthy respect this Path has in common with its predecessor a unique feature unparalleled anywhere else on the entire Tree. The central point of balance in both cases forms a right-angled Cross having the Archangels of the Quarters at the ends of the Paths. They are not in the same Elemental relationship as is usually found in the Magic Circle, being simultaneously rather than sequentially combined. Thus, Fire-Water defines the Middle Pillar Path, and Earth-Air joins this one. They are so arranged as to produce a point of maximum negative influence by any single Element in the exact center. In other words, anyone able to hold a position of poise along this Path where the previous Path intersects it, would be theoretically able to decide issues by means of their own Wills, since it would be exactly equal to them all ways, and therefore whatever they did would lock the Wheel on its decisive notch. If indeed a human entity could gain this precise position, he would find himself free from being influenced by thoughts, swayed by emotions, blinded by excess of Light, or bewildered by shadowy reflections. Being in the center of his Wheel of Fortune instead of at its edge, he could relate himself with its rotation from the most favorable point of vantage. In gaining control of any Path, the general procedure is to reach the middle and hold one end in either hand so to speak, but here we have to reach the center of two Paths simultaneously. What is more, it is a point where Spirit, Soul, Mind, and Body meet, and anyone establishing a central Life-relationship with these Four Vital Principles is in the best of positions indeed. RAPHAEL and AURIEL between them have the Keys to lock us in place on this Twenty-Seventh Path, and our chances in Life are bound to improve as we learn their use.

Formatively, this Path is administered by the Angel Orders of the ELOHIM and the BENI-ELOHIM. The "Gods," and the Children of Gods." From our human angle, "Gods" are formalized concepts of what we realize to be decisive factors in the feelings of our Inner Life, and their "Children" are the outcome of relationships, between these factors and ourselves. It is fashionable in purely materialistic circles to suppose that Man invented the Gods himself from imaginary projections of his own basic instincts. Occult Tradition rather reverses this by postulating that the Gods are, in fact, specific categories of Cosmic Consciousness which translate themselves in human terms according to the abilities of human consciousness to conceive them. Different types and classes of humanity therefore recognize the same Aspect of Divinity in very many different ways and varying nomenclatures. We make up our Gods from our own reactions to actual spiritual Identities. Humans do not invent Gods, but they build up relative imaginary concepts around the Inner realities which affect them basically far deeper than their ordinary waking awareness will reach. Thus the Identities of the Gods are real, but our conceptions of them are necessarily an outcome of adaptive imagination.

Everyone conceives Gods of some Atheists probably make more for themselves than they would care to admit. Our Gods may not be noble conceptions at all, but the crudest ideas concerning the principles upon which we believe our lives are based. It may be remembered that the vulgarian millionaire Trimalchio of the "Satyricon" was at least honest enough to call his personal Gods "Fat Profit, Good Luck, and Large Income." Revolting as this may sound, such were truly Trimalchio's ideas of Divine beneficence as far as he was concerned. Another, and far more advanced individual, might have called the same Gods "Life-progress, Grace, and Responsibility." As we evolve, we view the Gods by a better and better Light, until in the end we hope to recognize them for what they are in themselves, Immortal Individuations of Cosmic Consciousness. Millions of people would still agree with Trimalchio, however, and have no interest whatever in any sort of God higher than concepts deriving from their cupidity, lusts, or immediate material desires. No entity will evolve higher than their God-Concepts, and those who refuse to rise above their Greed-Gods must stay with that level until they learn better.

The Elohim on this Path are supposed to help us feel the need of ever ennobling God-Concepts so that as we steadily refine and raise our Inner ideas of Divine Aspected Identity, we shall also raise ourselves with them. The Beni-Elohim should encourage us to think and meditate about these Concepts so that we come to Inner-Life companionship with them. Again we have the "Feeling-Thinking" combination of energies for the single purpose of putting power into practice along this Path. In this instance the goal is identification and recognition of whatever Life-Principle we regard as indispensible for the integrity of our own Inner identity. These are our Gods, whatever else we may call them or whether we personify them or prefer to keep them amorphous.

How many people today could accurately identify, recognize, and form intentional relationships with their Gods? Not the Supreme Spirit of Life Itself, but specific projections of It far nearer the Life-forms of our conscious capabilities, through which we may relate ourselves with that remote Ultimate Reality. Pantheists got lost in their attempts to conceive a God-Form for absolutely every imaginable occasion. Christians over-masculinized or else hopelessly neutered their Humano-Divine Christ-Concept. Qabalists proposed a decimalization of Divinity through Ten Concepts covering all the properties and qualities of the Spheres. These are the so-called "Magical Images," and serve a very practical purpose of identifying ourselves with any Divine Aspect presented through the Tree. Whether we accept "ready-made" God-Concepts which have already passed through innumerable minds and souls and so gained an indestructible Inner actuality in their own right, or demand new ones worked out for ourselves with the aid of the Elohim and Beni-Elohim, this task must be tackled on the Twenty-seventh Path, and we cannot very well avoid it in one form or another. Sensible Initiates settle for purposeful God-Concepts which bring them in touch with the circles of Inner Awareness they seek, and go on building Cosmos from there.

A practical Qabalist, for example, would accept the God-Concepts offered by the Tree because they are proved and useful Inner Images projected from Archetypal levels of Awareness, and then set about forming personal relationships with these by means of Feeling activated through the ELOHIM, and Thinking channeled through the BENI-ELOHIM. That is the specific job of these particular Angels, so we might as well make good use of them. They have the Keys to this part of the Path, and we are entitled to ask for them.

Expressively, we meet the elusive but delightful combination of Hermes and Aphrodite (Venus) on this Path. Wit and winsomeness. They also typify the blending of the Male-Female principles into a virtually ideal partnership. Once again, Hermes is Thought and Aphrodite Feeling. These are the two aspects of awareness we have to marry on this Path to produce the "children of consciousness."

The sexual attributions of Venus are usually so overstressed that we tend to lose sight of her other and equally wonderful qualities. Her feelings and love extend over a very wide cultural field altogether. Love of children, the home, arts, pet animals, floristry and gardening, clothes, and all the pleasant comfortable amenities of joyful living are typically Venusian. She and Hermes between them cover everything civilized and pleasing which helps to make our lives in this world not only bearable but actually enjoyable. We owe their promptings in us a very great deal indeed.

This Hermes-Aphrodite coupling certainly provides us with the ups and downs around the Wheel of Life. Hermes gives easy riches with one hand while filching them with the other, and the ecstacy of Aphrodite's attentions is alternated with anguish because of her indifference or infidelity. Tortured by twisted thoughts and flayed by agonized feelings, humans are liable to have terrible lives until they manage to gain some degree of control over the force encountered on this Path. This is only accomplished by means of what are best called the "Hermetic Nuptials" in which a happily harmonious mating is accomplished between the Male and Female principles inherent in every entity.

No human beings are exclusively male or female despite their preponderant polarity as proclaimed by their reproductive and glandular characteristics. Whatever we are on the Outside, we have both sexes Inside. Either our Internal sex-polarities are happily related to each other or they are not. If not, a state of balance is usually sought with another human having compensatory qualities, and biological reproduction ensues. We suppose that we obtain sex-satisfaction from other humans, but strictly speaking we do not. The satisfaction is obtained by contriving harmonious balanced relationships between the two sexes in ourselves. True, we have had to borrow energy from others to supply self-deficiencies, and the satisfaction can only be temporary.

Really happily married beings are those in whom both Male and Female sides of their nature are perfectly mated. The happiest marriage is In (but not *to*) ourselves. That is the "Hermetic Nuptials" which the Rosicrucians had to publish originally under the heaviest disguise of allegory and allusion.

This remarkable classic of imaginative Inner adventure in search of spiritual serenity was most carefully coded to conceal ideas and sentiments which would have been considered blasphemous, seditious, revolutionary, outrageous, and even downright immoral by the strictly orthodox authorities of most European countries and Churches at the time of its publication. Nevertheless, the Rosicrucians were good enough psychologists to realize that if they could propagate their Inner Intelligence in mytholo-gized and apparently fictional form, it would enter a great number of minds without resistance, arousing interest as it went, and then descend to deep levels of subconsciousness where it would eventually translate into terms compatible with the clarity behind its original coding. A simple process. Take an idea which may be unacceptable as it stands to others, wrap it in a connective and coded coating so that something desirable appears on the outside, then throw it in the direction of greedy minds who devour it. Later on, after a process of Inner digestion takes place, the hidden idea will come to light in the very minds that would have rejected it previously, and the chances are that they will think they have discovered it for themselves. Sugar the pill!

Among the allegorical figurations of the Hermetic Nuptials was a description of the "Lion-Fountain" which on one occasion had an interesting Tablet attached to it. Freely translated it said:

The Principles of Hermes.
Behind the worst of Humanity is the best of Divinity.
Our art is our Aid.
The restorative of our health
Emerges from this.
Drink of me who can; wash in me who will, but—
dirty me who dares!
Drink, brothers, and Live.

In other words: "Drink in these ideas as the story flows along, but don't dare make anything dirty out of them because they are meant in a clear and pure way like Water, intended to impart spiritual strength and courage like the Lion, and no matter how bad humans seem, Divinity designs everything for an ultimately perfect purpose. Spiritual skills are our surest support." A very great deal indeed that applies to this Path may be learned from the "Nuptials."

Later in the story, the narrator, like Eros, has an unauthorized sight of Venus naked. The penalty of this was to be burdened with the task of Doorkeeping to the Innerworld where this action occurred, until such time as another offender might be found to take over the job.

If the beauties of Aphrodite arouse no more in us than sex-slobberings, then we shall condemn ourselves to hovering on the draughty threshold between Inner and Outer realities until we become so disgusted, weary, or just plain bored by that very behavior in other people that we shall walk away from our positions and leave them to get on with what we have freely relinquished. Only Hermes has the ability to reveal Venus to us in her loveliest and most radiant Light. When the science of Hermes and the sensuality of Aphrodite equate on this Path, anything may happen along this line at all!

There are untold combinations of consciousness to be made with Hermes and Aphrodite, and this is truly a Path for producing fertile results from an Inner marriage of our spiritual sex-principles. Our chances of happy marriage with other humans are very slight if we cannot remain happily married Inside ourselves. It has been said that marriages are made in Heaven, and so they are, but we have again and again been told that Heaven is Within us. How long will it take before our consciousness "clicks in" and the Wheel deciding our Fortune stops for us in its most favourable position? Perhaps Hermes and Aphrodite are hiding the Keys between them here, but hunting for these Keys can be the greatest sport imaginable.

The Twenty-eighth Path

SPHERE—LETTER CODE: Victory 7 W 9 Foundation
DIVINE ORIGINATION: IHVH SABAOTh— The
                          SHADDAI el CHAIIM Inquisitor
ARCHANGELIC CREATION: Auriel—Gabriel Sentiment
ANGELIC FORMATION: Elohim—Ashim Style
APPARENT EXPRESSION: Venus—Moon Sublimation
TAROT SYMBOL: THE HIGH PRIESTESS

This is the Path of sensitivities and feelings devoted to Divinity through living emotions. It is essentially a conviction of consciousness at foundation level that Life is worth living for the sake of achieving emotional depth and stability of soul, without which, progression along other ways of Life would be dangerously one-sided. Human Life devoid of feelings is a frightening thought. So is a life full of uncontrollable and wildly unstable emotions resulting in every type of insane activity. Here is a Path where the whole of our emotional energies may be channeled through dedication and devotion into every wonderful and entirely satisfying way which can be discovered by Initiates who seek its secret rightly.

On this Path, we are supposed to achieve victory in living and conquest over the factors of Life which tend to overbalance us through emotional pressures and strains. Everyone knows that these Inner tensions and stresses are behind a huge proportion of our troubles on Earth, but the problem has always been how to cope with them and divert their energy into helpful courses. This is the very Path for that vital solution to be found. Emotional motivation is half our Life at this point of the Tree, just as intellectual instigation is the other half. We shall never live successfully or victoriously by rigidly rejecting emotions and feelings as unworthy activities to be excluded from any Inner Initiatory curriculum of consciousness. Those who regard emotions as enemies are fighting the finest friends humanity has, once it becomes allied with them on this Path.

To live victoriously, we have to learn how to make full and free use of all the emotions and feelings we need in exactly the right way to achieve whatever purpose of Life is in us. This does not mean any spectacular Outer demonstrations or declarations whatever, but an ability to release and experience these typified energies through Inner fields and areas where they will best build us into souls worthy of attaining an ultimately immortal identity. Only those with firm intentions of extending their existence past the limits of ordinary Earth-life need expect real success on this Path, for the Victory of Life is over its alteration by Death.

The Tarot Symbol here is the High Priestess, displayed with deep esoteric significance in the Waite pack. Its background is almost totally concealed to indicate the mysterious nature of Life behind our beings. Sky, Sea, and Sand form the backdrop of this picture, hinting again at the emergence of humanity into this world via the Sky in space-borne spores, gestating and developing for unknown millennia in the depths of the Sea, until eventually appearing in forms adapted to Earth-life and crawling ashore on the Sand. Who knows in what shape we shall ultimately depart into Space again with our payload of Earth experience in all we have felt and thought here?

The sides of the picture are fully occupied with the two Pillars of the Principles. They are in the Egyptian "Palm" form, representing the Life-Tree between Earth and Heaven portrayed as a Palm whose fruits keep humans alive, whose wine makes them rejoice, whose height affords mortals a refuge from carnivorous creatures and a vantage point for observation, and whose wood provides them with a firm support for their homes and roofs. It is necessary to appreciate what life meant to early Middle-easterners in order to realize just how vital and essential the Palm tree has always been, both literally and also symbolically.

These Pillars here have been given identity by the initials "B" for Boaz on the left-hand Black column, and "J" for Jakin (or Iakin) on the right-hand White column. Those names mean "The Lord has established firmly," and this undoubtedly links the Tarot Symbol with the Spheres of Foundation, while the Palm capitals of the Pillars associate with Victory rising from a well-founded Line of Life. We might remember that the Pillars of Solomon's Temple whose names were Jakin and Boaz, were the Porch or Portal Pylons, and as such of major mystical importance. "Passing the Portals" is that vital step in the process of Initiation where the aspirant is accepted from the Outer Court into the actual precincts of the Temple, and is therefore dedicated to the service of the Deity from henceforth.

The Porch and its Pillars have always been of special significance in connection with Temples of the Mysteries. It is an area or platform which divides the "profane" Outer-world from the "sacred" Inner-world represented by the Temple. As such, it constitutes a sort of common meeting place for those "inside" the Mysteries, and those "outside" them. At one time, all money offerings or transactions concerned with the Temple had to take place on the Porch, so that no financial affair would enter and profane the sacred precincts. The Temple prostitute-priestesses made their bookings and took fees in the Porch of the Temples, before passing inside for the intimate relations which were regarded as a religious act. This custom eventually came down into Christian practice purely as a formal declaration of dowries and even a simplified form of marriage service before the couple went into the church for nuptial mass. Poor people, unable to afford full church weddings, often had the wedding vows read and the declaration made in the church porch. Porches always associate with dedications in the sight of Deity and Humanity combined and this Porch on the Twenty-eighth Path is no exception. Between its Pillars we must plight our troth to Life and promise our faithful support of its processes in us on all levels. The Priestess is there to solemnize our marriage with the Living Mysteries, as she waits in her place at the Pylons to receive our pledges.

From top to bottom of the Pillars hangs the Tapestry of Life. We ourselves are the threads woven into its pattern by the fingers of Fate. The design here consists of pomegranates and palm against a background of olive leaves. All symbols of vitality, fertility, and the very best factors of living. The actual lay-out is obviously a Tree of Life Glyph with the pomegranates as Sephiroth and the palms as Paths. The figure of the Priestess herself obscures the Middle Pillar because she takes its place. Pomegranates were once reckoned as a fertility fruit because of their great quantity of seeds. They are actually a vermifuge, but have the lesser known property of being the best immediate treatment for saving life in cases of severe thirst-dehydration in desert conditions. As desert dwellers know, it is fatal to give dehydrated people at their last gasp large quantities of water. Pomegranate juice is the answer as an immediate restorative, little by little, until the body is able to take water safely. By analogy, it is equally fatal to dose humans who thirst insatiably for intelligence or affection with unlimited supplies of either. The equivalent of a pomegranate applied Inwardly solves this problem. Once again also, we have the Palm (Victory) and Pomegranate (Fertility) symbols together to show the linkage between Netzach and Yesod, so there can be little doubt of this Tarotic position. In fact, there is a great deal of symbology in the Palm-Pomegranate combination which will repay deeper investigation.

The Priestess-Figure is very definitely a Moon-Venus Concept. She is shown as seated on the Cubic Stone of our Life-Foundation, clad in the traditional blue cloak of the Sky and white robe of purity. What little can be seen of her hair is dark, and her face is delicate and attractively serious. At first glance she seems to wear a horned head-dress with a central globe, until we realize this has a double significance. First, it shows the three phases of the visible Moon: new, full, and old in that order, then the central Lunar disc also serves for the top, or Mirror part, of the entire symbol of Venus, the bottom half of which the Priestess wears as a white cross on her breast.

This head-dress lines up with the Kether-Chockmah-Binah points of the Tree-design on the Tapestry behind the Priestess, and indicates the reflection of those qualities of Supernal Consciousness which are to be experienced on this Path along very fine emotional lines. Both the Moon and the Mirror of Venus may echo to us reflectively the distant Divine Light behind our lives if we devote our living towards that purpose. The Priestess will be our Initiator here.

The mystery of this Priestess is that she is a constant Virgin, yet capable of sexual activity with all sincere suppliants, passing the Life-force through herself into other vehicles for gestation and subsequent development. Her gown from the neck downwards has nine moon-shaped folds to signify the waiting womb-period, but she herself is specifically the Guardian of the Gates to

Life, or Priestess of the Portals, whose task is soul-selection for spiritual birth into Inner Existence. How does a soul reach a condition of fitness for selection as a suitable candidate for independent Inner entity? By the relationships they form with their deep emotional energies and their forces of Life-feeling. The ideal state of this condition is here symbolized and personified by the Priestess. If we pass her standards and tests we shall be In, so far as Inner living is concerned.

The white Cross on her breast is equilateral to signify balance between all points. It centers over her heart, and points to her head (higher feelings), her belly (lower feelings), her left (The White Pillar of "Yes"), and her right (The Black Pillar of "No"). This expresses the problems most of us have on this Path. How do we determine which of our feelings to follow in order to decide the Yes or No of anything? What is the difference between a higher feeling and a lower one? The Priestess must help us find the answers we need, and come to terms with all the emotional crosses in our hearts.

On her lap, the Priestess holds the Tora Scroll of the Law, but in this case we should also read "Lore" in the deepest sense. This Lore comprises all the fundamental Legends and Myths that contain the "feeling patterns" of Humanity which are so important for our ultimate evolution as souls. We have come along our Cosmic course to our present point because of all that our ancestral selves felt about Life and its affairs. Our generations will add our contributions to the Scroll, and it will steadily roll up into the genetic tape which activates our lives in the future. The Priestess is the Guardian of this Scroll, helping souls to read and understand it for themselves if they approach in the proper spirit of love and devotion. The Inner facts indelibly inscribed on the Scroll only look like fairy tales to the uninitiated, and cannot be appreciated except by the "Child-consciousness" which recognizes the Kingdom of Heaven anywhere. Yet these are the basic energy-imprints within us which impel us into courses of action that affect and alter our whole lives and progress along every Path. On the correct and harmonious balancing of our emotions and feelings, the entire future of Mankind may depend. Let us hope the Priestess will help us read and interpret her Scroll rightly.

The lower half of the Priestess presents a more puzzling picture. Everything angles down toward her left and the base of the White Pillar. Her right hand is not shown, and we do not see the other end of the Scroll. This should remind us that the Inner ends and "hidden hands" behind our ordinary Life-feelings are concealed from us by the covering of external consciousness represented by the cloak. We must feel for ourselves beneath the cloak if we would touch the Priestess on the hand which holds the Scroll. She will not prevent us from making this move, and neither will she hand over the Scroll of her own accord. Initiative for access to the Scroll and contact with the Priestess has to commence from the approaching entity.

The draping of the cloak over the knees and down to the left directs our attention to the Netzach position of Victory at the bottom of the White Pillar. It reveals that the right leg is crossed over the left to signify a check or control over impulsive tendencies. We also notice the strange and unusual absence of any feet to the Priestess-Figure. The robes become vague and inchoate, almost as if they are materializing from a golden crescent leaning against the base of the White Pillar. A causal observation might suppose this crescent to be the Moon, but it is actually the edge of the Sun eclipsed by the Moon whom the Priestess personifies and the significance of all this is deep indeed.

By taking light from the Sun, the Moon proclaims her presence to Earth. So do we proclaim our own personalities by taking Life from its Universal Source and re-radiating or reflecting it through our various vehicles. We materialize out of Ultimate Light into Life and realize we are alive because we feel and sense the happenings of Life in and around us. The two Pillars of Perception on sensory levels amount to Pain and Pleasure, having a Middle Pillar termed Peace. Here we find the dedicated feelings of Life arising from sensory pleasures associated with the White Pillar Tree-activities, when, as old astrologers would say, "The Moon is embraced by the Sun in the courses of Venus." The tranquility of the Priestess assures us of the quiet sense of fulfillment awaiting those able to poise their passions between the Pillars. This eclipses all other sensations.

The tip-tilted Solar crescent is indicative of a rocking motion, as if the Priestess were rocking the Cradle of Life rhythmically. So she is, because our lives are based on fundamental rhythms alternating between Solar and Lunar forces, or male-female frequencies which interlock with emotional variations of living energy. These bio-rhythms are right at the roots of our lives (the unseen feet of the Priestess) and whoever learns and practices the dance-steps of Life is attuned to the Rhythm of all the Spheres. We are on the Orphic Path here, and Music means much more than sex-stimulating sonics. These certainly have validity, but only apply to one end of an Inner frequency field covering a consciousness-area of the hidden Music of Life but also respond to it with appreciation and rapture, so that they become welcome partners for the Priestess who sits at the Portals, tapping out the Solunar rhythm while she awaits their invitation to dance with Divinity Itself. The initials on the Pillars beside her might stand in plain English for "Be Joyful." Whyever not?

Originatively, IHVH SABAOTh and SHADDAI el CHAIIM control this Path. I will be Everyone and the Lord of Lives. This means Divinity intending to become Itself through every living soul, and Divinity projecting souls into the courses of Life as human and other entities. The Spirit of Life in the process of feeling Alive. A concentration of Superconsciousness comprising all the feelings and emotions of every living creature in existence. The Sum of every sensation there is. Here, this Divine combination is termed the Inspiritor, because It inspires souls and selves to seek some emotional form of relationship with Itself and each other, aiming at a fully compensated and perfectly balanced state of spiritual satisfaction all round the Cosmic Circle.

It does not need a qualified psychiatrist to realize perfectly well that emotion-energies are major factors of our lives, and we make ourselves into whatever we become, largely because of our feelings—or lack of them. Obviously there must be feeling patterns suitable for every soul to achieve its best state of being during an Earth-life or a series of incarnations. Such patterns would not be the same for everyone, despite general similarities, and it is most likely that each of us has our own personal pattern-requirements when very fine details are taken into account. The question is how we may discover this vital information and apply it beneficially. This Path is where we should seek Initiation into that very mystery.

We usually suppose feelings to be no more than reaction results associated with Inner or Outer promptings. Something hits us physically so we feel pain and hurting inside us. Some moral or ethical issue connects with our Inner reaction points, and we promptly feel keenly about the subject. Incident first and feeling-reaction after. What we have to learn on this Path is the secret of experiencing any feeling or emotion we Will, quite independently of phenomenal causation from Inner or Outer Life. Difficult as this may be to a very considerable extent, it is not impossible, and this Path exists for cultivating the art, for art is truly is. On the complementary Path, we all acknowledge the skill and artistry of those who make their minds and thoughts take up intentional power-patterns for specific purposes, so why should we not equally admit the qualified abilities of souls who undertake the same experiential exercise along emotional lines?

In minor ways everyone can maneuver emotions to some degree, though possibly without deeply skilled effects. There is no use whatever concealing or suppressing the outward emergence of emotional energy unless it is equated and dealt with properly at the depth-level of its primal emergence in the entity concerned. To show a pleasing smile on the surface while boiling with rage underneath may be essential in some social situations, but it is also dangerous to spiritual health. The underlying condition must be satisfactorily neutralized as soon as possible or that soul will have trouble later on. In other words, initiated individuals on this Path do not hold their emotional energies fixed to their personality projections, but release them straight away into the Divinity behind themselves which is seeking to absorb that energy as Its own Life-experience.

This is a highly important technique, for on it depends the spiritual, emotional, and physical health of humanity. In the old days it was known as "offering up experiences to God" so that the "God Within" felt and partook of whatever souls enjoyed and endured on Earth. As, for example, the old Temple prostitute-priestesses were trained not to retain their sex-enjoyment purely for their personal pleasure, but "pass it back" to the Goddess Within them so that an Earthly experience became more completely part of the Great Life behind our mortal living. As with enjoyment, so with suffering. Sorrow and pain has to be "passed back" also, just as Divinity is said to experience human agonies in the death-passions of Divine Kings. Even today, Christians dying in pain or suffering grief are often advised to "offer it up to God," yet told no reasons for this, or trained in procedures.

To illustrate the principles involved, it is almost as if Divinity extended a sensitive nerve-probe through every soul alive. What happens to that soul is transmitted back through what might be called the "Divine sensorium," and thus the Lord of Lives, and "I Will Be Everyone" feel alive through the human section of Creation. Ideally, all this energy should pass through as into Divinity behind us and be dealt with as Divinity Wills. Where we go wrong is in trying to retain an impossibly great proportion of that energy in ourselves, and so suffer severely or irreparable in consequence. If we hold on to one end of an emotional charge, so to speak, while Divinity behind our personalities is pulling the other end toward Itself, a mounting condition of tension sets up which can only result in ill-effects both ways when it inevitably breaks or perishes. For the sake of spiritual health, we must learn on this Path the art of having emotions and feelings associated with Life which we make no attempt to retain on Earth-level, but allow to be fully absorbed through us by the Divinity Within which alone is capable of coping with energies of such intensity. It is really extraordinary how humans who would never attempt to hold a white-hot coal in their naked hands will hang grimly on to an emotional equivalent until it burns holes in their psyche which several lifetimes can scarcely repair.

On this Path, we have to establish the best possible conscious contact between our Life-experiencing emotional extensions of identity, and the Living Spirit Within us of Whom this process is a particular part. In this way, we ourselves identify more and more with the Divine Life Itself. Like the Priestess Symbol, we devote ourselves to Divinity through every smallest feeling we can possibly find as extended individuals. Life becomes progressively easier and more purposeful for those souls who become Initiates of this process. IHVH SABAOTh and SHADDAI el CHAIIM will explain it to us, because they have the Keys between them.

Creatively, Archangels AURIEL and GABRIEL govern this Path. The Light and Virility of Divinity that brings us all to Life. The fertile Field, and the life-bringing Rain. The Shield and the Cup. Between them they cover all the creational field of our feelings for Life on all levels. Gabriel deepens our experiences and helps us to contain them while they are being processed, while Auriel assists us to stabilize our emotional gravity, and affords us a protective shield against injury to our Inner sensitivities.

Here Gabriel is engaged in receiving pure Life-energy in his Cup, and pouring it out again into our souls so that we may receive it in our minor cups for our spiritual sustenance. This is almost like reflecting Life as the Moon reflects the Light of the Sun, and so Gabriel is aptly a Lunar Archangel. In this way, Gabriel is metaphorically dipping his Cup into the Stream of Life itself, and offering us vital fluid a cupful at a time according to our capacity. We have all watched mothers feeding infants with a cup. Careful, loving women let the child sip a mouthful at each effort, withholding the cup until the fluid is quite swallowed before putting it to the child's lips again. This, of course, takes a lot of time and attention. Careless mothers try and make the child choke down all he can in slipshod ways which lead to ill effects later on. This is analogous to adult humans and their Cups of Life. If an overdose is forced down our throats it makes us spiritually and physically sick and if we fail to get our proper supply, we shall suffer from thirst on more life-levels than one. If we rely on Gabriel for our Inner life supply of what amounts to the "Waters of Life," and only drink from the Cup he controls then we shall always be satisfied and never intoxicated by what we are offered. With Gabriel as our Ganymede, our cups will never fail us.

It is so easy to be drunk with Life. So convenient to grab at everyone's cup and attempt to drain their life-fluid as well as ours. Like Tantalus, the more we try to slake our thirst for life from the wrong source, the further it recedes from us, and the more maddened we become. The Cup which Gabriel bears is the "Cup which runneth over," or the Living Grail, and we can only partake of its contents in our "Temples not made with hands," or Within ourselves. There, we shall discover on this Path, that the Cup we are offered has just the right amount in it for our spiritual needs, and when we are fully prepared for more, it will be available. We shall be fed as a loving mother feeds fluid to her offspring, properly and adequately. Of course, if we behave badly like so many humans, losing our tempers and thrusting the Cup away with flailing fists, or grasp greedily for it with grunts and gulps, well—we shall only have ourselves to blame for what happens to us afterward. Here on this Path, the Initiate must learn how to accept the Cup of Life from Gabriel and savor it like a true connoiseur, extracting the most exquisite experiences from its contents—even if this is just plain water. Those who drink the Waters of Life and relish it as the rarest Wine, have participated in the miracle of the Cana Wedding Feast. Gabriel knows the secret and will impart it to souls asking properly at the Portals of this Path.

The Shield of Auriel is also the Platter-form of the Grail. Whenever Christians and others take Communion, they might spare a thought for Gabriel holding the Cup, and Auriel carrying the Platter. The combination of the two makes up the Holy Grail, and the supporting Symbols of the Lance and Sword bring in the other two Archangels of the Great Four. Auriel, being the Earth-Archangel, bears the Bread on his Platter, and without literal and metaphorical bread, we shall not stay alive very long. Here, Auriel offers Life on a Platter to us, even if some people's platters are piled high, while others can scarcely see the scraps available. How do we take our pieces of Life from Auriel's Platter? Well or badly? Selectively or senselessly? Watch people's behavior with their food, and they reveal their basic life-characteristics. Hence the important influence of table-manners. It is for Auriel on this Path to teach aspirants how to behave at the Round Table of Life whereat the Companions of Cosmos commune. This is his own Shield in a different scale of symbology.

The task of Archangels Auriel and Gabriel in their joint relationship with Mankind is to initiate us into cultured, cultivated and civilized circles of Cosmic behavior. As long as humans are virtually in a savage and crude state of spiritual evolution, they are scarcely fit for admission to more exalted and refined categories of living. Crudity and insensitivity are necessary during the primitive and cataclysmic stages of Earthly existence, and indeed such is the refuge that Auriel's Shield offers in those times. First we survive here cowering behind or beneath this Shield, but later on as we grow up Inwardly, we must come out from underneath and learn how to sit up properly around the Shield as the "Table which has been prepared before us amidst all threats to peace."

From Auriel and Gabriel we learn how to deal with every feeling and emotion we shall encounter in our lives, creatively, constructively, and in a truly Cosmic manner so that our Inner identities become really worthwhile Lives of Light. The Priest-ess-Symbol stands for a schoolmarm as well, and our initial Life-lessons are best learned at her knee. If we equate Life with Light, and assume all the colors of the spectrum to be the gamut of our distinctive feelings and thinkings in connection with conscious living, this will provide us with a useful working analogy. The White Light is all Life at once. The colors are the components of Life separately and sequentially by themselves. We must learn how to put them together in ourselves in order to shine with our own White Light. This is done by revolving the colors at a rate which will restore them to an appearance of White Light again. If we think of Gabriel scattering the contents of the Cup into indi-vidual drops so that these break up the Life-light into a rainbow of all colors, then the Shield of Auriel revolving its mirror surface so that the reflected Rainbow is restored to terms of Life-Light again, this will give ideas of procedures for this Path. AURIEL and GABRIEL know all the secrets of this, and will initiate us into them if we apply in the proper fashion. They have the Keys.

Formatively, the Angelic Orders of the ELOHIM and the ASHIM administer the Path. The "Gods" and the "Upright Ones." They represent the ideal images into the likeness of which we should become fashioned by our feelings, and our fitness to es-tablish ourselves as Initiates of Life and worthy members of the Divine Family. It is a well known anomaly of Life that its quality is only a fractional proportion of its quantity. In a sense, Life is pyramidal, its point being at the top in contact with Fire (the Sun) and Air, while its base material is at the bottom with Earth and water. Since this is an Earth-Water Path, we may expect to find upon it all the basics upon which to build both personal and collective Pyramids of Life. Even in primitive times water and clay were mixed to make bricks which were dried in sun and air so that structures in which humanity could live were con-structed. The same principles apply today with our modern mon-strosities. On Inner levels of Life, the Ashim and the Elohim are supposed to help us build ourselves selectively from our base ma-terials of emotional energies into the wonderful souls, "like unto Gods," which we may become if we Will.

Taking the whole of humanity as a basis, if it were possible to extract even a little from the best qualities in each individual and recombine these into other and quite new people, an amazing race of super-souls would suddenly appear. Over many millenia, this may be the case if the human race remains long enough on Earth to complete the process, but the principles of this meta- morphosis apply to all of us in every lifetime. If we could take the best experiences of our lives and the most deeply moving emo- tional events of our existence, then draw from these in order to design ourselves anew, we might achieve in a single incarnation what usually takes very many. The Ashim and Elohim are there to assist us in this very work. How many of us have clear ideas about the sort of God-form (Eloh) we would choose to assume, or in other language the Ideal Person we would like to become? The Elohim exist for that purpose. and it is for us all to find an Eloh for ourselves and devote our feelings toward achieving a relative condition of being human, equivalents.

The Ashim are the "Upright souls" in the sense of fit and proper beings to found families. They represent all that is good in any human ancestry, and the qualities in any of us that are worth passing on to our descendants for us to pick up again in future births. In other words, worthwhile genetic factors. They also stand for a steadily perfecting strain in human breeding until a point is reached where no further progress is possible through human bodies, and a changeover in consciousness then com- mences into Life-states beyond embodiment. Metaphorically, this may be likened to arriving at the top of the Life-Tree or Pyra- mid, and taking off from thence into other dimensions of living. On this Path, the Ashim urge us along toward attainment of the highest points of our lifetimes as sentient souls, pushing us as near a sensation of "Godhood" as they dare. In fact, many human fatalities occur among those who mistake this encouraging re- flection for reality, and misjudge their actions accordingly. We have to balance and equate the formative influences of the Ashim and Elohim here, so that a reasonably accurate estimate of our Inner abilities along this line will control our conduct.

Even a few casual thoughts about the Pyramid of Life will reveal that breeding should become increasingly selective and proportionately lessen in amount as the higher courses of the Pyramid are reached. Quantity at the bottom, quality at the top. There is no doubt at all that the indiscriminate and almost criminally careless breeding habits of the human race are a seri- ous menace to both Inner and Outer evolution. Whether or not it is possible to bring this collision-course with disaster under Cosmic control before its ultimate explosive ending-only the Ultimate Itself can know for certain. All others concerned must fulfill their functions in the Life-Plan with unremitting devotion. The Ashim and the Elohim are responsible for encouraging humans to accept and adopt increasingly higher standards and principles in regard to their reproductive programs. This world will not become a better place until only the best types of soul are allowed access to it, and however-unpalatable this fact may be, it is undeniably true. Even all the old ideas of human Heavens and Hells were built up on the principles of segregating advanced from retarded souls, establishing an Inner civilization of the highest type for evolved entities to live in, and making such a Life-level inaccessible to all save souls able to exist in such concentrated conditions of Cosmos. Those refusing to raise themselves to these requirements remained in Hells of their own making to suit their respective states of imperfection.

It is at this point of the Tree that souls select themselves for progression beyond the Portals of Life toward specific states of Inner existence that used to be called Heaven and Hell, but are actually widely differing spiritual conditions of Otherlife which are only comprehensible to those who live within their ranges of reality. They are not conditional upon temporal-spatial determinations, but solely upon the degree or category of evolutionized entity attained by souls in their own right. In other words, discarnate entities tend to group and associate strictly in accordance with their intrinsic natures, which automatically means segregation into spiritual states of differentiation. As an illustration, we might imagine a number of glass balls filled respectively with air, water, and earth. These represent embodied humans in this world, all mixed up together and sharing a common state of separated self-hood. Now let the glass containers be broken at a single stroke to signify death. All the air rushes together, the earth and water first become mud, then separate by settlement, and the elements become pure again. Analogously we shall take up our natural soul-states when we quit body-life here, though, of course, we retain our essential identity.

Since we become what we make of ourselves by Life-experience, which in terms of consciousness consists of feeling and thinking, this Path proves our soul-values as sentient beings.

Here we achieve what might be called our spiritual style or usage of emotional energy which determines what sort of soul-selves we become, thus deciding our eventual spiritual destiny. The ELOHIM and the ASHIM will show us how to develop ourselves in depth here. They have the Keys.

Expressively, the influences characterized by Luna and Venus control this Path. Although most people think of the Moon as being feminine, the Magical Image is a virile male. Both are valid concepts signifying fertility through feeling, on a far broader basis than physical sexual relations. We ought also to consider the auto-sexual circuit operating between the masculine and feminine elements in every individual soul which should result in a fertile Inner life, producing the "children of consciousness," or independent ideas arising out of what amounts to subliminal sex activity.

Venus, or Aphrodite, signifies "sex with everything" in a very wide way. Though she certainly links with human coital acts, she also extends the sentiments relative to those acts everywhere else. Why should we assume that the feelings and sentiments which move us emotionally when directed toward souls of opposite sex must be limited to that one field alone? Sexual feelings are no more than our emotional energies channeled and concentrated toward that particular aim in some specific set of circumstances. We can turn those same feelings wherever we Will in Life, and relate ourselves with any objective we choose. We do not have special sets of feelings for sex, and totally different ones for everything else. The object differs, but our feelings are our own energized attempts to relate ourselves with the rest of Living Consciousness in whatever form we find it. Sex between humans is but one way of expressing feelings. If it comes to fine shades of meaning, we might say that all our relations with everything and Divinity Itself are sexual in character so long as we ourselves remain sexed beings. Sublimate our feelings as high as we will, they remain characterized by the sex of our own souls.

The Moon, or Luna, has such a wealth of associative attributes that it is difficult to select a minimum of apt items for consideration here. Since we are dealing with a Moon-Venus combination, it may be best to stay with the sex-fertility angle. Surely the Moon and lovers go together through the most wonderful dream worlds Life can possibly offer? Let none dismiss or despise those inspired dreams as romantic nonsense and unrealizable rubbish. Where would humanity be without dreams? Who wants to live utterly without love and affection? Imagine a world wherein everyone is in love with everyone else. Such has ever been a human concept of Heaven, and although it is unlikely to materialize among Mankind in the foreseeable future, our Inner contacts along the Sphere-states of this path will provide us with the helpful encouragement we need to cope with many otherwise insurmountable obstacles of Earth life. The dreams we encounter on the Lunar end of the path may engender the Faith needed to carry us through everything to the Victory of Venus, which amounts to an ability of Loving at Will.

Failure to achieve balance upon this Path leads to the opposite of Victory—Disaster. Probably this and its companion Path from Yesod to Hod are the two most dangerous Ways humanity has to travel during early evolutionary attempts to ascend the Tree. Fail on this Path and we become depraved and vicious. Fail on its opposite extension and we become vainglorious and insane. Yet neither of the paths can be avoided except by those of such unusual spiritual natures that the Middle Way is possible for them. Usually, this is only likely after many incarnations of experience in other directions. The vast majority of us must attempt mastery of the paths leading to Victory and Glory, pay the price of our failures, and ultimately learn how to keep our balance upon both.

The balancing of Luna and Venus is the control of our emotional energies by means of our imagination and basic beliefs in Life, coupled with genuine love and affection for all that lives. Initiates of this Path have their feelings entirely in command to Do What they Will with, because those feelings have been devoted to the Divine purpose in every person, and can be sublimated up to any level of action. Here we become free from emotional compulsions of all kinds, sexual and otherwise, yet retain an ability of response over an emotional range unguessed at by unextended entities along this line of Light. It is not that sexual or other instincts become any less in themselves, but that the scope of application through fresh Inner fields becomes so very much wider, far more wonderful, and offers such a richer variety of experience than purely physical opportunity affords.

An expert Initiate of this Path should be able to run up and down the gamut of every typified emotion like a musician is able to cover a complete sonic keyboard. For instance, the most intense and powerful sexual feelings are convertible by processes learned on this Path into the highest and noblest devotion to Divinity, then all the way back again to complete the cycle. Eventually we realize that we can tap and use this identical energy at any particular point we choose. It is all one energy, so why not get the best results for ourselves with it?

This Western way of Initiation does not exclude emotion from the Path of Progress at all. Emotional feelings and experiences are not in the slightest way regarded as undesirable, ignoble, or something to be spiritually ashamed of. The ice-cold, utterly impersonal and emotionless sort of superhuman Intelligence which masquerades as a "Master-image" among some schools of opinion, can have no real place in the hearts and souls of all who feel really alive in that Inner Kingdom where the Tree of Life grows naturally. We are truly told, "conquer feelings," but this does not mean expel or abandon them, only that we should make them obey the True Will in us, constructing control-circuits and metaphysical mechanisms for them to work by the well-known magical methods of creative imagination.

From the Moon-base of Yesod, we must learn how to project ourselves into Inner Space by both emotional and intellectual Paths. Creative imagination alone makes this possible, but the one factor which prevents degeneration of such a state into futile fantasy is Will-control by the individual entity over his Inner spiritual situations. On this Path, we must learn about "Love under Will," which may not be the whole of the Law, but is certainly a very large part of it here. When we can "call up" and "banish" again any emotional condition we intend to use for specific purposes, we shall have progressed a good way along our Twenty-eighth Path. Luna and Venus will help or hinder us according to the way we deal with them. The Keys of Control await us if we Will.

The Twenty-ninth Path

SPHERE—LETTER CODE:	Victory 7 X 10 Kingdom	
DIVINE ORIGINATION:	IHVH SABAOTh—	The
	ADONAI ha ARETZ	Personifier
ARCHANGELIC CREATION:	Auriel—Sandalphon	Practice
ANGELIC FORMATION:	Elohim—Kerabim	Placement
APPARENT EXPRESSION:	Venus—Earth	Solidity
TAROT SYMBOL:	THE WORLD	

Here we have reached ground level at last, and emerged into the world of humanity just as we find it at present. There are three traditional Ways linking the ordinary Outer-world of material Mankind with the Inner-world of Initiated individuals. The Hermetic, the Orphic, and the Mystic. This is the Orphic Path of Experience connecting Earth and Venus together. Hereon we go inside ourselves through all conscious activities concerned with artistic, emotional, and cultural practical procedures. Music, dancing, gardening, poetry, painting, the erotic arts, floristry, and, in fact, any means at all of sending and sensing our souls beyond bodily boundaries. Every attempt we make as mortals to extend ourselves Inwardly through feelings and sensations of spiritual realities, constitutes a step along this Path. To ensure that our steps are wise or beneficial is the main problem we have to solve here.

This is where we personify ourselves into the people we are in this world through the sort of souls we become. Conversely, we feed back through those same souls the reactive effects of of mortal living translated into spiritual terms. For instance, some physical happenings may result in deep emotional changes in us which we transmit through our psychic structures back into our Group and World-soul life-levels. Thus, everyone is affected to minimal extent by individual experiences, and individuals are affected to perhaps maximal extent by what goes around the whole world. On this Path, the equation must be found which relates each individual entity with every other for the sake of sharing a common state of consciousness.

In effect, this is comparable to the Ketheric state, when evolved entities merge into a common condition of Cosmos at the other end of the spiritual scale in order to unify with Absolute Awareness. Here, we are a lot of people projected from One Life Spirit, and there we shall be a Single Living Spirit comprising every individual in Existence. It has been truly said that "Kether is in Malkuth after another manner," with the implication that we cannot learn how to live in the highest of Heavens before we find out how to live within this very world.

The entire Path of Initiation is nothing but a systematic and steady spiritual progression of entity from the least to the loftiest levels of Light-Life. Here we have to study how we shall set our feet firmly on that Path in this very world, so that we at least start off in the right direction toward Divinity. The first steps in any life are always the most difficult, and in the case of Inner Life these important attempts at making spiritual strides usually take more than a single incarnation on Earth to succeed. Such, however, is the Victory we must achieve in soul while still linked by this Path to the Kingdom of the World in body. The Names and Symbols of the Path should have a great deal to tell us.

The Tarot Symbol of the World, or Cosmos, shows Humanity as representative of Life in its natural environments. It is a deceptively simple Symbol, presenting an outer ring of Elemental concepts, an oval "Chain of Life" within these, and a stylized Human in the central field. The overall picture is one of external Elemental energies and Cosmic forces concentrating themselves on Humanity as the hub of their cyclic relationships.

If we look at the four familiar "Creatures" of the Eagle, Lion, Ox, and Man, we shall first note that their positional sequence is astrological, or according to their Zodiacal places, where they become Scorpio, Leo, Taurus, and Aquarius. These are the "Fixed" Signs, and also line up with the old Fertility Feasts of the cross-quarters, commonly called Candlemas (or Brigitta) in Aquarius, May-Eve in Taurus, Lammas in Leo, and Hallows in Scorpio. These old pagan times of commemorating the natural occasions of Life-tides indicate the continuity of our contact with the original Life-Elements from which we emerged. We and our world are all made out of these Elements, and an occasional conscious acknowledgment of this fact will help us along our life-courses quite considerably.

The "Creature-concepts" are surrounded by the usual clouds to signify they are conceptions of the Divine Consciousness whose Imagination brings all Life into Existence. An interesting point about them here is that they present differing facial angles to the observer. Scorpio, the Eagle, is left profile, Leo, the Lion full-faced, Taurus the Ox three-quarter right, and Aquarius the Man right profile. This indicates many things. The turning of the Earth on its axis, the Quarternity of the Word and Worlds upon which Qabalistic doctrines and speculations are arranged. The revolution of Life through its stages of Birth, Growth, Fulfillment, and Maturity. In fact, the only angle of the head we do not see is the back, which would show retirement from Life, or disincarnation. This obviously takes place at the Winter Solstice position or point of least Light between Scorpio and Aquarius. If we follow the Creatures around again, we might think of Man incarnating "out of the blue" like the Air of Aquarius, materializing and becoming involved with affairs of this world like the Earth of Taurus, using up strength and energy in life-work like the Fire of Leo, then flowing into the Ocean of Consciousness like the Water of Scorpio, from which evaporation occurs as Spirit into the Air of Aquarius the Water-carrier again, ready for another Life-cycle to commence. A really beautiful symbology of Life in Cosmic continuance.

These Creatures support the "Chain of Life," which is shown as a Victory Garland or Crown consisting of leaves which are representative of both olive and laurel with perhaps a touch of bay and myrtle thrown in. Such a combination obviously signifies the sort of environmental surrounds most humans would like to find around themselves. Peace, success, prosperity, and happiness altogether. In fact, the whole of this card seems to portray the world as we want it, rather than the world as we have actually altered it. Nevertheless, unless we realize what life in our world should and ought to be like, we can scarcely make this a practical proposition at all. Therefore, we might as well accept this Glyph as an emblem of encouragement in living.

The connection between this Circlet of Victory and the Four

Life-Elements certainly points to the Netzach-Malkuth nature of this Path. Moreover, it is only when we achieve victory over the natural forces operating in our world that we shall become free souls and Initiates of its life-way. In its oval form of presentations the Life-Chain also signifies the Zodiac, which word derives from "zoos," living, alive, and "zone," a woman's girdle, implying the life that came from the womb beneath that girdle. Esoteric teaching was to the effect that every life-type associates with its particular Sign or Space-Symbol in a Cosmic Circle awaiting its "call-up" into incarnation as and when its individual summons came. Each of the twelve Signs represents a special type of living soul, and entities of that character come and go from this Earth according to Cosmic circumstances which afford them opportunities. Hence the validity of a horoscope, or chart of known Cosmic situations under which individual humans incarnate, and discarnate.

In a sense, this Life-Chain is also every single leaf upon the Tree of Life, which is to say every one of us, gathered together into an endless Belt of Being right around the World for as long as we continue living here. If we look at the top of the picture, we shall find that two leaves in particular are standing out from all the rest. One is returning back to the Outer areas of the Elements, and the other is entering the Inner area of spiritual individuation where the central Figure typifying Humanity in triumph appears. Each of us has that choice. Either we revert back to the Elemental energies we came from, or we individuate into the beings we must become if we are to earn eternal entity or "Life-everlasting." Be it noted that the individuation leaf goes Within the Life-chain, or adopts the Inner Life as its *modus vivendi.*

These "Leaves of Life" link with the crossing point of a red "Eternity," or shaped band securing the Life-chain at the top. Another such band holds the Life-chain together at the bottom. There is deep significance in these seeming pieces of decoration. They are the Life-links, or bonds of blood that bind humanity in to a single spiritual family among themselves, and also with their Divine progenitors. It should be noted that the crossing of these links is right over left, to indicate the mixing of blood via the male and female lines of parentage. One rather fascinating connection here is with a custom which still persists to this day of tying a piece of red ribbon to some special or "magic" tree, and making a wish. This goes back to much deeper roots than might be supposed, namely to the Divine King sacrifice.

In early times, sacred Kings were frequently sacrificed by tying or hanging them to Trees, then stabbing them so that their blood ran down as a Stream of Life in which worshippers shared in fact or by token. This constituted a blood-link with Divinity Itself. The Christian Mass is established on this ancient principle, and attempts to deny or disguise the fact are not only futile, but utterly unworthy of even a moderately initiated intelligence. Eventually, however, the general principles of the practice became symbolized in quite a number of ways, one of the simplest being to tie a red cross-knot on some tree. The Tree of Life, the Life-link of Blood, an act of devotion for a particular purpose, the binding of Word and Will with the Bond of Belief—all the elements of the Rite are there. Almost a Mass in miniature, providing the practitioner knew or realized what was involved. So we have those vital Life-links on the Chain of this Symbol, to remind us how we should join Inner and Outer life into the Cosmos we intend to live with as our World. Ritualists might note that these links are shown at the solstices as being the most favorable occasions for contracts of this nature.

The central Figure represents Humanity, both individually and collectively, engaged in the Dance of Life which liberates us into Light. Again the human form shown is androgynous, its breasts being female, while its male organs are concealed by the center of a long purple wrapping. The Figure is in minimal contact with the ground, being balanced on the toes of the right foot; it bears a rod in each hand and has its head turned toward its right shoulder. Apart from the wrapping, which only touches across from left shoulder to right hip, the Figure is naked, save for a red ribbon binding its golden hair.

Some believe the Figure to indicate alchemical sulphur on account of its cross leg and triangular arm position, but the triangle over the cross signifies more than that. In solid form it can show the quartered cone, or the Circle-Cross of Cosmos emerging from its primal Nil-point into infinite extension, or conversely, concentrating everything in all quarters of Creation back to their original focus. The triangle-cross also shows a widening ray of Light shining down on Earth, the Divine Eye observing Mankind, and a great deal else besides. "Three over Four" indicates the constructional principle of the Life Pyramid in practice.

The loose wrapping from which the dancing Figure is emerging has much meaning of its own. It is purple in color, which is a blend of Severity (Red) and compassion (Blue). It also links the infra-red and ultra-violet ends of the Light spectrum in both physical and spiritual Dimensions. Purple is the color of Royalty, and is only associated with sorrow on account of our failings which lead to the sacrificial death of a Sacred King. For that reason perhaps, purple is the Veil color in the Holy Mysteries of Light. Here, we see this veil falling away from the Truth of Humanity Inside. If we visualize the Figure as being originally wrapped tightly in the veil, it is shown on this Symbol as being clear of the eyes and face to release sight, hearing and speech, also the feet are free to dance and the hands to maneuver. Only the sex organs are still veiled, to show we have not yet liberated ourselves from this bondage, because we have failed to fully grasp the meaning of its Mystery. The Figure is dancing a spinning movement deosil, or Lightward, which is unwrapping the veil, and ultimately will become altogether in a state of revealed Truth, when the veil lies at the feet of Humanity Triumphant. The Sign of Seven can also mean the dance of the Seven Veils, and this Symbol depicts the last veil being disposed of.

In each hand the Figure twirls what look like identical rods until we note the one in the left hand is shaded to give the impression of a measuring rule, while that in the right hand is plain. Whether by design or not, these rods are angled at twenty-two degrees from each other. If by intention, this shows that we must plot and plod all the Paths of Life on the Tree, reducing its Pillars to rods within our range of manipulation. The rod in the left hand is marked to indicate all that we have previously measured and learned, and the one in the right hand is plain since it stands for everything we have yet to do in this world. It should be noted that the rods are being twirled in opposite directions. Rod twirling and striking always formed an important part of the old Mystery dances, and study of this in folk-dancing even today will repay serious students of Symbology, especially those interested in this particular Path.

The expression on the face of the Figure is one of calm dedication to Life, or "Middle Pillar mood." The golden hair indicates an enlightened consciousness. It was a favorite trick of symbolic artists to use a hair coloring which suggested the sort of consciousness or outlook supposed to be in the subject's mind. This golden hair is bound with a red band which signifies devotion by blood to beliefs in Life. It says in effect that only the deepest beliefs for which we are prepared to give our Life-blood are worth holding. Paradoxically, this means that only what we are willing to die for makes life worth living.

So there is our World-Figure. Each of us in this world, yet within another world of our own the whole time, maintaining our measured balance in the Dance of Life between both Inner and Outer Living. If we follow and develop all the points outlined by this Path Symbol, we shall earn enough to live in any World of our choice, but until we live properly in this one, there is little sense in trying others. Our Cosmic citizenship must be earned on Earth before we become acceptable in better states of Being.

Originatively, the Divine Aspects of IHVH SABAOTh and ADONAI ha ARETZ govern this Path. I will be Everyone, and Lord of the Earth. They are keyed together as the Personifier. Divinity intending control of Cosmos here through every life on Earth, or allowing those lives to revert into their Elements again. We are not only considering Mankind here, but all that lives on Earth, including the Earth itself. If Man were the solitary Life-form on this planet, elimination of the human race entirely would solve a lot of problems, but Man on Earth is in the rather unique position of being on spiritual probation, so to speak, for the overall purpose of making right relationships through himself with all else, and individuating into higher types of entity. Therefore, while Mankind, individually and collectively, is still in a state of actual evolution and spiritual growth, there is no point in eliminating the human Life-species. Should such development cease beyond hope of regeneration, and the species deteriorate past a practical point of resurgence, then of course the Life-Spirit can scarcely be expected to support forms which are no longer suitable for manifesting Its force.

ADONAI ha ARETZ is virtually another way of saying the "World-Soul," or the spiritual sum of every life on Earth, or in any World, expressible as a whole entity. Just as we all have our individual souls, so do we share in greater soul-groups, such as those of families, countries, nations, etc. A soul may perhaps be described as a distinctive and individuated organism of spiritual energy, maintained in existence for the sake of its inherent characteristics relative to its condition of Cosmos. In this World, we need human physical bodies organized from the Life-energy natural to this type of planet in order to be here at all. To extend our living beyond those limits into Inner Dimensions, we need souls organized out of super-physical energies natural to Cosmic conditions in more subtle states of existence.

These souls are built up and kept going in ways very analogous to material methods. They are derived from what might be termed Divine Parentage, must be nourished, guarded, exercised, trained, instructed, and treated along similar lines to our bodies. We can neglect, ill-treat, and abuse our souls like our bodies, too. Though they survive our physical deaths, they are not immortal, and if they die, we disappear with them. Only pure spirit is immortal, and if we succeed at individuating into that state of Being, then we automatically become immortal also. Our souls, together with our conditioned consciousness we term "Mind," are the necessary intermediates between our highest and lowest levels of Life. They are exactly what makes us distinctly ourselves. Our state of Mind-Soul is who we are at any given instant. Our animating Spirit belongs to Life Itself, and our bodies belong to this Earth, but what we develop between those extremities on our own accounts is properly ours to do with What We Will.

Just as a lot of separate and specialized cells are combined and organized to make up one human body for a soul to personify, so may a lot of separate souls be related and combined to personify some distinctive spiritual entity needing such a medium of manifestation and operation. "Where three or four are gathered together in My Name, etc.," is literally true. Combine souls together in the name of a family, a group, a race, or a nation, and there will live among them a spirit uniquely theirs, yet exercising a pervasive influence of its own among them which will have a decisive effect on their destiny. Mankind on Earth is capable of soul-grouping (after a fashion) up to a national level, but seems singularly unsuccessful in holding the World-Soul together properly. Until we are able to fit ourselves properly into the World-Soul without endangering its entity, we can hardly be welcome members of its Inner Cosmos. Nor should we imagine that in order to have one harmonious world it is necessary to do away with all distinctive groupings of nation, race, family, and even individual character. To the contrary, a world deprived of its soul-distinctions has no more living unity than a body crushed into a homogenous jelly, or perhaps disintegrated into atomic dust. We all need each other for what we are and will become in ourselves and by associative groupings. A sound World-Soul would consist of everyone being themselves for the sake of Cosmos.

The purpose of this path between IHVH SABAOTh and ADONAI ha ARETZ is personalization into the sorts of soul which make Cosmos worth sharing by everyone. It is inevitable during this process that souls of specific categories will form into their own natural circles of Cosmos for the objective aim of personal perfection, for no perfect Whole can be constructed from individually imperfect parts. This is the function of Initiation in the Holy Mysteries. Namely to provide facilities for souls and selves to fulfill their individual Cosmic callings toward Divinity and one another. It is not, and never was, part of any genuine System of Initiation to offer unfair or unearned advantages over others. We are here to gain our qualities of Lordship on Earth by our own achievements along spiritual lines. Hence the Kingdom-Victory connection along this Path. We cannot qualify as lords of any sort unless we personify and bring into Life on Earth the particular purpose of Divine Will which is behind our incarnation as it were.

Initiation works through individuation. Initiates are those people prepared to leave the mass-level of humanity and evolve at increased rates of Inner progression through specialized systems of conscious procedures and behaviors. How much natural nobility and inherent aristocracy exists in a soul? Here on this Path we must discover this for ourselves, and recognize it in others. We can only adopt two attitudes to life at this point; either we become its lords in our own right, or remain its lackeys to everyone's detriment. In the old Mysteries no slaves were admitted. Nor will modern slaves in a different sense be any more acceptable to a spiritual society founded on principles of Inner freedom and achievement of all that is best in a soul which elevates that soul to a condition of lordship in life. By lordship is meant an actual attainment of quality, and this had nothing whatever to do with meaningless titles or pointless social promotions. True lordship is a responsibility, not a rank, and we must plod this Path if we are to deserve it. IHVH SABAOTh and ADONAI ha ARETZ are the only authorities through which we may gain such a distinction. They sponsor admission to the Inner aristocracy, because they hold the Keys between them.

Creatively, Archangels AURIEL and SANDALPHON control the Path. Sandalphon is the "Earth-end" of Metatron, so to speak. His name is said to derive from roots signifying "cobrother," and he is supposed to be the immediate superior of all guardian angels attached to humans. He is imagined as being so tall his feet are on Earth, and his head in Heaven. His job is to help us take the right steps along this Path on Earth if we aspire towards our Heavenly heritage. Between them, he and Auriel can assist us in making our Inner imaginings practical. The accent on this Path is one of positive practice rather than vague day-dreaming, or ineffectual amusement with visionary astral scenery.

Auriel reminds us we are on this Earth to achieve enough enlightenment in order to exist in other and higher conditions of Cosmos. Sandalphon tells us again and again that the Keys of Heaven are to be found on Earth, and every level of Life must necessarily hold the secrets of those immediately beyond its extensions. Just as astronauts have to learn how to live in Lunar conditions while still on Earth, before they can be safely sent to the Moon, so do we have to simulate our spiritual life while yet incarnate before we shall be fit to extend it otherwise. On this Path, we have to feel our way Inwardly, guided by what our equivalent Inner sense of touch and smell tells us is true about inner living. We are still on the Orphic side of the Three Ways here.

Our physical emotions of love are linked most strongly with touch and smell. Sight and hearing may trigger the finer aspects of Earthly love, but for maximum, and most intimate, experiences of the emotion, we must participate in exchanges of tactile and olfactory energies with our love-objective. As the Archangel of Earth as an Element, Auriel will put us in touch with spiritual contacts so that we may feel their reality just as if we held a physical object in our bodily hands, or discovered a rose garden by its fragrance. Since such an experience by itself might seriously unbalance an incarnate entity, Sandalphon's job is to relate it rightly for us in Earth-terms, so that we maintain our stability as personified people of this planet. While we are feeling the wonders of Heaven with our fingertips, guided Inwardly by Auriel, Sandalphon should make sure our feet will not slip on Earth. Between them they have to teach us the schoolboy's ruling of climbing any tree. "Never let go of a lower grip before you have firm and positive hold of the higher one." This is also how we must climb the Tree of Life, and here we learn not to take our feet off Earth unless we have a firm enough grip in Heaven to bear all our weight. So many souls fall on this Path because they instinctively grab at Inner sensations for spiritual satisfaction while at the same time they ignore or remove their footholds on Earthly incarnation. This often happens with young and inexperienced souls not yet tall enough in Inner Dimensions to reach Auriel's hand securely before releasing their grip on Sandalphon's robe. Sandalphon is a very tall Archangel, and his advice is to continue growing until handholds in Heaven feel as firm and secure as footholds on earth, then "walk tall" between both.

Our task upon this section of the Path is making practical and workable creative relationships, with our feelings for immediate Inner and Outer Life experienced or incarnatory levels. This is not a speculative path at all, but a strictly realistic one, on which we have to come to terms with physical phenomena and their metaphysical counterparts, linking them together through ourselves to that a common denominator of consciousness may be arrived at. Auriel puts us in touch with the physical ends of spiritual energies, and Sandalphon should connect us with the spiritual ends of physical forces. In this way we balance our experiences of Outer and Inner worlds and maintain our integrity in both. If we find ourselves becoming too materialistic we should invoke Auriel, and if we start losing our grip on Earth-life, we need Sandalphon. Best of all, we might try keeping to the middle of the path between the two Archangelic administrators.

Here we have to acquire the art of practical creative fantasy which will enable us to operate successfully along Inner and Outer living. This is an absolutely essential requirement in all magical or occult practices. It means relating ourselves with Life on any level by means of self-constructed situations created for this purpose within the perimeter of our personal consciousness. Our very lives may depend on our degree of skill and precision with fantasy control. Rightly used, it can raise us toward Divinity; wrongly applied, it may dash us down toward destruction. In fact, we really ought to make sure that we have Auriel on one side of us and Sandalphon on the other before we employ it all along this path of feeling.

For example, some materialized event or information may precipitate us into an agitated condition of Inner reactive feelings. We fantasize this into dangerously unreal concepts of our own construction in which we are forced to live with ourselves and suffer all sorts of spiritual injuries or disadvantages. If, on the other hand, we have learned how to act in accordance with the Sandalphon-Auriel system, the same original happening would only stimulate us into fantasizing an Inner condition of counterbalance calculated to restore our personal poise in relation to what is happening. The really important issue is that we should equilibrate ourselves emotionally between the Inner events of Netzach and the Outer realities of Malkuth along this particular Path. Since fantasy control is such a valuable means to this end, We should ask AURIEL and SANDALPHON for the Keys thereto, because they hold these together.

Formatively, the Angelic Orders of the ELOHIM, linked with that of the KERUBIM operate here. Kerubim are the Chioth ha Qodesh on a Malkuthic scale. At the top of the Tree, they are the pure Elements of Living consciousness. Here at the bottom, they are really that same Consciousness translated into terms of Life-Energy specifically expressed as Earthly existence. The Kerubim are personifications of the elemental energies in and around us within this world of matter. Hence they are depicted as being four-fold, having the semblance of Ox for Earth, Lion for Fire, Eagle for Water, and Man for Air. The choice of concept for Water and Air (Scorpio and Aquarius) of Eagle and Man often puzzles people, and is somewhat recondite in origin, but they connect quite well. The Eagle represents the noblest aspect of Scorpio, or Water evaporating in the Air in order to become life-bringing rain to Earth and complete the cycle of life. The Man, Aquarius, is Air bearing Water, which was anciently considered the seed of the Sky-God, which in turn must pour on Earth-Mother to create her children.

Put into another pattern, this rather lovely sequence of concepts shows our human cosmic cycle from a spiritual viewpoint also. Starting from Earth, we are liberated from the Waters of Life by the Light and Fire of Love and Devotion. Rising high into the Air of Heaven, we become as perfect as possible before being precipitated into Earth-incarnation again for another life-round. Thus, the Cycle of the Kerubim is ours, too, until we are able to exist otherwise.

To live properly in this world, we need our elemental energies balanced to as fine a degree around their point of poise as can be arranged. The Circle-Cross of Earth-cosmos revolving on its central axis effectively is the Symbol of healthy and harmonious living as humans, and the Kerubim are the Angelic types through which control of this cosmos becomes possible for initiates of this Path. Here especially, they deal with emotional angles of our elemental energies, which means our love-hate relations with everything and everyone on Earth. Once these are balanced and set running smoothly on a point of poise within us, life in this world gets so very much easier and better for us all. Only the Kerubim may show us the secrets of this arrangement, and these are obviously well worth learning.

Success or failure in life here depends so much on our emotional balance, and we might remember that one end of this Path connects with Victory while the other ends in just plain Earth where the fallen are buried until they rise and fight again. Furthermore, it is senseless to suppose that all emotions are nasty, dangerous, unpleasant expressions of energy to be strongly suppressed or eliminated from human entities. Feelings are the fuel in our elemental engines which they must either drive properly or explode dangerously. How are we to take humans with all their loves, hates, sensations, sex-instincts, and the rest of their reactive behavior, so as to make sensible and successful living for everyone a practical possibility? This is exactly the problem to be tackled on this Path, and our future depends on its solution. If the Kerubim can help us, then we certainly ought to establish the best of relations with them.

What the Kerubim in fact show us is that emotional energies, like all other types of force, are reducible to basic elements and have natural orders of sequence like the Seasons or any other cyclic phenomena. They also have their spectra like light, or scales like music. The Kerubim have to teach us how to put our forces of feeling into the right order of combination, and keep them turning at the correct cosmic rate. The Elohim now come into the picture and instruct us in the art of setting up our scales and spectra of emotional energy so that we may make harmonious melodies or paint perfect pictures with them. If we like to think of the Kerubim as the rotor of our emotional engine, and the Elohim as its field, while this Path becomes the pivot relating the two, we shall have a sound analogy to work with.

As God-Images, the Elohim present to us along this Path the patterns of emotional perfections we should strive to attain. Everyone must have at least some idea of the being he would like to become as a human of heart and soul, enjoying his empathy with others in a world where all is wonderful and welcome. A world in which we can be friendly and kind to one another without fear of ill-treatment or abuse in return. A world that brings out the best in us and allows us to live "Lightfully." If we were "Gods" or Elohim, this might be easy and natural for us, but being only humans, we must do the best we can with what we have until our spiritual scope widens. This is why we need contact with the Elohim and Kerubim here, in order to learn and practice the secrets of placing our feelings properly so that we may use them to build ourselves in whatever Elohic form we Will, and at the same time benefit other souls in contact with us who are affected by our emotional emanations.

Mankind in general has not yet experienced the higher range of emotional expression and achievement which are above the ordinary scale and spectrum of humanity, That will come with spiritual evolution on this Path. An entirely new world will open up for us in this one, when enough souls have evolved to the point where they can make such a proposition practical. In the meantime, Initiates must continue searching the Path here for those precious secrets. The KERUBIM and ELOHIM might lend us their Keys if we ask them the right way—with real feeling and a Will towards a better World.

Expressively, Venus meets Earth through this Path. Half our heavens and half our hells mixed up. Ever since sex was invented it has muddled Mankind into the most amazing states and situations of soul, largely through inability to control its courses, or recognize its applications outside of copulative activities.

Esoteric tradition is to the effect that human souls were not originally intended to live in animal types of body, and that since our physical progenitors "fell" into the practice of biological reproduction we, their Earthly descendants, have had to pay the price of their sin until we "redeem" ourselves by learning how to live beyond the necessity of incarnation. There is obviously a very great fundamental truth behind this belief, but unless we learn how to live with it successfully, as we should upon this Path, we shall probably come to more harm than good.

One striking difference between Mankind and other entities inhabiting physical bodies on Earth is that their copulative capabilities and inclinations are connected with seasonal and other fertility factors, while ours are irregular, unreliable, and to say the least, extremely irresponsible. Moreover, they are complicated by conflicting codes and compulsions, methods and morals, which have accumulated during our past ages and led to a very great deal of human unhappiness and discord which prevails in our world today. Conversely, the same energy stirring humans into their worst behavior, also provides drive to produce our most wonderful works or best ways of life. The difference between Divine or demoniac behavior here turns on purely personal pivots.

If humans worked by computer, the answer would be simple. Re-programming. Faulty basic patterns removed, and a set-up substituted which would automatically clear up and re-adjust all the rest of the tangle. We might solve the worst of our problems if we could either change our ancestors, or failing that, alter our own natures at the genetic base. The first proposition is obviously impossible, and the second is a very long term policy on which we have already spent several millennia, not entirely without success, though as yet inadequately if we seek to achieve independence from our Earthly evolution. Individually, we may follow Systems of Initiation which lead us to finer living levels with the most efficient evolutionary economies, but no soul dare start breaking up its spiritual structure with impunity, and neither does it help humanity as a whole to start smashing spiritual inheritances, however unsatisfactory these may seem, until something better is available to replace the superseded form of faith. The way of an Initiate is not that of an iconoclast. Old spiritual structures are not carelessly broken or wantonly abandoned, but if possible evolved the whole while with constant care, so that both Inner and Outer states of being keep pace with each other and no undue stress occurs between them on account of basic beliefs. Thus, the initiated followers of the oldest ideologies and spiritual systems known to humanity are always up to date and contemporary with whatever metaphysical conditions prevail among Mankind in general or particular.

At present on Earth, human technology has temporarily gone beyond our spiritual ability to adjust ourselves properly with all the novel and revolutionary changes this has brought about in terms of material living. Our minds may compromise consciously, but our souls need a lot more care and emotional cultivation before they can catch up with and even outstrip the spiritual significance of what is emerging on Earth. As Jung made abundantly clear, when Man is faced with severe spiritual crisis, there is an automatic return to our ancestral roots, and refuge is sought in our Mythological and Magical Traditions where we know instinctively that our basic beliefs began. Moreover, we are absolutely right in such an action, which is not regressive, but restorative and recuperative. The keys to our future lie in the past, but we must look for them in the present, then use them to alter ourselves into the sort of souls who are capable of living in a World which ought to be first built Within us, before being projected in solid shape as a physical phenomenon.

It is certainly the things of Venus which make our World worth living in emotionally if we are able to handle them rightly, and obtain victory over them instead of becoming their slaves. That is what we have to work out on this Path. How to enjoy our physical and spiritual senses in this and other Worlds with full control of our faculties and facilities for such experiences. How to fulfill ourselves as feeling souls with harm to none and happiness to all. This may sound unlikely, but it cannot be impossible *per se*. Probably such ideal conditions will only occur in the close future as they occasionally did in the remote past, for brief intervals, among connected circles of initiated souls, but ultimately the whole of Humanity is bound to benefit thereby.

If there are to be radical changes in human outlooks and behavior in this world (and who doubts this need?) then we must get back to our roots in order to make them, and those roots, as we have seen, may fairly be described as Magical, or basic to the Holy Mysteries of Life. There alone are we likely to learn how to alter our Key-codings so that we become competent to use our sensations and feelings in accordance with the standard required from us as responsible Companions of Cosmos. This will not be suppressive in the least, but will certainly be the most selective ever known on Earth. Therein lies the clue to future conventions and moral measures likely to prevail on this planet. Providing injury, injustice, or malicious damage is avoided, people will probably be permitted considerable liberty of conscience and action in the fields of sexual or other extensions of sensation. Nevertheless, out of all those souls, only those developing an ability to direct the energies of these activities into the finest spiritual channels will be selected into more exalted Cosmic Circles. This is the only practical way in which souls are likely to sort themselves into their Inner categories in the shortest and surest way.

Much must happen in this world which bygone moralists would have condemned outright because they would never have grasped the causes of circumstances leading into such unexpected changes of human character. There will emerge out of apparent confusion and indecision an entirely altered "inlook" concerning sex and religion, two major factors affecting our evolution through our feelings connecting with deepest levels of life. From many varied and perhaps peculiar stages of experiment, will come into our world a strange new sense of respect for and responsibility toward spiritual and sexual subjects. They will be extended into practical applications undreamed of previously except by advanced Initiates. The overall trend will lead toward all that is really lovely and worthwhile on this Path where Earth and Venus celebrate their united victory together.

There are only these three main streams of spiritual procedures linking our Earth-world with Inner Life: Hermetic, Mystic, and Orphic. In the Tree-Glyph they are shown as being straight, leading directly from this world to their respective Spheres, and this is the ideal way they should be. Once we were told "make straight the Paths," and that is precisely what we must accomplish throughout the Tree of Life. Here in particular, we have much to do in order to straighten and clear the tangled mess we have made of our Orphic Paths, but until this is done, we shall neither hear the music of the Spheres properly nor enjoy the vision of Venus without becoming blind like Eros. Clear Inner sight and hearing will come through this Path only to those who feel their way along it first, grasping its principles and practice with capable hands. Then we shall find good solid sense at last to whatever we will experience with our emotions for the sake of leading our souls to an immortal identity in Eternal Light.

The Thirtieth Path

SPHERE—LETTER CODE: Glory 8 Y 9 Foundation
DIVINE ORIGINATION: ELOHIM SABAOTh—   Thc
                           SHADDAI el CHAIIM Instigator
ARCHANGELIC CREATION: Raphael—Gabriel   Science
ANGELIC FORMATION: Beni-Elohim—Ashim   System
APPARENT EXPRESSION: Mercury—Moon   Precipitation
TAROT SYMBOL: MAGICIAN

This Thirtieth Path is Hermetic and intellectual, characterizing Mind as distinct from Soul, though neither Mind nor Soul should be considered as alien concepts in relation to each other. Here, Glory and Foundation are linked together as Principles. Our Foundation in this case is the basic collection of all our beliefs and ideas concerning Life, while our Glory is that we make use of these in reasoned and rational chains of consciousness so as to relate ourselves to life by means of Mind.

Here, in particular, we have science and system combining to produce a precipitation of commonsense out of the entire conglomeration of subconscious information and unclassified items of intelligence stored away in the stockrooms of both individual and collective awareness. Every experience in our existence is indeed filed away somewhere on Cosmic computer tapes, but this would be useless without the skilled operative knowing how to set and select these in order to come up with the needed answers, or perhaps suggestions on how to present questions in such a way that they will evoke whatever reply is required.

On this Path, imagination is converted into intellectual ideas and trains of thought. Fancy and fantasies become focused and factual, making the mental material from which we build our most remarkable Inner and Outer Cosmic constructions. It may not be sufficiently appreciated by many people that our advanced and apparently adult thinking is only possible by extending our consciousness skillfully from the fantasy-foundations created in us as children and inherited along our Inner Lines of Light. That is why myths and fairy-tales are so important. They contain every possible basic idea out of which we may grow into mental and spiritual adulthood AS WE WILL. Feed them rightly into a child's consciousness, and they will not only unlock all the knowledge from previous lives and make links with genetic information, but will also provide the best possible means for projecting both Intention and Ideation into the future in order to bring the best of Life into being, or in the words of fairy tales: "Make it come true."

This is just the Path for making things come true not only in, but with, our minds. There is an old Chinese proverb that wisely says whatever a human mind can think of must necessarily be possible for the thinker at some point of Existence. It does not mean that all we think about will actually materialize here on Earth, but it implies that we cannot bring anything into material manifestation unless we do sufficient and properly processed thinking about it. Strange to say, thinking is not a natural propensity of humans at all, but an acquired art, and an evolutionary development which has only become possible for us through the influence of Inner intelligences in contact with our consciousness on very deep levels of living indeed. Perhaps this sounds very magical and mysterious, which is possibly why the Tarot Symbol of the Magician is so apt here.

The Magician is depicted in the Waite pack not as the market-place mountebank of the Marseilles Tarot, but a veritable Magus of the Mysteries in operation. We see this Figure proclaiming an Intention of Will in a magical Garden which has no background except Golden Light. Since a Magician is a transformation or conversion Symbol, this indicates the Magus is actually converting or "thinking up" the foreground details out of the Light representing a state of pure consciousness behind every thing.

Throughout all traditions of Magic, a Magus is regarded as a Changer of some description, or one who intervenes for specific reasons in a situation, and alters it by unusual means into something different. The method of effecting such changes is what constitutes the Magic, because a Magician employs energies and methods beyond the scope of average individuals. He is a skilled specialist in the art of altering effects by influencing their causes, and since the causes of our external Life-effects lie deep within Inner circles of consciousness, those are the Magic Circles in which true Magicians must operate. Ordinary people tackle externalities of awareness with other externalities of their own, but a Magician probes and penetrates right down to causal levels of consciousness seeking for sensitive points at which to make the relatively small adjustments which will reprogram that particular issue from thenceforth. That is the kind of Magic the Tarot Symbol refers to here.

The entire framework of the picture is a floral motif. Flowers are shown hanging from Heaven and growing from Earth. No fruit or vegetables, but only flowers in full bloom, and only two species of flower—roses and lilies. The Heavenly flowers are red roses alone, two garlands of five each, but the Earth-flowers are represented by five red roses, four white lilies, and one golden flower at top center. This arrangement should tell us quite a lot.

Red roses are expressive of passionate devotion and also the sacrifice of life-blood in whatever cause we devote our lives to. They are the legendary bloom mentioned by Apuleius which had to be eaten by asinine humans in order to liberate them from their stupidity. They typify the "Perfect Purpose," and its reflection in our human purposes of striving to perfect ourselves. Red is the Rose of the Cross which holds in its calyx the Divine dew (ros) or essential distillation of Divinity within every truly devoted heart. The ten red Heavenly roses here symbolize the sacrifices needed to enter every Sphere on the Tree of Life, and the Garland of Glory due to all who partake of this privilege. Be it noted that a Crown of Roses is also a Crown of Thorns, for we cannot achieve very much Glory without some degree of suffering in the process.

The Earthly flowers are the red roses of passion and white lilies of purity, both these Principles being linked with the Pillars between which our Life experience extends crosswise. There are five red roses to represent our physical senses, and four white lilies standing for our spiritual scruples of Dedication, Devotion, Duty, and Discretion which should control our senses within safe limits of tolerance. In the center of these and higher than them all, is a Golden Flower of perfection. This is the Magical Work on which the Magician is engaged. Raising the finest possible flow-

ers in the Inner Garden where consciousness is cultivated. That
is to say, thinking the best thoughts, evolving the noblest ideas,
bringing awareness to an acme of perfection in terms of mental
achievement. Such is the Magic of Mind we should concern ourselves with here.

It should be particularly observed that the accent and emphasis throughout this whole Symbol is upon the theme of cultivation by art. There are no "natural" or wild flowers shown, nor
for that matter anything except one item that is not an artifact of
some kind. Roses and lilies are carefully cultivated flowers, needing horticultural ability to produce. This indicates that our task
on the Path should be the training and cultivation of our
thoughts from a "wild" state of growth into conditions of splendor
and perfection fit for consideration by our spiritual superiors in
Cosmic Inner Consciousness. Roses and lilies on Earth produce a
perfume that attracts the best side of our natures, and induces in
us a state of amiability and admiration. So should our comparable cultivated thoughts produce an equivalent Inner fragrance
which will attract the attention of Otherworld entities who are
likely to enjoy our company and bestow on us the benefits of contact with their specialized consciousness. All this is Magic of the
most wonderful kind, yet we can practice it for ourselves in our
own Inner Gardens just like the Magician in the picture.

The Mage in person is shown in simple traditional robes of
the Magical Mysteries. A white inner gown signifies purity of intention and dedication to Light as being the underlying motive
for all Magic practiced by whomever wears it. Normally a girdle
cord would secure this gown centrally, but here there is a snake-
belt with the head of the serpent pointing to the right of the Magician, which symbolizes his standpoint within the Eternal Cosmic
Circle of Light and Right. Perhaps the old phrase "Heart-girt-
with-a-serpent is my Name" occurs to our minds at this point. At
all events, we must certainly be compassed by the Serpent of Wisdom when engaged in or contemplating any operation of Magic.

Over the inner gown, our Magician wears a red robe of con-
cealment. This represents his entire Life-blood dedicated to Divinity, and the Inner mystical "Blood-link" with that branch of
the "Faith-family" to which he belongs. It is the burden of responsibility toward his whole lineage of Light which he must bear on
his shoulders, and a reminder that failure to uphold Inner ances-

tral honor with sufficient devotion must be paid for in his blood. As a rule, an ordinary practicing magician would have an outer robe of a much more purple shade to temper Blood with Beneficence, but here we seem to have a Magician Figure well aware of every risk ran, and prepared to pay every penalty incurred. Let this remind those hoping for rich magical rewards that payment for debts on this Path is often demanded at most inconvenient moments with inescapable insistence.

Another, and less-known, reason for the red-over-white order of robing here is because this inverses the In-Out nature of appearances, allowing us to objectify what is normally beyond our immediate reach in the realms of subconsciousness where Magic must be worked. Looked at with ordinary sight, we are beings with white skins on our outsides, while behind and within this is our red life-blood. Consciously we know the skin is there, and subconsciously we realize the blood must be somewhere at the back of appearances. To alter our Outwardness, we must first change our Inwardness, and this applies metaphorically even more than materially. So to wear a red robe externally signifies bringing our Inner Life-intentions to Light objectively and making these manifest through the art of Magic. We "turn ourselves round" so to speak, and interchange Life-laws between Inner and Outer living. This is the unusual method of activity by which Magic operates.

The Magus holds a right arm up to Heaven, clutching a white rod at center with the closed grip indicating firm resolution and tenacity of purpose. The left arm angles at ninety degrees to this, the hand extended with the last three fingers closed, index finger pointing directly at the Earth. This entire attitude says, "As above—so below," or "Thy Will be done on Earth as it is in Heaven." Divinity and humanity must meet and relate themselves in the Magus, for that is the secret nature of the Operation depicted in progress here. So much is made plain by the Eternity symbol of "Truth-twist" shown over the Magician's head. To get some idea of how this applies, an endless loop of cord will illustrate the process. If opposite parts of the loop are grasped by each hand, or by two people facing each other, then both parties wind their portions of cord in the same direction relative to themselves. The cord will twist up tightly into a state of tension which amounts to potential energy capable of driving whatever it becomes connected with. Children do this with rubber bands and matchsticks frequently. If this simple physical formula is translated into Inner terms of energy, it will explain many of the Magician's secrets. In Magic, our thoughts literally have to "turn into" things, with the accent on "turn." We have to learn how to "twist" our thinking into Cosmic courses of consciousness so that we rotate (or "Tarote") our thoughts in partnership with Inner intelligence and thereby wind up the energy for making Magic with our minds. In this way we truly "wring the last drop" of essential information out of Inner matters, and set the tension ready for the swing-back which accomplishes the mental mission intended. There are other methods of consciousness-conversion, but this torsion-technique is a useful one to associate with the Magician here.

The white rod in the Magician's grip signifies purity of intention and single-mindedness, two indispensible attitudes of mind for any worthwhile Magical Operation. The way in which the right hand grips it indicates that we should hold the Middle or mean position between Earth and Heaven, upholding our beliefs in God and Man alike. The single index finger of the left hand pointing to Earth means that we must know exactly where we stand relative to the rest of humanity, and precisely what our purpose is in making Magic. We must be able to "put our finger" unerringly on the point of all we do in our Magical work. Only when our magical standpoint is completely clear to us may we expect any success in the art.

When we look at the face of the Magician, we find the features of Eternal Youth set in a slightly serious expression due to calm concentration of Inner attention. The hair is dark, yet bound with a circlet of white, signifying clear circlets of consciousness around all dark areas of the mind, thus limiting them by means of Cosmic enlightenment. Closer observation reveals the hair is differently cut on each side, and again the unobtrusive androgynous character of these Figures becomes apparent. The right side of the Magician is male and the left side female. The left hand is rather more feminine than masculine, and the left inner sleeve is yellow instead of white. Then, too, we must remember that the magical Image of Hod, Sphere of Glory, is an Hermaphrodite. All these details provide us with clues and data for use when building up a Magical personality, and working along this Path.

Before leaving the Magician to consider the remainder of the Symbol, it might be noted in passing that there are indications of an apron being worn, of which no specific design is evident. The apron is associated with Hermeticism and is the receptacle for whatever secrets may be written. Since an apron covers the genital area, we may assume those secrets to be "written into" our genes, and through Hermetic practices we have hopes of interpreting them.

Level with the Magician's genetic point is the corner of a square table which the Magician is circumambulating. In its center is the Cup of the Mysteries above which is poised the Rod in the Magician's right hand. The connection of Rod into Cup is sex-symbology which here means the conception of fresh ideas and "mind-children" born of intercourse between Heavenly and Earthly intellects. On the table with the Cup lie a Sword, Shield, and Staff. The point of the Sword is covered by the Shield, to show that a good Magician protects himself against occupational injuries, and also that a Shield ought to be taken up first, before employing the Sword for any purpose. On the Shield is the Pentagram, or Sign of Man, with its points away from the Magus to repel evil.

Furthest from the Magician on the table is a Staff, which is quite distinct from a Rod. This particular Staff is of the "blossoming" kind, which grows Magically when planted in the right sort of Garden. There is one tiny shoot just emerging, and we assume the whole Staff has been detached from the Tree of Life itself. All kinds of legends exist around the "burgeoning staffs," and in general they point to propagation of Life by other methods than sexual congress. Do we read here a hint of extending Life Magically into other Dimensions by such means translated into metaphysical terms? If so, the Magician seems to know the secret, and we may seek to discover it on this Path.

The table surface signifies our "working level" of consciousness forming the middle distance of our minds in relation to which we extend our thinking either above or below this Magical mean. All the Magician's work here is strictly above board, though it is *sub rosa*, as the roseate garlands testify. Masons might note that the Magic shown in this Symbol is planely presented on the square. Others should translate this as meaning the Magical Operation to be one of absolute honesty compatible with the clearest conscience. Around the edge of the table are hieroglyphics, while its surface is blank. This tells us to read the edges of our conscious working areas while we feel our way round them, keeping a clear field within for projection of whatever patterns we shall make with our information by mental Magic. That the table is square rather than round, shows we must corner our consciousness here by means of art, reaching the conical Cup from all angles. A square also declares the Fourfold basis, or Foundation on which the Qabalistic System is set up.

These past considerations are only some of the obvious ideas indicated by the remarkable Symbol of this Path. The more they are meditated on and mediated into living actualities, the more Magical they will become for Initiates. Now we should see what the other parts of the Path have to tell us in their own ways.

Originatively, we meet the Divine Aspects of ELOHIM SABAOTh and SHADDAI el CHAIIM. The Divinities we would be, and the Lord of Lives. Between them, we come to terms with the fundamental aspects of Life as a whole, and from this basis begin to individualize ourselves into the sort of beings we think we should eventually become.

With the Lord of Lives, we are units of Life just as our blood cells are units of our lesser lives. With the Gods of Everyone, we join in with the general ideas of what everybody thinks he ought to be if he were God, and make our own Magical marks along this line. Out of all that happens to us in Life, we think ourselves whatever Likeness of God we choose to resemble. From the Foundation of our Inner beliefs and experiences, we Glorify ourselves towards our God-becoming by this Path. It can be a truly dangerous process which has damaged or destroyed many minds, and yet we must all make the venture for ourselves if we are ever to become emancipated entities living in Light for the Right Reasons. Since it takes a mental Magician to achieve spiritual stability on this Path, the Tarot Symbol was well chosen.

We instinctively seek Glory of some kind, and ambitions in this direction have probably ruined more lives than could be guessed at. Why? Mainly because of inadequate Foundation and lack of skilled mental balance, coupled with inability to use imaginative concepts clearly and constructively. Nothing blinds

Inner vision on this Path quite so effectively as our own chances of Glory going up in flames of fanaticism or folly. On the other hand, unless the incentive of Glory induced humans to branch out for themselves toward the higher levels of Tree-Life, we should remain very stick-in-the-mud creatures of Earth altogether so far as mental enterprises are concerned. Our problem on this Path is how to gain a fair measure of Glory, yet remain reasonable, rational beings.

Our first necessity in this direction is obviously a solid Foundation or basis from which to build up our mental projections along the Path. This originates with the Lord of Lives in whom our genetic patterning begins. In each incarnation, these factors of heredity, ancestral characteristics, and individual intelligence quotas are fixed at birth, and have an inherent rate of growth or development, and we cannot exceed or make unnatural demands of them without serious risk to our sanity and reason. The personal potentials we are born with are our total capital credits of consciousness for a lifetime. We may augment or extend these according to circumstances, but we are all limited in living by our particular capabilities of consciousness which carry with us into incarnation. The vast majority of humans do not organize or use more than a fraction of these, but many are pushed beyond or away from their margins of mental safety, and trouble occurs all around them. Keeping mental balance in this world of ours is presenting more and more of a problem and this is the Path on which we must find our individual and collective answers.

Every mind has its own capacity and its safety-strain factor. Attempts or compulsions to exceed or depart from this are bound to cause insanity. Minds will take just so much along various lines, and after their limits of tolerance are reached will become unstable and unreliable, like any mechanism put to wrong use or overloaded. Finding this essential factor and applying it properly is a major task here. This is where accurate and competent astrology can be of enormous help, for if the inherent birth-potentials at the SHADDAI el CHAIIM end of the Path are realized, the safety degrees for seeking glorification at ELOHIM SABAOTh can be calculated very reasonably. Providing such information or advice is acted on, level mental living becomes a more practical proposition.

We may suppose as we live that we are improving so marvellously in our minds, but what we are really doing is developing our original potential as a plant grows out of a seed. The possibilities were there to start with, and if the right advantage is taken of favorable environments and stimuli, the rest follows. Yet no matter how favorable our chances are all round us, we must always draw the secret supply of evolutionary energy right up from our deepest roots to whatever level on which our Golden Flower of consciousness may be blooming. As we discover, no matter how we prefer to disguise the fact, the roots of Mankind are best reached by means of what are usually called Myth and Magic. This is true both mentally and mystically. Through our myths, we may reach right back to the "Life before our lives," or the body of collective consciousness behind our embodied beings connecting us to Cosmos, or the "Universal Mind." Through our Magic, we mentally manipulate and "call up" the underlying energies of this unseen Universe which enable us to grow toward the glory of a truly enlightened intelligence. That is how we become more advanced with each life and commence every fresh cycle or incarnation with increased potentials. Be it very clearly understood, however, that each one of us is responsible for reaching his own individual roots and keeping the channels clear from thence through the remainder of our mental and spiritual systems.

We cannot cut outselves away from, or inhibit, contacts with our mental roots connected with our causes, and expect to remain sane and soundly balanced beings. Moreover, these vital roots do not directly connect with our ordinary mental expressions and the stimuli experienced in this world at all. Those are effects, not causes. Our thinking arises from our deepest foundations which lie with the Lord of Lives beginning every birth. Once we realize what this profundity amounts to, and put it into Magical practice along this Path, mental health and happiness come closer to all seekers of this secret.

The combination of Divine Aspects here may be thought of as the Instigator, because we are impelled thereby to investigate Life with intelligence and make rational meanings out of things to satisfy our standards of reason. We do this for the sheer sake of Glory experienced because of what we have accomplished, and the changed conditions of consciousness we undergo on this account. Unless thinking brought us some kind of Glory we should make no real advances of awareness in any direction mentally. At the Glory end of this Path ELOHIM SABAOTh shows us unmistakably what our thinking ought to do for us in Divine ways. ELOHIM SABAOTh is the incentive actuating our minds to perform their proper part in the Holy Mysteries of Light-Life. Only when we are able to follow the conscious connection between our Life Foundation basis with SHADDAI el CHAIIM, and the Glory of being a living intelligent thinking entity with ELOHIM SABAOTh shall we hold the Keys of this Path properly. At least knowing whom to ask for these is a useful step toward their personal possession.

Creatively, Archangels RAPHAEL and GABRIEL control the Path, mainly through their instructive and informative aspects. Raphael, Archangel of Air, is a teacher and healer. His Symbol is the Sword. A Sword is symbolic of a keen mind and intellect, sharp, to the point, polished, flexible, and maneuverable at any speed in any direction by its wielder. It can also hurt and cause injuries. What human being has not been hurt to some degree by mental activities while engaged in learning how to live by means of mind? We might remember that the human mind has now arrived at the solution of ethnic extermination on this planet, and few are likely to survive that degree of injury.

What is hurtable is healable one way or another. Raphael exists to teach us methods of healing and repairing whatever harm we cause with our minds if regeneration is possible. He is the archangel of recuperation. Should injuries be too serious for this process to be practical, then Gabriel must take over after regeneration is complete, and at the conclusion of the death-cycle, re-issue the reconstituted subject into objective living again. Gabriel is the archangel of resurrection. Between them, they get us through the life-death-life cycles of our evolution so that we may learn as we live until we are able to follow along these lifelines on our own initiative. The whole object of this Cosmic operation is to produce individuation of entity to degrees of Consciousness which we might consider Divine, because it becomes capable of auto-intentional existence, or being As It Wills.

Gabriel has been called the "Messenger of God" insofar as he is supposed to relay Divine instructions or orders to human beings. The importance of Gabriel is that he represents the connection between our ordinary state of awareness and all the consciousness behind and leading up to our individual lives. The "Horn of Gabriel," apart from being phallic, signifies the channel connecting us throughout life-roots with the essential supplies of energy we need to increase and improve our individuation process through linking and intelligence. Raphael tells us what to do with these energies once we have surfaced them successfully, but it is Gabriel who keeps us in touch with the deep-down reservoirs of concealed consciousness from which we draw whatever mental conclusions we are likely to reach in any lifetime. Gabriel's Symbol, the Cup of Consciousness, is a well chosen one.

Again we are back to the question of basic roots and foundations of being. What are they, where are they, and how do we reach them? Only Gabriel answers those vital issues on this Path. Whatever these basic factors are, they may be traced back to our birth-conditions before we lose direct sight of them behind our incarnate identities. All of us have our particular familial, ethnical, racial, cultural, and even more selective branches of being to which we fundamentally belong as entities. To reject or deny our inherited connections with Inner Cosmos is to repudiate Life itself and seek suicide on a spiritual scale. Our task as living beings is to perfect our own species along with individual lines of Light-life so that we become fit and worthy Companions of Cosmos. Therefore we must learn how to receive the messages Gabriel delivers to us through our direct line to Divinity connecting bia the roots springing from our sources of Life as conscious and rational creatures. Willful ignorance of, or refusal to accept, Gabriel's Inner instructions only leads to unbalance or insanity of mind from slight to severe degrees.

Once we have made satisfactory arrangements with Gabriel for our fundamental intake of intelligence from basic courses of supply, we must then reach a corresponding agreement with Raphael as to how we should make use of this mental material. It is natural that everyone should want to make the most of himself because of what he thinks, and this is the Glory which Raphael should reveal to us. Our part of the bargain is that we must remain within the rules of Reason if we are ever to gain such Glory in reality, and not come to grief through insane and unbalanced behavior while in pusuit of it. We ought to remember that Raphael's Element is Air, and we must learn to swim before we can fly. Provided that we take the precaution of not seeking more from Raphael than we can equate by our provisions from Gabriel, or accepting from Gabriel anything we cannot reason out with Raphael's aid, we shall achieve the Glory of an Initiated Intelligence on this Path.

Between the two Archangels, we have to learn the science of thinking, or how to arrange our mental make-up into satisfactory presentations of personal power and constructions of consciousness. Despite the publications and promises made by ambitious authors, thought-science is something we must all learn for ourselves from Inner instructions. Other people's ideas and notions may be helpful in suggesting courses of action or giving encouragement, but until we discover how to make our own minds operate according to our inherent capabilities of consciousness, we shall never be thinkers in the true sense of the word, and that is exactly what we must become upon this Path.

To maintain our balance of reason and mental stability while exploiting the possibilities of the Path to their full, we have to remain in close contact with Raphael and Gabriel together. No other way will work the Magic of Mind for us properly. We dare not turn our backs on either Archangel, but must walk between them toward wisdom. If we listen and learn, they will teach us the science of thinking, and that is a magic the whole of mankind would be better for practicing. With RAPHAEL on one hand and GABRIEL on the other, Temples made by mind will open to those who ask their mentors for the Keys.

Formatively, the Path is administered by the Angel Orders of the BENI-ELOHIM and the ASHIM. They are the "Children of Gods" and the "Family-founders." Once more we are firmly presented with a picture of sound structural foundations and the best ideas of what should arise from such a basis by thinking along such lines. There can scarcely be a clearer connection. Our program of the Path says here most plainly, "Consider what you came from. From thence project a reasonable focus ahead, make a mental link between the two concepts, and follow this faithfully." Easy to say, undeniably difficult to do, but essential to attempt. Whether we achieve our aims in any one lifetime or not, it is much more important that we should set up Inner systems having these aims in clear view. Initiates of this Path realize well enough that it may take several incarnations to establish systematic channels of consciousness resulting in mental ability to

make the type of Mind-Magic they intend to work with. Furthermore, they regard all the time and effort devoted to this project
very well spent indeed. If we even reach such a realization on this
Path during a lifetime, that particular incarnation will have been
justified for this single point alone.

There used to be an old quip that the only guarantee of a
good life was to be born into the right sort of family, and there is
more truth in this than might be supposed. How does any individual human arrive on Earth except through some kind of an ancestral line leading to reproductive activities at Earth level? According to the category of entity, so will be their available incarnatory
opportunities. As human entities develop themselves along their
own Inner lines, they tend to become increasingly selective about
conditions of embodiment. There may be many reasons why advanced individuals accepted incarnation into very difficult or
dangerous conditions. They may have needed certain experiences or volunteered for specific services, or simply returned because they felt a call of love or duty. It is almost a *sine qua non*
that such people have a high order of intelligence and mental
ability, so they need suitable lines of heredity and genetics leading up to individual human incarnation. These may not emerge
into wealthy, powerful, or influential circles at all, but the Angelic agencies responsible for arranging suitable birth-conditions
for those of enough mental development to request these for
themselves with sufficient reason are the Ashim. The thinking of
entities undergoing this process is characterized by the type of
Beni-Elohim involved.

We are, at any given moment, the mental mediators of all we
have thought ourselves from, and whatever we are thinking ourselves into. If we consider those factors to be formatively represented by concepts termed the Ashim and the Beni-Elohim, there
seems no reason why this should not be a satisfactory system of
thinking. Angel-agencies are a perfectly valid proposition if we
are prepared to forgo the harp-nightshirt-and-wings notion.
Since we are concerned here with making the most of our minds
during our lives in any condition of consciousness, it is natural we
should seek relative terms with our mental extensions each side
of our living focus.

The ultimate aim of Mind, so far as we are concerned, is discovering how to live successfully beyond necessity of embodi-

ment. Before this becomes practical to other than highly advanced human intelligences, we shall have to cope with our incarnatory problems with the aid of the Ashim and Beni-Elohim along this Path, keeping in balance between them as best we may. In early times, humans were kept in touch with their antecedents by family histories and legends or tribal tales and traditions. Their possibilities were opened up to them by personalized projections of ideas into mind-moving stories of super beings and suggestion-sagas of future fulfilments of Will. Just what have we available today to replace motivations linked so deeply with our Life-basis and all we become therefrom? If humans repudiate their ancestry, and refuse to consider continuity of identity outside of incarnation, what have they to live for worth thinking about? Luckily for most mortals, we have an inbuilt instinct which advises us not to abandon our Inner inheritances along these lines too hastily, even if circumstances call for cautious and circumspect external behavior. We cannot sensibly afford to ignore what the Ashim and Beni-Elohim are trying to tell each one of us deep down in our minds.

It may be as well to ask ourselves quite plainly where our best personal interests lie as intelligent entities. Are we really content to accept that we have just one isolated incarnation during which we must grab what we can before we become extinct? Is anyone of advanced mental ability convinced beyond doubt that such is the inevitable destiny of all mortals? Why should anyone submit to such mental and spiritual suicide unless he genuinely intended to utterly disintegrate his identity? What would motivate him in such a direction? All these are key-questions to be meditated upon this path.

Conversely we must consider our possibilitities of aligning ourselves with energies of Mind that exist independently of incarnation, even if associated with incarnate awareness. We should remember that what humans think about for long enough and with Will enough, eventually comes true for them once they discover systems for making their mentalizations manifest. Man in general has certainly been thinking about intelligent existence apart from mortal embodiment for a very long time, so this can scarcely be an impossible attainment for us, even though our systems of achievement are very far from perfection or practicability. For those who affirm and adhere to the principles of identification with Mind as a way of Life through its own energies, this method of personalized power-projecting must sooner or later become a normal and even average system of living.

When we think of all the previous impossibilities for humanity which have been realized in the last few decades because of systematic mental activities geared to available materials, any Mind-project of ours is obviously only a question of sustained application. Within living memory, the fantasy of man on the Moon was a fond fiction of intelligent imaginations only. Now, as these very words are being written on paper, men are actually living and working with their minds on their way to that identical Luminary. Perhaps their most glorious achievement of all is the undeniable proving of Man's mental capabilities when systematically and collectively concentrated along imaginative lines. Just as Man is learning to live independently of Earth, so shall we also learn the magic art of living otherwise then by association with animal bodies. The system toward this objective we must learn here with the ASHIM and BENI-ELOHIM, is simply that of maintaining sound mental relationships between our Life-roots and the force-formations toward which we are projecting our growth as intelligent entities. If we ask these Angel-agencies for the necessary Keys, they are constitutionally bound to offer them.

Expressively, Hermes and Luna govern the Path. Hermes is the Master Magician, and special mentor or "Mind guider" of Mankind, while Luna represents the "Magic Minor" of Life wherein every reflection passing through our minds comes to light, and from whence rays of otherwise insupportable brilliance are re-directed with modified intensity into our receptive consciousness. Together they precipitate the workings of our minds into recognizable channels of activity.

Hermes is certainly a Master of Mind-maneuvers, and the acknowledged patron of inspired thinking. His job here is to help us make sense and reason out of all the vital mental material condensed at Lunar level into relatively safe reservoirs of consciousness which would otherwise prove too confusing for rational minds to deal with. We should remember the old Lunar symbols of the Maze in which we become lost without clues of leadership, and the Thorn-bush, with which we get entangled and torn when we try to free ourselves from its clutches. These are important to those following this Path.

The absolute Light of all revealing Truth would be fatal to human minds in their present state of evolution. Our surest and safest way toward increasing Illumination is by the reflected Inner rays of Lunar Light which become brighter and brighter by tolerable degrees until our Inner sight is strong enough to stand Solar radiation for brief periods which will gradually lengthen as our Inner lives mature on higher mental levels. On this Path, Hermes is the mediator who guides our minds between moonlight and sunlight, but makes sure that we are capable of directing our thoughts through the Moonmaze first, and keeping clear of thorny problems afterwards.

As a mental Luminary, Luna consists of an incredible miscellany of mind-matters from all kinds of sources. These are reflections, representations, Symbols, and suggestions of Inner actualities which our consciousness cannot cope with in their Solar states of being. Such Moon-modifications, however, are very mixed and muddled from a rational mental viewpoint. From our angles of awareness they appear unclassified and uncategorical. They are not unlike all the letters of the alphabet shaken together and dropped in a heap. Every letter would be there for anyone to write all the books in the world with, providing they were sorted into sense, and the rules of writing realized. So things are relatively with Luna. This seems so confusing to unaccustomed Inner explorers, they sometimes think of it as the "Lower astral," and imagine it may be avoided or ignored, which is not quite the case at all. On this Path we must learn how to conduct ourselves clearly through these tangles, and here Hermes will assist us, because he guides minds as well as souls.

The Maze-matters of the Moon come from everywhere. Ancestral memories, idea-images concerned with everything, wishful thinkings, fears, baneful and beautiful beliefs, every variety of imaginable mental impressions, fearful or fascinating by turn. We might wander forever among these bewildering byways for the sheer sake of their strangeness and the curiosity they arouse, but this would not be recommended by any rule of reason. Hermes tells us sensibly, "Your thought-needs are in there somewhere. Go in and get them while I guide you, but leave everything else alone except what you enter for, then return with your findings so that we may deal with them in more suitable surroundings." Perhaps we are reminded here of the Magician's instructions to Aladdin outside the Treasure cave. He was supposed to enter, touch nothing except the Lamp, take this alone, and return without loitering. The same rules apply when we enter the Treasure Cave of accumulated consciousness on the Moon of Mental Magic. At least Hermes is a helpful Magician if we continue to follow his clues.

If we allow ourselves to drift aimlessly around the confusing corridors of Lunar consciousness with no intentional control over our course, we run the risk of delusional insanity. Again, if we only play with our fantasies in Lunar areas of awareness for the sake of idle indulgence or some ill intention, our mental stability will be deranged to some degree. Yet our fantasies are the very materials from which our finest and soundest mental conceptions are constructed. We need them like a builder needs sand and cement, but those would be useless if builders just threw water on them and tramped around in the mess until it set solid. Our task on this Path is to confine our fantasies in the Lunar levels of our lives, then enter these as freely as we will and use what material we choose, providing our purposes and decisions connect with higher realms of reason indicated by Hermetic mediation. We should also avoid thorny issues of unnecessary entanglements such as useless arguments and controversies which do nothing to clarify consciousness and only add to the normally confused Inner Lunar landscape.

By and large, the Lunar Sphere of awareness is the realm reached through dreams and drugs by minds unable to make clear and reasonable conclusions with that type of consciousness, and so they sustain even more mental damage by their excursions. The only reasonable way to make mental Magic out of Lunar Mind-matter is by this Hermetic Path of precipitation. We should neither lose our wits in Lunar conditions of consciousness, nor permit ourselves to be isolated into pure Hermetic intellectualism, remarkable as this may appear to the insufficiently initiated. Either event leads to mental unbalance, and as this is essentially the Path of Reason on all Life-levels, it is therefore necessary to keep ourselves in sound states of Mind so that we stay poised between its extremities.

Hermes carries many clues among his Symbols. His caduceus suggests that if we are seeking mental fertility of ideas, we should extend the pine-cone point into the realm we intend to reach, such as Luna, then swiftly obtain what we will by means of the direct return center-staff through alternating serpentine coils of consciousness on either side. This system brings what we seek to hand. In a way, the caduceus is our computer card which selects and delivers what our reason requires. If we can make our minds work in the same way as a caduceus, we shall become true Initiates of Hermes. He will show us the secrets of successful mental life enriched from Lunar supplies, and Luna will modify our mentality so that our minds remain human rather than mechanistic in operation. They hold these major Keys between them, and we have every right to earn them also on this Path.

The Thirty-first Path

SPHERE—LETTER CODE:	Glory 8 Z 10 Kingdom	
DIVINE ORIGINATION:	ELOHIM SABAOTh—	The
	ADONAI ha ARETZ	Hearer
ARCHANGELIC CREATION:	Raphael—Sandalphon	Innocence
ANGELIC FORMATION:	Beni-Elohim—Kerubim	Amenability
APPARENT EXPRESSION:	Mercury—Earth	Plasticity
TAROT SYMBOL:	FOOL	

Here, Mind meets Matter as we recognize both Principles on Earth. Divinity discovers what Life is like when observed through the limited and fallible consciousness of Humanity, and Man thinks how wonderful it would be if only he were a God. It is a novel experience for both parties, whether or not they are objectively aware of each other.

On this last point, we must be very careful to distinguish between Ignorance and Innocence. Strictly speaking, these are attitudes of Mind toward Existence. Ignorance signifies a deliberate state of unwillingness to learn. A refusal to make realizations for any particular reason. That reason may be good, bad, or indifferent, but Ignorance means to ignore by intention. Innocence is a condition of uninvolvement, or a consciousness entirely clear from direct contact with whatever might obscure or contaminate such clarity. It depends entirely how the principle of Will is employed. We may be wisely ignorant or foolishly innocent. An idiot is innocent. So is an Avatar. We may be innocent in some areas and ignorant in others. Wise fools and stupid sages. This is the Path where we must sort ourselves out mentally and come to terms with our thinking along its lines.

Our thinking ability, and the use we make of it, has a great deal to do with our lives in this world. What we work with our wits determines at least half of our living. In order to develop a good intelligence, our minds have to be amenable and open to reason, possessing sufficient degrees of plasticity for molding into whatever mental shape may be necessary for coping successfully with any perplexing problem we may meet on Earth. We need the adaptability of Hermes, coupled with every mental resource available to Earthly humans, in order to live here at all sometimes! Here is the Path whereon we must learn how to organize our mental faculties around the issue of remaining relatively reasonable and sane creatures on this mundane level of living Cosmos. Only a fool, or someone quite innocent of Earthly experience, is likely to believe that living on Earth is an easy matter. On the other hand, without such carefree confidence, what intelligent being would willingly attempt living here in the first place?

This is probably why the Tarot Symbol of the Fool, or Innocent, is so apt here. We are the fools or innocents who rush into this world where angels fear to tread. Our heads get full of nonsense and idiotic ideas concerning life and everything to do with it, and so we make every mistake possible to possessors of even the most feeble wits. Sooner or later we learn better because we have lived here, or we are silly enough to muddle our mental affairs so badly that we must return in search of our lost reason. Only when we discover how to transmute Ignorance into Innocence, by the process of Experience, shall we become free from the necessity of human incarnation. This is what used to be called the "redemption" of Man, or regaining our condition of Primal purity. Such purity had nothing to do with sexual connotations, but meant a state of unmixed being or, as a chemist would say, a pure isolated element. To regain purity of Mind means that it should be operative in its own state, unmixed with Matter. The same applies to the Principles of Soul and Spirit. On this Path, we should learn the secret of Mind-Life independently of Body-Life, the Keys of which are held by a type of consciousness once called "Divine Folly." It must be clearly grasped in concept that this has no connection with insanity at all, and the meaning must be sought in metaphysical terms rather than medical ones.

The Tarot Fool has been considered the most important Trump of all. It stands for each one of us as individuals for what we amount to as thinking creatures of Cosmos at any given Time-Space-Event focus, and also indicates the state of absolute Innocence and uninvolvement with Existence we must reach in order to effect our Liberation into Ultimate Light. As far as the Paths of the Tree are concerned, the Fool may be attached to any of them, but for the sake of orderly arrangement, he is shown in this System upon this Path at the commencement of our Cosmic climb, because he represents Mind in the condition of "making itself up" or "knowing Unknowing." The Fool meddling and muddling among mortality and matter is the same spiritual Symbol as the Enlightened One released from Reason into the Unknowable. The Mystery of the Fool is indeed a most profound one. At one end of this Path we meet Mind in a state of subtle cleverness, ready to reason its way in any direction. At the other end, we find such a simple sort of Mind that it is capable of being impressed by any intelligence intending to influence it. As usual, in following a Path, we have to balance precariously between both like the Fool in the picture, standing poised on the edge of Earth and Air. We must neither be caught by "clever-cleverness," nor snared by stupid simplicity. On the one hand we should not conclude we know everything and close our minds completely, and on the other hand we should not open our minds to invasion by anything. Only one sort of fool acts that way. The Tarot Fool remains at the edge of abysmal ignorance and solid opinion, allowing selected thoughts to slip past sideways. He is evidently not quite so silly as he seems.

The background of this card is plain yellow, indicating a state of blissful ignorance/innocence. In the middle distance are icy expanses of mountainous regions with ten peaks showing. The region of unrealized opportunities and unscaled heights of thought. Perhaps they also stand for the frozen assets of awareness in the remoteness of subconsciousness. The foreground consists of a solid rocky platform with a dangerous overhang above a precipice. Below lie more icy wastes with two visible protuberances. At the right edge of this hazardous height can just be seen part of a throne-like rock formation—probably the "seat of reason" which the Fool has quitted.

This setting alone gives an impression of remoteness, danger, barrenness, and solitude, yet at the same time a sense of exhilaration and "Godlikeness" such as climbers of lonely heights often experience. There are several mountains in this world with legends attached to them that whosoever spends a night alone upon their summits will greet the dawn either without the wits they began with, or with all the wisdom that mortal mind can achieve in a single birth. Our Tarot Fool seems to have risked his reason on one of those "Holy Mountains," but which condition of consciousness has he reached? All must answer that question for themselves.

All this indicates an Inner state of isolation to which most of us must be exposed at some peak-point of life in order to discover just how much our individual minds amount to. Are we capable of thinking for ourselves at great heights of mentality or not? Just as there is a "Dark Night of the Soul," so is there a "Point of Peril" which we must surmount with our minds or fall from sanity and reason for perhaps very long periods of wasted life-time. We see the Fool right on the edge of that fatal moment. His supreme instant is upon him. What will become of him? Who knows, except the Divine decider of destiny ruling all Reason? That is the test of our thinking we must endure and pass successfully on this Hermetic Path of Initiation. Maybe we shall obtain some useful clues on coping with it from the rest of the symbol, which could be a vital issue, because the way we make up our minds at any given moment may determine every other moment we shall be given.

The figure of the Fool looks simple on the surface, but conceals quite a considerable quantity of meaning. First we should note its androgynous character, which is natural enough, since Mind (or mindlessness) is common to both male and female Life-principles of polarity. The general attitude suggests an open cross over a triangle, or an incomplete Cosmos at the apex of an awareness. Extensions of consciousness into Inner Dimensions in search of conclusive encirclement. We note also that the left side of the Fool is turned toward us, and everything in the Symbol slopes down toward the left. This is Kether reversed, or rather returning through the cycle of Life back to itself again. What emanates from Kether down the right hand side of the Tree from the Right Profile of Divinity must turn the Cosmic corner at the nadir of Malkuth and start climbing back by the left hand side of the Tree-circuit. The lowest levels of the Divine Mind are the highest reaches of the human mind, so here they connect through the Fool, at the bottom left-hand Path of the Tree. The three planes of rock, iciness, and sky space are relative to the three Veils of Negativity in pre-Ketheric Cosmos.

Interpreting the Fool's clothing calls for rather careful scrutiny and opinion. His white shirt, signifying Inward innocence, has folds at the neck capable of reading into many Hebrew phrases. Most significant are, possibly, "Vision of God," "Concept of God," "Walk with God," and "Praise ye God." We can also read "Freedom" and "Terror." Everyone of these phrases applies in some way to our Fool. Over the shirt, he wears a richly embroidered tunic, with wide-flowing, impractically cut sleeves. They are the sleeves of a playboy, not a craftsman of any kind. Fool he may be, but poor Fool he is not. His clothing speaks of style, elegance, and individualism. His tunic is black velvet, symbolizing softness and ignorance. It is covered with a pattern of green leaves, amid which are scattered a number of eight-rayed Life-wheels, plus a gold ornament on his chest of circular design, with a trefoil red inset. Assuming his right sleeve also has a Life-wheel, or "compass of consciousness," on it, we shall see he bears (unknown to himself) the tenfold Tree-Pattern upon him, even to the six-belled golden belt around his waist indicating Tiphereth.

Swinging from his waist is a pouch-purse of the same black and green material. What it contains we may only guess, but it looks light, and its fastening is a gilded turn-buckle. Evidently the Fool carries little material wealth with him, or is indifferent to the weight of monetary responsibilities. An empty purse seems to bother him not, so confident is he of living by credit. The green on his tunic matches the green in his eye—if his eyes were open. Hidden on the top front of the tunic is the sign of Air, which seems to link the Fool between Air and Earth as this path indicates, and he is certainly adopting a "Johnny-head-in-air" attitude. Also concealed on his left shoulder is a tiny Golden Ass, indicating that for which most men make fools of themselves.

The Fool's headdress is interesting. It is a cap of green leaves, green being the traditional color of simplicity, and it almost conceals his golden hair. This shows he has no evil thoughts or ill-will in his head, but is scarcely capable of formulating very complicated or forceful ideas. Rising from the cap is an elaborate plume, in scarlet, of twenty-two small tufts. The Fool's feather-brained thinking ought thus to be guided lightly toward the Paths of Life on the Tree.

In his right hand and resting on his right shoulder, the Fool bears a Staff which is really the Black Pillar of the Tree. This is the left-hand Pillar to an external observer, but becomes the right-hand one to those who look out upon Life from Within. Attached to the top end of the Staff or Pillar is a satchel just about the same size as the Fool's head. Since the Sphere of this position is Binah, Understanding, it seems clear where the Fool keeps his mother-wit without realizing what a treasure he has with him. In line with the Staff at top right of the picture is the Sun of Reason, to which the Fool's back is turned. Rays from this source of Light also fall upon the White Rose of dispassion which the fool bears between the thumb (Will) and forefinger (Attention) of his left hand in the circling gesture of inclusion. With its four petals and six leaves attached to a single stalk, we meet the Tree-Emblem in flower form again. The important question is where did the Fool obtain the Rose in such a unlikely spot?

In all likelihood, the White Rose reached the Fool because the White Dog brought it to him. This little animal is symbolic of his best instincts, which now try to warn him of peril by barking furiously and reaching up with eager paws. Obviously, the small creature could not save him if the Fool insisted on going over the edge and throwing away his chances of rationality with his life. The Dog has done as much as it can by offering the Key-suggestion which would save the Fool from fatal ends. If the Fool continues to ignore the very vital Key which he holds in his own hand, then the faithful Dog can only lament the missing wits of his erstwhile master. It might be noted here that the Rose and its leaves are the pattern which will unfasten the satchel of Understanding above the Fool's head.

On his legs and feet, the Fool wears the traveling-boots which must take him through all his imaginative journeys. His left foot still supports him on the piece of solid ground between himself and disaster. His right foot is hesitantly lifting, and another stride forward would be his last on this Life-journey. What must he do to avert calamity? First, heed the frantic warning of the dog. Second, come out of his dream and open his eyes to his situation. Third, tuck the Rose in the breast of his tunic, and getting the Staff off his shoulder, test the ground ahead of him with it, as he should have done in the first place. Struck by the Staff (consisting of Understanding, Discipline, and Intelligence), the treacherous piece of rock, upon which the Fool was going to trust his life, will break away and fall into the Waste where it belongs. In passing, we may note that this dangerous lump of rock sug-

gests a stupid and idiotic face, vapid and valueless. Nothing to regret demolishing.

This is the message of the Fool-Symbol to all on this difficult
Path. "Awake to the actualities of the mental situation around
you. Open your eyes from Within, and see where you really are.
Listen to the voice of your trustworthy instincts, and accept what
comes from thence as a saving suggestion. Do not rely on even the
firmest appearing ground beneath your feet, until you have
probed and tested it thoroughly with the Staff of Understanding,
Strictness and Intelligence. If anything breaks away, and you
find yourself on the edge of insanity, retreat to the Seat of Reason
and think things over. You have on your person and in your possession every necessary Key and Clue which will lead you to
safety and sanity along the most hazardous Paths." Who but the
wisest of Fools can lead us from the Mountains of Madness to the
heights of mental achievements, and ultimately the Apex of
Awareness? That is the only type of folly we should indulge in
upon this Thirty-first Path of Life, for it is our foolishness from
which we must learn every lesson that makes Life worth living in
this world.

Originatively, the Path is ruled by ELOHIM SABAOTh and
ADONAI ha ARETZ. Everyone's God, and the Lord of the whole
World. The God and Gods we all think about in various ways, and
the actual Lordship of Divinity which is common to the consciousness of everyone on Earth.

Whether or not human beings are subscribing members of
any religious System, or believe in any form of force or Deity,
makes little difference except to themselves. Every mortal with a
mind must realize themselves in contradistinction to all else they
are not and admit "Here I am, and there That is." What kind of
relationship they make between themselves and That depends
on their characteristics of consciousness. Here we are concerned
with maintaining satisfactory mental balance between ourselves
as human creatures in whatever unknown Energies of Existence
account for everything within reach of our experience leading to
ward our eventual destinies.

To paraphrase a well-known couplet, we might say:
> "Man has most odd
> Ideas of God."

First of all, primitive Man recognized Entity of some de-

scription in the natural forces he feared. Later, these were personified and projected into more sophisticated ideas and images.
Then they became conceptualized as spiritual degrees of a Divinity whose Consciousness controlled entire Cosmos. After this, the
mind of man denied the Principle of Divinity as such altogether
and approached the same old problem mathematically and intel-
lectually through systems of science confined to purely physical
phenomena of Life and Existence. Now we are faced with making
fresh extensions of Mind for ourselves into new Dimensions of Inner Life which obviously connect with what we used to think of as
Divinity. We have to realize that we are reaching mentally toward an entirely different type of Mind than ours, but a Mind
nevertheless, and what is more, a Mind whose thinking affects us
very considerably. If, in some way, we can manage to link our
very limited and imperfect mentality with a Consciousness capable of conceiving Cosmos, then commonsense alone should tell us
that our lives in this, or any world, are bound to become truer to
the Intention behind the inception of their being, and therefore
must be improved because of our increased contact with whatever Controlling Consciousness is the real Lord of this World.

We shall only become rulers of our own destinies to the degrees we "think back" or respond to what might be called the
"Mind behind Mankind." Whatever controls the consciousness of
humanity on this Earth decides our destiny as mortals. Hence
the continual "Battle for the Mind" waged by the various contestants for control of mundane human affairs and resources on this
planet. Our world has always been the battleground of those who
try and "take-over" the thinking of everyone else in order to establish their own temporary supremacy as "Lords of the World."
Every so often comes a culminating point which decides issues for
a period, and then the fight for mental freedom recontinues along
other lines. There can be no ultimate outcome of this struggle until the Mind of man as a whole comes to agreement with the Mind
behind Mankind, and the Lord of the World governs this Earth as
a Kingdom from the Throne of Reason in our Court of Consciousness. This cannot eventuate through compulsion or coercion of
human thinking, but must be arrived at freely as the result of all
coming to the same conclusions through their own lines of reasoning, thus becoming truly "of one Mind" together.

We are on this Path so that ELOHIM SABAOTh which gives

rise to everyone's idea of Divinity, relates reasonably with ADONAI ha ARETZ, or the type of Divine Mind we believe should best control our affairs as creatures of Earth. Individually, this means we must come to terms in our minds with our own "God-ideas," and our conscious convictions concerning an Overlordship of Mind holding Mankind in harmony together. How we arrive at this we arrive at this point of balance is a discovery we must make with the aid of those two Divine Aspects. We may have to push our Inner points of perception right to the very peak of their possibilities, risking our reason like the Fool in the symbol, unless we learn what he has to teach us. It has been rightly said that Sages teach us what to do, while Fools show us what not to do, and each tells the truth in their own way, so both should be regarded.

It might be noticed in the case of the Tarot Fool that no trace of an ear is showing. He does not listen to the warning given by the dog which might save him; but then, Fools are famous for ignoring advice. He might hear better if he grasped the plume representing the Paths of Life, and pulled off the confining cap of his green notions which closes his ears to the audio-atmosphere of awareness around him. This is what we have to do also on this particular Path. The Divine Aspects are termed the "Hearer" for that very reason. We must learn how to listen to the still small Voice Inside which speaks calmly and clearly of Right and Reason. Nor must we despise messages reaching our minds from the humblest sources, as the Fool rejects information from the mouth of a mere dog upon which, unrealized by himself, his very life depends. Even though it be but a moment or so a day, those who seek Initiation on this path must be prepared to raise their minds Inwardly and intentionally toward the Overmind which should eventually rule the reason of everyone on Earth, if our divine destiny is to be fulfilled. Perhaps the simplest and finest formula here is: "Speak, Lord, thy servant heareth."

Conversely, the Divine Mind must necessarily "hear," or receive, whatever we think at It, even though no response may be recognized by us. Establishing clear connections of thinking by means of mental imagery that links Mind between mortal mundane levels and Inner immortal ideology is a major task for Initiates working along this Way of Life. Man and his Gods have much to think over together concerning their common problems

in this World, and here is the Path where they must reach acceptable mental agreements which should lead toward Lordship of
Life on Earth. ELOHIM SABAOTh and ADONAI ha ARETZ are
the Aspects of Divinity offering us the Keys of this vital secret.

Creatively, the Path is governed by the Archangels
RAPHAEL and SANDALPHON. Raphael appears here in his
role as Teacher or instructor of our intellects, his Sword showing
how a sharp, keen, and polished mind should work to a point.
Sandalphon, the "Big Brother" of Humanity, tells us there are no
limits unreachable by Mind Ultimately, if we patiently proceed
along the Paths leading to Limitless Light. Yet we dare not demand that Sandalphon will lift up our little minds to look at the
Light while we refuse to be conditioned by the points of reason
which Raphael endeavors to insert into our consciousness with
his Sword, if nothing else will penetrate our Earth-bound mentalities.

Raphael's job, as Archangel of Air, is to try and move our
minds even a few degrees away from and above mere materialism on Earth. Sandalphon's task is to keep our mortal feet in firm
touch with this world until our Inner "wings" are sufficiently developed to carry us safely through Inner atmospheres. After that
point, we must be encouraged to fly steadily up the Tree, perching on every branch, until we come level with Sandalphon's head
and are fit to share his Vision and Awareness. Altogether, there
is a nice analogy here between our fledgeling minds attempting
first flights and baby birds venturing into their proper Element.
Still, even birds must come back to Earth sometimes, and while
we are human this is where we have to live, so between Raphael
and Sandalphon, we come and go like birds from Earth to Air.

It may puzzle some students of Qabalah why Sandalphon is
not Archangel of Earth rather than Auriel, who occupies a higher
place on the Tree. An unfortunate confusion in terms of the word
"Earth" makes this possible. We term our whole world upon this
planet "Earth," although, of course, it is actually composed of all
the elements. That is the "Earth" with which Sandalphon connects in particular. Auriel relates with the pure, or unmixed, condition of Earth as an Inner Life-element, and therefore locates
with a higher level on the Tree than mundane Malkuth. We must
never forget however, that although Sandalphon's feet are upon
our Earthworld, his head reaches into the highest of Heavens.

Moreover, he is capable of movement around the Tree while the others must remain attached to their proper stations. In this connection, we might be reminded of the traditional Fool in the old dance-patterns who is free to go at will among the other dancers or around them, while they must all move strictly according to the prescribed time and tune. So do our minds wander until we learn how to make them dance whatever mental measure we will.

Raphael should make us mentally appreciate the point and purpose of our being alive in this Earthworld while we turn our thoughts toward possibilities of living elsewhere in finer creations of Cosmic Consciousness. Sandalphon is represented as weaving crowns for the King of Cosmos to wear, or, in other words, constructing the highest patterns of thinking possible for any mind to take upon itself. We must neither wander witlessly in vaguely foolish ways toward the general direction of Sandalphon, nor keep sharpening our wits in such a perpetual engagement with Raphael that we fail to balance the forces of this Path properly and come to grief at either end of it. As always, we have to hold metaphorically the hands of both Archangels and mediate the influence of each through our own minds.

Between Raphael and Sandalphon, Initiates of the Path will learn how to maintain their mental balance even on the precipitous edges of peril which have to be negotiated in search of Inner intelligence. The Fool is indeed an apt Symbol for this Path. The shock of his awakening to his surroundings will either incline him to insanity or illumination. That was the symbolism of the hoodwink snatched from the candidate's eyes in Temple or Lodge initiation ceremonies. How would they react mentally to their strange environment? Everything depended on how well their previous training and instruction had been carried out. The same applies to Inner Life. How shall we react and deal with quite different conditions of consciousness than those we are accustomed to on Earthworld levels? Raphael and Sandalphon must be the proper sponsors of this Inner Initiation. They will help us perceive and practice with types of thinking which might seem very peculiar to Earth-minded mortals, and yet remain reasonable and rational beings.

The relative factor here is innocence, in the sense of guiltlessness or absence of guile. Innocence should not be taken as inexperience, but is to be understood as an intentional abstention from ill-will and a positive purity of motive in making mental moves or thinking in any direction. Inherent innocence is actually no safeguard against error, accident, or misfortune, but it does establish good relations with Inner realities and maintains an "open line" with intelligence devoid of malice or harmful intentions toward humanity. Why do we seek increase of our mental abilities? What are our underlying motives for what we do with our minds? We may intentionally deceive other humans, or even our own lower ranges of personal perception on these important points, but we certainly cannot make falsehoods appear very convincing to a consciousness operating at Archangelic creative levels. It is simply silly to suppose so. Therefore we should clear ourselves from pointless pretenses, and keep the Inner way of intentional innocence open toward categories of consciousness completely capable of knowing for themselves just what our minds amount to, and what can be accomplished through those minds if they are kept in correct working order. Only fools stand in their own light, and this is what happens if we block our Inner Lightways by our stupidities. RAPHAEL attempts to persuade us away from follies with his Sword, and SANDALPHON tries to hold us out of harm's way by indicating higher courses of action, but in the end we must learn the way we will, however hard this may prove. It might be best in the long run if we asked Sandalphon and Raphael how to use the mental Keys of this Path connecting the height of stupidity with the zero-Zenith of Intelligence. They hold these in trust for us.

Fomatively, the Path is administered by the Angel Orders of the KERUBIM and the BENI-ELOHIM. The Elemental Angels, and the offspring of the Gods. In terms of mentality, this means the basic elements of our thinking in this world, and the results of our thinking toward extensions of ourselves in the direction of Divinity, whatever we choose to call this perfecting Principle of Being.

Our mentality constructs Cosmos from Elements of Mind just as Matter is formed up from Elemental Forces. The Kerubim represent here the mental equivalents available to us in the Earthworld as the Chioth ha Qodesh are the pure Life-Elements available to the Life Spirit at the commencement of consciousness. With the help of the Kerubim, we built up our Inner Temples of Thought from the Elements they supply us with in this mortal sphere. Remembering that Kether and Malkuth are inversed images of each other, we shall see that if Malkuth were in Kether's place, we should now be upon the Path leading to Wisdom between Kether and Chockmah. If, in fact, we continued drawing this Path through the center of Malkuth to commence another Tree, it would become the Eleventh Path of the contiguous Tree-System. Here, however, we shall remain with our present Tree-excursion, and consider the Kerubim as Elements of thought encountered during normal Earth-life.

The Beni-Elohim, Children of Consciousness, or results of Reason, are formative forces building up our beliefs into serviceable Inner ideas along lines leading toward the immediate stages of our mental evolution away from sheer materialism. They inform us that exclusive materialism is also entirely unreasonable, and extremely foolish. We cannot escape the Fool at any point on this Path. If we live with our heads in the clouds like the airy Fool in the picture, that is quite wrong. If we come down to earth and bury our noses in the mud of materialism, that is wrong, too, and probably more foolish. Unless we learn how to live with our foolishness so that it balances between the solid Elements of thinking offered by the Kerubim, and the air aspirations afforded by the Beni-Elohim, we shall never find the secrets of this Path, and keep falling over the edge of the precipices we build up in every lifetime. At least while we keep one foot on the ground like the Tarot Fool, we might still retain our poise, providing no violent wind of chance blew us off balance. Then, too, we note the Fool leans slightly backwards, as if he might be in fact retreating away from the edge, rather than leaning too far forward in the direction of danger. These are useful suggestions to think about on those points.

Between the Kerubim and the Beni-Elohim, we have to make ourselves up with our own minds out of what we find in the way of elemental materials in this world and the issues of our thinking in extended terms of metaphysical personal projection. We are doing this all the time to some degree, and Initiation on any Path is only an extension Inwardly of Outer expression, linking consciousness along various levels. Here we encounter anything at all in material manifestation which makes us think, but the question is what it makes us think *of*, and how far into ourselves we think. Do our thoughts simply bounce off the surface of material phenomena and associated thinking, so to speak, or do they lead us to the Inner realities those externalities represent? Can we even see some connection between objective surface symbolism and subjective actualities? How far do we see into brick walls? This is the Path where we are supposed to perfect the skill of imaginative thinking, and the art of mentally arranging our thought-elements in order to make Cosmic constructions of consciousness between mundane and supra-mundane modes of living. Any craftsman or artist does this by taking the materials of his profession as elements, then processing these in and with his mind so that a masterpiece emerges physically as a material product, and mentally as all the thinking it evokes in everyone concerned with it. Actually, the material arrangement is really a symbol, and the mental energies evoked around it constitute the true work of art. The Kerubim assist us to modify matter, but the Beni-Elohim are the agents who make this mean something.

No artist could do anything with his mental or material elements unless these were amenable to the motivating intention. Therefore, we must discover on this Path what mental elements connected with Earthlife are amenable for any given purpose. It is no use employing the wrong elements of mind when we intend to do Inner constructional work with our consciousness. We must learn what our minds will do with available supplies of awareness, and how to extend our scope in both directions. All such training and experience belongs to this Path, and the BENI-ELOHIM and the KERUBIM have the Keys.

*Expre*ssively, this Path is governed by Hermes and Earth. Earth to be understood in its planetary and not Elemental sense. We most certainly need all our wits about us to live in this world, and Hermes is the Initiator who stimulates our thinking and wakes up our minds both to Inner and Outer events concerned with our consciousness. Nevertheless, Hermes is not exactly noted for dispassionate and undistorted truth, although he will lead us thence in the end through all sorts of enthusiasms, inaccurate conclusions, and a whole tangle of thinking for the sake of its fascination. Hermes does not lie, but he expects us to develop enough commonsense to test his catch-questions for ourselves. Let us be charitable with Hermes, for he is the most approachable and companionable of Inner entities, and say that he makes deliberate mistakes for our own good in relatively harmless ways so that we may learn how to look out for ourselves when more serious issues are at stake. We might be right in thinking that Hermes tries to trick us out of our foolishness.

One special quality must be particularly recognized with Hermes. A sense of humor and fun in the wittiest and happiest way. There is nothing nasty, bitter, vicious, or unpleasant about Hermetic humor. It can be as sensual or "naughty" as possible, but it always has subtlety and gay wit as its explosive element, depending on cleverness for its effects, yet never "clever-cleverness." If only we can beg, borrow, or especially steal some sense of Hermetic humor, our mental problems will be solved far more swiftly. On the other hand, while we are mortals, we need the solid and quiet type of amusement usually associated with Earth which, though it can be crude, is never unkind. Both approaches to life are attitudes of mind to be mediated on this Path.

Earth is best thought of as a natural Mother of Mankind, and the home of humanity in our planetary projection of personal appearances. The place and country of our Earth-births or incidence of incarnation is so important to everyone because it relates with the Cosmic influences associating with our individual characteristics. The whole science of Astrology is founded on those factors. People say unthinkingly, "I didn't ask to be born as this, that, or the other sort of person," but basically they had made themselves available for birth in this world and accepted the opportunity most in accordance with their Inner line of Life. It takes four beings to account directly for birth in this world. The two physical parents, the incarnating individual, and the Associative Entity, or "Group-Soul" with which the incarnating ego belongs, outside of and apart from physical living. When we disincarnate at bodily death, we return to that Inner condition of existence and live mostly out of the conscious capital we have acquired during incarnation. This might be a heavenly or hellish experience according to individual and collective living, so the mental abilities and assets we gain on this Path will be invaluable in developing and evolving our Inner Identities.

It may be true that we are born with inherent limitations and characteristics of mind, but these are for cultivation and growth while we live in this world. Our minds are made to live in and care for, not neglect, ignore, and abandon. This is the particular Path where we must tend and cultivate our Inner mental fields with the equivalent skill and effort of an agriculturalist bringing the fruits of the Earth to perfection. These two processes are really the same in different Dimensions, and they depend on each other to a greater degree than might be obvious. A good, sound, well-developed, and finely balanced mind grows out of Earth-experience, just as much as the finest flowers or fruit in creation. True, we can cultivate minds in the equivalents of hot-houses with forced growth and artificial fertilizers, but these are fragilities and fantasies with no fundamental strength or nobility of structure resembling the natural home-grown species.

It should scarcely be necessary to remind ourselves, however, that our Earth-products did not cultivate themselves, and it is Inner intelligence evolving through us that has helped them toward their present conditions of Cosmos. We are the Earth-agents of an Awareness with a conscious concern for Cosmic perfection, and whether we fulfill that function faithfully, or fail to keep such faith with the Intention behind our beings, depends entirely upon the sort of selves we are and become because of our living. This means as we interpret our own wills and intentions relatively to the True Will and Intention which should be worked through us in this and every World. That is the whole purpose of the Hermetic Mysteries. To help us discover for ourselves by means of Mind our purpose in being on Earth, and the practice of modifying Matter by Mind in conformity with Cosmic Consciousness.

The rustic, countryman, or typical son of the soil, has frequently been regarded as an unsophisticate verging toward simplicity or even folly. A fool used to be called a "natural" or unteachable individual. In fact, the basic mother-wit drawn directly from native soil of body and mind is the root of Reason and rationality we should be most unwise to sever, however high we may rise above it. We shall learn this, perhaps upon this very Path, where the simplest folly and the most sagacious mental faculties meet, and must be mediated through the Initiates who learn the secret of transmutation by thinking. We might also learn some day the secret of the legendary "Mind-food," or plant substance which was reputed to turn the silliest fool into a man of mighty mind if sufficient was eaten over a prolonged period. The chemistry of consciousness may yet establish the connection between soil and sense. Perhaps the flower held by the Fool has something to suggest here? If so, Hermes is certain to know the trick of using it.

Just as Mercury, the metal of Hermes, is virtually a liquid, and the matter of our Earth can be molded into almost anything we need, so should we cultivate the principle of plasticity in our minds so that we may make what we Will out of them. The whole of our world now bears the marks of Mankind because of what we think. This does not imply that we have remodeled the world in the best possible way, but merely that our thoughts are traceable all over this poor old planet. We have known Stone ages, Bronze ages, Iron ages, and now the Plastic age is upon us. Its physical utility is obvious, but there is a mental equivalent to master on this Path. "Mind-material" is no myth, but a practical possibility to investigate and put through thinking techniques here with the help of Hermes and good old Mother Earth. All the Mysteries of Mind are theirs for the Initiation of Mankind from first follies to final freedom. They know the Sacred Secret with which only a Perfect Fool may be trusted in Truth, and the mental Zero-Zenith which only a pure Zany is likely to reach. There is a profundity of mystical meaning here that is reachable from our world by the Earth-Hermes held Keys. We may as well ask for these with all the might our minds may muster.

The Thirty-second Path

SPHERE—LETTER CODE:	Foundation 9 Th 10	Kingdom
DIVINE ORIGINATION:	SHADDAI el CHAIIM—	The
	ADONAI ha ARETZ	Omnipresent
ARCHANGELIC CREATION:	Gabriel—Sandalphon	Propagation
ANGELIC FORMATION:	Ashim—Kerubim	Distribution
APPARENT EXPRESSION:	Moon—Earth	Reflection
TAROT SYMBOL:	MOON	

At last we arrive at the final Path linking the Middle Pillar of the Tree with the Kingdom of this Earthworld. It is usually supposed the Tree of Life has its roots in Heaven and grows down to Earth, but it is equally true to say that our purpose here is growing a corresponding Tree, the roots of which are strong enough to support our Cosmic climb toward Heaven by its branches. Somewhere in the Scheme of Life, there has to be a point where Humanity becomes a distinct species of its own kind, capable of reproductive functions, and emerging on Earth as a product of Life peculiar to this planet. A nadir of Life, so to speak, below which we cannot fall without loss of human status altogether. This point is here, and it is from the lowest levels of our Earthlives that we start our highest spiritual journeys. Our Cosmic climb begins with a crawl.

The Spirit of Life is Omnipresent in essence, but enters this Earthworld through processes of propagation and distributes itself according to the way its images are reflected by the force-foci of its multiple facets we term "families," or species of living creature. The Lord of Life as a Cosmic Entity becomes focused down to this planet in particular as an Earthlife Controller. The remotest Archangelic Intelligence touches metaphorical toes to Earth, and the Angelic Order whose function is concerned with good breeding, links up with the Earthly elemental energies which distribute the various types of living specimens around this world. In the immediate Heavenly vicinity of Earth, our Moon, traditionally connected with cycles of fertility and reason, shines serenely upon humans as a whole, awaiting the first touch of Man to awaken the latent forces represented by Lunar Light. As we know, this has now happened, and in consequence the entire history of Mankind must alter from that point. All babies eventually grow up and leave home, even from planetary points of view, and it cannot be long in Cosmic time before streams of Earth-children quit this old home of ours in search of Life in other spheres of Space.

What happens physically must have metaphysical equivalents, and so we must also learn to live as functioning Life-entities in conditions of consciousness apart from, if connectible with, ordinary physical embodiment. Sooner or later, we shall discover that the humano-animal bodies we live in at present and accept as normal are, in fact, both abnormal and inadequate for operating the sort of Consciousness into which advancing entities among us are evolving. In time, we must become more than animated lumps of meat, and alter the atomic structure of our Life-force foci so that we are able to live far more comfortably and naturally in states of being which at present can only be described as spiritual or super-physical. Far from being pure fantasy, this must ultimately become fact, and our fantasies do indeed become facts if they make Earth appearance.

Man has always instinctively realized his Inner possibilities of immortality, or entitized existence apart from association with bodies which rightly belong to the animal kingdom. Our struggles to achieve even the smallest degrees of Inner independence make up the story of our stay on this Earth. Our religions and philosophies have dealt with the question as a life-after-death issue. Strictly speaking this is scarcely a very accurate way of approach. The births and deaths of our human bodies are incidental events in chains of consciousness which should be linked with far more extensive ranges of awareness in quite different dimensions of living experience. Ultimately, the crux of our entire confinement as humans of a sub-spiritual Life-species on Earth, is whether or not we ever discover how to exist otherwise. That is our primal and final problem of Earthlife, and the real reason why we concern ourselves with climbing the Holy Tree. Here, at the base of the main trunk or Middle Pillar, we have to discover how to look above Earth levels for Light, and follow the Inner impulse which induced us to direct our attention toward Divinity in the first place.

The Tarot Symbol of the Moon takes us right back to the start of the story. We see a strangely desolate world of wild and cheerless aspect, unfriendly in character, and with a bleak outlook. A full Moon shines down upon this landscape, revealing two weird towers presumably not set up by or for humans, since there is but a single small aperture at the top of each, and the sides are smoothly unscalable. A dog and a wolf howl miserably at the Moon on either side of a narrow path reaching from a river in the foreground as far as the eye reaches to the ragged horizon. At the riverside edge of this peculiar path is a crayfish. Not a flower, tree, or anything very happy is in sight and, strangest of all, this is the one and only Tarot Trump with no visible aspect of humanity on it. Even the Wheel of Fortune shows a humanoid Sphinx, and the Man symbol in a corner. If there are traces of humans on this card, they are well hidden and it may be difficult to locate them. Let us attempt translation of this mysterious Symbol into more comprehensible terms.

First we notice the face in the Lunar disc is looking directly downwards from the midst of a thirty-two rayed circle. If the rays represent the Life-Paths of the Tree, this certainly indicates the connection of this Trump with the Thirty-second Path we are now following. The face-image could be either male or female, and it displays a left profile in contradistinction to the right profile of the traditional image at Kether. Apart from the thirty-two points of the Life-compass, what may this Moon signify?

The little secret lies in the arrangement of the "living flames" depicted in what looks like disorder between Moon and Earth. These connect with the Ashim Angelic Order, and to interpret them the right hand three must be pushed down in order to make the rest read properly. The flames will then outline the words "IHI ChI," signifying Life will Live. One flame for every soul alive here. Surely there is something very deeply significant in the symbols for individual souls hovering in the atmosphere of this world? Does this indicate the true mission of Mankind upon our planet? Everyone to find their own souls by living here until we either succeed or fail in this vital project. How many lives are needed before we become securely established in our living souls? An unanswerable question, but the injunction to live each moment as if it were the whole of a lifetime, and every life as if it were an entire existence, is a good one. One soul is worth more than the entire world when decisive moments are forced upon Mankind. Here are shown souls to be gained, and only those placing proper values on them are fit to keep them.

To the right and left of the picture the peculiar towers rise to the level of the Moon's lower edge. The left-hand tower is female on account of its rounded top and curved sides, while the right hand tower stands for the masculine principle of living polarity. They are not entered on Earthlife levels at all, and their secrets may not be penetrated until we have risen above ground level at least Moon-high. The towers stand silently and firmly as boundary markers for Mankind to pass between upon our Earthly pilgrimage of Life. They are monuments to the Mystery of Life itself, and it is enough for our purpose to realize they are where they are. It is their height and location which is of real value for us to obtain our bearings from, and we should only waste good living-time trying to break into them. Even if we succeeded, there would be nothing for us to find. They are empty except to those able to look into them from the correct angles through their apertures.

It should be noted that the towers of Mystery are standing in the wastelands that represent remote regions of consciousness and uncultivated areas of Life. Then we might observe we are slightly closer to the right hand tower than the left. This tower stands on a small promontory connected with the main section of grassland, while its companion is more isolated and difficult to approach. A cheerful cynic might take this to mean that females are always more mysterious than males, but it actually indicates that we should "Keep to the Right" along the Inner Way leading us to the Light of Dawn beyond the mountains of uncertainty, where the Sun takes over from the Moon.

This stony and difficult Path, with all its ups and downs, is traceable from the remotest central mountain peak, meandering from side to side generally in the middle of the scene until it reaches the edge of the River of Life, or stream of Consciousness, in the foreground. Oddly enough, its curvatures can be interpreted as "YLL," from a Semitic root meaning to yell or howl in the sense of animals howling in a wilderness, which is exactly what is happening on either side of the Path.

On the right of the path is a male wolf, sitting down, and standing on the left is a female bitch of the retriever type. They are wailing their timeless Lunar Lamentation, or as the old pagans would have said, "Calling down the Moon." More probably they are instinctively asking the Lady of the Moon to bless their intended union with fertility, for they typify the mating between wildness and domesticity which we must all arrange in our own natures on this Path. These creatures have been carefully chosen as symbols here, because the wolf is well-known as the most faithful father of all wild animal life, fighting for his family to the death if necessary, individual in character, yet gregarious and selective in choice of pack-associations. He has many qualities Mankind needs for survival during primitive progress along the Path. The sort of spaniel-retriever crossbreed of bitch is normally affectionate and faithful, capable of seeking and finding indicated objectives and bringing them back for consideration. She will cherish her offspring, and carry them around until they find the use of their own feet. These again are basic and fundamental qualities needed by all of us on Earth, most especially in the earlier phases of our evolution. If Man could mate the characteristics of these creatures when commencing evolutionary life on Earth, very sound genetic traits would follow us down the ages as faithful companions and old feral friends.

So where and when is Man to emerge into this picture? He is already there in the symbolic personification of the lowly crayfish. We may well look with disapproval on this crawling creature dragging itself slimily out of the Stream of Life on to unfamiliar ground at the very point of a Path leading to some Ultimate Unknown destiny. So were the highest archangels said to look with Heavenly eyes at Earthman, in the distant day of our invention by the Living Spirit. Some of these High Beings were indeed reputed to be so revolted by the idea of humans ever becoming able to reach their rightful realm of Life that they rebelled altogether and determined to destroy our species. In one way, can we blame them? Are we not also capable of destroying ourselves? Do we not appear as alien to higher lifetypes of Inner intelligence as the clumsy crayfish seems to us? Yet even high species of living beings may have come from the humblest origins, and in watching the crayfish crawl ashore on the Land of Life, we are really looking back at the early times of our own evolution.

The creature representing us is coming from a sort of whirl-pool in the river. This compares with the Nebulae at the top of the Tree, but here it means all the spinning cycles of Life-species eventually throwing to the top the most suitable for adaption into humanly habitable force-forms. It could survive out of water for a while, but needed to return for restorative periods. We can survive in these present bodies for some time, providing sleep-states are available, and we can return to our Life-river for discarnate renovation. The crayfish has opposable claws capable of grasping materials and manipulating them. This principle of thumb and finger dexterity has enabled us to rise above all other forms of animal activity. Moreover, if the forefinger signifies attention and the thumb means will, the meeting of these two factors alone surely accounts for very much of our evolutionary advances? Again, the crayfish is an armored creature, and without a fairly tough exterior we are unlikely to survive the rough going along primitive parts of our Life-Path. Despite its externally rugged construction, there are quite sensitive feelers for gaining finer information from its environment and imparting light touches to Life. We shall need much the same equipment along equivalent lines of living. Granted the crayfish has scarcely a high order of intelligence, but neither have we when we begin tackling Earthlife. The beast has one essential quality to keep it going—tenacity, and if we have this also, we can crawl along our primal Paths quite well.

What are the chances of the crayfish on the Path? According to the signs, three to one in favor. Just ahead of it lie four stones, three white and one black. They represent the elements we encounter in life. Three of them are relatively safe, but the fourth—Fire—constitutes both our chief danger and main asset. Everything depends on how we deal with it both physically and metaphorically. The little black stone is a coal, with the secrets of the Sun locked up in it. At first it lies almost insignificantly on the Path, and we shall not realize its possibilities for a very long while to come. In the same way, we have to carry unused potentials of power and undeveloped qualities of character along with us in Life until occasion arises for their full employment. There are the elements of living lying in our way to be picked up as we go along, and, once we have acquired them, our journey ahead becomes much easier.

Where are we going to? The first ridge in the narrow road has a concealed IHVH in its folds, the tail of the V being lengthily exaggerated. Since V is the Fire-letter, it provides a clue on how to trace Divinity through Light. The narrowness of the Path tells us that each single one of us must find our own individual ways toward this same Light. There is no room for more than one traveler to each track. It is a lonely way through life for everybody. especially those on the Way of Initiation which is particularly indicated here, but so it must be.

The little heap of six stones, one a reddish one, at the water's edge, speak the message: "Be guided on the Right by the primal Principle of the Life-Tree, and pay particular attention to the Middle point of Harmony." Of course, the unheeding crayfish is making for the left-hand edge of the Path, but it will learn later— the hard way. That is how we distinguish the Path from the wasteland. It is hard by contrast, and the feelers of the crayfish should discern the edges of the Path all the way along. So should ours. All must find their side-limits in order to keep going along their proper Paths which have no perceptible limits ahead in this world. That is the plain message here. Stay in the average Middle Way, guided by the Right.

Above all, the Moon tells early comers to the Path of Inner evolution to seek Lunar Light before attempting exposure to the Sun. Again and again we are given this instructional warning, and constantly we find the sad results of failure to observe it. Our Inner way to the Sun lies through the Moon, and that is why the Lunar Symbol occupies this first section of the Middle Pillar connected directly to Earthlife at Malkuth. We must pass through the Lunar Mysteries and emerge as Initiates of the Moon, before we can possibly hope to succeed as Solar candidates for Inner Cosmos. This means we must master the techniques of reflection, meditation, fantasy-working, coping with mental Maze-patterns, finding our way through twilight thinking, and all the rest of such essential preliminaries, before we arrive at a point of training and experience where it is safe and proper to proceed Sunwards. To ignore the Moon and attempt strides toward the Sun is a folly which frequently results in insanity. Every event on the Inner Path of Initiation should have its proper position and proportion. Here, we are supposed to learn and live as faithful

Children of Light according to Lunar Laws. They will take us safely along our initial sections of the Path leading us gently and gradually away from our primeval slime through the cleansing Stream of Life to the firm grounds of progression toward our destiny beyond the furthest boundaries of belief. On this Way, we shall gain our most precious Life-possession—a soul of our own to be ourselves with forever, if we care for this sufficiently.

If we wonder just how long or difficult this journey is likely to be, the chances are it will take us until we are as different from our present Life-states as we now differ from our earliest evolutionary appearances, and will probably present equivalent degrees of difficulty. Still, if we have arrived so far on our Path, some of us stand good chances of staying the course of Cosmos while it continues.

This thirty-second Path is the hardest of all to travel up the Tree. On it, we have to gain the makings of Mind, the rudiments of Reason, the stirrings of Soul, and learn at least the elementary Laws of Life as we crawl steadily up to Lunar level. For a long time our prospects may seem quite bleak and unpromising in the rugged landscape of Earthlife, and if it were not for the soft shining of the Moon like the Shekinah Presence on Earth, we might die out from sheer discouragement. Man, like the wolf and the dog, has been crying for the Moon the whole of his spiritual babyhood. Now that we have touched it literally, our Earthliving should enter another phase in the course of Cosmos. Yet no matter how far advanced some souls may be, countless others are still in the Moonwailing stages, and while their Life-needs exist, the Lunar Mysteries must remain to serve them on this Path as this Symbol shows.

Originatively, the path is presided over by SHADDAI el CHAIIM and ADONAI ha ARETZ. The Lord of Lives and the Lord of this World. At every point of Qabalistic teaching and practice we are faced with a *Living* Spirit, a *Living* God, and a Lord of *Lives*. Never a Deity of the Dead, or a concept of "Afterlife." To a Qabalist, we are *always* alive while we exist at all, whether we are associating with a physical body or not. Thus there are no Dead, nor an Afterlife, to a Qabalist, since those are Non-concepts. There are states of incarnation, excarnation, or intercarnation, during which we are living entities in some kind of existence, consciously or unconsciously. Spirit does not die, but either Is, or Is-not. Souls are not immortal until they unify with Spirit finally, and Mind is the condition of Consciousness achieved by Life-entities of all types, while our poor flesh bodies are arrangements of organized cell-units suitably constructed for Earthlife purposes of personal force-foci. These are perishable and expendable, being our available means of entry and exit to and from our Earthly arenas of experience. The Lord of Lives in conjunction with the Lord of the Earthworld are the Divine Aspects wherein originate our energies of embodiment. Between them we bounce back and forth, as it were, from physical to nonphysical conditions of living.

We get into Earthlife via genetic chains extending into Otherlife existence which correspond with our individual and collective personalized patterns. Just as our fingerprints (which follow fingertip nerve patterning) are peculiar to each of us, yet come within various broad categories, so have we distinctive and original Life-patterns, or Cosmic circuitry, imprinted into our Inner Identity which make us exclusively what we are as and in ourselves. The more evolved we become, the more distinctive and individual these patterns are. In order to incarnate, we must either do so through Life-channels appropriate for our proper spiritual Inner Pattern, or try and force ourselves through unfit entries. The ill effects of miscegenation and faulty breeding procedures in this world are too obvious to need comment.

Once humanity had begun the habit of incarnation, essential rules of breeding should have been learned and observed strictly. The higher Initiates of the old Mysteries seemed aware of these, but genetic damage was occurring at a faster rate than it could be put right, and we have not yet sorted ourselves out into balanced sets of species. Theoretically, our Inner linkage with physical birth goes roughly like this. As entities of Life, we all have our particular Life-keys or personal patterns which constitute the sort of beings we are. A mass type of Key fits a mass type of lock, so unauthorized entry is relatively easy into Earthlife on lower levels. Nevertheless, there are proper Paths leading into Earthlife which match up exactly with the Key-patterns of every living soul. The Lord of the World holds the physical genetic end of the Path, and the Lord of Lives holds the corresponding ends of those Life-lines in a spiritual state of living associated immediately with this Earthworld. As and when such patterns coincide along the Path, the best conditions for birth by suitable individuals occur. Since this relates with externally observable Cosmic phenomena such as planetary motions, astrologically based calculations and judgments are made possible in connection with Earthliving entities and events.

Really the whole process is like an elaborate combination lock with tumblers at each end and Keys in the middle. Once our corresponding combinations come together we can slip through the Gate of Earthlife if we intend to. While we are here in this world we actually alter our Inner patterns to some extent for better or worse by the way we live, and how we make deep structural changes to our souls which survive the passing of our purely physical bodies. Those changes have a marked bearing on our spiritual Life-status and they also determine many factors about our next entry to Earthlife. After all, if one bends, files, or alters the wards of any Key, it will open quite a different lock. In today's analogy, we might say that if we change the frequency of a radio it will communicate with another sort of station. This is the opportunity which this Path offers us—alteration of our Life—Key characteristics for the better during an Earthlife.

The really important item to consider in connection with finally focusing Life-forces into Earth incarnations is the Inner equivalent of Luna. This is like the last contact that must be cleared before a Life-circuit operates and incarnation eventuates. In modern times, it is not unlike the final firing point of a spacecraft motor that aligns the ship with its proper Earth target. Boiled down to basics, it makes every difference to our lives. The instinct of the ancients which connected Life and Lunar cycles together was fundamentally correct, although it is the Inner rather than the Outer Moon which affects our Life-tides, and the two are not precisely coincidental, though they do relate with each other.

By and large, the Lunar Inner Sphere of Life ruled by SHADDAI el CHAIIM consists of associated discarnate Life-entities and groups who are Life-linked with the Earthworld for any number of reasons, and may or may not be seeking immediate or future incarnation here. There are not dead people at all, but very much living ones, though in different conditions to ours in Earthlife now. Nor is this state Heaven, Hell or Purgatory, but simply a Sphere of Life containing a very mixed company of souls who are neither more nor less capable of managing their own affairs than we are on our side of Life. They come and go from their Sphere just as we do, perhaps back into physical bodies, or perhaps to higher circles of Cosmos. The position is that relationships between this Sphere as whole and our World as Life-location have rhythmical variances comparable with Lunar cycles. There are incidences which favor the incarnation of the most evolved souls, and others during which even the most undesirable entities may get across. The former seem far fewer and rarer than the latter. Centuries ago, early Initiates tried to counterbalance this tendency by training tribespeople to copulate only at specified lunar intervals. This might have worked if the plan had been followed faithfully, but there is no use regretting lack of results now. We have too much to learn on this Path about how to arrange plans for the future along such lines, aided by our present experience.

With these Life-ends in view, Qabalists make the Tree of Life their personal basic Pattern upon which they arrange the circuitry of their Inner consciousness. This produces a Life-Key which opens very well worthwhile opportunities of Life on all levels. It is furthermore a primal pattern clearly recognized by SHADDAI el CHAIIM and ADONAI ha ARETZ, who are the Aspects of Divine Omnipresence as the Life-Spirit concerned with our incarnatory existences. They hold the Keys of all Earthlife patterns here, and we have every living right to ask them for these Keys on this Path.

Creatively, Archangels GABRIEL and SANDALPHON govern the Path. Gabriel here is the Archangel of the Annunciation and Resurrection (birth and rebirth), while Sandalphon links even the lowliest life on Earth with the highest purpose in Heaven.

Gabriel's task and function is controlling the creative forces behind birth processes. This, of course, includes the resurrection part of the Life-cycle which makes new bodies out of old ones. It also relates with the construction of Innerlife vehicles which do not incarnate at all, but are for use in different Dimensions of Life. Whether we are born back to Earth or are ready for rebirth on higher Life-levels, Gabriel personifies the creative Power behind such events.

Sandalphon in this position is supposed to ensure that only individual lives intentionally linking themselves with the Highest Living Spirit come into incarnation. This obviously is not happening in fact, since if only the right types of people were born in this world at the right times, places, and in correct quantities, our Earthlife conditions would be much nearer perfection than they are. Human interference with natural breeding patterns and creative cycles has strained the limits of tolerance applying to our Earthlife scheme almost to the very edges of their extent. Short of eliminating humanity from Earth altogether and starting afresh, little seems possible in the propagative process of human life which concerns these Archangels, except selection of survival strains and realignment of Life-streams into Cosmic categories conformable with the intentions of Creative Consciousness.

In effect, this means a steady sorting out of human souls by a kind of grading and classification system, so that everyone is not only enabled to live in conditions compatible with his conscious development, but will also find every opportunity and encouragement for increasing his evolutionary entitlements. Thus, "every soul will go to its own place," and yet remain free to change that place for the better by evolutionary efforts of will and work. No simple solution, but the only eventual alternative to abrogation of Earthlife as a means of initiating Mankind into the early stages of Cosmic Consciousness. Failing such course, Earthlife might otherwise become isolated from Inner Cosmos and left to deteriorate and die out naturally over whatever period was needed to complete the process. Whatever we may prefer to suppose, all the human population of this planet would not be an irreparable loss to a Cosmos capable of creating far more advanced Life-types. On the other hand, such a calamity could indeed prove a real regret to a Consciousness reluctantly coming to such conclusions on Divine Life-levels. No one would be responsible for our extinction but ourselves.

Providing Gabriel sorted out the souls to be incarnated, and transferred these along the Path for Sandalphon to fit into their appropriate living conditions, all would be well with our world. As affairs stand, we must make our own individual arrangements with these Inner authorities with complete confidence that not a single soul will be lost to life on Earth or otherwise except by their own choice. Those who prefer to remain with the rotting remnants of a decaying and degenerating planetary body for corrupt reasons, can scarcely expect to avoid its final fate. Our world is by no means at this stage yet, and its eventual end may be many multiple generations away, but it is advisable to commence conditioning of consciousness well in advance of actualities. Initiates of this Path must learn living between their Innerlife connections through Gabriel, and their Outerlife contacts among Mankind pertaining to Sandalphon.

We not only belong to Earth-families of fellow-humans in this world, but we also have an Inner line of ancestry with which we relate discarnately, though not, of course, by any sexually reproductive process. Earlier in our evolution, the Earthlife system proposed among humanity was to keep clear and distinct categories of entity by birth-entry alone, so that specific sorts of soul developed within their own family areas among most favorable conditions. This turned into the caste system, founded on perfectly sound principles offering advantages to everyone, but eventually wrecked through irresponsibility and lack of loyalty to the fundamental ethical standards involved. Once the spiritual structure of the system degenerated into socio-economic segregations regardless of character qualifications, it became doomed. Yet sooner or later we have to work out a satisfactory classification of Earthlife entities and restrict entry to suitable souls only, or Earthlife itself will be doomed. Either we learn and respect the Laws of Life dealing with good breeding or pay the penalties of neglecting them. Gabriel administers these laws at one end of this Path, and Sandalphon at the other.

The ancient ideas of ancestral lineage and its importance to human individuals, their families and descendants were, and always will be, based on completely correct Inner laws of living. Difficulties and trouble arose through misuse and mismanagement of the arrangement, and mainly because Inner Life-linkages become out of alignment with physical family genealogies. Our physical birth-lines differed more and more widely from our spiritual heredity, until virtually the whole of humanity was affected by the unhappy results. One very important function of the Holy Mysteries, ancient or modern, is to reestablish the direct linkage between Initiates and their Inner familial Life-lines so that they literally "inherit the Kingdom of Heaven." The Initiator here is Gabriel, whom we may regard as a directing genealogist, working in conjunction with Sandalphon who acts as a sort of selective screener, helping everyone find his own proper folk-lines and real Inner relations.

Humans realize this instinctively, as they run round this world in frightened circles looking for some kind of spiritual heritage where they might at last feel entirely at home with their own true families and friends. Our world is full of such seekers, and until the whole unhappy situation sorts itself out into more or less correctly established family circles with harmonious Inner and Outer lineage, we are unlikely to live on very good terms with each other on Earth. Meanwhile, Initiates of this Path will quietly reach a state of right relationship through themselves between their true soul-families and spiritual heritage located with Gabriel's aid, and the Earthlife connections Sandalphon links them to. Eventually both these lines may level out if the Keys of the Archangels are properly employed.

Formatively, the Angel Orders of the ASHIM and KERUBIM administer this Path. Here again we have the family issue, because the Ashim signify those fit to found families, or "gentlemen," in the sense of well-bred people. The Kerubim, of course, are the personifications of Elemental energies applying to Earthlife. Thus, we have an overall concept of well-founded Life types deriving from sound spiritual stock, and being built up from Elements available on Earth. This is as things should be, rather than actually are.

The Ashim, sometimes termed "Souls of Fire," and possibly connected with the "Anshe Shem," or "Men of Name," said to have had untimely relations with the "daughters of men," are our genetic links taking us right back along our Lines of Life through our physical ancestors until contact is established at the Foundation point in Yesod (Foundation) of our Inner families located at Lunar levels of Innerlife. The Kerubim provide the Elemental qualities necessary for constructing the finest familial Life-types available from Earthly supplies. For example, we might expect of the Kerubim endurance and patience from the Ox, courage and regality from the Lion, discernment and view from the Eagle, and intelligent feelings from the Man. There are other combinations, of course, but they provide the Earthlife basics, which, translated into Inner terms, signify a good specimen of human breeding.

No amount of instruction or education can substitute for good breeding, or the lack of it obviate sound fundamental factors. Not that education or training of any kind is wasted, far from it. All such enhancements of consciousness feed back through the formative channels cleared by the Ashim, and result subsequently in gains for the Inner family with which the living individual in this world is connected. It may ultimately lead to entry into more exalted family circles. Therefore every use should be made, and advantage taken, of the Elements from which our Life-characteristics are modified and altered for the better on Earth.

It is of the highest importance for anyone on this Earth that they achieve at least some sense of "belonging" to an Inner Family, or even Group-Soul, which has actual existence and reality quite apart from Earthlife, yet connects with this World through its incarnated members. In times past, individuals could accept this vital linkage along their own ancestral lines which they were taught like a catechism. Those long and boring lists of names, meaningless to those outside their circles of contact, actually provided Initiated humans with a practical means of meeting up with, and sensing the solidity of, their own rightful Inner kinfolk. No wonder they were advised to "honor their fathers and mothers," or in other words respect their own true lineage leading to Light. Physical parentage today has lost so much significance, and the ancient patterns are so attenuated or broken, that entirely different circles and groupings will have to be formed up along reconstituted lines. This is a major operation involving the Ashim and Kerubim to the full extent of their capabilities.

Everyone with the slightest pretensions of a soul, and, perhaps most of all, those who never think of such subjects at objective conscious level, needs an undoubted assurance of belonging to, and being accepted by, some inclusive overgroup among which their Inner or true Identity is "at home." Rejection by and expulsion from such an Inner Circle brings a sense of horror and desolation which is almost the ultimate unhappiness. We all need spiritual shelter with and inclusion in some particular family, tribe, clan, or associative circle of other entities on our own Life-levels. During our past history, it was possible to experience quite deep degrees of this in conjunction with friends, families, clans, and nations, from social standpoints, and with creeds, faiths, cults, churches, or philosophical systems along meta-physical lines. We could all feel ourselves substantially part and parcel of something bigger than ourselves which would last longer, lead to great possibilities, and to which we could return in another life. Who knows where their Inner loyalties lie now? Who feels they are truly loved and wanted by any circle of Companions living apart from Earthlife? Who can be certain where and with whom they actually belong as selves of soul and Spirit? However we try to answer or ignore such important questions, we shall need the services of the Ashim whether we know them under that name or not. One way or another, we have to know where we line up with Life, and the Ashim lead us to this discovery if we also call upon the Kerubim for the energies and qualities necessary to sustain our search.

The Kerubim are the agencies by means of which we build up our general attitude to Life and apply ourselves to the problems and practice of living in this world toward a finer condition of existence. They are symbolized via the traditional Elements and Creatures. We may accept and use them in any appropriate form. For instance, the Ox may typify Endurance, the Eagle Discernment, the Lion Nobility, and the Man Imagination. Those are four qualities of basics which are absolutely necessary for making ourselves into specimens of humanity worth using as a Foundation for higher systems of Life altogether.

What else are we humans on Earth for that gives Earthlife any depth of meaning at all? Nothing less will put real purpose into our living, or justify our occupation of this planet. Somehow or other, we must eventually come to realize that we are here for the purpose of developing the Inner or spiritual side of our natures so that we, like the Ashim, become "fit and proper people" to be founder-members of Life-chains extending into totally different conditions of conscious Cosmos. This was once called the "Kingdom of Heaven," and we are the "rough ashlars" to be squared off and so finished that we shall at last be worthy of inclusion as "Foundation Stones" upon which the whole Inner Kingdom of Life is established at Yesod. The Kerubim will help us do the work on ourselves until we have attained the needed degree of perfection, and the Ashim will help us put this finished product exactly in its right position to fulfill its true function for the construction of the Temple "not made with hands," in which dwells the Holy Living Spirit. Between them the ASHIM and the KERUBIM deal with our distribution both in and out of this world. They will supply us with the Keys of this process on this particular Path, if we learn how to ask properly.

Expressively, this last and most difficult Path lies between Earth and Moon. Since the Earthworld means to everyone neither more nor less than their own personal experience of Life therein, we shall take that much for granted and concentrate here on the Lunar effects of enlightenment toward those lives.

Our "lift-off" away from Earth, both in a physical and spiritual sense, begins with the Moon. It first drew Man's attention to the mysteries of star-filled space, and awakened contemplative consciousness, imagination, and what are often called our magical faculties. Man could look directly at the Moon while none dared to stare at the Sun without risk of blindness. The first Mysteries organized on Earth were Lunar-feminine rather than Solar-masculine in character, and in all genuine traditions of the Holy Mysteries of Light, initiates are taught and advised to look for Lunar illumination first and foremost before attempting Solar styles of working. "Look for the Sun by means of the Moon" is still the soundest of Mystery principles.

In effect this means procedural patterns adapted to Lunar rhythms and traditions. For example, regulating Inner work programs by the month so that the active practical Earth-side is inaugurated at New Moon, increases to culmination at Full Moon, then goes into devotional and meditational phases during the Moon's waning, and pauses for depth-contact at the last period before New Moon again. The Lunar side of the Mysteries is especially concerned with gaining control of our imaginative faculties and the fantasies out of which we can construct so much of our Inner Cosmic life. The myths, legends, folk-tales, and other constituents out of which our elementary Inner education arises, are so much Lunar lore to be assimilated and rearranged into progressive patterns leading us gently and gradually toward more intense degrees of Light. Those who fail in these first degrees of the Path tend to insanity, not because of the subject-matter involved, but through their own lack of ability or training in conceptual and conscious use of it for higher ends. Others who suppose their own superiority to Lunar Light levels and think they can plunge boldly past them, straight into spiritual Sunlight, are liable to be severely burned for their foolhardiness. The Lord of the Sun punishes those who offend the Lady of the Moon, as older writers would have phrased it.

If we consider some of the Lunar symbols, we shall easily see how they connect with the Lunar Mysteries of Life. The Maze, for example, signifying confusion of consciousness easily sorted out when the overall pattern is discovered. The Thorn-bush, or the tangled thoughts that tear at us, yet have so many valuable uses when properly employed. The Bridge of Moonbeams, or safe way across the gulf dividing madness and sanity. The Silver Castle, or Dream-dwelling, where we take refuge from the hostile issues of Life while we conceive ways and means of coping with them otherwise. All these, and many more, tell the story of what the Moon means for Man on Earth. They speak of fertility and fecundity of Mind and Soul as well as Body, and those who are Wise will listen carefully to what they tell us in our dreams.

This, in fact, is the Path of Life where we begin as ordinary human beings to put Mind and Soul together with Body and Spirit in order to make Selves out of this Cosmic combination. The Selves we dream of until they come true. The poet has said we are such stuff as dreams are made on, but we might also say that dreams are the stuff we make ourselves from. Those without dreams are those without vision, and it has been said that without vision the people perish. All this and much more along such lines must be mediated upon this Path. The Lunar Light of reflection and alternation of intensity through reiterated cycles of consciousness reveals these elementary stages of our Inner evolution away from Earth. We must learn how to make ourselves live by Lunar laws along such lines, recognizing the rise and fall of Life-tides, the waxing and waning of periodic spiritual illumination, the right times and places to plant ideas and aspirations into suitable soil, and every such kind of Lunar Life-lore. Not until we have properly grasped the principles on this Path should we venture to climb to other branches of the Tree. By this period of our Earth-evolution, even average humans have become practical Initiates of the Path to quite a fair degree, but those who intend deepening and extending their Life-abilities through the Holy Mysteries of Light will be required to recapitulate the Lunar Initiations through much more concentrated courses of consciousness.

It might help travelers along this Path to remember the Shekinah, or that perceptible luminous cloud on Earth which bore testimony of the invisible influence from highest Heaven. The probability that this was actually some form of static electrical phenomenon does not invalidate its mystical significance. Just as the Moon bears witness at night to the continuance of our Solar Cosmos, so do equivalent Symbols on Earth reflect the Light of a Heaven we cannot see while we remain in human obscurity. It is a question of finding the right conditions for making such observations, or achieving a clear, serene, and unclouded state of consciousness, with no interventions between our Inner eyes and the reflecting surface of the Symbol. When we discover how to make almost anything on Earth act as a mirror like the Moon, revealing the Light of a Sun hidden from us by Earth, we shall have climbed this main stem Path to a very considerable degree.

Divinity is said to look at Humanity from four Faces. First the Vast Countenance of starry Space itself. Then the Lesser Countenance of the Sun which we dare not look upon while we live as mortals. Next comes the Mystical Countenance of the Moon, seeing us through dreams, visions, and reflections. Last, of course, is the Close Countenance, or the face of this very Earth we are living on, where we can be viewed in our normal habitat through the eyes of all our fellow-creatures, human or otherwise. Here, upon this proximal Path, we are daring to lift our line of vision from Earth toward Heaven. Even though we should scarcely expect insight at first, the fact that we have realized there is something to find, if we look long and faithfully enough, will be sufficient to keep us pointed in the right direction for finding what we seek as we go along.

If we stand here at the foot of the Living Tree, and give the traditional three knocks on its trunk while we listen for an echoed reply, we shall perhaps realize something of its structure and extent above and beyond us. Even the faintest response from the Tree should convince us that here is a Way from Earth to Infinity which will not only bear the weight of our most strenuous attempts at Cosmic climbing, but must infallibly support all that lives in the whole of Existence. Having so knocked, we must ask in the right way, and the Keys will surely be given to us which admit every soul, one by one, along the Paths of Perfection, into the Presence of the Living Spirit who alone makes it all possible.

Leaf, Fruit, and Seed

Having toured every branch of the Tree of Life in the briefest possible way, only one thing remains to be done. Live it. We have seen how the amazing Tree covers every aspect of Cosmic Life and Consciousness under a few principle headings schematically related with each other. By this time, it becomes clear enough that another twenty-two volumes of equal or greater size could quite easily be written to cover each Path in far deeper detail. Becoming ambitious on behalf of future workers, we might even imagine an entire Encyclopedia of the Tree in eighty-eight volumes, four per Path. Possibilities are never ending. We have but to touch the Tree at any point, and it is capable of expansion by experience to infinite extensions, providing we remember the operative rule of setting up our Pillars as limits, and streaming our consciousness between them in the Middle Way toward the desired direction.

That, after all, is the secret of using the Tree. Channeling, or beaming our consciousness along lines of deliberately limited width, but limitless in depth of reach. This is the pattern of the Tree itself. Limits at the sides, and bounded at the bottom by initiating inertia, but absolutely unlimited in the direction of Divinity. We may imagine ourselves constructing a sort of projection tube on the principles of the Tree. The two side Pillars are the barrel, the base our own standpoint, and the Middle pillar our projectile and its power. The other end of this mystical Light-launcher is freely open as long as we keep pointing it into the Ain Soph Aur as we should. To Project consciousness by this means, we bring an aim into view between the point of our projectile and Ain Soph Aur, then press the release button. There are many other ways of working this analogy, but the principle of "guiding

401

the sides while we extend the end," applies to all Tree-work.

Such is life in any case. Making our way from one known birth-beginning toward an unknown exit into Eternity, keeping as much in the middle as we can between extremities on either side. This is exactly the pattern of the Tree, except that we set the proper width of view, or "Pillar distance," for ourselves, according to the proportions shown by the Tree-Plan. Magical ritualists will realize this ideal measurement to be proportional with their personal passage, and regulated by the Rod, so that held horizontally it will just engage its ends against the Pillars enough to prevent passage. Vertical position of the Rod allows an advance to be made like a Key turning in a lock, which is what the action symbolizes. To live our Tree, we simply relate it to ourselves and our existence by means of some practical symbology such as ritual, and gear in our lives with it as we go along.

There are so many ways of doing just this, that it is largely a matter of the personal selection employed. The Tree itself is supposed to inform its Initiates of their individual needs. Nevertheless, it seems a deficiency in some respects that reliable ritual and liturgical material is not readily available for those in the early stages of Qabalistic practice. This might help them over the first few difficult hurdles until such time as they were able to supply their own necessities. Some tentative steps are already being taken in this direction, as witness the *Office of the Holy Tree*, published by Sangreal Foundation (USA). This useful and entirely original work comprises a complete set of invocations and prayers, one for each Sephirah and Path. When related together, they form into a systematic "Pathworking" from one end of the Tree to the other, so that a Path a day can be taken consecutively throughout a lifetime if required, something on the style of the "Divine Office" based on the Psalms. Provision is made for brief meditations on each Path, and apart from providing a sense of continuity and linkage with the Tree, the whole exercise results in ever deepening contact with the Consciousness operating through the Tree-Concepts as a system of communication with human awareness. Schemes such as this are likely to prove of very great value if they are used to assist, and not supplant, individual experience of the Life-Tree.

Once the major difficulties and obscurities of Qabalistic principles, practice, and parlance have been straightened out in accordance with modern mentality, yet retaining the fundamental truths and teaching of our oldest spiritual Traditions, a great stride will have been made toward our future as a Life-species destined for fulfillment of a Divine purpose. What this will amount to is offering every single soul capable of individual spiritual initiative all the necessary Keys, clues, and means for finding his or her own Life-Path and coming to direct relationships with Inner Life-dimensions and Divinity itself. At the same time there will be the closest sense of Companionship with all others living in similar circles of consciousness linking the Light-lines of Cosmos through a common bond of belief. There is little likelihood, however, of Qabalah ever becoming an acceptable Tradition among the masses of Mankind who reject responsibility for their personal spiritual progress and expect to find all their demands catered to by ready-made religions, automated artificial thought-tracks, and purchaseable philosophies. Qabalah is for spirits of sufficient stature to stand by themselves and ask of Cosmic Consciousness whatever they would be answered in terms of their own.

There are three principle products that fall from trees to be gathered up by those beneath them. Leaves, fruits, and seeds. The leaves we can look at or learn from, the fruit will refresh and nourish us, and the seeds grow more trees to perpetuate a living process. We may gather leaves from the Tree of Life almost everywhere if we know how to recognize them. They are whatever informs us of the Tree in any way, or tells us of its works either directly or by suggestion. This book, for instance, is such a leaf from the Tree. So are a set of Tarot Trumps, or a set of circumstances connecting consciousness with the Tree. Just as leaves put together make up a book, so do leaves from the Holy Tree tell the Story of Life, or any single life-story at all, to those who can interpret the script.

The fruits of the Tree are what we obtain from it and assimilate into ourselves so that this becomes essentially part of us through what might almost be described as spiritual biochemistry. Each Path has its especial fruit, so that once we know our Inner needs, we may reach out and help ourselves from whichever branch bears the appropriate provision. It is these fruits of the Tree which afford us the sustenance of our Inner lives and keep us in good conditions of spiritual health. Like physical fruit, they take time to grow and ripen, having their seasons and proper occasions for plucking. We cannot very well expect a good crop until we have cultivated our Trees to a state when they are ready to produce wholesome specimens for Inner eating.

Each individual Tree springs from seeds found in the fruits of former Trees. This means to say that every aspiring Qabalist faithfully growing a Tree must have obtained its seed from the fruit of others cultivated previously by past planters. So indeed Qabalah continues from spiritual generation to generation. Sometimes the harvest seems very sparse, and now and then comes a most fruitful period for everyone. Naturally we all have our individual seasons of fruitfulness which should supply us with more seeds for more Trees, but so far as there can be a fruiting time for Humanity in general throughout this world, once in a century seems a fair average. So grows the Tree of Life among us.

Much has been made in Qabalistic literature of letter and number interchanging in order to learn the spiritual secrets encoded by the Tree-arrangement. To attempt this on literal lines is unlikely to reveal more than consonantal combinations capable of whatever interpretations we like which fit around them. The real value of these practices lies with the systematic training and use of consciousness during their exercise. They make us use our awareness in a way which extends our Inner life experience toward areas of existence not generally accessible to average mortals. Regular practice and exercise of our intellectual faculties in such ways certainly tends to develop a consciousness capable of Qabalah.

The principle behind these letter-number procedures is very simply a compression or limitation of consciousness so that it expands or extends in another dimension of awareness. This process is necessarily reversible, so that a complete cyclic exchange of conscious energy occurs. Thus we begin, say, by taking a number of words which concern any particular concept or concepts. Each word consists of a lesser number of basic concepts called letters, and these we now convert to numerical values according to an acceptable alphabetical conversion tariff; e.g., "A equals 1, B equals 2, etc." Now with another conversion effort we alter these values into a new arrangement by totaling the numbers of each letter word by word, so that a number stands in the place of each word. This has resulted in an overall group of value-concepts to the same total as the original number of words, but capable of being inter-related with each other according to quite different laws. That is to say we could add, subtract, multiply, divide, or do anything with them which is mathematically possible and obtain an end product relative to the process employed. Having done this, we may continue the cycle by reconverting resultant number values back into alphabetical components of letters, which are then arrangeable into new combinations of words giving us quite different concepts and conditions of consciousness from those we had at the commencement of this entire operation.

What we have done, in effect, is move our working consciousness from the field of word-thinking to the much more universal field of value-thinking, yet kept a practical connection open between the two entirely different states so that energy-exchanges are possible between them. For an initiated Qabalist, a yet more remarkable development should have occurred during such an operation. Having changed consciousness from word-working to value-vision, a further change becomes possible which is the secret aim and intention of initiates engaged in these activities. From a state of consciousness operating constructively or cosmically in a force-field composed of pure values, it becomes possible to enter yet another state higher, wherein contact is made and sustained with orders of intelligence far in advance of human thinking or awareness. Once it becomes possible for an initiated human being to make and hold conscious contacts with Life on those levels, then a re-conversion of energies must result in a force-flow which emerges at our end as concretions or manifestations of consciousness in word-concepts, which are bound to change our living to lesser or greater degrees, according to the nature and extent of any such exchange.

The whole of this action is not unlike the stages of Space-travel. We start on Earth with a word-language working in alphabetically arranged sequences separating one concept from another. Then we are projected into a Space-state where conscious communication is converted into pure values co-related by means of a computer since humans are incapable of such thinking-scales in time-terms. Assuming a safe landing is made on an alien world, the combined sensory and consciousness systems of the spacecraft itself and its human crew will engage in exchanges of awareness with those new entities and environments coming into contact with the circle of consciousness set up round the craft and crew like a magic circle round a magician in old times. After this momentous event, the return cycle is made in reverse order, and later on the experience is coded into words which are likely to alter our concepts of Life in Earthly terms.

This is just the sort of adventure we are expected to undertake through Inner Space by means of methods available from Qabalistic sources of supply, and unless we understand what this entails, Qabalism will provide nothing more than mere intellectual entertainment. Those who are content to push numbers and letters around on paper in the hope of some Higher Being attending promptly to human wants, or for the sake of even worse motives, are doomed to remain "number-letter twisters" for at least the remainder of their Earth lives, if they do not find a way out of their self-made maze toward deeper levels of truth. Unless a field of consciousness can be converted stage by stage from ordinary verbalizing levels to purely innate intuitional intelligence linked with higher than human living, then re-routed back to complete the cycle, we might stare aimlessly at Qabalistic symbology for ever. The numbers and letters are only a means to an end. That end is raising our reason, intelligence, and all processes of consciousness toward a more advanced order of Life than our purely human status. In old terminology this was called, "Knowledge of and Conversation with the Holy Guardian Angel." Whether we still choose to employ the term "Angel" (Agent or Messenger) or prefer some alternative phraseology, the implication of humanity seeking contact with a consciousness belonging to higher orders of entity is the same.

There are naturally other methods of extending our awareness into Inner fields than via word-letter-value conversions. Music and dance-mime, for instance, will serve similar ends. So will other combinations of field-shifting. Why then, should we bother with comparatively complicated Qabalistic procedures? What is their advantage over other systems? The principal reason is on account of the entity-classifications closely concerned with the Tree-System, and using it something in the nature of a call-sign, frequency, and specialized code for closer degrees of contact between human consciousness and their own. By no means every type or species of discarnate entity and Innerworld intelligence is necessarily favorable toward our best chances of development in a Divine direction. This does not imply such beings are evil, or even inimical to us, though we should not dismiss such a possibility altogether. These "others" may well be perfectly pleasant and harmless entities of no great efficacy or even as much value as vague good wishes from casual acquaintances in Earthly embodiment. Inner contacts made via the Tree-System, or through Qabalistic procedures, are most unlikely to be of this nature, or to allow intentional or accidental contact with types of entity which might be considered "evil" or inimical to right-meaning Initiates. With the Tree-System, we have quite a sound assurance that our Inner contacts made through its means will be true Companions of Cosmos with whom our best hopes and interests lie. In addition, we have as good a guarantee against adverse effects as may possibly be offered to Initiates of the Inner Way. These are very sound reasons for selection of the Qabalistic approach to Cosmic Awareness by those able to adopt its principles and practice its disciplines.

None of these considerations implies that Qabalism is productive of easy living, comfortable conditions, high incomes, or any of the material advantages connected with Earth life which attract the least spiritual and worst motivated members of our mortal species. To the contrary, Qabalah has a Tradition running with roots among quite poor or else very wealthy people. The common bond between these two social extremes is non-attachment to money or power for ill intentions. One side seeks not that of this world which they do not possess, and the other seeks not the same because they have it already. Both parties actively seek the same Inner aims from motives transcending the sheer lust for power and possessions causing so many mortals to reject all else and remain with lowest life-levels on Earth for the meanest reasons. It is not that poverty is particularly ennobling, riches degrading, or the other way around. The issue is one of force-flow polarity. If any entity deliberately binds up its being with its will, and devotes all energies exclusively to the power-position-possession self-cycles of Earth living, then they are diverting and applying, to those areas alone, forces which should flow freely around the Nadir of Earth-existence and return on their Cosmic course toward Divinity. We might say they were rendering to Caesar the things of God. A poor person whose entire life-aim is directed into greedy and avaricious channels is equally guilty of this as the richest person alive with a similar character. The whole question is one of motivations and attachments. Qabalah is for those whose directing drive is not confined to or originating with Earth life living levels. Coming from higher origins entirely, this driving motive must descend to Earth and actuate humans who are able to translate it into terms of their own consciousness, react according to their capabilities, then send the combined energy-stream back toward its Inner origin to complete the remainder of the cycle.

Qabalists of old frequently remained poor because when faced with the choice between committing their lives to a course of cut-throat commercialism or spiritual service, they unhesitatingly chose the latter. The decisive factor was whether or not anything interfered with their most direct line of Light from Inner spiritual sources. Rather than lose contact with those vital rays leading them toward a Life they valued above all others, they took whatever course kept their conscience clearest. Providing their spiritual principles and purposes were not threatened, Qabalists have never been barred by their beliefs from worldly wealth or office. The one absolute and rigid restriction has always been upon using Qabalah as such for moneymaking or personal profit. The inflexible rule was and is yet, "Live for the Law, and never by It." This is why so many sincere Qabalists earned their livings by manual or craft work, becoming wood-carvers, shoemakers, farmers, artists, musicians, scientists, etc. They sought to earn their livings in ways which would neither impede their own spiritual Light nor that of others.

Altogether, there is nothing in Qabalism for the get-rich-quickers, and the find-fame-fasters. That is the surest hope for the System of remaining relatively sound through its spiritual structure and only attracting the sort of souls suitable for living out its Tradition at all levels. Nor, despite its accent on Inner life, and directions toward Divinity, is Qabalism an easy escape route from unsatisfactory Earthlife conditions into a cloud-cuckoo-land of pleasant fantasy. There is no magic in Qabalah which will save its adherents from themselves or their circumstances while they make no efforts to apply its principles to both. Anyone foolish enough to approach Qabalah with vague ideas of coercing supernatural agencies into abnormal activities on human behalf is doomed to well deserved disappointment—if not worse. Qabalah is a practical means of Life-relationship between ourselves and the Living Spirit. We might even think of the Tree and its Spheres as a sort of interrelated gear system for gearing ourselves in with God. Everything else about it is subservient to that prevailing purpose.

With this ultimate end always in view, contact is needed between the consciousness of advancing humans and those entities who are most closely concerned with human Cosmic destinies. Since we of this world think so much in words, and those of immediate Otherlife do not, some means of translation has to be found. The nearest comparable Units of consciousness to ours they work with, are senses and sequences of values relative to our mathematics but based on quite different conceptual principles. Thus, if we can arrange a common meeting ground in literally figurative fields and bring results from this region back to words we understand as Earth-entities, the problem of communication between these varying states of Life will be well on the way to solution.

This is exactly what the Letter-figure relationships and all associative coded consciousness of the Life-Tree and its Paths are for. They work like a cipher machine which takes in an Unintelligible communication at one end and produces a readable rendering in English or any language at the other. In the case of the Tree, these communications come out in whatever language the System is set up for. Hitherto, it has only been set for Hebrew, and therefore has been limited to that tongue. Now at last an attempt is being made to set the Tree for English so that it can be used with practical purpose by those of us who talk, think, and act in accordance with Traditions of the West bound up with English as a Mother language. No matter what reactions to this transition may come from conventional Qabalists who automatically challenge the least innovation, this development of the Tree-design for living must take its proper place in a Plan aiming for human advancement in the future. It is a twentieth-century contribution for the consciousness of twenty-first century Qabalists to work with.

It is obvious to any human of average intelligence that in order to cope with the pressing problems we are presented with during our modern Earthlives alone, we shall not only have to alter our thinking values very considerably, but will also have to change and expand our methods of consciousness and extent of Inner awareness. How we think is of greater importance than what we think of and we are faced with learning how to live and extend our existence along quite different life-lines than those we are following on Earth during our present period of history. So much can scarcely be questioned, but the real query is just how the courses of consciousness which control our future fate can be altered into different dimensions. The Tree-System of the Qabalah offers an exceptional answer to this all-important issue.

We have seen how Path concepts may be built up and made into an accumulation of awareness by alternating between Polarity points from whence supplies are drawn. Theoretically, the limits to this amount of intelligence are unknown. If each Path is coded by a letter of the alphabet and a figure combination, that code-symbol by itself should provide a Key to the whole Path working. Every time we meditate upon or work with any Path, we increase our stock of consciousness by the amount we put in. Suppose we are meditating on the Eleventh Path, which lies between Sephirah 1 and 2, letter B in the English System. Perhaps we begin by imagining a large letter B between the Sephiroth values of 1 and 2. Then, we allow the B to fade gently into whatever we are Pushing through the 1 - 2 Pillar gap in to the Universal Mind beyond. When finished, the B should reappear to "seal things in." To reverse the process, we set up the Symbols and receive what comes through the opened B Portal, remembering to close it again afterwards.

After our consciousness has been conditioned in this way for a sufficient period, we shall have programed a sort of Inner computer keyed by Letter-figure codes of a simple nature, and containing our whole conscious Cosmos with leads extending indefinitely into Inner Dimensions of Existence. Entities living in, and employing codifications of consciousness natural to such states, may therefore work back along those lines until the energies we receive from them are converted into intelligible terms of our own native tongue. The actual translation into English is made by ourselves out of what we received from other sources, so that accuracy or extent of communication does really depend on our interdimensional linguistic ability. For instance, we receive and register a unit of energy emanating from another type of entity. The category into which this must go in order to release the right letter-code relating to it in our minds is decided by how correctly we have constructed our Inner circuitry. If this is muddled and inaccurate, then only a garbled version of an original contact with Inner communicator will emerge.

However well we program our Paths with Letter-codes, we shall always need the values of Vowels before we get much sense in English from consonants. Vowels have not been attributed to the Paths in this System because they equate with concepts ommon to Paths, namely the Four Elements and the Principle of Spirit Itself. The Four Life-Elements equate with the Vowels as:

A - Earth, or solidity of Concept.
E - Air, or inspiration of Concept.
I - Fire, or relevance of Concept.
O - Water, or fluidity of Concept.
U - Universal Element of Meaning in Concept, or Truth.

Those are the essential Elements of every verbal Concept we need to receive or impart via the Tree of Life. Each should have a certain solidity we designate by the Vowel "A," an inspirational content we term "E," some special relevance denoted by "I," and a fluidity which allows for adaption or connection with other concepts represented by "O." In addition, there has to be a Universal Element capable of translation into any terms, so this is shown by the vowel "U." With these four main factors and their common point of union, we can proceed to link up our Consonantal Concepts so that a Living Language of spiritual speech comes to life through the Tree.

This special treatment of vowels stems back to the Inner Traditions which have always used them as "Great Names of Power," or sonic symbols of Divinity in the purest possible sense relative to human speech. They bring life, meaning, and intelligent consciousness to otherwise pointless (unvoweled) collections of consonants.

Thus, they are like the Life-Spirit, imparting Itself to every item of living Existence and creating Cosmos of Chaos. No word can really come alive for us without vowels any more than inanimate material of other descriptions could hold intelligent communication with us. The vowel makes all the difference between "dead letters" and the "living Word." Hence they are used for animating our otherwise lifeless secret Inner speaking. This was one reason why the "Sacred Tetragram" of IHVH, the "unpronounceable Name," became so revered of old. It was not the actual written letters which were revered, but the unwritten vowels which appeared in between them purely to the awareness of initiated readers. Therefore the IHVH meant whatever might be made of it through vowels suggested straight into Inner awareness by inspiration from the Living Spirit of Cosmic Intelligence. Man set up the Letters of the Law, but God sent in the Spirit. So it was that the Name could not be spoken by Man, for only Divinity might utter the life-giving vowels to a consciousness opened along the right Inner lines.

An initiated human intelligence trained in working this way eventually becomes accustomed to accepting the "face value" of anything or anyone as a series of Letters, and expecting the true Inner value to be imparted through information gained on deep contact-levels as equivalents of vowels spoken by the Spirit of Understanding at that depth of Divinity. The belief is that if we pick up the Letters, looking at them with faith and asking with hope, the compassion of the Cosmic One will tell us the vowel-values in our hearts which complete the Word we should take them for. So do Qabalists seek speech with God, by using consonants as symbols for the framework of consciousness constructed by human efforts, and accepting vowels as symbolic of that Divine Awareness which makes entire spiritual sense of All that Exists.

Equating vowels with suitable Inner values and then applying them through the Tree-Symbols is largely a routine matter of associative procedures. If we accept the easy Elemental attributions, such courses are quite simple to follow. We might start with literal simplicity by means of some solid Earth object such as a stone, a candle or lamp, and a cup or bowl of water. Air might be provided by our own breath or a fan. When handling the stone we resonate "A" with all our attention of body, mind, and soul. When lighting or carrying the candle or lamp, "I" is treated the same. "O" is sonated while we deal with the water, and "E" as we activate the air. When going from one Element to another or dealing with them sequentially we resonate "U." All sorts of really pleasing little rites may be worked up in such fashion.

Another literal device which is most useful because of its

conscious associations, is a plain four-sided teetotum with A, E, I, and O written on its sides. The vowel U is indicated by the actual spinning of the top as the Elemental Letters whirl around in their Life-dance of the Cosmic Circle. We visualize this action going on automatically the whole time we are "Lettering the Tree." Appropriate vowels will thus select themselves relatively to Letters once practice has extended this exercise into the realms of possibility. We should not attempt to stop the teetotum ourselves, or let it keep spinning to indicate "U." All we have to do is supply the idea of the thing, and leave the vowel selection to Inner Intelligence associating with us in the operation

By means also of straightforward meditation, we may link the Vowels with their Inner values. It is a useful idea to hum or resonate each vowel while meditating on its deep Significance. "A," for example, should mean the weight, appreciable quantity, consistency, and all the qualities of any concept which might associate with Earth as an element of Awareness. "E" must bring to mind Airy qualities, such as inspiration, atmosphere, etc. "I," being Fire and Light, signifies relevance, illumination, warm feelings, and so forth. "O," as Water, implies potability of a concept, fluidity of its nature, its depth, content, and the like. "U," is a Universal link among all these Elements of Life. Sometimes this "extra" Element is termed Aether, but if we take its hidden meaning to be concealed by the first and last letters of the Alphabet, A - Th, this may well signify the Element of Truth: Amath. Therefore we have our perfect linkage with the Elements of Living as a thread or cord of Truth running universally through them, and represented by the vowel sonic "U."

For those who find ritual Procedures of chanting helpful in establlshing workable relationships with Inner realities, the entire Path-Alphabet and Vowel-Elements have been rhythmically arranged and set out for ceremonial or instructional usage by a litany-like procedure known as "The Telling of the Tree." This consists of bare associative statements concerning the Spheres of each Path, their numbers on the Tree, and the letter of the Path linking them together. In addition, the particular taps of the Spheres may be given at the end of every Sphere-line, so that a very pleasingly complete exercise can be made out of the whole affair. Its script runs:

THE TELLING OF THE TREE

Path No.	*Spheres*	*Knocks*	*Letters*
0.	NIL is Zero. CROWN comes First	0-1	
	The Path of Life between says—		Naught
11.	CROWN is First, and WISDOM second	1-2	
	The Path of Life between says—		B
12.	CROWN is First, UNDERSTANDING Third	1-3	
	The Path of Life between says—		C
13.	CROWN is First, and BEAUTY Sixth	1-6	
	The Path of Life between says—		D
14.	WISDOM Second, and MERCY Fourth	2-3	
	The Path of Life between says—		F
15.	WISDOM Second, and MERCY Fourth	2-4	
	The Path of Life between says—		G
16.	WISDOM Second, and BEAUTY Sixth	2-6	
	The Path of Life between says—		H
17.	UNDERSTANDING Third, SEVERITY Fifth	3-5	
	The Path of Life between says—		J
18.	UNDERSTANDING Third and BEAUTY Sixth	3-6	
	The Path of Life between says—		K
19.	MERCY Fourth, SEVERITY Fifth	4-5	
	The Path of Life between says—		L
20.	MERCY Fourth and BEAUTY Sixth	4-6	
	The Path of Life between says—		M
21.	MERCY Fourth and VICTORY Seventh	4-7	
	The Path of Life between says—		N
22.	SEVERITY Fifth and BEAUTY Sixth	5-6	
	The Path of Life between says—		P
23	SEVERITY Fifth and GLORY Eighth	5-8	
	The Path of Life between says—		Q
24.	BEAUTY Sixth and VICTORY Seventh	6-7	
	The Path of Life between says—		R
25	BEAUTY Sixth and GLORY Eighth	6-8	
	The Path of Life between says—		S

26. BEAUTY Sixth, FOUNDATION Ninth, 6-9
    The Path of Life between says— T

27. VICTORY Seventh and GLORY Eighth 7-8
    The Path of Life between says— V

28. VICTORY Seventh, FOUNDATION Ninth, 7-9
    The Path of Life between says— W

29. VICTORY Seventh and KINGDOM Tenth 7-10
    The Path of Life between says— X

30. GLORY Eighth, FOUNDATION Ninth, 8-9
    The Path of Life between says— Y

31. GLORY Eighth and KINGDOM Tenth 8-10
    The Path of Life between says— Z

32. FOUNDATION Ninth, KINGDOM Tenth, 9-10
    The Path of Life between says— Th

The chanting of the Elements may either be done by itself, or interspersed among the Paths as desired. In fact, this Element-chant might be taken as an entirely separate item where and whenever intended. As a rule, however, the Path-letter chanting should always be completed or accompanied by the Vowel-chant, whereas this may be treated as an independent item. It makes a suitable accompaniment if recordings of the actual Elemental sonics themselves accompany the chanting of the Vowels. For example, there might be a noise of a rushing wind for Air, a crackling blaze for Fire, breaking waves for Water, and thudding sounds for Earth. The "Sound of Truth" for the Universal Element may be anything from an echoing gong to a vibrating string of piano or harp. Such refinements may not be absolutely necessary, but they do help especially the early practice in exercises like this. The chant of the Elements goes:

THE ELEMENTS

The Living Element of AIR
Is sensed and symbolized by   E E E E E E E E E E

The Living Element of FIRE
Is sensed and symbolized by   I I I I I I I I I I

The Living Element of WATER
Is sensed and symbolized by   O O O O O O O O O O

The Living Element of EARTH
Is sensed and symbolized by   AAAAAAAAAA

The Living Element of TRUTH
Is sensed and symbolized by   UUUUUUUUUU

Blessed be the Holy Living Name   E. I. O. A.   HU-U.

These chants may either be worked by a single person, or in chorus between many. They are among the many ways we might choose to "give the Vowels to God, and keep the Letters of the Living Law" ourselves.

All this processing of consciousness is easy enough to describe with a few sweeping sentences, but it may well take many generations before any remarkable changes among humans are noted through what might be called "Qabalistic consciousness." Nevertheless, it is perfectly possible to produce quite definite alterations of awareness, and a much richer relationship with Life as a whole, over a few short years of theoretical and practical work with the system. Existence, Ultimate Identity, and Infinite and the Individual, and all our vital issues of living become quite different, and markedly more important to those enquirers into the Eternal Enigma who link them through the Tree-patterns they construct in their own consciousness. All that lives around and in the awareness of a Qabalist seems to proceed quite naturally into its proper place and assume its correct proportions. The point and purpose of living becomes clearer every day, and entirely new vistas open up on living levels beyond the boundaries of Earth, though invisibly touching them for the majority of mankind. A sense of direction from a Divinely constituted authority is experienced, and the meanings of everything encountered in Life become deeper and more relevant all the time. In short, confidence and competence in living, even through the worst conditions Earthlife may inflict, comes to those who conscientiously attempt Qabalistic consciousness, including the early stages of its inception, covering a decade or so of Earthlife. With some souls more rapid results yet may be Possible.

It is highly unlikely and also very undesirable that mysterious voices will whisper all kinds of dubious instructions or gratuitous information about the workings of the Universe. Any such event should be severely suspected and put to every possible test. Objectified aural phenomena heard as if spoken into the ear rarely come from the most reliable Inner sources. The communion we seek with trustworthy Inner Intelligences associated with the Qabalistic Tree normally comes from inside us through very deep contacts which reach our personally focused consciousness as conclusions or convictions arising from realizations we have made by our recognition of truth on those fundamental levels of Life. Insofar as these can be verbalized, they generally do so as a kind of "word-experience" so that we live the words into terms appreciable by our normal awareness. We do not so much *hear* words as *be* them and resonate them into recognizable sonic symbols at the focal point of our personal consciousness.

The principles of this are tied in with the Magical practice once known as "Vibrating the God-Name," or sonic sequence, with such effect that every nerve in the body and sense of the soul is modulated by and resonates to the particular frequency of that Name and its meaning. That is why such Names are traditionally chanted at great length in a variety of pitches. This is an art needing considerable practice and perseverance before results can be expected. From the physical sound, resonance is transferred to mental meaning, spiritual sense, and then released toward the Inner realms of recipience for which it is intended. This can be done with any word at all actually, but "God-names" are usually sonic combinations especially suitable for this purpose. Our reception of replies or intentional communications from these "God-guarded" Inner areas of awareness returns to us along reversed lines. From Inner sources, the spiritual sense of a contact becomes coded into mental equivalents which may result as condensations of our consciousness into such potent phraseology that even our physical bodies resonate as we recognize its meaning. Thus do the Gods we invoke "answer back" in echoes, and so may we expect to hear the Tree talking to us as it rustles its leaves in reply.

Growing a physical tree is a lifetime experience of very great meaning. To hold the original seed in the hand, look at it, realize its potentials, and hopefully plant it in proper conditions. Then waiting and wondering while it develops in the dark for perhaps a prolonged period. The thrill and joyous excitement when at last a tiny green tip reaches the light of day and announces its intention of living with us as a companion in this world. We follow the growth, count each leaf, protect the little tree from harm, and as we do so find ourselves growing into a very definite relationship of friendliness and affection toward it. As it gets older with us, we tend to take it more and more for granted, but there are still all the magic moments to come of admiring its flowering and especially plucking its first fruit to eat, or climbing into its welcoming branches. Over the years, an affinity between that tree and ourselves grows steadily stronger and deeper in a strange sense which cannot be explained any more than love is explicable. If the tree were to die, something of ourselves would die with it. It has become part and parcel of our lives, interrelated with our inhabitance of this world in a way that makes living here mean just that much more, and maybe we have an unuttered hope the tree will remain here to tell our story after we have departed. So long as it stays on Earth, it will be our living memorial and a trysting-tree for those of our kind who love us. Perhaps there might be a feeling that the tree will act like a link between ourselves and those we leave behind when we quit mortal life, and provide some means of communication with one another. Who knows the extent of hope a human heart may hold?

All this, and very much more, applies in metaphysical equivalents with the Tree of Life, except that it cannot be cut down and destroyed like a physical tree. Nor will the Trees of Life we grow within ourselves die with our human bodies, for we shall continue living according to their pattern whether we are incarnate or not. Indeed it becomes a great advantage for us to have a common Pattern of consciousness connecting our incarnate and discarnate living. Just as eventually the fragile and delicate green stems of a seedling tree on Earth grow into strong and secure branches to bear our weight as we climb upwards in search of fruit, so will an Inwardly grown Tree of Life ultimately develop equally reliable supports for our searching souls and spirits to rise up and reach realization and fulfillment of our highest purpose in Life. It is all a matter of tending our Trees with persevering patience during the spiritual Seasons we pass through, as we progress around the Cosmic circles of the Sun behind the Sun.

Everyone should grow a Tree whose life is bound up with their own. Sometimes this was done literally when a child was born, and both tree and child grew up together with an odd bond of understanding between them. In the long ago, when people believed that Divinity dwelt in all that lives (as It does) they would sometimes seek out trees that seemed specially magical for them and tell the Life-Spirit, through the tree, all their sorrows, fears, troubles and problems, praying for help and comfort. Physically, the tree provided something to hold, a shoulder to lean on, a coat of bark to cry against, a crevice to whisper secrets in, a gentle rocking like a mother's arms, a soothing murmur of leaves moved by the wind of compassion. Spiritually, the tree mediated what the helpless humans needed most. An unmistakable Inner assurance that the Life Spirit was entirely aware of them as individuals, was concerned about their cares, would look after them in Its own way, did love them and want them to continue living, however difficult this might seem. The tree gave them our greatest asset in Life: Confidence in Cosmos. We may have come many centuries from the period when mankind ran automatically to trees for safety and assurance of Life, but the Pattern is still with us in principle, and the Tree of Life fulfills this vital function for us now and forever.

Nothing will ever be out of date about the Qabalistic Tree of Life. From any present point of conscious contact with it, we may penetrate its past or fare forth into its future as far as our ability allows. There is no end to the exploration possible except the extent of our awareness, and the limits of our will to follow its ways. Qabalism is no cut-and-dried set of outworn opinions, but a constant of consciousness growing continually from the Tree-Tradition as we grow with it toward Living Light. Qabalah is the faith in Life we achieve through listening to what it teaches us from Inner depths leading to Divinity. That is the Tradition we receive handed on to us by those ahead of us in living, and which we are expected to pass back to those behind us, with our added contribution of consciousness.

It is precisely this last factor which makes Qabalah so utterly different from any other spiritual System. Though it is neither a religion nor a philosophy in an ordinary sense, it fulfills the functions of both and offers opportunities in all fields of Life, where these apply, which seem unique when contrasted with more widely recognized codes. Most of these outline a mythology which may or may not be related to historical data, lay down a specific set of dogmas, laws for living, doctrines for learning, set up a socio-spiritual hierarchy of their own, then expect support-

up a socio-spiritual hierarchy of their own, then expect supporters of the System to devote their life-efforts and earnings to the
upkeep and expansion of the entire combine. Qabalah works in
quite another manner. It has no recognizable hierarchy in this
world, although its exponents and adherents have existed
through the centuries and occasionally offered various publications which seemed appropriate for their era. None has claimed
infallibility, Divine authority, or made any demands whatsoever
of fellow-mortals. Any writings or teachings concerned with
Qabalah are simply free-will offerings for the acceptance or rejection of whomsoever is capable of making such decisions for themselves.

There are no inflexible dogmas or doctrines in Qabalah. The
lessons of Life have to be learned as we go along, which calls for
constant changes in consciousness to cope with the spiritual side
of any situation. What the received and handed down Tradition
of Qabalah has done to date is set up a Decimal System of related
Principles in a Pattern of Life from which we can coin the currency of our consciousness to supply our spiritual needs in living
as these arise. It offers freely the components of a construction-
set out of which we may build up our means of communion with
Cosmic Life. Advice and instructions are available with this for
assembly and operating purposes. Whatever we receive or transmit therewith is Qabalah. As simply as that.

No one need join Earth-based associations or subscribe to
Societies and Lodges in order to qualify for Qabalah. Such are entirely optional issues of personal decisions and choice, having the
normal advantages or disadvantages of any human organizations. True Qabalah transcends far beyond remotely Rabbinical
researches, or the occult opinions of Semitic specialists and scholars. It is the teaching we receive from the Talking Tree of Life de-
livered directly into the depths of our consciousness by Inner
agencies of Divine Cosmos. Whoso learns the language of this
spiritual speech may listen and answer of their own accord.

The parrot-cry of "God is dead!" will never be heard from
those who live by the Tree of Life and have awakened to awareness of the Living Spirit in the least degree. Life does not die, nor
death live, and for the Qabalist, God is Life, and Cosmos is con-
ceived and continued by Divine Consciousness. Through Cosmos,
GOD LIVES! Our imperfect appreciation of that Life changes as

we continue in its courses, and in that sense our concepts of Divinity may be said to die as we outgrow and bring them to rebirth in our consciousness as finer forms of enlightenment. Those pronouncing God dead only proclaim their own extinction, for if the Life-Spirit ceased Living, no-one would be left in existence to announce the fact of Ultimate Finality. God is not only maximally alive, but is Life Itself through the whole of Cosmic Consciousness and Continuity. No less, and Nothing more. Qabalists encounter evidence of Divinity everywhere, and they piece this together for themselves in their Pattern of Perfection called the Tree of Life, which in its inimitable way tells them the facts of Life outlined for Children of Light as they approach their coming of age in Cosmic Living. With so much to thank the Life-Spirit for through the Tree, sincere practitioners of Qabalah chant a concluding hymn at the end of their daily Office which says simply:

> Glory be to Thee.
> O Living One of Light.
> May we forever be
> Upon Thy Path of right.
>
> Direct us from above,
> According to Thy Law.
> And may Thy boundless Love
> Be with us evermore.
>
> Let Thy sublime design
> The Tree of God and Man,
> Both Human and Divine
> Prove our most perfect Plan.

AMEN

SO MOTE IT BE INDEED,	in the Name of the	WISDOM
	and of the	LOVE
	and of the	JUSTICE
	And the infinite	MERCY
	Of the One Eternal	SPIRIT
		AMEN.

Appendix

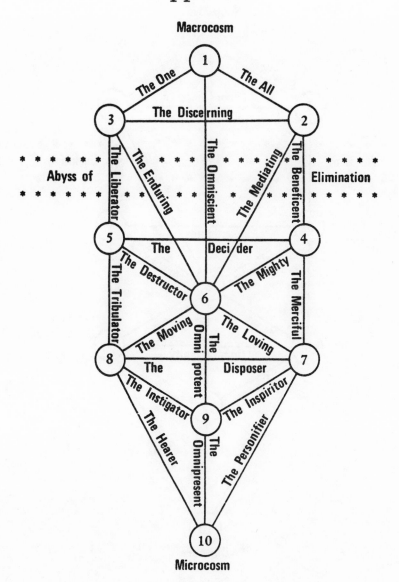

Macrocosm

The One
The All
The Discerning
The Omniscient
The Mediating
The Beneficent
The Liberator
The Enduring
Abyss of
Elimination
The Decider
The Destructor
The Mighty
The Tribulator
The Merciful
The Moving
The Loving
The Omnipotent
The Disposer
The Instigator
The Inspiritor
The Hearer
The Omnipresent
The Personifier

1
3
2
5
4
6
8
7
9
10

Microcosm

ORIGINATIVE PATH-QUALITIES
(DIVINE)

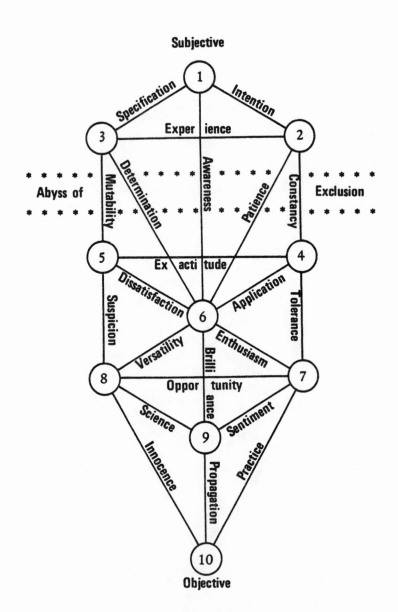

CREATIVE PATH-QUALITIES
(ARCHANGELIC)

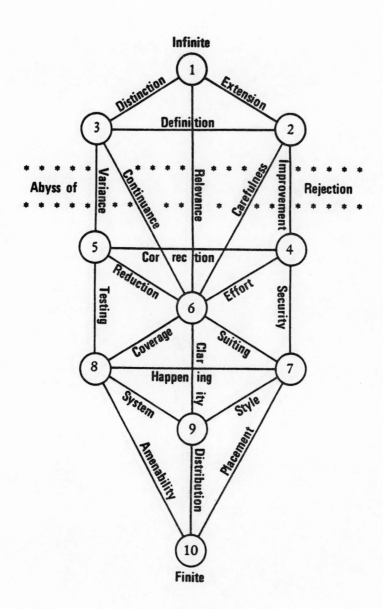

FORMATIVE PATH-QUALITIES
(ANGELIC)

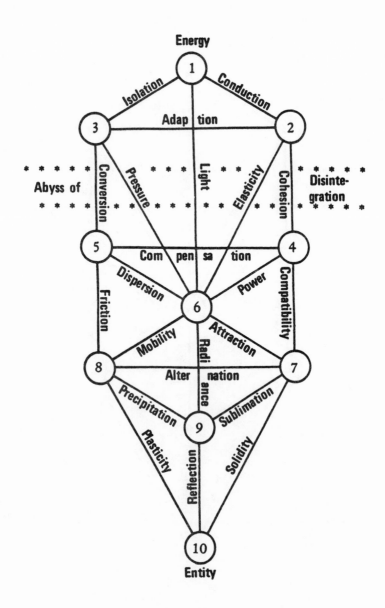

EXPRESSIVE PATH-QUALITIES
(MUNDANE)

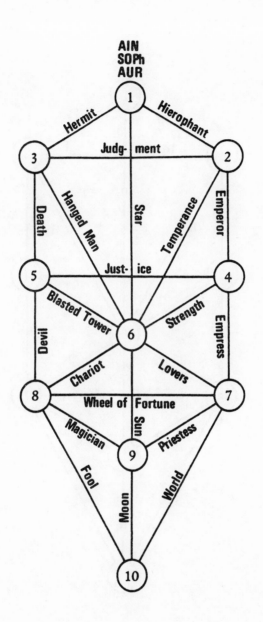

IDEOLOGICAL TAROT ATTRIBUTIONS
ON THE TREE

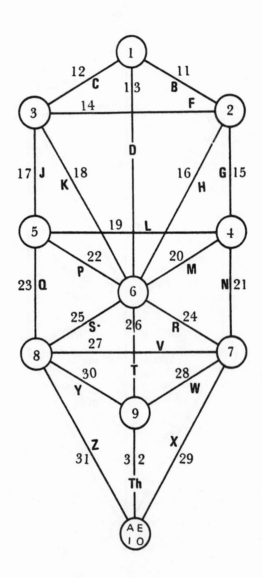

**ENGLISH LETTERS AND PATH NUMBERS
ON THE TREE**

Postscript:

A Note on the So-Called "Traditional" Tree System

Queries have often been raised concerning why this series system of Path-working should differ in any way from what is sometimes styled the "Traditional" method, because of increasing familiarity with its last century lay-out. The implications seem to be that an immutable and infallible set of Path attributions have already been officially fixed by some unquestionable authority, and any deviancy from that decree smacks of heresy, blasphemy, and other unmentionable occult aberrations.

A leading British publisher rejected the work outright on those very grounds. He wrote "... The book is interesting, but because you have changed the traditional Hebrew letter attributions, and altered the way in which the Tarot trumps are allotted, the book would be meaningless to a lot of readers. *I am sure your way is probably correct*, but because it is not the traditional one, I fear we would find it very difficult to publish, and so am returning the typescript herewith."

Surely an extraordinary admission. Leaving aside all the obvious inferences to be drawn from it, let us metaphorically pick up a challenging cudgel in reply and query bluntly: "Who says there is any such thing as a Traditional Tree of Life in the sense of a printed diagram which none dare deny on pain of excommunication from initiated circles?" Fifty years ago, only the slightest percentage of Western literates had ever heard of the Tree of Life. It was not until after World War I that any appreciable amount of information about it became available to a wider class of readership, and even that was made possible in English by fewer authors than may be counted on ten fingers. So how did all this purported "traditionalism" emerge during the last three decades after World War II, and precisely who or what insists on its

429

authenticity to a degree forbidding all further investigation of advancement within its field of inner influence? What reason could there possibly be for opposing individual and original research in that area which might result in fresh light leading to new solutions of old spiritual problems? Why in particular should this book be virtually banned in Britain, ostensibly on account of its originality alone, while presses are pouring out dreary and depressing "permissive" pornography in ever-mounting heaps of printed excrementa? There could be some very interesting speculations involved, but instead of considering these, let us look back a little towards the origins of this Tarot-trump Hebrew-letter Tree-Path business and see just what its rights of authorization amount to in terms of our present times.

The familiar and fairly frequently published form of the Tree-Path-Tarot-Letter combination, met with in most modern books, traces to a presumed finalization of these by the Golden Dawn Hermetic Society of the last century. Those are traceable again mainly to Eliphas Levi (Alphonse Louis Constant), the noted nineteenth-century French magus who linked the Tarot trumps with the Hebrew alphabet according to his own ideas of them. Levi thought very highly indeed of the Tarot, being convinced that it contained every secret of theoretical and practical Qabalah. Strange perhaps to say, he makes no significant mention whatsoever of the Tree of Life or its Paths in all his published writings. He was, however, a friend and connection of Bulwer-Lytton and the small yet influential group of English esotericists who were instigators of the subsequent Golden Dawn Society.

As an actual glyph of any kind, the Tree of Life did not appear in anything like its present form among Western occultists until the last century. It traced to a set of creative concepts outlined in a work of unorthodox Hebrew mysticism entitled the *Sepher Yetzirah* or *Book of Formation*, first published in the sixteenth-century from reputedly much older oral traditions. Herein, the letters of the Hebrew alphabet were attached to astrological and human functional ideas, while the ten Spheres were associated with spiritual and elemental energies. Later attempts to pictorialize these in two-dimensional diagrams produced various versions of circle, square, triangle, and linear combinations until eventually the sheer mathematical relationships of ten equal spheres or purely positional points became obvious.

The Tree as we know it now evolved over quite a period of pushing its proportions around.

Once the conceptual values of the ten fundamental Life-Spheres had been arrived at by much spiritual study and meditation among those working with a system still evolving through their efforts, some means had to be found of identifying relative values between those Spheres themselves. In order to form a framework for this, connecting channels of consciousness were conveniently numbered with letters of the Hebrew alphabet. The idea was simply to use the letters as "call-up-keys" for evoking whatever concepts were held by individual or collective workers concerning the particular Sphere-linkage a letter indicated. In reverse terms of course, such a concentration of consciousness could be used by intelligences living on higher than human levels to communicate back through the channels so formed. Nevertheless, if Hebrew nomenclature and symbology alone was employed, then the "print-out" reaching humans had necessarily to be in Hebrew equivalents. This might be fine for whomever thought naturally in Hebrew, but could scarcely be much use outside those limited circles.

If indeed the attributions of Hebrew letters to the Tree-Paths were made by actual Hebrews in the first place (about which there could be legitimate doubts), it does seem somewhat odd that the path numbered eleven is identified by the letter Aleph, or number one in Hebrew numerical values. Of course this Path is indeed the first Path *per se* between Spheres, though in that case why not simply call it "Path One"? If Hebrew letters are to be used as values throughout the Tree, why is Aleph not associated with Kether, and so on from there? How is it we have come to think of the Spheres in Arabic numbers and the paths in Hebrew letters? Then again, why have the Paths not been numbered sequentially as they should have been, but by an "inside out" arrangement according to a supposed "Serpent Path" system which works quite as well with a correct sequence of Path numeration? Since this "Sword and Serpent" attachment to the Tree is of relatively late date like the Three Pillars, it would seem that Path numbering may not be as old as some might unthinkingly claim. This is a discrepancy no one appears anxious to explain.

When we come to current linkage of the Tarot Trumps with the Paths via Hebrew alphabetical means, good sense is asked to suffer and swallow some severe shocks in the cause of credulity. We are expected, for instance, to connect our "Devil" concepts with our beliefs in the Principles of Beauty and Honor. We are supposed to see Death between Beauty and Victory, Ruin (the Tower) relative to Honor and Achievement. The Moon between Victory and the World. Other attributions show different absurdities, inconsistencies, and incongruities, until it becomes painfully obvious to any deeply thinking observer that something must surely be seriously out of gear in the overall presentation. One is reminded very much indeed of the old puzzles set for children and entitled: "What is wrong with this picture?" The reputed "traditional" attachment of Tarot Trumps to the much-published Tree of Life shows a picture so obviously wrong as to almost shout for conscious attention to the problem.

It could presumably be claimed by autocratically minded esotericists that such was the intention behind the whole thing in the first place. Publish a picture of the Tree with enough deliberate mistakes in its design to attract the attention of those capable of solving the enigma, and such souls would prove worthy of being dealt with in a more direct fashion by "Inner Masters." Deliberate misdirection, to discover who fell for foolery and who was bright enough to see through trickery, used to be very much part of past occult policy. It seems to have hung over somewhat into our times too.

In this century there have, in fact, been quite a variety of Tarot attributions to the Tree Paths. Apart from the Golden Dawn system, there is one by the Swedish Qabalist Knut Stenring, one by Zain in America, "Frater Achad," and several much lesser known people. In the Golden Dawn, especially, it was hinted to initiates that however they managed to associate the Tarots with the Paths, there would always be a more recondite method which could only be known to very high Masters and initiates of much more exalted grades. Arthur Edward Waite, then an ex-member of the Golden Dawn, believed he had actually found such a secret system, and it is with the Tarot he designed that this present work has been partially accomplished.

Therefore to talk about "Traditional" Trees of Life as if only one officially approved design could ever exist is both meaningless and misleading. What is Tradition anyway, or rather—what should it be? Certainly not a dead and gone left-over of some kind from our romantic past. Tradition should be a *living spirit*, persisting among people from one generation to another, and consequently leading them constantly from past learning to future illumination. This means that Tradition ought to be in a continual state of evolution and improvement. It is essentially the spiritual *growth* of human souls both individually and collectively. It stands for regenerative replacement and never for degenerative decay. Each generation of humans owes a Traditional debt to its ancestors and descendants which can only be paid by processing a common chain of consciousness in the present. This is especially true with spiritual structures supporting us through the centuries like Qabalah and its Tree of Life Master-Mandala.

Over the last few generations in particular, the Tree of Life formula and Cosmic Circle Cross have been the basic genetic patterns of Western esotericism. It is thus the perpetual duty of all those who love and work with them to cultivate and develop them with every care and consideration. This includes both pruning off dead wood and training new growth in the right directions for future fruiting. That is precisely what has been attempted with this present work, which represents a whole lifetime of effort for such a single purpose.

As a Western "Perfection Pattern," the Tree of Life needed to speak modern English rather than ancient Hebrew, however much pure concepts may be above all human language. Our consciousness as Western humans of our times has been constrained into English and other European linguistic channels employing an Anglo-Latin alphabet. So, therefore, we should have a common esoteric Master-Glyph geared to those integrals of our intelligence. The Tree of Life *should* do just that. The Tree of Life *has* done just that. Q.E.D.

The difficulty with the reputed "Traditional" connections between the Tree and the Tarot had lain entirely with the existent Trump numberings being forced into unreasonable relationships with Path positions determined by Hebrew numerology regardless of ideas, symbology, or intrinsic metaphysical meanings. Either there had to be some better way of working this, or else the scheme was a bad mistake in the first place. So a happier and more harmonious method of relating Trumps with Paths by means of pure consciousness-content alone was duly sought and providentially found. Nevertheless, acceptance or rejection of this must necessarily lie entirely with personal perceptions or prejudices.

At least there can scarcely be any serious disagreement as to numerical placements of the four decades of Tarot "minor arcana." Arguments are thus confined to the Trumps and court cards. It could well be asked why there should be exactly twenty-two Trumps if they were not meant to belong with the Hebrew alphabet which has that many letters. The answer here is that if any decade *commencing with Zero* is related with itself through a common circular design (Tarot-Rota), there will be eleven separations and eleven connections in all, making twenty-two relationships altogether. This is no more than a matter of mechanical and mathematical principles. The Zero, or "Fool-trap" factor has to be the commencing and concluding Key.

In the last analysis there can only be one Traditional Tree of Life. That which is lived with and within at any instant of individuation. A truly Living Tree cannot be other than a growing Tree if its people are making the very least progress towards perfection. Hence we have here no "breakaway" version of the Qabalistic Tree scorning its ancestry by cocking some modern snook in the direction of its derivations. It is neither more nor less than the Tree of Tradition wearing suitable clothes for this century. These can be changed again as often as necessary to match conditions, providing the principal pattern of the Tree always points in the direction of a Divine Perfection-plan, which people may follow however they are able, in their own terms and times.

Strictly speaking then, no one at all, except maybe the most case-hardened anti-progressive staticist, should see any sort of an alien Tree, hostile to their immobile beliefs, lurking among the leaves of this book. We shall only meet our own good old Tree telling the latest installment of its story in its own words through the channels it chose for this occasion. It is most likely to tell other tales and surprising stories in different ways and words through many more mouthpieces yet, and keep unfolding its endless legend in languages best understood by human hearers.

For the time being, therefore, will all ladies and gentlemen sitting at the Round Table made for mediating these matters please pay attention and pray silence for: THE TALKING TREE OF OUR WESTERN INNER TRADITION!

STAY IN TOUCH

On the following pages you will find listed, with their current prices, some of the books and tapes now available on related subjects. Your book dealer stocks most of these, and will stock new titles in the Llewellyn series as they become available. We urge your patronage.

However, to obtain our full catalog, to keep informed of new titles as they are released and to benefit from informative articles and helpful news, you are invited to write for our bi-monthly news magazine/catalog. A sample copy is free, and it will continue coming to you at no cost as long as you are an active mail customer. Or you may keep it coming for a full year with a donation of just $2.00 in U.S.A. ($7.00 for Canada & Mexico, $20.00 overseas, first class mail). Many bookstores also have *The Llewellyn New Times* available to their customers. Ask for it.

Stay in touch! In *The Llewellyn New Times'* pages you will find news and reviews of new books, tapes and services, announcements of meetiongs and seminars, articles helpful to our readers, news of authors, advertising of products and services, special money-making opportunities, and much more.

The Llewellyn New Times
P.O. Box 64383-Dept. 268, St. Paul, MN 55164-0383, U.S.A.

• • •

TO ORDER BOOKS AND TAPES

If your book dealer does not have the books and tapes described on the following pages readily available, you may order them direct from the publisher by sending full price in U.S. funds, plus $2.00 for postage and handling for the first book, and $.50 for each additional book. There are no postage and handling charges for orders over $50. UPS Delivery: We ship UPS whenever possible. Delivery guaranteed. Provide your street address as UPS does not deliver to P.O. Boxes. UPS to Canada requires a $50 minimum order. Allow 4–6 weeks for delivery. Orders outside the U.S.A. and Canada: Airmail—add retail price of book; add $5 for each non-book item (tapes, etc.); add $1 per item for surface mail.

FOR GROUP STUDY AND PURCHASE

Because there is a great deal of interest in group discussion and study of the subject matter of this book, we feel that we should encourage the adoption and use of this particular book by such groups by offering a special "quantity" price to group leaders or "agents."

Our Special Quantity Price for a minimum order of five copies of *Growing the Tree Within* is $44.85 cash-with-order. This price includes postage and handling within the United States. Minnesota residents must add 6% sales tax. For additional quantities, please order in multiples of five. For Canadian and foreign orders, add postage and handling charges as above. Credit card (VISA, Master Card, American Express) orders are accepted. Charge card orders only may be phoned free ($15.00 minimum order) within the U.S.A. or Canada by dialing 1-800-THE-MOON. Customer service calls dial 1-612-291-1970. Mail Orders to:

LLEWELLYN PUBLICATIONS
P.O. Box 64383-Dept. 268 / St. Paul, MN 55164-0383, U.S.A.

ATTAINMENT THROUGH MAGIC
by William G. Gray
In this newly titled reprint of the classic *A Self Made by Magic*, the author presents a "Self-Seeking System" of powerful magical practice designed to help seekers become better and more fulfilled souls. The source material is taken from standard procedures familiar to most students of the Western Inner Tradition, procedures that encourage the best of our potential while diminishing or eliminating our worst characteristics. To that end, Gray deals extensively with the dangers and detriments of maleficent or "black" magic.

The lessons follow the pattern of the Life-Tree, and guide the student through the four elements and their connection of Truth, the Ten Principles of "Spheres" of the Life-Tree, and the associations which bind these together. Gray includes an in-depth study of the Archangelic concepts, with exercises to "make the Archangels come true" for us through the systematic use of appropriate words of power.
0-87542-298-5, 5-1/4 x 8, 308 pgs., softcover $9.95

BY STANDING STONE & ELDER TREE
by William G. Gray
This is a compelling firsthand account of the fascinating and mystical Rollright Ritual. It is an intriguing journey into ancient times—a journey into the heart of the monumental Stones that have marked the rise and fall of our civilizations, cultures and developments.

This is a timeless, rewarding exploration of the spiritual principles, practice and inner realities of a significant psychodramatic experience which can be carried out anywhere at all, because it is based on a fundamental Cosmic Pattern imprinted in the Consciousness itself.

The Rollright Ritual holds traces of the oldest mysteries celebrated among humankind, and is at the same time positively pointed toward a mystique that is reincarnating through rising generations.
0-87542-299-3, 5-1/4 x 8, 185 pgs., softcover $9.95

EVOKING THE PRIMAL GODDESS
by William G. Gray

In our continuing struggle to attain a higher level of spiritual awareness, one thing has become clear: we need to cultivate and restore the matriarchal principle to its proper and equal place in our conceptions of Deity. Human history and destiny are determined by our Deity concepts, whatever they may be, and for too long the results of a predominantly masculine God in war, brutality and violence have been obvious.

In *Evoking the Primal Goddess*, renowned occultist William G. Gray takes you on a fascinating, insightful journey into the history and significance of the Goddess in religion. For the first time anywhere, he shows that the search for the Holy Grail was actually a movement within the Christian church to bring back the feminine element into the concept of Deity. He also shows how you can evoke your own personal image of the Mother ideal through practical rituals and prayer.

It has been said that whatever happens in spiritual levels of life will manifest itself on physical ones as well. By following Gray's techniques, you can re-balance both your male and your female polarities into a single spiritual individuality of practical Power!

0-87542-271-3, 5-1/4 x 8, 192 pgs., softcover $9.95

BETWEEN GOOD AND EVIL
by William G. Gray

If you are seeking Inner Light, read this important book. *Between Good and Evil* provides new insight that can help you take the forces of Darkness that naturally exist within us and transform them into spiritual light. This book will help you discover how you can deal constructively, rather than destructively, with the unavoidable problem of Evil. Our lives depend on which way we direct our energy—whether we make the Devil in ourselves serve the God, or the other way around. We must use our good intentions to understand and exploit the Evil energies that would otherwise prove fatal to us.

In order to confront and control our demons," Gray has revived a centuries-old magical ritual technique called the *Abramelin Experience:* a practical, step-by-step process in which you call upon your Holy Guardian Angel to assist in converting Evil into Good. By following the richly detailed explanation of this "spiritual alchemy," you will learn how to positively channel your negative energies into a path leading directly to a re-union with Divinity.

The power of altering your future lies in your own hands, and within this unique book you will discover the means to move forward in your spiritual evolution. You will find the principles discussed in this multi-faceted book valuable and insightful.

0-87542-273-X, 304 pgs., 5-1/4 x 8, softcover $9.95

TEMPLE MAGIC
by William G. Gray
This important book on occultism deals specifically with problems and details you are likely to encounter in temple practice. Learn how a temple should look, how a temple should function, what a ceremonialist should wear, what physical postures best promote the ideal spiritual-mental attitude, and how magic is worked in a temple setting.

Temple Magic has been written specifically for the instruction and guidance of esoteric ceremonialists by someone who has spent a lifetime in spiritual service to his natural Inner Way. There are few comparable works in existence, and this book in particular deals with up-to-date techniques of constructing and using a workable temple dedicated to the furtherance of the Western Inner Tradition. In simple yet adequate language, it helps any individual understand and promote the spiritual structure of our esoteric inheritance. It is a book by a specialist for those who are intending to be specialists.

0-87542-274-8, 5-1/4 x 8, 240 pgs., illus., softcover   **$7.95**

THE RABBI'S TAROT
by Daphna Moore
In its striking, in-depth interpretation of the symbology of the 22 Major Arcana cards, *The Rabbi's Tarot* will lead you to profound depths of self-development and spirituality. You will learn how the practical occultist develops the pineal and pituitary glands by energized currents coming through the seven golden candlesticks and the seven churches of Asia. When the pineal gland is energized by the transmuted sex force, the result is the White Light, as depicted by the seven White Stars in the Tarot card The Star. This occult magic can be worked in your body and outside your body. It is also referred to as cosmic consciousness, illumination or enlightenment.

The object of this book is not merely to show you the Laws of the Universe, but how these laws work out in you. The teaching of the book is that the self-conscious, by assiduous endeavor, may bring into your body more and more of the superconscious in the form of the Cosmic Mind-Stuff. The symbols of the Major Arcana suggest how you set about realizing your own perfection. They show that we evolve only by desire, and that no matter what desire we cherish, it is but a stepping-stone to a higher one.

The Rabbi's Tarot is one of the most intense studies of the Major Arcana ever published. It is a must for all who work with the Tarot and for all who want to develop themselves to the utmost.

0-87542-572-0, 6 x 9, 385 pgs., illus., softcover   **$12.95**

GODWIN'S CABALISTIC ENCYCLOPEDIA
by David Godwin

This is the most complete correlation of Hebrew and English ideas ever offered. It is a dictionary of Cabalism arranged, with definitions, alphabetically, alphabetically in Hebrew, and numerically. With this book the practicing Cabalist or student no longer needs access to a large number of books on mysticism, magic and the occult in order to trace down the basic meanings, Hebrew spellings, and enumerations of the hundreds of terms, words, and names that are included in this book.

This book includes: all of the two-letter root words found in Biblical Hebrew, the many names of God, the Planets, the Astrological Signs, Numerous Angels, the Shem Hamphorash, the Spirits of the Goetia, the Correspondences of the 32 Paths, a comparison of the Tarot and the Cabala, a guide to Hebrew Pronunciation, and a complete edition of Aleister Crowley's valuable book *Sepher Sephiroth*.

Here is a book that is a must for the shelf of all Magicians, Cabalists, Astrologers, Tarot students, Thelemites, and those with any interest at all in the spiritual aspects of our universe.

0-87542-292-6, 6 x 9, 500 pgs., softcover **$15.00**

THE LLEWELLYN PRACTICAL GUIDE TO THE MAGICK OF THE TAROT
How to Read, and Shape, Your Future
by Denning & Phillips

"To gain understanding, *and control*, of Your Life." Can anything be more important? To gain insight into the circumstances of your life—the inner causes, the karmic needs, the hidden factors at work—and then to have the power to change your life in order to fulfill your real desires and True Will: that's what the techniques taught in this book can do.

Discover the Shadows cast ahead by Coming Events. Yes, this is possible, because it is your DEEP MIND—that perceives the *astral shadows* of coming events and can communicate them to you through the symbols and images of the ancient and mysterious Tarot cards.

Your Deep Mind has the power to shape those astral shadows—images that are causal to material events—when you learn to communicate your own desires and goals using the Tarot.

0-87542-198-9, 5-1/4 x 8, 252 pgs., illus., softcover **$7.95**